Great Ideas in Psychology

GREAT IDEAS IN PSYCHOLOGY

A Cultural and Historical Introduction

Fathali M. Moghaddam

ONEWORLD
OXFORD

GREAT IDEAS IN PSYCHOLOGY

Oneworld Publications
(Sales and editorial)
185 Banbury Road
Oxford OX2 7AR
England
www.oneworld-publications.com

ISBN-13: 978–1–85168–379–6
ISBN-10: 1–85168–379–8

Cover design by Mungo Designs
Typeset by Saxon Graphics Ltd, Derby
Printed and bound by WS Bookwell, Finland

Cover photograph: Portrait of a Pensive,
Young Man Looking Down © Digital Vision Ltd

To Maryan

CONTENTS

PREFACE

I have found that, wherever I teach, great ideas in psychology stir passions and engage students directly. I wrote this book because, like many other professors, I feel there is an important gap among the texts available for introducing students and lay people alike to modern psychology. The available texts for introductory psychology, history of psychology, social psychology, cross-cultural psychology, and a number of other central courses typically present thousands and thousands of names, dates, terms, and are generally "factual" to the extreme. In the midst of such mountains of information, insufficient attention is given to great ideas, which get pushed into the background and become neglected. This is a shame, because what most people find really interesting about psychology are the great ideas central to the field. Insightful teachers recognize that great ideas help to focus attention on thematic issues that really matter, and will still be remembered decades after a student has graduated and forgotten the thousands of names, dates, and other "facts" crammed into standard texts. By placing the great ideas in cultural and historical context, this book helps students grasp the "big picture" and arrive at an overview of modern psychology in world context.

This book presents a selection of the greatest ideas of the greatest psychologists. Modern psychology is often considered a young science, but it is already rich in great ideas, *these being ideas that have had a lasting and widespread impact on our understanding of human behavior.* Many of these ideas, such as the ego and IQ (intelligence quotient), have become so much a part of our everyday language that we use them without necessarily reflecting on their roots in the discipline of psychology. In addition to great ideas that are now part of the history of psychology, I have selected a few great ideas, such as feminist psychology and multicultural psychology, that reflect fairly recent trends. But irrespective of the vintage of the idea discussed, both strengths and weaknesses are highlighted.

This is a *critical* introduction to great ideas, meaning that readers are taken on a journey not only to learn the great ideas, but also to evaluate and assess them. We discover that even great ideas should be considered as works in progress, that they have limitations, and I do not shy away from pointing these out. Often such limitations become apparent when we step back and review a great idea from another cultural perspective and in historical context. The cultural and historical themes in the book help the reader to consider the great ideas of psychology in the world context.

Each chapter is devoted to one great idea, presented in an informal style, and followed by references to a small number of both classic and cutting-edge studies. I have adopted a style that keeps the focus on the great ideas themselves and frees up the text from distracting technical details, dates, and references.

This volume has been taking shape over the last decade and has benefitted from critical feedback provided by numerous professors and students in the US and abroad. I want in particular to acknowledge the great joy and privilege I have had of learning from Rom Harré and Karl Pribram, who perfectly fit Chaucer's description "And gladly would he learn, and gladly teach."

1

INTRODUCTION: WORKING OUT AND WORKING IN

Albert Einstein worked out. Those who work out have grand visions, outside the constraints of available empirical evidence. They use their creativity to construct pictures that show the world in a new way, unconstrained by the known facts. Their visions concern the big picture and broad ideas, rather than the details of experiments. Albert Einstein did not do any experiments, but he had great ideas; ideas great enough to change our views about the universe. Sometimes it takes decades or even centuries before experimental research catches up with the ideas of such thinkers; it is only now that we are capable of testing some of Einstein's great ideas, such as the idea that the universe is expanding, and finding them to be accurate.

Sigmund Freud also worked out, crafting intricate and elaborate stories about how the conscious, the pre-conscious, and the unconscious take shape, and how civilization molds individual personalities. He did gather evidence, mostly through case studies of his own patients, and he made some efforts to tie his ideas to evidence, but the link remained rather loose. For the most part, Freud worked out; his ideas were based on sheer flights of creative imagination. He worked rather like a fiction writer. The genius of Freud, Einstein, and others who work out is in their flights of imagination, soaring well beyond experimental evidence of the time.

The great Russian scientist Ivan Pavlov, on the other hand, worked in. Researchers who work in try very hard to stick close to empirical evidence. Their point of departure is often an observation of unexpected events in everyday life or some unexplained findings from empirical research. From such a puzzling fact, the researcher develops an explanation, always working back in toward the hard evidence that was the point of departure. Pavlov worked in and kept his ideas tied to hard facts, as far as he could recognize them.

In scientific research, great ideas have come from either working out or working in, and some of the best ideas have come from researchers working both routes. For example, Charles Darwin amassed a great deal of evidence about geological and biological change when as a young man just graduated from university he traveled on board the ship HMS *Beagle* around the coast of South America for five years (1831–36). He gathered more and more evidence about evolutionary change, and was inspired to develop the theory of evolution to explain the various bodies of evidence he and others had accumulated. He worked out, and he worked in; and the fit between his revolutionary ideas and the mass of accumulated evidence eventually convinced most of the die-hard critics. Piaget, the Swiss developmental psychologist, also tried to work both in and out. He did most of his research on his own children, and originated a stage-wise model of human cognitive development.

Since the mid nineteenth century, psychologists have conducted hundreds of thousands of experiments, many of them inspired directly or indirectly by a very small number of great ideas. Some such ideas, such as the unconscious, displaced aggression, and the self, have evolved by researchers mostly working out. In these cases, the great idea is not very closely tied to empirical evidence. Other great ideas in psychology, such as attachment, learning, and obedience to authority, have evolved by researchers mostly working in. In these cases, the ideas have evolved on the basis of hard evidence, and often such ideas were developed explicitly to explain puzzling evidence.

WHAT MAKES AN IDEA GREAT?

Most psychologists agree that ideas such as the unconscious, artificial intelligence, and learning are great. However, key questions about great ideas are seldom explicitly addressed. Why should we identify great ideas? Why should students care about great ideas? We should identify great ideas and be concerned about them because they tie together the central issues in psychology. Great ideas in psychology engage us in what is most central and essential in the science of psychology, stripped away from what seem like endless bits of detailed information, dates, names, and references that cram the typical introductory texts. The great ideas are what should be attended to and remembered because of their centrality, even decades after the detailed information about facts, dates, and names may have been forgotten. It is through the great ideas that we too can join the long debate, stretching back thousands of years to ancient Greece and beyond, about the nature of humankind and our potential for change and genuine progress.

What makes an idea great? What are the criteria by which we recognize one idea as great, and another idea as not so? By examining the hundreds of books that selectively discuss foundational issues in psychology, such as books on the history and current state of the discipline, we can see that there are many possible criteria for selecting great ideas. I have arrived at the following four as the most important criteria.

Influence on perceptions

First, to be judged great an idea in psychology must in a major way influence our interpretation of human behavior; it must alter how we view ourselves, rather like a mirror that reflects back a new, changed image of ourselves. Often, such ideas change our conception of human nature. For example, Freud's interpretation of the unconscious dramatically shifted the emphasis, from seeing humans as rational to irrational, creatures who often do not know the real motives for their own behavior. This change came about not only among academics but also among the lay public. Also, Freud fundamentally changed the way artists and writers portray humans in novels, plays, paintings, films, music, and other creative works. As another example, the idea of attachment, an enduring and strong emotional bond between an infant and a care provider, has in important ways influenced how we approach child rearing, by highlighting the importance of the emotional bond between a primary care provider and an infant. The implications of attachment are part of controversial ongoing discussions on child care, adoption, and divorce, and this links to the next criterion.

Applied impact

A second criterion that must be met in order for an idea to be judged great is that it should prove to be effective in application. Such application can be in the professional arena. For example, the idea of IQ has been applied widely by professionals in educational and other settings. But the application may also be by lay people in their everyday lives. An example is the wide use lay people have found for the concept of IQ. Despite the severity of critical attacks by some experts against the idea of IQ, it thrives in popular culture (for example, talk about 'high IQ' and 'low IQ' has entered prime-time TV, the popular press, and political debate, as evident in discussions about the IQ of President G. W. Bush), presumably because people find it useful. Similarly, personality assessment techniques (such as the Minnesota Multiphasic Personality Inventory, MMPI) have had a profound and widespread impact in both high-income and low-income societies around the world, by influencing how abnormality is assessed, for example. Again, despite avowed weaknesses of traditional personality assessment techniques, even critics would not deny their tremendous applied impact. The widespread applied impact of certain psychological ideas, such as in the areas of intelligence and personality, has been associated with highly productive research.

Stimulate research

A related, third, criterion for assessment is the ability of an idea to stimulate new research. Great ideas in psychology, such as personality traits, stimulate tens of thousands of studies involving an enormous number of researchers and research participants around the world. Such research often leads to new questions, both wide-ranging and narrow in scope. For example, research on personality traits led to major questions about the consistency of personality across contexts (Does personality stay the same across different situations? Or, is the consistency of personality an illusion, arising out of our expectations and biased judgments?), and narrower questions about the possible universality of particular traits (Are certain consistencies in behavior, such as neuroticism, shared by all humans?).

Ideally, a psychological idea should be proved either valid or invalid through cumulative empirical research. This is a similar point to what the philosopher of science Karl Popper refers to as *falsifiability*, making sufficiently precise predictions that we can at least imagine what evidence would be needed for an idea to be disproved. Put another way, falsifiability begins with the premise that, rather than trying to prove a hypothesis as correct, researchers should focus on demonstrating the conditions in which the hypothesis cannot be falsified (proved incorrect). In practice, we find that some of the most influential psychological ideas, such as the unconscious and the self, have not yet been proved or disproved. This could be because we do not as yet have sufficient empirical evidence to make the judgment. However, in the long term some of the psychological ideas we consider "great," such as the unconscious, may not prove to be falsifiable, despite their historic importance and widespread international impact.

The criterion of time

These different criteria for assessing ideas and identifying great ones are all relevant, but a strong argument can be made for the view that these criteria are subsumed by one overriding criterion: time. The surest way to determine the greatness of an idea is to chart how well it survives over time. An idea that in a major way influences the way we interpret human behavior, has wide application, and stimulates a great deal of research is bound also to survive a long time. The criterion of time is applicable to art, science, or any other domain of human endeavor. For example, we consider an athletic record, such as world record for the one hundred meters dash, to be particularly great if it lasts a long time.

Although I believe the criterion of time is the most important one for identifying great ideas in psychology, two qualifications are necessary. First, we must be careful not to confuse the survival of terminology associated with an idea with the survival of the idea itself. For example, the continued use of terms such as "Freudian slip" and "ego" in everyday language does not by itself demonstrate that Freudian psychology is surviving over time. Such terms may have become detached from the original ideas from which they originally derived. Consequently, we must seek evidence of the survival of the broader original idea, and this is where the first three criteria – "influence on perceptions," "applied impact," and "stimulate research" – prove invaluable.

A second qualification concerns the interpretations of a great idea during different historical periods. As culture changes, the ways in which a great idea is interpreted can also change. For example, over the last century there have been major changes in culture, in most societies, in areas such as gender roles and gender relations. In turn, such changes have altered the ways in which men and women evaluate Freudian psychology generally (for example, Freud's views on the so-called "Oedipus complex" have undergone serious re-evaluation, in part as a result of the feminist movement), and possible great ideas articulated by Freud particularly (for example, Freud's ideas on so-called "penis envy"

in the early development of girls and how this influences the unconscious have been critically re-assessed and found wanting, particularly
given the modern role of women). In a sense, a great idea is continually
being reconstructed by different generations of psychologists and lay
people. However, the core of the idea must survive through such recon-
structions if it is to be recognized as a great idea.

Although the vast majority of the great ideas I have included in this
book are very well established, I have also included four newer great
ideas, on the well-founded conviction that they will pass the test of time.
These four newer ideas are: artificial intelligence (AI), multicultural
psychology, feminist psychology, and the self. Two points need to be
highlighted about these four newer ideas. First, they are strongly influenced by multiple disciplines and reflect growing multi-disciplinary
trends in psychology. For example, artificial intelligence is influenced by
developments in biology, engineering, linguistics, philosophy, as well as
psychology. The disciplines that influence multicultural psychology,
feminist psychology, and the self include sociology, political science,
anthropology, as well as psychology. Second, these four ideas have
already had deep and wide impact on psychological research and practice: this is self-evident from the contents of psychological publications
and psychology training programs at major institutions around the
world. Thus, there are very strong reasons for adding these four newer
ideas to the longer list of more established great ideas.

The challenge of change

The criterion of time raises a number of other thorny issues when
applied to ideas in psychology. Since the decline of behaviorism and the
first "cognitive revolution" of the 1950s, psychology has been viewed by
most researchers as the science of thinking and activity, mental life and
overt behavior. Most psychologists would also agree that mental life and
overt behavior are at least to some extent influenced by the cultural
environment. Over time, the cultural environment changes, and so does
human behavior. For example, in Western cultures, at least, males and
females think and behave in ways that were fundamentally different in
2002 compared with 1802. Thus, an idea that would have been considered "great" because it accurately described the behavior of men and
women in 1802 (in the domain of personality, for instance) might not be
accurate in 2002, because cultural conditions have dramatically changed
and so has behavior. Does this mean that the criterion of time is not

applicable to assessing ideas in the discipline of psychology? Or, does it mean that the criterion of time is actually the best criterion for identifying great ideas that characterize human thought and action despite cultural change? An answer can be found by looking back to the origins of modern psychology.

GREAT IDEAS AND ORIENTATIONS IN PSYCHOLOGY

From its beginnings in the mid nineteenth century, modern psychology has been characterized by different orientations, formalized as "schools" influential during different eras, including structuralism, behaviorism, psychoanalysis, Gestalt psychology, cognitive psychology, evolutionary psychology, and social constructionism (see Table 1). These schools are different from one another in their major goals as well as the historical eras in which they enjoyed the greatest influence. For example, behaviorism was most influential for much of the first half of the twentieth century, whereas cognitive psychology has been most influential since the mid twentieth century. Behaviorists attempted to study publicly observable behavior and rejected any reference to thought processes, whereas cognitive psychologists study thinking.

Although the major schools in psychology have fundamental differences in goals, at a deeper level they share a concern for discovering the causes of behavior. Thus, a foundational division that is even broader than the types of psychology schools is between psychology as a *causal science*, attempting to identify cause–effect relations in thought and action, and psychology as a *normative science*, exploring regularities in thought and action in association with norms, rules, values, and other features of culture. These two broad orientations both have legitimacy as part of a science of psychology, and they both have their roots in the pioneering work of nineteenth-century researchers.

Students of psychology learn that 1889 is a foundational year for the discipline, since it is taken to be the year that the first laboratory for experimental research in psychology was established. The innovator of this laboratory, and the person who has come to be regarded as the father of modern experimental psychology, is the German scholar Wilhelm Wundt (1832–1920). The American scholar William James (1842–1910) also set up a psychology laboratory about this time, but perhaps because he did not continue to invest much time in experimental research, his early contribution to the psychology laboratory is seldom remembered. At

Table 1. Schools of psychology, their goals, and eras of greatest influence

School	Goal	Historical Era Most Influential
*Structuralism	Explain behavior by reference to the smallest possible "elements" of the mind	Latter part of the 19th century
*Behaviorism	Focus exclusively on behavior that can be publicly observed and measured, and reject all reference to mind and thought	First half of 20th century
*Psychoanalysis	Identify the impact of unconscious motivations, desires, fears, and the like, on thought and action	From the early 20th century
*Gestalt Psychology	Follow the idea that "the whole is more than the sum of its parts," and explore how in-built characteristics lead us to impose structure and meaning on the world	Particularly in 1930s and 1940s
*Cognitive Psychology	Study of thinking toward discovering universals in mental processes	From the 1950s
*Evolutionary Psychology	Explore the adaptive functions of behavior to show how certain behaviors have helped humans to survive	From the 1970s
*Social constructionism	Explore how humans construct meaning systems and use norms, rules, and the like to regulate social interactions	From the 1980s

the heart of modern experimental procedures is the manipulation of independent variables, assumed causes, to examine their effects on dependent variables, assumed effects. The goal of experimental psychology is traditionally seen to be to discover the causes of behavior.

But Wundt also worked on a second type of psychology, a non-experimental field of study that might best be described as "cultural psychology" (it is often translated as "folk psychology"). Between 1900 and 1920, Wundt completed ten volumes on cultural psychology, reflecting his deep commitment to this "second" psychology. The main areas of cultural psychology for Wundt were the products of the mind, such as myths, language, and customs. The community comes to create collectively shared phenomena, such as myths and values, and these in turn have an influence on individuals. In this way, the behavior of individuals is influenced by the cumulative effects of social interactions over years, sometimes centuries. Obviously, the precise measurement of direct cause–effect relations is not the goal in cultural psychology as it is in experimental laboratory-based psychology. However, Wundt's second psychology is a *bona fide* psychology, and is different from anthropology, sociology, and other such disciplines, because his focus remains on explaining individual thought and action.

A useful way to re-conceptualize the "causal versus normative" distinction is to think of all behavior somewhere on a dimension with less or more *degrees of freedom*, referring to the range of options available to an individual in a situation. In some circumstances, a wide range of possible behaviors are available to an individual and so the degrees of freedom are high, whereas in other situations the range of possible behaviors available to an individual is narrower, so the degrees of freedom are smaller.

Research on behavior with less degrees of freedom has been more rigorous and representative of the side of psychology nearer to the hard sciences. Examples from the early history of the discipline are found in the research of Gustav Fechner (1801–87), the father of psychophysics (a precursor to modern signal detection theory), and his contemporary E. H. Weber (1795–1878). We are indebted to them for the understanding that the human nervous system is sensitive to relative rather than absolute differences in stimuli. For example, suppose Jane can just notice the difference between 10 and 12 units of noise in a room (but not between 10 and 11 units). Then she will be able to notice the difference between 20 and 24 units (but not 20 and 22 units), and 40 and 48 units (but not 40 and 44 units).

Research on behavior with greater degrees of freedom is also well represented throughout the history of psychology, from Wundt's folk psychology in the nineteenth century to contemporary research in areas such as social, cultural, developmental, and cognitive psychology. A great deal of ongoing research in these domains is fundamentally influenced by cultural trends. For example, changes in gender roles have influenced behavior in areas such as prejudice, discrimination, and leadership. Cultural trends have also influenced seemingly more objective research areas, such as intelligence testing (as we shall see in chapter 7, scores on intelligence tests have been increasing over time, perhaps as a result of people becoming more test savvy). Whereas in the nineteenth century medical and psychology texts assumed the female brain is less capable of taking on the challenges of university education, in the twenty-first century some researchers looking at the school perform-ance of girls and boys are asking, "Can the boys keep up?" In both the US and the UK, girls are now outperforming boys in all but a few school subjects, mathematics being the most notable exception.

Most of the great ideas selected for discussion in this text fall between the polar extremes of very low and very high degrees of freedom. For example, learning has an inbuilt biological component that allows low degrees of freedom, but is also largely based on cultural conditions that allow higher degrees of freedom. However, some great ideas are clearly closer to one pole rather than another. To give clear-cut examples, long-term potentiation (LTP), discussed in chapter 4, is closer to the extreme of low degrees of freedom, but conformity, the topic of chapter 15, is nearer to the extreme of high degrees of freedom.

Change and continuity

In general, biologically determined behaviors (such as reaction time) have lower degrees of freedom, whereas behaviors influenced by culture (such as gender relations) have higher degrees of freedom: there is very little I can do to change my reaction time, but I can change the way I interact with other women and men. On the surface it may appear that ideas closer to the low degrees of freedom pole of the continuum, reflecting biological processes, will be more long-lasting than ideas closer to the higher degrees of freedom pole, reflecting meaning systems in society. After all, it could be argued, the biological characteristics of humans change very slowly over long periods of evolutionary change, whereas cultural meaning systems can change relatively quickly. Thus, for example, it would seem that we can apply the criterion of time to assess great ideas in an area such as the biological basis of memory, because behavior in this domain changes very slowly. Presumably the biology of the brain, for example, has not changed significantly over the last few centuries. But applying the criterion of time to ideas about behavior characterized by higher degrees of freedom would be more problematic, because presumably human behavior to do with how things are done, and the meanings people ascribe to phenomena contin-uously change over time.

This theme of change has been highlighted by scholars throughout the ages. The Greek scholar Heracleitus pointed out twenty-five centuries ago that one cannot step into the same river twice, because the waters in the river are continually flowing past. The American psychologist Kenneth Gergen argued more recently that social psychology, at least is like one big history, because the topic of research, social behavior, is continually changing. This seems to suggest that we cannot have great ideas where there are higher degrees of freedom for individual behavior, because the "river is continually flowing." How can an idea about behavior be great if the behavior being described is always in a state of flux?

On closer inspection, however, we find that the picture is not so clearcut. For example, neuroscience research is highlighting the plasticity and changing nature of the brain in association with environmental conditions (this is discussed in more detail in chapter 4). Our brains are not static, but continually changing as we experience changes in life. This suggests that the criterion of time is applicable even to ideas associated with low degrees of freedom.

On the other hand, the criterion of time is also applicable to ideas describing behavior with higher degrees of freedom, because there is also strong continuity in meaning systems and the ways in which things are done. This continuity is sustained by *carriers*, which act as hooks on which values, meanings, sentiments, and the like are hung (Moghaddam, 2002). For example, a national flag acts as a carrier, as do labels referring to stereotypes of men, women, Black, White, Hispanic, and so on.

The continuity supported by carriers is complicated by changes in the meanings of the carriers themselves. For example, the United States national flag has changed meaning to some degree over time, as have the values associated with this flag. However, there are certain continuities as well, such as in terms of nationalism and sacrifice for country. Similarly, although the roles of mother and father have changed in major ways over the last century, they have also remained the same in other ways. Thus, despite the changes that take place in thoughts and actions over time, we can validly apply the criterion of time to evaluate great ideas in psychology.

CONCLUDING COMMENT

Since the gradual emergence of modern psychology in the middle of the nineteenth century, a number of ideas have become both central and great. The ideas selected for discussion in this book are not exhaustive, but they are ones that best meet the criteria we considered earlier in this chapter, particularly the key criterion of "time." A fruitful way to evaluate the selected ideas is as works in progress, since in most cases these are ideas still being tested and some of them may well become even more influential in the future, while others may lose their vitality.

The discussion of each "work in progress" is designed to stand separately, so that each chapter can be read on its own. However, there are also important themes running through all of the chapters, such as the relationship between the great ideas and their cultural contexts. Other themes running through the chapters are the issue of degrees of freedom, and the extent to which each great idea is associated with working in or working out. Consequently, each chapter can be read separately, but chapters can also be read as part of a longer story about the characteristics of great ideas, and the relation between ideas and their cultural and historical contexts.

FURTHER READING

Danzinger, K. (1990). *Constructing the subject: Historical origins of psychological research*. New York: Cambridge University Press.

Gergen, K. (1973). Social psychology as history. *Journal of Personality and Social Psychology, 26*, 309–320.

Harre, R. (2005). *Key thinkers in 20th century psychology*. London: Sage.

Leahey, T. H. (2004). *A history of psychology: Main currents in psychological thought*. 6th edn. Upper Saddle River, NJ: Pearson/Prentice Hall.

Moghaddam, F. M. (2002). *The individual and society: A cultural integration*. New York: Worth.

Sternberg, R. J. (2003). *The anatomy of impact: what makes the great works of psychology great*. Washington: American Psychological Association Press.

Wundt, W. (1978). *Elements of folk psychology: Outlines of a psychological history of the development of mankind*. Washington: University Publications of America.

2

THE PSYCHOLOGY LABORATORY

For thousands of years philosophers speculated about the characteristics of human thought and action, but it is only relatively recently that systematic and controlled methods for testing such speculations have been developed. The progress made by modern psychology has been possible because of one method in particular: the *psychology laboratory experiment*, an experiment conducted in a separate physical space in which all the important characteristics can be controlled. The laboratory has gained a uniquely important place in psychology. The currently dominant school of psychology, cognitive psychology, relies heavily on the laboratory method. The cognitive approach pervades all research domains, including the domain of *social psychology*, the scientific study of individual behavior in social contexts, where over eighty percent of studies are conducted in the laboratory. What explains this dominance of the laboratory method in psychology? Why are survey methods, or observation methods, or open interview methods, or discourse analysis methods not the most often used by psychologists?

A major reason for the popularity of the laboratory method is the superior level of control achieved by studying specific features of the individual isolated in a laboratory, relative to that achieved in other research methods, including surveys, observational procedures, and interview methods. Through a high level of control of all the factors in a situation, researchers can examine connections between independent variables, assumed causes, and dependent variables, assumed effects. This I call *the causal assumption*, which proposes that all behavior is determined by cause(s). Greater control achieved in the laboratory leads to higher *reliability*, meaning that experimental procedures can be replicated and results can be repeated. However, critics have raised questions about *validity*, the meaning of what is measured in the laboratory and how results from laboratory experiments can be interpreted.

Another way to view the laboratory method in relation to other available methods for psychological research is in terms of the degrees of freedom afforded. The laboratory method allows for lower degrees of freedom, so that the range of behaviors available to participants is smaller relative to other methods, such as observational and interview techniques. The tighter control and lower degrees of freedom have some advantages, but they also have possible disadvantages, and these have been debated throughout the history of psychology. In essence, this debate is associated with working out and working in, because the laboratory method is more in line with working in, keeping close to hard data derived under controlled experiments. In this chapter, I critically highlight key aspects of the debate on the laboratory method. An example of research based on working in and affording lower degrees of freedom are behaviorist studies using the so-called "Skinner box" (see chapter 6 in this book). A rat is placed in a small box and the only behavioral options are for the rat to press a lever or not (i.e. low degrees of freedom), and data gathered by observations of this behavior are used to formulate laws of learning (working in, keeping closer to hard facts). The characteristics of the laboratory method that made it more appealing to traditional psychology have roots in the early days of modern psychology, which we turn to next.

THE LABORATORY BECOMES CENTRAL TO PSYCHOLOGY

The central role of the laboratory as a hallmark of modern psychology first evolved in the mid nineteenth century when psychology attempted to become a science in the mold of the hard sciences, such as chemistry and physics. The German researcher Wilhelm Wundt (1832–1920) is traditionally credited with establishing the first psychology laboratory, in 1879. But a number of other researchers exploring psychological questions were also testing individuals under controlled conditions, such as Herman Helmholtz (1821–94), who contributed to research in sensation and perception, and Gustav Fechner (1801–1887), the founder of psychophysics. The Englishman Francis Galton (1822–1911) in the early 1880s tested close to ten thousand people in an attempt to measure intelligence by administering a battery of tests under controlled conditions.

Galton measured reaction time, auditory ability, and other aspects of sensory capacity which he believed determine intelligence (this assumption was later seriously criticized; see chapter 7).

In the United States, William James (1842–1910) had set up a physiological psychology laboratory as early as 1875, and in 1883 he established a psychophysics laboratory. But James was not keen on experimental work himself, much preferring to spend his time on writing broad, theoretically rich texts, such as his monumental *Principles of Psychology*. In other words, James preferred to work out rather than to work in. James's personal skepticism about the value of experimental work may explain why Wundt, rather than James, is credited with establishing the first psychology laboratory. One can hardly credit a skeptic of a new idea with being its founder.

The three most dominant schools of scientific psychology since the mid nineteenth century – structuralism, behaviorism, and cognitive psychology – have all relied heavily on the laboratory method. In the latter part of the nineteenth century, psychological research was dominated by the laboratory studies of Wundt and those he influenced, such as Edward Titchener (1867–1927). In this early phase, among the phenomena studied extensively in the laboratory, perhaps the most "social" was association, first introduced by Galton and adapted by Wundt to study types of word association. Wundt and his students used *introspection*, self-reports by respondents about their private thought processes and experiences, to systematically study aspects of cognition, such as association and memory.

Wundt did not believe the laboratory method to be appropriate for studying topics such as values, myths, language, and other social features of human life. These phenomena would be part of Wundt's proposed folk or cultural psychology, a second kind of psychology to be studied through a variety of qualitative and quantitative methods outside the laboratory. Wundt's proposal for a second psychology is in line with researchers who work out, developing grand theories without being tied closely to experimental evidence. In the first half of the twentieth century, behaviorism was the most influential school and heavily relied on the laboratory method. Since the late 1950s, cognitive psychology has dominated, and again given central place to the laboratory method.

The laboratory method in behaviorism and cognitive psychology

Early in the twentieth century Wundt and his followers became far less influential in psychology, in large part because the method of introspection they had adopted was criticized as fatally flawed. Some laboratories using introspection reported that thought was only possible through images, but others reported that "imageless thought" does take place. Supporters of these opposing views locked horns at the start of the twentieth century, but introspection was judged to be unable to resolve this kind of dispute, because it did not seem to offer an objective way of evaluating contradictory reports provided by different research participants. When Jane claims she always has images associated with thoughts, and Judy claims she can have thoughts without associated images, how can we decide which of them is correct if we rely on introspection? The answer, declared behaviorists, is "We can't!" According to J. B. Watson, who launched behaviorism with much fanfare through his "behaviorist manifesto" (1913), psychology can only become a science by focusing exclusively on observable phenomena, the publicly observed stimuli that impinge on behavior and the responses they cause.

Behaviorism was the dominant school of academic psychology for about half a century after Watson's manifesto, and this served to give the laboratory an even more prominent position in psychology. Irrespective of whether studies involved animals or humans, behaviorists focused on the control of all other factors in the laboratory except the stimuli serving as independent variables, to measure their impact on the responses serving as the dependent variables. Famously, behaviorists conducted laboratory experiments using a Skinner box, often with rats or pigeons as participants. This consisted of a box that typically had nothing in it except a food dispenser. A rat could press a bar or a pigeon could peck at a disk in order to get food. As a starting point, it was demonstrated that a response that was reinforced by a positive stimulus, such as food, was more likely to be repeated. On the other hand, a response that was negatively reinforced, by an electric shock for example, was less likely to be repeated. Through extensive and detailed studies involving different reinforcement schedules, researchers systematically formulated the "laws of learning," and made particularly important contributions to applied domains, such as behavior therapy through which dysfunctional behaviors, such as phobias to open spaces or dogs and other common animals, can be treated.

The behaviorists worked in, attempting to reduce behavior to stimulus–response units, and the laboratory was well suited for this task. The laboratory method as traditionally used in psychology has been associated with *reductionism*, the attempt to explain behavior with reference to smaller units. By reducing behavior to smaller units, it is assumed, the task of explaining behavior becomes more manageable. After all, human behavior is extremely complex, and simplification seems like a good route to understanding this complexity.

The dominant position of behaviorism was coming to an end by the late 1950s, but the dominance of the laboratory methods continued. From the late 1950s, the so-called "cognitive revolution," spearheaded by the psychologist Jerome Bruner, the linguist Noam Chomsky, and others, was putting forward a serious alternative to behaviorism. Cognitive psychology brought the mind and thinking back into scientific psychology. But bringing the mind back into psychology did not change the favored method for conducting studies, which remained the laboratory. In some respects the laboratory method has been even more central to cognitive psychology than it was for behaviorists. For example, the traditional approach to studying memory in cognitive psychology is to examine how a person isolated in a laboratory remembers bits of information, typically designed to be as meaningless as possible, under different conditions.

Also, reductionism was still adhered to. For cognitive psychologists this means reducing behavior to cognitive processes, heuristics, and the like, and seeing causes in cognitive mechanisms. More recently, *cognitive neuroscientists*, who study the biology of the mind, reduced "causes" to the level of "brain centers," neurons, and neurotransmitters. For example, they have studied the impact of brain lesions on memory functioning. Also, both behaviorism and cognitive psychology have adopted a causal model of behavior, meaning that their research is intended to discover assumed causes for behavior. The causal model closely matches the incorporation of independent and dependent variables in the traditional laboratory experiment, and we critically assess this issue later in this chapter.

The laboratory and social behavior

Our hero suddenly found himself in a changed world; everything was now going against him. Just a few months before, his life had been wonderful. He had fallen madly in love with a beautiful and talented girl, who seemed to be passionate about him as well. His studies were going well, and he had a close and caring relationship with his mother and father. Then, without warning, his world turned upside down. His father died, and very soon after the funeral, far too soon our hero believed, his mother married his uncle. Our hero began to hate his uncle, first because his uncle had married his mother, and second because he suspected that his uncle and mother had somehow been involved in the murder of his father. But by now all the family power and fortune was firmly in the hands of his uncle, a usurper and murderer!

To make matters worse, our hero was plagued by doubts: How could he be sure of his uncle's guilt? What if he was wrong? Should he revenge the death of his father by killing his uncle? What if he killed his uncle in revenge, and it was never proven that his father had been murdered by his uncle?

Doubts, self-questioning, all kinds of uncertainty plagued our hero. And what of the girl he loved – would he have to abandon her and devote himself exclusively to revenging the murder of his father? Life did not seem worth living. He even contemplated suicide at this point. Our hero needed certainty; he needed proof of guilt or innocence. With proof, he could take action and not be plagued by doubts. The uncertainty seemed to be driving him insane. Everyone started to see him as mad. He had to act, but first he had to have proof.

Then, in a flash of inspiration, a brilliant idea came to our hero. He would set up an experiment. He would be the experimenter, and a number of confederates would cooperate with him to set up and run the experiment. They would re-enact the exact way in which his father was supposed to have been killed by his uncle. All the script for the experiment would be worked out in detail, and only one part would be left open: the part to be played by the participants, the audience for the "play" that was going to be put on. The hero's uncle and mother were to be part of the audience.

Our hero devised a brilliant method for manipulating an independent variable in order to test its effect on the dependent variable. The independent variable in this experiment was the two different types of behavior presented in the play: in *Condition 1*, normal scenes in life would be presented; in *Condition 2*, the murder scene would be presented. The dependent variable in the experiment was the emotional reactions of the participants: the reactions of our hero's mother and uncle would be compared with the reactions of other participants observing the same scenes. The emotional reactions of the participants would indicate their guilt or innocence.

Our hero runs his experiment. In *Condition 1*, all the participants display normal emotional reactions. In *Condition 2*, when the murder is committed, by poison being poured into an ear of our hero's late father, two participants, our hero's uncle and mother, show unusually strong emotional reactions, noticeably different from the reactions of other participants in the audience. Our hero interprets this as evidence of guilt. His inference proves to be valid. His uncle is guilty of murder. His experiment has worked.

Our hero is Hamlet, in William Shakespeare's play of the same name. The social experiment conducted by Hamlet in order to "catch the conscience of the king," is in important ways like an experiment a modern social psychologist might devise and run in the laboratory. Hamlet's experiment is a play within a play. Can all laboratory experiments be thought of as drama? I argue that the answer to this question is "No." Laboratory experiments on only some, not all, types of behavior can be usefully interpreted as drama.

The laboratory method has been extended to include the study of social behavior, through studies on topics such as prejudice, aggression, altruism, group and inter-group dynamics, conformity, and obedience (for detailed examples concerning conformity and obedience, see chapters 15 and 16). Researchers attempt to identify the key factors in a situation and operationalize these factors as quantified variables in an experiment. For example, in studies on inter-group relations starting in the late 1960s, Henri Tajfel and his students at Bristol University, England, identified "social categorization" (the placing of people into groups) as a fundamental factor that, under certain conditions, could by itself lead to inter-group bias. Tajfel's experiment was termed the "minimal group paradigm," because it reduced inter-group relations to its barest form: simply knowing whether one is in group X or group Y. First, participants were placed in groups X or Y on the basis of a trivial criterion such as how many dots they estimated on a screen. Next, participants allocated points to others in groups X and Y, without knowing the identity of these others, but knowing that they themselves would not receive any of the points they allocated.

The finding that even minimal group membership can lead to inter-group bias proved to be surprising and controversial, and serves to highlight some of the pros and cons of the laboratory method. On the one hand, the minimal group paradigm has proved to be reliable, with hundreds of replications conducted since the initial studies. On the other hand, questions have been raised about the validity of the method: how meaningful is it to be arbitrarily placed in groups labeled "X," "Y," and the like and asked to allocate points to people you never meet? How can such an experiment inform us about bias in the real world involving deep-rooted passions, hatreds, historical injustices, and so forth? Tajfel and his supporters argue that the point of their experiment is that, rather than trying to mimic the real world, it demonstrates that inter-group bias can occur even under the minimal conditions they set up. This is part of the ongoing debate about the validity of the laboratory method, to which we shall return again in this chapter.

In summary, although there have been fundamental changes in the kinds of schools of thought dominating psychology during different periods of the last 150 years or so, the dominance of the laboratory methods has not wavered. The vast majority of studies published in traditional journals are conducted in the laboratory. The main advantage of the laboratory is still seen to be the control of variables, so that the link between cause and effect, independent variable and dependent variable, can be objectively studied.

CRITICAL THINKING QUESTIONS

1 If Hamlet could have conducted a more formal and better controlled experiment, what might he have changed?

2 What do you believe are the two most important reasons why the laboratory method is favored in traditional psychology?

CRITICALLY ASSESSING THE PSYCHOLOGY LABORATORY

The laboratory method is included as a great idea because it is truly revolutionary: after thousands of years of armchair speculation about human thought and action, we now have a method for studying human thinking and behavior under controlled conditions. The laboratory method has brought a higher degree of reliability in psychological research and gained psychology some level of scientific respectability. However, there are also limitations associated with the laboratory method. First, the psychology laboratory arose out of a particular cultural context and has limitations associated with this context. Of course, all methods arise out of particular cultural contexts, and are in some ways limited by this. Second, in interpreting the results of psychology experiments, it is important to keep in mind the degrees of freedom afforded, the behavioral options available to participants.

The cultural context of the psychology laboratory

The psychology laboratory arose out of the Western context, and became firmly established as the main research method particularly through the influence of US culture.

A first way in which the psychology laboratory reflects Western and particularly US culture concerns the "implicit research knowledge" that individuals need to have in order to successfully participate in laboratory studies. Imagine going to a village in a non-Western country, as I have done, and asking villagers, who may be illiterate, economically poor, and technologically unsophisticated, to participate in a laboratory experiment. Typical responses from villagers are very likely to be: "Who are you, a government agent?" "What is a laboratory? From what you describe it seems like a kind of prison." "What law have I broken that you want to put me in a room by myself?" Even if you offer to pay such villagers, they will be very suspicious about your intentions and will be bewildered as to what you want from them. Some of the same reactions will be evident among some groups in Western societies, but Western populations are generally far more knowledgeable, and better prepared, for participation in laboratory experiments. This higher level of implicit research knowledge is part of Western industrial culture and goes hand in hand with the extensive use of laboratory methods in psychology. The implication is that the laboratory method is not suitable for research in all societies and all groups, so there are possible limitations to basing a science of *human* thought and action on this method.

A second way in which the laboratory method is in line with Western and particularly US culture concerns individualism. The US is the most individualistic major society in the world, dominated as it is by an ethos of "self help" and "individual responsibility." The "American Dream" espouses an ideal of individual mobility: anyone can make it, as long as she or he has personal ability, is hard-working, and so on. If Jane is a millionaire and Carole is penniless, it must be because Jane is hard-working, talented, motivated, and so on, and Carole is not. Given this cultural background, it is perhaps inevitable that the use of the psychology laboratory has been influenced by individualism and reductionism. The assumption has been that one can come to a valid understanding of human behavior by studying individuals in isolation, and that the causes of behavior lie within, and can be reduced to, factors inside individuals.

Social relationships are seen as secondary and unimportant in explaining behavior. For example, in studying memory, the focus is on how isolated individuals remember, and not how people reconstruct the past through interactions with one another. In other words, it is "isolated minds" remembering and not collective remembering that is important. Also, the context of behavior is ignored. For example, the context in which remembering takes place is not taken into consideration. The implication is that the laboratory method can inform us about certain underlying psychological processes but not necessarily about what will happen in the world outside the laboratory. Thus, we need to constantly move back and forth from laboratory research to explorations in the world outside.

Degrees of freedom, physical objects, and human beings

The traditional use of the laboratory in psychology has assumed *causal universalism*, the assumptions that cause–effect relations (1) explain all human behavior and (2) operate in the domain of human behavior in the same way as in the physical world, studied by chemists, physicists, and other hard sciences.

These assumptions are clearly present in standard research methods texts that discuss the use of the psychology laboratory. For example, Solso, Johnson and Beal (1998, chapter 1) explain the idea that behavior is causally determined. Pelham (1999, p. 42) explains that an important reason for the central role of the laboratory method in psychology is that it allows for the study of the assumed causes of behavior under controlled conditions. Also, it is clear that the goal of psychology, according to received wisdom, is to emulate what is assumed to happen in the physical sciences in the search for causes. For example, Solso and colleagues describe Galileo's demonstration that objects of differing weight fall to the ground at the same speed. Where Galileo studied accelerating objects, the authors point out, psychologists study thought and behavior. However, according to these authors both physicists and psychologists research in a "lawful universe" (p. 8), one in which all events have a cause. According to this widely shared view, the goal of psychological research is to discover the causes of thought and behavior, just as physical science research examines the causes of events in the physical world, such as the speed of falling objects.

A critical question demands to be asked: Is all human behavior causally determined? The role that we assume for free will in everyday life strongly suggests that not all human behavior is causally determined by factors outside individuals. For example, when I am driving down a road and arrive at a red light, does the red light cause me to stop in the same way that the ground caused objects released by Galileo from the top of the Leaning Tower of Pisa to stop? Obviously not, because I could choose to ignore the red light and continue to drive through the road crossing. We have all witnessed instances of people driving through red lights, sometimes with fatal consequences. The red light is a cultural signal, with a specific meaning for motorists and pedestrians. But people can and sometimes do choose to disregard this signal.

However, it might be claimed that if we have all possible information about the individual and the context, we will be able to predict when a person will stop at a red light and when, if ever, a person will go through a red light. There are two problems with this claim. First, this takes us out of the realm of science and into the realm of religion, because now we are being asked to have faith that some day in the future all such information will be available. There is a fundamental difference between having faith that such information will become available and having faith that, for example, cancer will one day be defeated: human thought and action arise out of collective social interactions and collaborative constructions, whereas the course of cancer can be accurately charted within the individual body. Second, this causal account based on faith about the complete information we might one day achieve flies against our common sense understanding of the role of free will in everyday life. For example, if I drive through a red light and claim in my defense that "my behavior is causally determined and I should not be held personally responsible for such an action" the response from a jury acting with common sense would surely be "you chose to drive through the red light, and you must face the consequences of your actions." In other words, common sense tells us that people do have free will, and the legal system acts on this basis to hold us responsible for our actions.

Consequently, we must presume that *some* (not all) types of behavior are not causally determined; at least, this is the assumption we work with in the law courts and in everyday life. Such behavior involves an individual selecting to act in one way rather than in other ways, choosing to stop at a red light rather than to drive through, eating with a knife and fork rather than with bare hands, waiting until the end of class to use a cell phone rather than during class, and so on. Most of the time most people do the correct thing according to local norms and rules. Because of the normative nature of most behavior, certain patterns and regularities are discernable. However, this regularity should not mislead us to assume that all behavior is causally determined and absolutely predictable. What we can predict is that there is a very high level of probability that most people within a particular society will show certain similar patterns of behavior. But the possibility is always open for individuals and groups to reject cultural norms and adopt new ways of doing things, and this is reflected in the counter-cultures and alternative life-styles that often characterize new generations. This viewpoint, emphasizing different probabilities for certain types of behavior, suggests that there is a better way than causal/non-causal to conceptualize behavior. My preference is to use the idea of degrees of freedom.

Certain behaviors are associated with a low degree of freedom. For example, my ability to hear is determined by certain features of my biological makeup, particularly the tiny bones (the hammer, the anvil, and the stirrup) connected to the eardrum, and the cochlea. If these bones or the cochlea are damaged, hearing impairment will result. In other words, there are zero or few degrees of freedom for me to shape the outcome. People with normal hearing can hear sound waves in the range of 15–20 hertz to about 15,000–20,000 hertz. Again, this is a biologically determined limitation and the threshold of hearing, the sound intensity that an individual can hear fifty percent of the time, can be studied in the laboratory on the assumption that the individual can do little to change this behavior.

But there are a vast variety of other behaviors, traditionally conceived under broad headings such as "social," "personality," "cognition," that when studied in a laboratory afford higher degrees of freedom. In laboratory experiments focused on such behavior, participants typically enter the laboratory wondering, "What am I supposed to do?" They look for clues in the context to inform them about the most appropriate behavior for the setting. The setting and the script have been set, and the only part that is left open is that of "participant." The research question is: How will the participant play this part?

The behavior shown by participants in such settings has higher degrees of freedom but is still guided by cultural norms and rules. Consequently, a pattern emerges in how people behave in the laboratory experiment. For example, in Milgram's famous study (1974) on obedience to authority, about sixty-five percent of participants in the US study obeyed the authority figure of the scientist in the lab coat and administered (supposedly) lethal electric shocks to a learner (actually, a confederate of the experimenter). Although most participants in Milgram's study saw it as appropriate to obey the authority figure, about thirty-five percent did not see it this way and refused to obey. This is a typical pattern of results for laboratory experiments in many social, personality, cognition domains, indicating that there are higher degrees of freedom for this kind of behavior, but it still does follow certain cultural patterns because most people do what they think is appropriate in a given context.

This discussion has important implications for how we should interpret the results of laboratory studies. First, the findings of studies on many types of behavior are indicative of norms and rules, and not reflective of cause–effect relations as understood in the physical sciences. Second, in many instances laboratory findings provide valuable information about basic psychological processes but do not necessarily tell us what will happen in everyday life.

The laboratory experiment and validity

There is general agreement that because of the high degree of control achieved in the laboratory setting, reliability of measurement is high, but critics have raised questions about validity and the meaning of behavior in a laboratory. For example, critics have contended that participants in a laboratory setting do not behave as they would in the real world, and that inferences should not be made about behavior in the real world on the basis of findings from laboratory research. The criticism of the laboratory as lacking realism has resulted in attempts to clarify types of realism. *Mundane realism* is the similarity of events in the experiment to events in the real world. This is seen as less important than *experimental realism*, the realism of the experimental situation for the participants, how much it impacts on them. I have pointed to the importance of *cultural realism* involving the recognition, first, of the context as requiring certain types of behavior and, second, that not behaving in the culturally appropriate way would be a serious transgression.

An alternative way to assess this controversy is to focus more on types of validity than on types of realism. The argument here is that the laboratory has high *internal validity*, the demonstration that manipulation of independent variable(s) caused a change in dependent variable(s), and this is what is most important. For researchers taking this approach, *external validity*, the extent to which findings would generalize to people and situations outside the laboratory, is far less important. In the continuing debate about the merits of the laboratory method, one point that most people agree on is that there is a fundamental difference between the physical objects that scientists such as Galileo have studied and the human participants studied by psychologists: humans self-reflect and have the power to think about the scientist studying them, whereas, as far as we know, physical objects, such as stones falling from a tower, have no such power. Also, as far as we know, stones do not change their minds about taking part in an experiment, whereas many human participants can and do change their minds about how they behave, both inside and outside the laboratory.

In summary, the psychology laboratory reflects the individualism of Western and particularly US culture and is more appropriate for use with participants who have a minimum level of knowledge about the meaning of scientific research, and some familiarity with research procedures and goals. This limitation is shared by many other research methods in domains outside psychology, such as political science surveys. If a political scientist is exploring relationships between voting patterns and political advertising, many populations in many regions of the world would not be appropriate for inclusion in such a study, because they would lack adequate experience with and under-standing of democratic voting and political advertising.

The laboratory is high on reliability, but critics contend it is low on validity. The laboratory is particularly effective to study the causes of behavior when there are fewer degrees of freedom, an example being perceptual thresholds. However, when degrees of freedom are higher, when behavior has to do with meaning systems, the interpretation of results becomes far more complicated and controversial. But patterns of predictability still do arise because participants can share interpre-tations of how they should behave, as in the case of Milgram's studies of obedience to authority (see chapter 18).

CONCLUDING COMMENT

A word of caution is needed on the matter of "the culture of partici-pants." Through travel and work in different countries, I have realized that young university students in different countries throughout the twenty-first-century world share many experiences and have lives that are in fundamental ways similar. The music they listen to, the films they watch, the clothes they wear, the food they eat, and even the books they read are very similar. In many ways, the students in the modern universities of Asia, for example, are more similar to Western students than they are to people in the traditional sector of their own Asian societies. Unfortunately, most so-called "cross-cultural" research continues to rely on university students recruited in Western and non-Western societies. The outcome is that behavior in the laboratory is often reported to be "cross culturally consistent" when in fact the participants are all from the same university student culture even when they live in non-Western societies. The inclusion of illiterate villagers from rural areas of Bangladesh, for example, would be a much truer test of the cross-cultural applicability of laboratory methods. My own attempts to include illiterate Asian villagers in laboratory studies proved to me that the laboratory method is highly limited when participants are from outside Western culture and outside the modern sector of non-Western societies.

CRITICAL THINKING QUESTIONS

1 Imagine you are stepping into a psychology laboratory to take part in an experiment. What kinds of thoughts are on your mind? What are your objectives? How do you see the situation? How would a study of you (with your thoughts, perceptions, and ability to self-reflect) be different from a study of a physical object?

2 In many psychology laboratory experiments, at least some participants consciously or unconsciously behave in a way that is different from the majority of participants. How should we explain such a different pattern of behavior?

FURTHER READING

Harré, R. (2002). *Great scientific experiments: Twenty experiments that changed our view of the world*. 2nd edn. Mineola, NY: Dover.

Moghaddam, F. M. (1998). *Social psychology: Exploring universals across cultures*. New York: Freeman.

Pelham, B. W. (1999). *Conducting experiments in psychology: Measuring the weight of smoke*. New York: Brooks Cole.

Solso, R. L., Johnson, H. H., & Beal, M. K. (1998). *Experimental psychology: A case approach*, 6th edn. New York: Longman.

3
THE PLACEBO EFFECT

What greater psychological idea than "mind over matter" in the domain of health? What greater psychological idea than that how patients think about their health, illness, and medical treatments determines the outcome of treatment? In essence, psychology is taken to be at the heart of health; mental life is assumed to powerfully influence physical being. Nothing less than this underlies the idea of a *placebo,* traditionally considered to be a medically neutral or "inert" medication, or other "hoax" or "sham" procedures or interventions, that the patient *believes* has certain therapeutic powers; the *placebo effect* is the effect on health brought about by the patient's belief in the placebo. Evidence in support of the placebo effect testifies to the power of psychological factors, and the idea that **subjective beliefs can determine the course of physical illness.** Moreover, the universal nature of the placebo effect is evidence that psychological factors have the same powerful impact among all humankind. This effect is not limited to Western societies, but is found in many different parts of the world.

The placebo effect is truly a great psychological idea, but, as we shall see, it is an idea that is being re-evaluated and may prove to be even more important than has been assumed. This re-evaluation includes a re-thinking of the traditional definition of the placebo effect. Received wisdom suggests we should distinguish between an *inactive placebo*, a substance that leads to no physiological changes in the patient, and an *active placebo*, a substance that does create physiological changes in the patient but does not positively impact on the illness being treated. However, this distinction may be too simplistic, because in some instances certain types of placebo have a positive impact through the physiological changes they bring about. In other words, the beliefs, expectations, fears, and other psychological characteristics of patients can lead them to experience improved health through physiological and not just psychological changes.

Another way to view this is in terms of degrees of freedom: the placebo effect suggests that psychological factors can increase the range of possible outcomes of a treatment. The degrees of freedom are determined not just by drug medication but also by patient psychology. The placebo effect is powerful and can come about in different ways, but it is also in some ways still controversial and the debate surrounding the placebo can best be understood in cultural and historical context.

HISTORICAL CONTEXT

Discussions about placebos coincided in the nineteenth century in Western societies with the adoption of a strictly reductionist approach in medicine, designed to discover and to treat pathologies that are demonstrably physiological. The attempt was to work in and to develop medical treatment based on hard facts. Through a gradual process of professionalization, medical practice in Western societies improved in status and separated itself from traditional forms of healing, including religious-based ones, which were dismissed by the medical community as "quackery" or "hoax." Shamans, priests, medicine men and women, non-Western medicine, and the like came to be seen as solutions that could please some of the public but not provide real treatment for patients.

The professionalization of medical practice in Western societies meant that professional bodies, such as the American Medical Association, could now control who had the right to charge fees for providing medical treatment and prescribing medications. It became more and more important that "real doctors" and "real medications" be differentiated from the "quacks" and "hoax medicines," and as part of this effort it was seen as important that the placebo effect be identified and pushed outside the boundaries of legitimate medical practice. After all, the placebo effect comes about because of the beliefs of patients in treatments, and in many cases patients can come to believe in persons and practices that are outside professional medicine. Thus, the placebo effect came to be seen as part of the non-scientific problems confronting modern physicians in their efforts to work in and to establish medical practice firmly on scientific grounds.

After the Second World War research on new medical drugs was routinely designed to identify and isolate the placebo effect – particularly after Henry Beecher's influential paper (1955) in which he reviewed the placebo effect in fifteen different clinical trials and concluded that an average of thirty-five percent of patient improvement owed to placebo alone. The title of Beecher's paper, "The Powerful Placebo," is also the main title of a more recent publication on the placebo effect by Shapiro and Shapiro (2001), in which they argue that until recently the history of medicine was basically the history of the placebo effect, implying that the reason why patients improved in health was because of their belief in the efficacy of the treatment rather than the actual efficacy of the treatment.

According to the prevailing research tradition in the health sciences, it is essential that placebos are used as a control in clinical trials. This requirement is now routinely met as part of the standard procedures of regulatory agencies responsible for approving new drugs, such as the Food and Drug Administration (FDA) in the United States. The standard procedure for clinical trials now also entails *double blind* procedures, meaning that neither the patients nor the researchers are aware which group is the experimental group (i.e. who receive the drug being tested) and which is the control group (i.e. who receive the placebo). The clear implication of all these efforts to try to control for the placebo effect is that, first, there is such an effect and, second, this effect is of fundamental importance in the domain of health.

However, some critics have argued that the contemporary emphasis on the placebo effect is utterly misplaced, because there actually is no such powerful effect. Since the mid 1990s a number of reviews with findings critical of the placebo effect have been published incorporating clinical studies in which patients were randomly assigned to experimental or control groups, typically with experimental groups receiving the drug being tested and control groups receiving a placebo. For example, after conducting a meta-analysis and finding little evidence for a placebo effect, Hrobjartsson and Gotzche (2001) argued that previous research purportedly showing a "powerful placebo" was flawed methodologically. Much more needs to be done, they argue, to try to isolate and demonstrate the placebo effect as an effect distinct from such things as recovery achieved through the natural course of a disease.

How should we interpret the current controversy about the placebo effect? On the one hand there is enormous evidence and experience suggesting there is such an effect, and that it is powerful. On the other, there have been critical attacks on the placebo effect. These attacks should lead to closer and more careful attention to factors that should be taken into consideration in research studies, so that the placebo effect is more accurately identified and measured. Two such factors are considered next.

FACTORS TO CONSIDER IN TESTING FOR THE PLACEBO EFFECT

In the following discussion two main factors are reviewed, with special attention to psychological issues rather than purely medical matters.

Natural course of illness

A first factor to consider is the natural course of an illness and the likelihood of eventual recovery. Depending on the characteristics of the illness and the patients, some or all patients will recover even when not given any treatment. For example, almost everyone can recover from the common cold without taking any treatment (the medications typically taken for the common cold alleviate pain, but recovery would take place without them anyway). It is important to identify recovery as part of the natural course of illness and differentiate it from the effect of the placebo and the experimental treatment. For example, consider cold sufferers randomly assigned to a control group, who receive a placebo, and an experimental group, who receive a new drug being tested. It may be that after two weeks both groups have recovered, so we might conclude that the placebo performed just as effectively as the experimental drug. However, such a conclusion would be misleading, because we have not considered the natural course of the illness. This implies that our research design should also include a "no treatment, no placebo" group, to identify the natural recovery rate.

Behavioral changes

Illness has an important behavioral component, in that we learn to behave like, and to present ourselves to others as, an ill person, a "patient." This learning process begins in early childhood, in part through the child imitating others. The child sees how adults play the role of an ill person and present themselves to others as "ill." For example, mom tells the young child that daddy can't play with him right now because daddy is ill and needs to take a rest in a quite room all by himself. Through such episodes, the child learns that an ill person should spend a lot of time resting in bed away from others, should be inactive, should not engage in physical exercises. In this way, what it means to be ill is arrived at in part by learning how one should behave when ill.

The child also learns to behave like an ill person through suggestions and instructions from caretakers. For example, when mom discovers that three-year-old Jimmy has a high temperature, she says to him, "You poor darling, you must be feeling so weak. Your head must be aching. Are your eyes sore? Try to eat some of your soup. You can't eat solids when you're ill like this." Jimmy is provided with guides, some more subtle than others, as to how he is supposed to behave when he has a high temperature. Soon, when appropriate, he is able to present himself to others as an ill person and behave according to societal expectations.

The social construction of illness is to some degree influenced by the physiological characteristics of the illness being experienced. This means, more specifically, that there are limitations on how the role of an ill person can be performed. For example, if a cancer patient is experiencing excruciating pain and can hardly move, it will be very difficult for the patient to present himself as agile and carefree. Or, to consider another example, a person suffering from migraine has fairly severe limitations as to how she or he can present herself during a migraine attack. However, even in such extreme cases the learning of behavior repertoires is fundamental to how the patient actually behaves.

Patients who are given a placebo may come to believe that the placebo has improved their health, and change their behavior to present themselves as a healthy rather than as an ill person. In such cases, the illness of the patient may continue, but the patient's behavior could (wrongly) indicate improved health. Thus, the impact of the placebo may be misinterpreted as improving the health of the patient, whereas all that changed was the patient's self-presentation.

On the other hand, it could be argued that in some circumstances and for patients suffering from certain illnesses, presentations of the self as healthy will lead others to treat one as healthy and may actually result in improved health. In other words, self-presentation style can act as a form of self-fulfilling prophesy. Individuals who are viewed as healthy by others may come to see themselves as healthy and to follow a regular diet, exercise in the fresh air, and generally adopt a more healthy lifestyle. As a consequence, their health may well improve. On the other hand, individuals who are labeled by others as "sick" are likely to take on the behavior of ill persons. This possibility is confirmed by the long line of research critical of traditional psychiatry, from the work of R. D. Laing and Thomas Szasz in the 1960s to more recent research that emphasizes the social construction of illness and the treatment of those labeled "ill" by society (Kitwood, 1990).

Researchers in the so-called "anti-psychiatry" movement share certain fundamental beliefs with humanistic psychology, a school of psychology that emerged in opposition to behaviorism and psychoanalysis and flourished particularly in the 1960s through the influence of Carl Rogers and Abraham Maslow, among others. Most importantly, the anti-psychiatry movement and humanistic psychology are both opposed to drug therapy in the realm of mental health, or at least drug therapy in the way it is traditionally practiced. Also, they both give importance to the collaboration of the "client" (patient) with the therapist, in what they see as an exploration of the inner self. They believe the role of the therapist should be that of a collaborator and guide rather than an expert giving directives and making changes in the behavior of a "patient."

Thus, critics argue that the placebo effect may actually not exist, but be (mistakenly) assumed to exist as a result of at least two series of events: first, recovery owing to the natural course of an illness; second, real or imagined recovery as a result of behavioral changes in the patient. The way forward, critics argue, is to conduct more studies that include not just an experimental and a control (placebo) condition but also at least a "no-intervention" condition. Patients in the no-intervention condition would experience the natural course of the illness, and their rate of recovery would act as the base line for comparisons. Although this is a constructive suggestion that should be taken up by researchers, the criticism that "there is no such thing as a placebo effect" is clearly wrong. As we shall see in the next section, the placebo is probably even more powerful than previously imagined. However, in order to understand the way the placebo works and how it achieves its power, we must consider the placebo effect in cultural context.

MEANING AND THE ACTIVE PLACEBO

Placebos work because they are ascribed meaning by patients. The full power of this meaning ascription can be better understood by considering the case of active placebos, which can involve physiological reactions brought about by belief. The active placebo not only underlines the power of the placebo, but forces us to re-think the traditional definition of a placebo effect.

Active placebo

In the introductory discussion we saw that the distinction between a placebo that leads to no physiological reactions in the patient (inactive) and a placebo that does create physiological reactions (active) is too simplistic and needs to be further clarified. In particular, the active placebo needs to be further differentiated at least in the following way.

The first type of active placebo I term *negative active placebo*, because the physiological reactions that result from the placebo do not *directly* improve the disorder being studied. However, these physiological reactions could still indirectly improve the disorder being studied if the patients come to believe that they are in the experimental condition and have received the experimental treatment. For example, Judy is in a study testing a new pill for treating migraine headaches. She receives a placebo pill, which results in physiological reactions that are detected by her. Judy comes to believe that she is in the experimental group and that she should be experiencing less migraine pain. This "positive illusion" could in itself be associated with and perhaps even influence improvements in her health.

But there are also what I term *positive active placebos*, which result in a physiological reaction that does improve the disorder being studied. More detailed evidence and information concerning this type of placebo is starting to become available. For example, researchers used positron emission tomography (PET) in a double blind study to assess levels of dopamine in the brains of Parkinson's disease patients who were administered either a placebo or an active drug (Fuente-Fernandez et al., 2001). In another trial, patients knew whether they had been given the active drug and at what level, or had been given neither drug nor placebo. Of particular interest was the level of endogenous release of dopamine in the part of the brain, the striatum, most seriously impacted by Parkinson's disease. The researchers concluded that in Parkinson's disease the placebo effect is mediated by an increase in the synaptic levels of dopamine in the striatum. The amount of dopamine increase resulting from placebo is at least similar to that brought about by an active drug.

Another domain in which the placebo effect has been shown to be powerful is depression. In response to an influential book entitled *Listening to Prozac* (Kramer, 1993), which argued for the positive benefits of the anti-depression drug Prozac, the results of a meta-analysis were published under the title "Listening to Prozac and Hearing Placebo" (Kirsch & Sapirstein, 1998), arguing that up to seventy-five percent of the efficacy of antidepressant medication actually represents the placebo effect. A more recent study used quantitative electro-encephalography (QEEG) examined brain activity in depressed patients administered either a placebo or an antidepressant medication. First, the decline in depression was similar for patients administered placebo and medication. Second, placebo responders showed an increase in prefrontal cordance that was not evident in medication responders. This shows that, in the case of some patients at least, what I have termed "positive active placebos" induce changes in brain function that are not the same as those associated with anti-depression medication.

But, as I suggested earlier, there are limits to the power of placebos, and this is reflected in the kinds of physical changes they can bring about. For example, in a study involving cancer patients, the placebo effect proved powerless to treat tumors (Chvetzoff & Tannock, 2003). Despite the limitations suggested by this kind of study, however, the placebo effect does lead to beneficial physiological reactions in domains such as depression.

Recent research trends suggest a need to re-think the traditional conception of a placebo. The idea of a positive active placebo, for which there is now some evidence, seems to contradict the traditional definition of a placebo as an inert substance or treatment. How can we claim that a placebo is inert if in at least some cases it does have a direct physiological effect that results in improvements in the illness being studied? One solution would be to distinguish between the predicted benefits gained from an experimental treatment and the unpredicted benefits gained from a positive active placebo. However, this approach is problematic in that in many cases experimental treatments and drugs also have unpredicted benefits. A second approach would be to re-think the types of things encompassed by the definition of the placebo effect and to re-define what I have termed "positive active placebo" as an effective treatment rather than a placebo.

Meaning systems and placebo

The placebo effect is best understood within a cultural and historical context, and more specifically the meaning system within which individuals live in a given time and place. The placebo effect comes about through the beliefs that individuals have about the healing power and influence of certain carriers that pass on the values of a culture (as discussed in chapter 1). For example, in Western societies science is highly prized, some think of it as a new religion, and medical doctors are carriers of scientific values. The medical doctor represents the authority and prestige of science. Advertisers know that a medication or a treatment that is recommended by medical doctors rather than, for example, members of the general public is taken more seriously and is more likely to be followed by patients. That is why medical doctors often appear in advertisements for medical drugs. Their word counts more for patients and sells more drugs.

The Western patient who is given a pill by a medical doctor ascribes important meanings to the pill, because the pill is seen as being endorsed by an authority figure, a scientifically trained doctor. The same pill given to a patient by a plumber, student, or painter, for example, would not be ascribed the same meaning. It is in this context that we can best understand the healing power of the various "healers," "shamans," "witchdoctors," and other local traditional persons who throughout the ages have specialized in treating the sick, sometimes with a surprisingly high degree of success.

For example, shamans play an important part in the lives of the Yanomamo, a tribe indigenous to the Amazon region in northern Brazil and southern Venezuela. Shamans influence the spirit world in the battle between health and illness. Among the Yanomamo, only men can become shamans, and those who aspire to do so have to go through extensive and rigorous training, including fasting and abstinence from sex. They learn magic chants and songs, and use hallucinogenic snuff to help them contact the spirits. The faith that Yanomamo patients have in local shamans influences the health benefits they receive from shamanic ceremonies. In a sense, the chants, potions, and practices of Yanomamo shamans act like placebos; they can improve health through changing the mental states of patients.

Viewing shamanism from a Western twenty-first-century perspective, we may (mistakenly) assume that our own practices are completely different. After all, we place our faith in modern science rather than in spirits. However, a closer examination of behavior in Western societies reveals that faith in the spiritual world also plays an important role in health and illness, at least for some groups of people. There is a generally positive association between religious belief and health. One reason may be because more religious people are less likely to indulge in drinking, smoking, addictive drugs, and so on. Also, prayers and religious services may serve to reduce anxiety and stress levels, in the same way that meditation and yoga have health benefits.

In summary, the meaning that patients ascribe to actual or potential treatments, be they physical interventions (such as pills or medical operations) or spiritual ceremonies, can be fundamentally important in treatment outcomes. Such ascribed meanings can be so powerful and influential that they give rise to physiological changes beneficial for the health of a patient. This underlies both the power of the placebo effect and its greatness as a psychological idea.

CRITICAL THINKING QUESTIONS

1   Do you approve of the definition of a placebo as an "inert substance or treatment"?

2   What does the idea of a "positive active placebo" imply for the relationship between mind and body?

COMPLICATING FACTORS

Despite critical attacks aimed at the very idea of a placebo effect, there is sufficient evidence to claim that the placebo effect does exist and is powerful, at least in the case of certain illnesses and certain patients. Of fundamental importance is the cultural context and, more specifically, the meanings ascribed to the placebo by the patient. But the questions raised by the placebo effect are more complex than I have indicated so far, one reason being that the placebo effect is not simply a technical issue; as we shall see in the next section, it is also a moral one.

Ethics and the placebo effect

The testing of new drugs now routinely involves at least two conditions: an experimental condition in which the new drug is administered to patients and a control condition in which a placebo is administered to patients. In such studies, patients are randomly assigned to conditions. Consequently, one group of patients will receive a drug that in some cases could be life saving, whereas the second group of patients will by chance only receive a placebo. From the start, the assumption of the drug developers is that the new drug will be effective and lead to improved health and longer lives in patients. Consequently, it could be argued that researchers are playing a lottery with the lives of patients, randomly picking one group to live better lives, or to live at all, and condemning another group to sickness and perhaps earlier death.

The general consensus among researchers is to agree that the use of placebos in research does raise ethical issues but is not in itself an unethical practice when considered in the light of the interests of humankind as a whole. The incorporation of placebos in research allows experimenters to better identify effective drugs and in this way to improve health and save lives in the future. Without the use of placebos, it is argued, humankind would live in poorer health in the future.

However, this generally adopted view is not without problems. There are alternative ways of designing drug-testing studies so as not to include placebos. For example, by varying the doses of different drugs administered to patients and plotting dose–response curves, it is possible to gage the efficacy of different drugs relative to one another without the use of placebos. This "non-placebo" alternative test design could still be criticized on ethical grounds, because not all patients will necessarily receive the most effective drug treatment when different doses and drugs are being tried out in comparison with one another. Consequently, defenders of the use of placebos could argue that such alternative non-placebo research procedures share the same ethical shortcomings as traditional designs that incorporate placebos.

Addiction to placebos

A very different type of ethical issue is raised by strong supporters of the placebo: given that the placebo effect is known to be positive and powerful in the case of some illnesses and some patients, why should doctors not use the placebo effect as another tool in the struggle between health and illness? What does it matter if a patient is cured by a placebo or a real pill, as long as health improves?

This reasoning seems sound on the surface, but when we dig a little deeper we discover shortcomings. One problem that can arise is that patients become addicted to placebos; they come to depend on all kinds of "wonder drugs" that are no different from sugar pills, and to treatments that are akin to quackery. In some cases, patients can come to adopt superstitious behavior, such as following certain ritual routines before going to bed or during a meal, as part of their dependence on placebos. This opens the door to all kinds of fraudulent practices and to "healers" who may do more harm than good.

Animals and the placebo effect

The use of animals in drug development research is common, and an intriguing question arises concerning animals and placebos: does the placebo effect arise in animals? The results of some studies seem to suggest that the placebo effect does arise in animal behavior, but this seems to contradict the idea that placebos depend on ascribed meaning. Are we to believe that animals ascribe meaning to drugs or to the scientists administering the drugs to them? Do animals share our meaning systems?

The solution to this riddle is rather subtle and has implications for placebos in studies with humans as well. Animals who are placed in a control placebo condition do benefit, but not from the placebo. The benefit they receive arises from the attention they get. Animals selected to be part of a study are typically given special treatment irrespective of whether they are placed in the experimental or the control (placebo) condition. There animals are handled regularly and monitored frequently. Often, special efforts are made to make sure they eat and drink regularly. The stimulation and attention they receive are very likely to have beneficial effects on their health. These benefits arise just from an animal being part of a study, independent of the placebo effect and the effect of the drug being tested. The same argument can be made about placebos and human behavior: that patients in a control placebo condition improve in health not because of a placebo effect but because of the increased attention they receive as a result of being in a study.

CRITICAL THINKING QUESTIONS

1 Do you believe it is ethical to give one group of patients a placebo and another group an active drug?

2 Given that placebos can sometimes bring benefits, should we use placebos more often as a regular part of medical treatment?

CONCLUDING COMMENT

The placebo effect is powerful and sometimes of considerable benefit in health. The traditional view that the placebo effect involves only psychological factors is being reconsidered, as a result of research demonstrating physiological reactions arising from the placebo effect; reactions that, for example, lead to better health in Parkinson's disease patients. The sheer pervasiveness and power of the placebo effect ensure its place as a great idea in psychology, although this idea may have been underutilized so far. Greater efforts could be made to explicitly use the placebo effect in treatments for some types of health problems rather than to consider the effect a nuisance and to try to nullify it.

CRITICAL THINKING QUESTIONS

1 The concern with placebos arose as the medical profession established its legitimacy in modern society. Why is it important for the science of medicine to identify the placebo effect and demonstrate that medical treatment is distinct from the placebo effect?

2 What are some examples of the placebo effect in everyday life?

FURTHER READING

Beecher, H. K. (1955). The powerful placebo. *Journal of the American Medical Association*, *159*, 1602–1606.

Chvetzoff, G., & Tannock, I. F. (2003). Placebo effects in oncology. *Journal of the National Cancer Institute*, *95*, 19–29.

Fuente-Fernández, R. de la., Ruth,T. J., Sossi, V., Schulzer, M., Calne, D. B., & Stoessl, A. J. (2001). Expectation and dopamine release: Mechanism of the placebo effect in Parkinson's Disease. *Science, 293*, 1164–1165.

Fisher, S., & Greenberg, R. P. (eds.) (1997). *From placebo to panacea: Putting psychiatric drugs to the test.* New York: John Wiley.

Harrington, A. (ed.) (1997). *The placebo effect: An interdisciplinary exploration.* Cambridge, MA: Harvard University Press.

Hrobjartsson, A., & Gotzche, P. C. (2001). Is the placebo powerless? An analysis of clinical trials comparing placebo with no treatment. *New England Journal of Medicine, 344*, 1594–1602.

Kirsch, I., & Sapistein, G. (1998). Listening to Prozac and hearing placebo: A meta-analysis of antidepressant medication. Prevention and Treatment article 2a. <http://journals.apa.org/prevention/volume1/pre0010002a.html>.

Kirsch, I., & Lynn, S. J. (1999). Automaticity in clinical psychology, *American Psychologist, 54*, 504–515.

Kitwood, T. (1990). The dialectics of dementia: With particular reference to Alzheimer's disease. *Aging and Society, 10*, 177–196.

Kramer, P. D. (1993). *Listening to Prozac.* New York: Viking.

Leuchter, A. F., Cook, I. A., Witte, E. A., Morgan, M., & Abrams, M. (2002). Changes in brain function of depressed subjects during treatment with placebo. *American Journal of Psychiatry, 159*, 122–129.

Moerman, D. E. (2002). *Meaning, medicine and the placebo effect.* Cambridge: Cambridge University Press.

Peters, D. (ed.) (2001). *Understanding the placebo effect in contemporary medicine: Theory, practice, and research.* Edinburgh: Churchill Livingstone.

Sandler, A. D., & Bodfish, J. W. (2000). Placebo effects in autism. *Developmental and Behavioral Pediatrics, 21*, 347–349.

Shapiro, A. K., & Shapiro, E. (2001). *The powerful placebo: From ancient priest to modern physician.* Baltimore: Johns Hopkins University Press.

4

THE FREUDIAN UNCONSCIOUS

Imagine if I jumped out of this page and asked you to explain your behavior over the last week, to tell me what you have been doing and why. How accurate an account could you give? Could you really tell me how you have been behaving toward other people, or why? For instance, why you spoke harshly to one of your friends, or why you fail to confide in your family members as often as you should, or why you "accidentally" overlooked the birthday of a close friend, or why you have started to dislike a person you used to like?

Are we really fully aware of what we do and why? Can we truly see our own actions and motives the way they are? If so, then we are conscious of our own behavior and the reasons for how we behave. In this sense, we are closer to being rational creatures, able to more accurately see our own actions and to give accurate accounts of them.

An alternative view is that we humans are less able to see our own actions and motives accurately, that we remain largely unaware of important parts of our own experiences. In other words, we often don't really know what we do or why. This alternative view depicts us more as irrational beings, not fully conscious of our own actions and motives. What we are not conscious of is part of an *unconscious*, the total memories we are unable to bring to mind but are still affected by.

The idea of the unconscious, particularly as explored so creatively by Sigmund Freud (1856–1939), is probably the most influential great idea in the history of psychology. The unconscious has had fundamental implications for therapy and applied psychology generally, as well as for psychological research, including in clinical, developmental, personality, social, and cognitive areas. More broadly, Freud's view of the unconscious has fundamentally influenced lay people in everyday life. This has happened in three major ways. First, a shift in common beliefs about the role of basic instincts, particularly sex, in everyday social behavior. Freud helped to bring sex to center stage in the mass media and among the lay public. Second, Freud helped to change our views of ourselves, so that we see ourselves as more irrational beings, who often are not aware of the motives and reasons behind our own behavior. The degrees of freedom for our behavior are far more limited than we assume, Freud argued; they are limited by unconscious forces that generally remain unknown to us. Third, Freud popularized the idea of *repression*, a mechanism through which feelings, thoughts, ideas, and so on that are anxiety provoking are pushed out of consciousness and into the unconscious (see chapter 12 for further discussion). After Freud, "repression" came into popular use and became part of everyday language.

For much of the twentieth century, and even now, Freud's view of the unconscious formed a dividing line between experimentalists, who preferred to work in (as discussed in chapter 1) and to try to stay close to hard data, and many therapists, who 'worked out.' However, the idea of an unconscious has historical roots well before Freud, and it is useful to trace some of these earlier roots. Freud developed the idea of the unconscious in revolutionary ways, but his ideas also came to be influential because they arose in a particularly historical era, and it is important to review the cultural and historical context of Freud's rise.

EARLY HISTORY OF THE UNCONSCIOUS

In the Western tradition we can trace discussions of the unconscious in some form or another at least back to the time of Plato around twenty-five centuries ago, such as in the famous simile of the cave. Unenlightened people are like prisoners in a cave. There is a fire behind them, but they cannot turn around to see the light of the fire, or the daylight outside the cave. All they can see are the shadows cast by the fire onto the walls of the cave. A person may break free from the chains and get to the daylight, but the dazzling outside light will make it more difficult to see shadows inside the cave again. The simile of the cave is part of a long tradition of scholarship about how people can be mistaken in their beliefs about the world and themselves. Implicit in this tradition is the idea that people are often unaware of what they do and what they do not know. As a consequence, they often act on the basis of mistaken beliefs.

Throughout much of the last two thousand years, though the Christian Church held such a dominant position in Western life, a widely influential idea has been that only God is perfectly knowledgeable. From this viewpoint, the best humans can do is to craft imperfect pictures of the real world, inaccurate to different degrees. With the rise of scientific thinking in the seventeenth and eighteenth centuries, and the decline of Church influence, the idea of humans as having an imperfect understanding of the world did not fade. Rather, scientific measurement allowed for more precise assessment of the ways in which humans misperceive the world and of the ways in which they are conscious of some things and unconscious of others.

Among the many different influences on the idea of the unconscious in recent centuries, five are particularly noteworthy.

Thresholds in perception

A first development that helped highlight the unconscious was research on psychological thresholds in *sensation*, the detection of stimuli, and *perception*, the interpretation of stimuli. Leibnitz (1646–1716) and other German philosophers had earlier discussed ideas around levels of consciousness, and how some things pass a threshold and enter consciousness and others do not. The idea of a threshold was explored empirically by Gustav Fechner (1801–1887), the father of psychophysics. Fechner experimentally studied the relationship between physical stimuli, such as light, and psychological experience, such as the intensity of light subjectively perceived by a person. Fechner devised a unit, *just noticeable difference*, which measures the amount of change needed in a stimulus strength for a person to just notice a difference. Fechner's innovation allowed for an objective measure of how much a stimulus would need to change, becoming stronger or weaker, for it to just slip either into or out of conscious experience. An idea of Fechner's that had a particularly profound impact on Freud was the notion of the mind being like an iceberg, with the greater part submerged underwater.

Freud took up and further developed the iceberg metaphor. Just as the vast bulk of an iceberg is submerged below water, most thoughts, wishes, motives, and so on remain out of consciousness. The small fraction of such psychological experiences that do come to consciousness show themselves as the "tip of the iceberg" above water. Most onlookers are only aware of the "tip of the iceberg," but to understand the movements of the iceberg it is important to be aware of its submerged bulk. In essence, the submerged part of the iceberg, the unconscious, has an enormous impact on behavior, but remains out of sight.

Unconscious inferences

The concept of the unconscious was also highlighted by research on perception pioneered by Hermann von Helmholtz (1821–94), and later by Gestalt psychologists. In his research on color perception, Helmholtz came to the conclusion that through *unconscious inferences*, hunches we make *without* conscious effort, contexts play an important role in how we see colors. Generalizing to other stimuli, we can say that each bit of sound or color is interpreted the way it should be in order to make sense. We hear a bit of a tune and we imagine the rest of the song to which it must belong, or we hear a sound and imagine the arrival of a friend we are expecting. Such inferences are automatic and come about without our conscious effort.

In the late nineteenth and early twentieth century, Gestalt psychologists also highlighted our tendency to infer "completeness" on the basis of fragmentary stimuli, such as perceiving a triangle even when three lines did not meet to complete the shape of a triangle. For Gestalt psychologists, certain inbuilt characteristics of human beings lead them to see the world in particular holistic ways, without individuals being aware of these tendencies. For example, when Anna goes to her new school for the first time and encounters thousands of unfamiliar faces around campus, she automatically categorizes people on the basis of similarity. Without consciously thinking about it, she uses similarity to place others into many different groups, including male/female, Black/White, friendly-looking/unfriendly-looking, and so on. By the end of her first day, Anna has arrived at a rough idea of different groups on the basis of similarity, without having consciously used similarity to form the groups.

Variations in idea intensity

A third influence on the idea of the unconscious comes from the writings of Johan Friedrich Herbart (1776–1841), who viewed the human mind as a collection of ideas of varying intensity. But not all ideas are strong enough to enter consciousness; many ideas remain unconscious. Ideas are not destroyed; they simply lose strength and slip out of consciousness. An unconscious idea can be brought to consciousness through associated ideas. Thus, from Herbart's writings there emerges a picture of consciousness as representing only a part of all the ideas present in the mind. Other ideas are housed in the unconscious but can be accessed by association. For example, Tom is unable to recall the name of his dentist, but remembers that her name is "Dr. Hunter" when he sees a documentary about Native American *hunting* methods.

Although Herbart worked out and his goal was to develop theories rather than to conduct experiments on the mind, his ideas are not far removed from the spirit of experimental work conducted half a century later by Hermann Ebbinghaus (1850–1909) on memory. Ebbinghous demonstrated that bits of information that were learned and then forgotten could more easily be re-learned, implying that the forgotten material was not completely discarded but lay dormant somewhere in the mind. This gave rise to the idea in memory research that items could be stored in memory but not necessarily be accessed or retrieved. Parts of our memories, this implies, remains buried in an inaccessible section of the mind. Thus, experimental research on memory also presents a picture of the mind composed of two major parts: a conscious part, consisting of material we can recall, and an unconscious part, consisting of material that we are unable to recall in most circumstances.

Hypnotism

A fourth development that fundamentally influenced the idea of the unconscious was the rise of interest in hypnotism, as part of larger efforts to discover new effective methods for treating mental disorders from the latter part of the eighteenth century. Hypnosis was initially popularized by the Austrian Franz Mesmer (1734–1815), but it gained more scientific respectability later through the efforts of the Frenchman Jean Charcot (1825–93) and his pupil Pierre Janet (1859–1947). The work of Charcot and Janet included systematic public demonstrations of hypnosis, during which patient-participants would be hypnotized and moved by suggestion to carry out various actions that they would or could not carry out in their normal waking state. For example, in some cases under hypnosis a patient-participant with peralysis in her hands would be influenced by suggestion to move a hand that she could not move in the normal waking state.

Studies of behavior under hypnosis by Charcot and others had a number of implications for consciousness. A first implication is that there are aspects of experience that lie outside the reach of introspection and conscious awareness. Each of us can only get at a part of our own experiences. A second implication follows: personality has a number of different strata, with "deeper" layers beneath the surface. Third, it is implied that some hidden levels of personality may influence behavior in ways that are not easily brought to conscious experience. That is we remain unaware of how deeper layers influence our everyday behavior. Hypnosis was seen as a key to mysterious hidden layers.

False consciousness

Finally, among the many developments that influenced the idea of an unconscious, we should also note discussions of *false consciousness*, the misunderstandings some people have about what social class they actually belong to, what their class interests are, and how their class interests differ from the interests of other social classes. Karl Marx (1818–83) argued that through control of media, education, the Church, and other sources of information, the major owners of capital also control the perceptions that most people (what he termed the *proletariat*, those who do not own capital but sell their labor in the marketplace) have of society and their place within the social structure. Most importantly, most people fail to see that capitalists and workers belong to different social classes and have opposing class interests; they are not conscious of the objective situation. Such false consciousness leads most people to lack loyalty to their own social class and their own personal interests. For example, Marx did not see capitalists as being engaged in a conscious conspiracy to create or perpetuate false consciousness. Rather, he argued that class interests act as a "hidden hand" to move capitalists to preserve the class system. The same invisible forces will move the majority of people (the proletariat) eventually to act in their own class interests. Although Marxist discussions of false consciousness focus on a lack of awareness about the nature of objective reality in society, they do highlight the idea that individuals are influenced by factors they are not conscious of, and in this way underline the limited nature of conscious experience as a basis for understanding behavior.

In some respects, then, the idea of an unconscious was already receiving considerable attention before Freud. However, Freud transformed the idea of the unconscious into something truly revolutionary. First, Freud used the unconscious as a door to past experiences, which he argued continue to shape present thought and action. Freud encapsulates the modern Western trend of seeing the unconscious as pointing to the past. Second, rather than having an impact just on academic psychology, Freud had an enormous impact on all of society. For example, Freud's ideas have greatly influenced films, novels, paintings, and other forms of artistic expression. Indeed, Freud's impact on academia has in large part been through his greater impact on the wider culture. Despite the disdain with which some critics view Freud's ideas, Freud has fundamentally changed the way humans view themselves. In order to appreciate this impact, we need to consider Freud's ideas about the unconscious in cultural and historical context, starting with the theme of the irrational.

CRITICAL THINKING QUESTIONS

1 Why does the unconscious support the idea of humans as more irrational?

2 In what way does hypnosis suggest the existence of an unconscious?

THE FREUDIAN UNCONSCIOUS

Marx and Freud were both historically important revolutionaries born in the nineteenth century, but whereas Marx saw conflict as centered on social classes in the larger society, Freud's treatment of the unconscious took the center of conflict out of society and placed it within individuals. In the terminology introduced in chapter 1, Marx was primarily concerned with societal restrictions on degrees of freedom for behavior, whereas Freud was primarily concerned with internal, intra-personal restrictions. In Freud's writings, each person is depicted as the stage on which is played out a lifelong struggle between opposing forces; the eye of a storm lies within. Freud took the idea of an unconscious, a submerged iceberg, and transformed it into a dynamic force with awesome power and often cruel and crippling consequences.

The conflict tradition

Freud is part of a conflict tradition that in modern history has roots in the ideas of Thomas Hobbes (1588–1679) and Jean Jacques Rousseau (1712–78). Both Hobbes and Rousseau saw a central tension in society, but each explained it in a fundamentally different way. For Hobbes, human beings are self-centered, egocentric, and motivated to satisfy their own desires irrespective of the interests of others. This becomes clear in times of war and civil conflict, when central authorities collapse and people suddenly find themselves free to rob, rape, pillage, and murder, which according to Hobbes they are apt to do. Hobbes would have interpreted a lot of events in modern times, such as continuing violent conflicts and efforts at "ethnic cleansing" in Eastern Europe after the collapse of communism, and international terrorism, as further support for his view of individuals as self-centered and potentially destructive. For Hobbes, then, individuals have to be controlled, and society has to be saved from them, if we are to have peace and progress.

Rousseau also saw tension and potential conflict in society, but only because individuals have to struggle to become free from the corruption of society. Everywhere humans are born free, he pointed out, yet they live in chains. There is evil everywhere, but the roots of evil lie in society and not individuals. Society is in need of radical reform in order that the natural goodness of humans come to fruition. But radical reform necessarily brings the forces of progress in conflict with those concerned to conserve the existing system.

For Marx, also, conflict is inevitable, in this case as part of the historical evolution of social classes. Just as feudalism had inevitably been replaced by capitalism, with capitalists overtaking traditional landed aristocracies, so capitalism will inevitably be pushed aside by socialism, with the working class (proletariat) gaining power over capitalists. The working class will, through successive and increasingly violent clashes with capitalists, come to see themselves as a distinct social class with unique interests. This class consciousness will lead to a final revolution to overthrow capitalism and establish the classless society.

Hobbes, Rousseau, and Marx developed fundamentally different views about a social contract, between individuals and a central authority, that would end conflict. For Hobbes, individuals must give up certain freedoms and accept restrictions (e.g. follow instructions given by police officers) under a central authority, who in return guarantees the safety and security of individuals. For Rousseau, a social contract is just and workable only in a reformed society, where the central authority is accountable to the citizens. Marx, on the other hand, argued that historical evolution would eventually lead to a classless society without a central authority, and so the social contract would be between citizens without the intervention of a central authority. What Hobbes, Rousseau, and Marx had in common was their treatment of the idea of a social contract at the societal level and in terms of the historical development of societies. For them, the social contract between individuals and a central authority came into existence (or, in Marx's case, disappeared) at a certain historical stage. Everyone born into society after that stage inevitably entered into the same contract.

The conflict within

Freud took the revolutionary step of individualizing and internalizing the social contract, so that it became something to be worked out by each single individual in her or his own lifetime, and within herself or himself. The starting point for Freud's account of individual development is Hobbesian: we come into this world self-centered, acting according to the pleasure principle, and motivated to satisfy our own needs instantly. The term *id* refers to personality at this point, unrestrained as it is by the practical limitations of the external world. The id knows no bounds, no space or time limitations. The infant wants gratification now, and even a slight delay in providing food, comfort, or anything else that is presently desired will bring immediate reaction in the form of ear-piercing screams.

But little by little the restraints of the external world close in and the id becomes boxed in. Infants find that in the real world they cannot be gratified instantly; they have to wait, and even then many wishes remain just that. New social skills develop to cope with these real limitations, gradually leading to a new layer of personality, the *ego*, which emerges with a view to satisfying the id in pragmatic ways. Now the *reality principle* guides behavior, as the little person learns the rules of politeness and how to cope with delays in gratification.

There are different kinds of reasons why the id cannot be completely satisfied. Some reasons are practical, such as limitations in time or money, but many limitations are moral and arise out of the value system of a culture. For example, a little boy finds it pleasurable to touch his penis while he is being bathed, but is told by his mother he is doing a bad thing. "Dirty, dirty," she says to him. "That's a dirty thing to do." Or a little girl comes running out with no clothes on in front of guests and is told she should be ashamed of herself. "Good girls don't show their body like that." Prior to these kinds of incidents the little boy and girl had no reason to see parts of their bodies as dirty or shameful, but now the association is made. Societal taboos, such as those related to bodily pleasures, begin to be internalized. In this way, cultures set limits as to how the id can be satisfied, particularly in the domain of sex.

Cultural ideas about good and bad, transmitted particularly by parents and other caretakers, have a powerful impact on the ego, and gradually these ideas become internalized to the child. This gives rise to the development of another layer of personality, the *super-ego*, which is the internalized moral order derived from cultural surroundings. In everyday language, the superego is a conscience, a police officer inside each of us, a warning voice within scolding us whenever we are in danger of crossing the line. But now that the scolding comes from within, it is not just actions that are kept under control, but thoughts also. The little boy now experiences anxiety each time he thinks about touching his penis even when he is completely alone, because the voice within him is now doing the job his mother did of imposing societal restrictions. The only way the little boy can avoid feeling anxious is through *repression*; that is, to push such thoughts out of his consciousness.

Wishes that get pushed out of consciousness are not the "politically correct," "acceptable" ones; rather, they are ideas that conflict with the moral order of a culture and are taboo according to the dominant local rules. After they are pushed out of consciousness, they do not just disappear and evaporate, but become part of an unconscious. Once in the unconscious, "nothing can be brought to an end, nothing is past or forgotten" (Freud, 1900–1, p. 577). Whatever is pushed into the unconscious lurks there, with the potential to rear its head at a later stage. Freud's is sometimes referred to as a hydraulic model, in the sense that energy does not just disappear, but if blocked in one way, it will reveal itself through other routes, such as "slips of the tongue" and other "accidental" behaviors. Thus, gradually as the child develops, the unconscious grows as more and more material is repressed.

Individualized social contracts

Each individual comes to work out a personal social contract with parents and other authorities representing the larger society. On the one hand, certain wishes, motives, and feelings are repressed by individuals, as they struggle to conform with the norms and values of their cultures. The cost of such repression is sometimes enormous, and so high that it cripples the individual and prevents healthy functioning. On the other hand, by conforming to the morality of their cultures, individuals gain acceptance and support from others; they become part of the human group. Clearly, then, joining civilization comes at a very high price,

> It is our belief that civilization and higher education have a large influence on the development of repression, and we suppose that, under such conditions, the psychical organization undergoes an alteration (that can also emerge as an inherited disposition) as a result of which what was formerly felt as agreeable now seems unacceptable and is rejected with all possible psychical force. The repressive activity of civilization brings it about that primary possibilities of enjoyment, which have now, however, been repudiated by the censorship in us, are lost to us. But to the human psyche, all renunciation is exceedingly difficult.
>
> (Freud, 1905, p. 101)

The difficulties of becoming civilized arise particularly in the domains of sex and aggression. These two primary human instincts are, first, seen as dangerous and curtailed by Western and other major civilizations and, second, in important ways linked in that Freud envisioned a direct relationship between cruelty and the sexual instinct. From a Freudian perspective, it is not surprising that novels, films, music, paintings, drama, and other art forms are censored for sex and violence in their content – it is exactly in the domains of sex and violence that our basic instincts conflict with the morality of modern civilization. But the unconscious is not under the control of civilization, or anyone, and thus there remains a "voice within us that rebels against the demands of morality" (Freud, 1905, p. 110).

This "voice within us" arises out of the unconscious, the home of complex thought processes, "the most complicated achievements of thought are possible without the assistance of consciousness" (Freud, 1900–1, p. 593). No understanding of human behavior can be adequate without access to the unconscious. Thus, for Freud it is not enough to know that there is an unconscious, because there also needs to be a method or "road" to reach the unconscious. Initially, influenced by Charcot and others, Freud believed that hypnosis was an effective method for reaching the unconscious. Over time, however, Freud came to view hypnosis as an unsatisfactory method. This is because not all patients could be hypnotized, and the effect of hypnosis on patients was erratic. Eventually Freud came to see dreams as a far more powerful tool.

The "royal road"

Freud became convinced that a powerful way to explore the unconscious is to study dreams. He referred to dreams as the "royal road" to
the unconscious, and the place in which repressed wishes arise in
disguised form. Disguise has to be used so that individuals do not recognize their own unconscious wishes, which if recognized would provoke
anxiety and end sleep. "All dreams are in a sense dreams of convenience:
they serve the purpose of prolonging sleep instead of waking up"
(Freud, 1900, p. 233). Consequently, a major part of training for psychoanalysts is the study and interpretation of the unconscious content of
dreams, the *latent content*, and how this is transformed through dream
work into the surface or *manifest content*. For example, David dreams
that on a cold, rainy, dark night he is walking across a narrow, rickety
bridge in the company of a stranger, a powerful older male. The stranger
constantly criticizes David and sneers at him. But when they reach the
middle of the bridge, the stranger slips and falls to his death in the thun-
dering river hundreds of feet below. David feels relieved and even happy,
although he does not know the identity of the stranger. One interpretation of this dream is that the stranger is David's father, and the death of
the stranger is David's wish fulfilled (latent content). But this wish, for
the death of his own father, is so anti-social that it could not become
manifest in the dream, otherwise David would wake up alarmed. Thus,
David only remembers the manifest content of the dream, the walk
across a bridge with a stranger who falls to his death, when he wakes up
the next morning.

Dreams organize and make coherent the scattered impulses and
wishes of the unconscious. In this sense, dreams are an expression of
wish fulfilment, a way in which those wishes that are deemed unacceptable by civilization become fulfilled without severe consequences. But
such impulses and wishes are also directly linked to the waking world.
That is, the content of wishes and desires is derived from experiences in
waking life. For example, the person to whom the dreamer is aggressive
in dreams is a real person and a source of frustration in the waking life
of the dreamer.

Apart from dreams, other paths to the unconscious include slips of
the tongue and jokes, both of which were researched extensively by
Freud. He began with the proposition that there is no such thing as an
accident in human behavior. For example, when Norm "forgets" to
order the birthday cake for his school rival's birthday party, this kind

of "forgetting" reflects unconscious wishes. Freud also saw slips of the tongue and jokes as revealing wishes hidden in the unconscious. For example, Joan says to the handsome car salesman, "Yes, I do need to change my husband and get something more exciting ... oops, of course I mean I need to change my car!" But from a Freudian perspective, Joan's slip of the tongue probably reflects hidden wishes to actually change her husband. In both slips of the tongue and jokes, the central topic is often sexual, exactly because it is the sex instinct that has been most severely repressed by civilization, "There is no more personal claim than that for sexual freedom and at no point has civilization tried to exercise severer suppression than in the sphere of sexuality" (Freud, 1905, p. 110).

CRITICAL THINKING QUESTIONS

1 In what way is Freud part of the "conflict tradition"?

2 How convincing is the idea of the "royal road" to the unconscious?

THE UNCONSCIOUS ASSESSED

The unconscious has become a great idea in psychology, in large part because of the enormous influence of Freud since early in the twentieth century on academic psychology. Freud is the one psychologist whose ideas, and implicitly or explicitly his views on the unconscious, are included in modern psychology texts in all the major sub-disciplines, including developmental, personality, social, abnormal, and cognitive psychology.

However, critics would contend that twenty-first-century research has turned away from the Freudian unconscious and is concerned with a different type of unconscious. The new research on *automatic processing*, the tendency for a cognitive process to run to completion without a need for conscious monitoring, is not directly concerned with emotions, repression, anxiety, and the types of motivations Freud was concerned with. An example of a well-known automatic process is the *Stroop effect*, which arises when participants are asked to name the ink color of letters that make up color words (e.g. the word "green" printed in yellow ink). Participants have a hard time not reading the words instead of saying the color of the letters (e.g. reading "green" instead of saying "yellow" when the word "green" is printed in yellow). The Stroop effect is used in contemporary research to further unravel the details of automatic processing (e.g. Tzelgov et al., 1997). Automatic processing is also a focus for researchers studying how people think about *category member-ship, such as being a member of a racial or gender group* (Lepore & Brown, 1997). This new research seems to be concerned with an unconscious based on "cold cognition" rather than the "hot" emotion-laden, repression-based unconscious Freud discussed. But, in defense of the Freudian unconscious, it could also be argued that the new laboratory-based research on automatic processes demonstrates how people could think under certain controlled conditions, not necessarily how they actually do think in everyday interactions. In everyday life, thinking is more often hot rather than cold; emotions and motivations tend to be fundamental to thought, not set aside.

Less controversial is the idea that Freud continues to have considerable influence on the general public and everyday life. Some of Freud's ideas, such as "ego" and "displaced aggression," are influential among both the lay public and professional psychologists. Freud wrote in a very creative, literary style, and he noted himself that "the case histories I write ... read like short stories" (Freud, 1893–95, p. 160). No doubt his imaginative writing style was in part responsible for his tremendous influence on the world scene. Through Freud, the idea of the unconscious has touched almost every aspect of life, including the arts, such as James Joyce's novels (particularly *Ulysses*), the paintings of Jackson Pollock, the operas of Alban Berg (particularly *Lulu*), and countless films, including classics such as *Psycho* (an Alfred Hitchcock movie).

The unconscious challenged

The Freudian unconscious has not gone unchallenged. A pertinent criticism is that Freud's conception of the unconscious is too vague to be tested empirically. This is a case of a researcher working out to the extreme and moving too far away from hard evidence (as discussed in chapter 1). In the terminology of the philosopher of science Karl Popper, the Freudian unconscious is not falsifiable; it is not specific enough to be disproved. This is one reason why empirical studies have not so much proved or disproved the Freudian unconscious as led to further questions and controversies.

An important line of research attempts to establish the existence of an unconscious by demonstrating that people repress traumatic experiences they had in their childhood (for reviews of this literature, see Bremner & Marmar, 1998). For example, when researchers followed up and recorded the experiences of women who had been sexually abused at an early age, they found that at least some of these women did not recall the incident. Such evidence can be interpreted in support of the idea of repression into an unconscious, but it is also possible that simple forgetting is involved, or that victims simply chose not to report such painful events even though they remembered them.

Reconstruction rather than repression

Critics of the unconscious find powerful ammunition in the research of Elizabeth Loftus (Loftus, 1993; 1997). Conducting research in the context of law courts, Loftus demonstrated how eyewitness testimonies can be influenced by "suggestion" and "planting" certain ideas into a cross-examination. For example, when a lawyer asks an eyewitness, "Did you see the red car?" the chances of an affirmative response is higher than if the question is asked using the word "a [red car]" instead of "the." Through similar subtle processes of suggestion, false memories can be planted of events that are supposed to have happened in our childhood.

Turning her attention to repression and dreams, Loftus has conducted research to show how "false memories" of events in childhood can be planted during the interpretation of dreams. Participants whose dreams were interpreted to suggest a history of (false) critical childhood events later reported that such events had actually occurred in their childhood (Mazzoni et al., 1999), and even "inflated" false events by adding to them (Paddock et al., 1999). Thus, Loftus argues that our "distorted" remembrances should be taken as evidence not that we repress past events but that we continually reconstruct them through ongoing social interactions, and the powerful influence of suggestion from others, particularly authority figures. Loftus's research does not falsify the idea of repression and the unconscious, but provides an alternative interpretation of how we remember the past.

Does the unconscious point to the past or the future?

"I've been very worried about you," I explained to my mother.

"No need to worry," she responded calmly, "I had a dream that told me I wouldn't be harmed."

The year was 1979, the place Tehran. A violent political revolution had been going on in Iran for the last year, with the center of the storm in Tehran, the capital city, where my mother lived. Thousands of people had been killed, the Shah and his government had been overthrown, the army and the police were defeated and in disarray, and there was sporadic looting and violence throughout the city. In the midst of this terrifying revolutionary change, my mother, a widower, lived alone, in a neighborhood that was at the center of the storm. I had been terribly worried about her, and was glad to have completed my studies in England so I could return to Tehran and be with her.

As a psychology student in England, I had been taught to think about dreams as relating to the past. Like most students, I had been particularly fascinated by the possible use of interpretations of dreams in therapy, and the idea that by analyzing dreams we can come to better understand our unconscious and our past experiences. Everything I read about dreams and the unconscious in the Western literature pointed *to the past*, but now I was back in Iran, confronted by Eastern cultural beliefs, and my mother was telling me how her dream had told her *about the future*.

"I was very anxious when the revolution first started," explained my mother, "but then I had a dream in which there was a sudden earthquake and all the city shook violently, and there was a lot of noise and confusion in the streets and many people died, but when it was over my house was among those that stood unharmed and I did not even get a scratch. When I awoke the next morning, I knew the dream meant that nothing bad would happen to me. The meaning of the dream was clear, and in fact no harm came to me throughout all the turmoil and violence of the revolution. So you need not have worried about me."

Here I was, then, on my very first day back in Iran, finding the assumptions of my Western training being challenged. But this challenge came from the everyday experiences of a mother, my mother (who I knew was invariably always right about things!), and not merely from some expert or other, like myself. More broadly, once again I found that by looking at Western psychology from a cross-cultural perspective, I could reflect back critically and raise constructive questions about received wisdom.

When I researched the topic of dreams and dream interpretation in the traditional Iranian and related Eastern literature, I found numerous "books of dreams" in which writers analyzed different dreams to explain what the dream content indicates *for the future*. This traditional future-oriented Eastern approach stands in contrast to the modern past-oriented Western tradition, imported to the East by Western-educated psychologists like me. Interestingly, both Eastern and Western traditions share the assumption that human beings are not always aware of what is influencing their behavior.

From a Freudian perspective the unconscious is a key to the past, a place where all the repressed feelings, thoughts, wishes of experience reside. The Freudian analyst uses dreams, the "royal road," to travel back to the patient's earlier experiences and to uncover the roots of psychological problems. But in at least some Eastern cultural traditions, dreams are indicators of future events. If dreams reflect an unconscious, from some Eastern perspectives the unconscious informs about what behavior will be like in the future rather than the past.

In some respects twenty-first-century cognitive psychology is also viewing the unconscious as future oriented. This arises from a long line of cognitive research demonstrating that often people are not conscious of the factors that lead them to think of particular things, but they are ready to provide inaccurate explanations of such factors. For example, a participant is shown a picture of a girl either throwing a temper tantrum or behaving politely. This picture is quickly flashed, so that the participant does not have conscious awareness of the picture. Next, the participant is shown a neutral picture of the girl, this time at a slow speed, and asked to evaluate her personality. Findings show that the earlier subliminal message, of the girl throwing a tantrum or behaving politely, influences evaluations of the girl. Participants explain their evaluations in many creative ways, without reference to the earlier subliminal message. For example, a participant who saw an image of the girl throwing a tantrum would describe her personality as "volatile" and "fiery," and give reasons like "her eyes tell me so" or "there's something about her," without realizing any connection with an earlier image of the girl flashed up quickly. An implication is that the unconscious can influence our future behavior.

Biology and alternative interpretations of dreams

Alternative interpretations for and against repression and the unconscious are also provided by research on the biology of the brain. From the early 1950s, a series of landmark studies by researchers working in and trying to develop ideas only on the basis of empirical data demonstrated that dreams occur regularly during REM (rapid eye movement) sleep (Aserinsky & Kleitman, 1953), and that people need to experience dreams as part of their normal sleep (Dement, 1960). The demonstration of a biological need to dream can be interpreted as being in line with Freud's depiction of dreams as fundamentally important. However, whereas Freud theorized that dreams stem from unconscious wishes, another line of research on the biology of the brain has fundamentally different implications.

Alan Hobson and Robert McCarley (1977) argued that all mammals experience regular cycles of REM and non-REM sleep, as part of programed biological functioning. During REM sleep, neural activity continues in the pons region of the brain stem, a primitive part located in the back and near the base of the brain, involved in automatic activities such as temperature regulation and respiration. When these random signals reach the more advanced parts of the brain that deal with higher-order functioning, such as comprehension and problem solving, past images and experiences are applied to try to make sense of the signals being generated. The result is the kind of disjointed, often nonsensical series of images or stories we experience in our dreams. In other words, dreams are nothing more than the attempts of the more advanced parts of the brain to make sense of random and meaningless signals being sent by a primitive part of the brain that remains active during sleep.

Have Hobson and McCarley (1977) dealt a death blow to Freudian ideas about dreams and the unconscious? Not so, because (as indicated by Hobson, 1989) even if the source of dreams is random electrical activity in primitive parts of the brain, exactly how the higher cognitive faculties make sense of random signals could tell us a lot about an individual. Also, perhaps surprisingly, there is more direct support for Freud in research using advanced brain-imaging technology. Researchers have discovered that the REM sleep of people with damaged pons regions of the brain was disrupted, but they continued to have dreams (Solms, 1997). This seems to suggest that dreams are not dependent on neural activity in the pons. Also, people with damage to centers of the forebrain that control motivation continued to have REM sleep but experienced loss of dreaming. One possible interpretation is that dreams are associated with motivational and emotional systems in the forebrain but not necessarily with REM sleep.

Also, a research team led by Alan Braun discovered that during REM sleep areas of the brain that control motivation and emotion were active, but areas that control the more rational cognitive activities – including attention, working memory, and logic – were inactive. These results correspond with Freud's views about emotional and instinctual manifestations in dreams. Thus, advances in brain research are in some ways supportive of Freud's views about wish fulfilment in dreams. However, in each case interpretations of results in support of Freud's position are only tentative.

CRITICAL THINKING QUESTIONS

1 Does evidence provided by Loftus and others showing that the past can be reconstructed demonstrate that repression does not take place?

2 Is Freud's idea on how dreams relate to wish fulfilment testable?

CONCLUDING COMMENT

My mother's dream, which she interpreted as foretelling a safe future for her even during a turbulent revolution and its violent aftermath, is a reminder of potential cultural limitations to Freudian ideas of the unconscious. The empirical social-cognitive research of Loftus and others suggests that the past may in some instances, at least, be reconstructed rather than repressed. Biological research also points to alternative interpretations of dreams and the unconscious, although some recent studies have provided evidence that fits in with Freudian ideas of dreams and repression. The power of the Freudian unconscious is that it has altered how modern people think, about themselves as well as the world around them. Globalization and modernization are likely to increase this influence, as Freudian ideas spread to non-Western parts of the globe. If sheer impact across the world is considered, the unconscious may well be the greatest psychological idea.

CRITICAL THINKING QUESTIONS

1 Can you think of an example of how the Freudian unconscious has entered the media or everyday life?

2 Do you agree with the criticism that the unconscious is very difficult to prove or disprove?

FURTHER READING

Aserinsky, E., & Kleitmen, N. (1953). Regularly occurring periods of eye mobility and concomitant phenomena during sleep. *Science, 118*, 273–274.

Braun, A. R., Balkin, T. J., Wesensten, N. J., Gwadry, F., Carson, R. E., Varga, M., Baldwin, P., Belenksky, G., & Herscovitch, P. (1998). Dissociated pattern of activity in visual cortices and their projections during human rapid eye movement sleep. *Science, 279*, 91–95.

Bremner, J. D., Marmar, C. R. (1998). *Trauma, memory, and dissociation.* Washington, DC: American Psychiatric Press.

Dement, W. (1960). The effect of dream deprivation. *Science, 131*, 1705–1707.

Easthope, A. (1999). *The unconscious.* London: Routledge.

Ellenberger, H. F. (1970). *The discovery of the unconscious.* New York: Basic Books.

Freud, S. (1893–95/1955). Studies in hysteria (written with J. Breuer). In J. Stachey (ed. and trans.), *The standard edition of the complete psychological works of Sigmund Freud*, Vol. 2. London: Hogarth Press.

Freud, S. (1901/1960). The psychopathology of everyday life. In J. Stachey (ed. and trans.), *The standard edition of the complete psychological works of Sigmund Freud*, Vol. 6. London: Hogarth Press.

Freud, S. (1900/1953). The interpretation of dreams (first part). In J. Stachey (ed. and trans.), *The standard edition of the complete psychological works of Sigmund Freud*, Vol. 4. London: Hogarth Press.

Freud, S. (1900–1/1953). The interpretation of dreams (second part). In J. Stachey (ed. and trans.), *The standard edition of the complete psychological works of Sigmund Freud*, Vol. 5. London: Hogarth Press.

Freud, S. (1905/1960). Jokes and their relation to the unconscious. In J. Stachey (ed. and trans.), *The standard edition of the complete psychological works of Sigmund Freud*, Vol. 8. London: Hogarth Press.

Hobson, J. A. (1989). *Sleep.* New York: Scientific American Library.

Hobson, J. A., & McCarley, R. W. (1977). The brain as a dream-state generator: An activation-synthesis of the dream process. *American Journal of Psychiatry, 134*, 1335–1348.

Jameson, F. (1981). *The political unconscious: Narrative as a socially symbolic act.* London: Methuen.

Lepore, L., & Brown, R. (1997). Category and stereotype activation: Is prejudice inevitable? *Journal of Personality and Social Psychology, 72*, 275–287.

Loftus, E. (1993). The reality of repressed memories. *American Psychologist, 48*, 518–537.

Loftus, E. (1997). Creating false memories. *Scientific American, 227*, 70–75.

Mazzoni, G. A. L., Loftus, E., Seitz, A., & Lynn, S. J. (1999). Changing beliefs and memories though dream interpretation. *Applied Cognitive Psychology, 13,* 125–144.

Paddock, J. R., Eber, H. W., & Loftus, E. (1999). Imagination inflation and the perils of guided visualization. *Journal of Psychology, 133,* 581–595.

Solms, M. (1997). *The neuropsychology of dreams.* Mahwah, NJ: Erlbaum.

Solms, M. (2000). Dreaming and REM sleep are controlled by different brain mechanisms.   *Behavioral and Brain Sciences, 23,* 793–1121.

Tzelgov, J., Porat, Z., & Henik, A. (1997). Automaticity and consciousness: Is perceiving the word necessary for reading it? *American Journal of Psychology, 110,* 429–448.

Whyte, L. L. (1960). *Unconscious before Freud.* New York: Basic Books.

5

LONG-TERM POTENTIATION

As you read this chapter, you are coming across information that is in some ways new to you. You are reading sentences you have never encountered before, as well as some new ideas and facts. For some time after you finish reading this chapter, you will be able to recall this new information. After reading this chapter for the first time, you will probably forget a lot of the new information after a few days or even hours. But if two minutes after you have finished reading I ask you to relate what you have just read, you will still be able to recall some information that you did not know before.

In addition to being able to recall new information, you will be able to evaluate what you remember from this chapter. For example, you will be able to debate in your own mind the merits of views presented. Imagine that at the end of the day, before going to sleep, you critically think over what you have read in this chapter, looking at the issues from different perspectives. By the time you fall sleep, you have worked through in your own mind a number of questions this chapter raises. Then, the next day when your parents ask what you have been reading lately (one of the habits many parents have!), you can tell them about this chapter and the questions it raised in your mind. This simple process of recalling information and debating it in your own mind raises a number of puzzling questions that are central to psychology, such as *where* you stored the new information and thought about it?

Presumably the bits of new information you learned are stored somewhere within you, and the memory you have of them has some kind of a physical trace inside your body. If we had the ability to record the exact, minute details of the biology of your body before you read the chapter, then examined your body again after you have read the chapter, what you remembered about the chapter, the new bits of information, should be identifiable as a "memory trace" in your body. This viewpoint is *materialist*, meaning that it assumes all thinking has a physical correlate within the person doing the thinking. This viewpoint is also *monist*, meaning that it assumes the mind to be nothing more than the function of the brain. A major challenge taken up in modern psychology, some researchers would claim the greatest challenge, is to work in (in the terminology of chapter 1) and tie a materialist, monist account of behavior with hard empirical evidence.

MIND AND BODY

At least since the time of René Descartes (1596–1650) the brain has been considered the storage place for information and the center of thinking. This much has not changed since the seventeenth century. But Descartes, keeping in line with the religious doctrine of his time, argued that the mind (which in his treatment was synonymous with the thinking part of the soul) and body are separate entities. This is why, according to him, the body can be damaged (e.g. a person could lose an arm) without a corresponding change taking place in the mind.

This doctrine of "Cartesian dualism," with the mind and the body considered to be two separate entities, has been rejected by most modern scientists. The currently prevailing view among scientists is that the mind and the brain are the same thing, and we should not be fooled into thinking they are separate just because we use the different words "mind" and "brain." The philosopher Ludwig Wittgenstein (1889–1951) has warned us that language can sometimes mislead us about the nature of the world. Imagine we look at the eastern sky at sunrise and, seeing Venus, call it the "morning star," then seeing Venus in the western sky at sunset call it the "evening star." The different names "evening star" and "morning star" should not lead us to assume there is more than one Venus.

A major challenge for psychologists has been to provide an empirical demonstration of the now generally held belief that the mind and the brain are the same thing. Rather than studying the mind and the brain in their entirety, researchers have simplified the challenge, by focusing on the memory trace that, from a materialist perspective, must come about when a simple act of learning takes place. Initially called an "engram," this memory trace is today referred to as "long-term potentiation" (LTP). An implication of the idea of LTP is that future behavior is afforded lower degrees of freedom, because future behavior becomes influenced by changed physiological characteristics of the person. However, if *plasticity*, physical changes in the brain as a result of experience, is assumed to be ongoing, then future experiences will also influence the brain, which further influences behavior, and so on. In some ways the engram, LTP, memory trace, or whatever we call the physical change assumed to come about as a result of learning, has become the holy grail of psychology. As we shall see, this holy grail is elusive, and many a would-be discoverer has come away with handfuls of dust.

PIONEERING IDEAS

A number of developments in the nineteenth century laid the foundations for the idea of a memory trace, although no development actually provided evidence to empirically demonstrate this idea. At this stage, researchers were working out, in the sense that they developed theoretical accounts without any supporting hard evidence.

Phrenology

The phrenology movement, pioneered by Franz Gall (1758–1828), popularized the view that the psychological characteristics of individuals are reflected in the shape and contours of their skulls. Cognitive and emotional characteristics are assumed to cause the shape of specific localized brain regions and these, in turn, are assumed to causally determine the shape of the skull. The more a psychological characteristic is dominant in a person, the more developed will be the part of the brain housing that characteristic and the larger will be the protrusion of the skull in that place. Correspondingly, a psychological characteristic that is less prominent will have a hollow in that part of the brain housing it, and so the skull in that place will also have an indentation.

Students of psychology now learn that phrenologists were misguided. The methods of phrenology were reliable – the same bumps and indentations could be measured accurately many times – but invalid, meaning the inferences made on the basis of the measurements were wrong: bumps and indentations in the skull are not indicative of psychological characteristics. Despite being invalid, phrenological research did help to focus attention on the relationship between the brain and psychological functioning, and specifically the idea of localization of psychological functioning in regions of the brain. However, phrenology emphasized inborn characteristics whereas, as we shall see, the later idea of memory trace is based on changes in the brain as a result of experience.

Associationism

A more interesting link between thinking and changes in the brain is found in the work of Alexander Bain (1818–1903), who built on the traditions of the British Associationists. In the eighteenth century a number of British scholars developed the view that movement from one psychological experience to another, from idea to idea or sensation to sensation, for example, is chiefly dependent on contiguity. That is, when two psychological experiences occur simultaneously or close together in time, the association between them is strengthened, thus increasing the probability that in the future one experience will follow the other. Put another way, when psychological experiences occur close together, they become associated. For example, when Paula repeatedly sees Joan out walking with an aggressive dog, the next time she thinks of Joan she is likely to also think of the frightening dog. Bain attempted to formulate a physiological basis for associationism, to show that mental phenomena have a material basis in the brain.

Classical conditioning and the brain

The biological basis of psychological functioning was also a focus in the work of two great Russian pioneers, Ivan Sechenov (1829–1905) and Ivan Pavlov (1849–1936). Both Sechenov and Pavlov believed that psychological phenomena can be explained in terms of physiological functioning; particularly reflexes, which can be innate or learned. They avoided references to subjective experiences. Pavlov's research before 1900 focused on the digestive system, for which he won the Nobel Prize in 1904. His research in the early 1900s on what became known as "classical conditioning," in which the pairing of two stimuli changes the response of one of them to become like the response to the other, excluded any references to subjectivity and focused exclusively on observable behavior.

During the course of his research on the digestive system, Pavlov noticed that the dogs used in his experiments salivated not only when meat was presented to them but also when they heard the footsteps of the attendant who brought them food. It seemed that the dogs associated the footsteps of the attendant with food, and this association led to salivation, a reaction originally exclusive to food. Through controlled experimentation, Pavlov demonstrated that when an unconditioned stimulus (UCS), such as food, is paired with a conditioned stimulus (CS), such as the sound of a bell, after a number of pairings the CS by itself will lead to a conditioned response (CR), such as salivation (see chapter 6). Of particular importance to the present discussion is that Pavlov theorized about changes in the brain that he believed arise through classical conditioning.

Pavlov believed that classical conditioning came about as a result of a strengthened connection between parts of the brain in which the CS and UCS activities are centered. Before the training of the dog, the UCS (meat) excites the UCS center in the brain, which then excites the unconditioned response (UCR; salivation) brain center, and this results in the salivation response. At this time, the CS (bell) excites the CS brain center, but the response is not salivation. After training, excitation of the UCS (meat) brain center also excites the CS (bell) brain center, so the response to the CS is the same as to the UCS. Although the technology was not yet available to test this proposition by examining brain pathways, the fundamentally important point is that Pavlov had made a key conceptual leap: learning must be accompanied by changes in particular centers in the brain.

James's principles

But we should not end this discussion on pioneering ideas without clarifying the monumental contribution of William James (1842–1910) to our understanding of the relationship between brain processes and learning. Students of psychology typically learn that Pavlov established the experimental foundations of learning in the early 1900s. But it is often neglected that William James taught a course on "The Relations between Physiology and Psychology" in 1875–76. In his monumental text *The Principles of Psychology* (1890), James made clear his belief that change takes place in the brain as a result of learning. For example, in the chapter on memory he discussed paths worn in the brain by experience: "The persistence or permanence of the paths is a physiological property of the brain-tissue of the individual, whilst their number is altogether due to the facts of their mental experience" (p. 621). James was undoubtedly influenced by the findings of the pioneering memory researcher Ebbinghaus, which demonstrate that through repetition bits of information can be remembered for longer periods. Presumably this is because repetition creates deeper paths in the brain. It was up to experimentalists to try to identify such changes in the brain in association with learning.

Thus, by the early twentieth century a number of leading scholars had discussed the idea of a memory trace, without having hard evidence to support the idea. A first step toward gathering this evidence was the demonstration of *localization*, the extent to which different regions of the brain specialize in controlling different functions. Some types of specialized links between biological and psychological processes were already being experimentally examined before the twentieth century. Technological advances in the nineteenth century had enabled researchers to distinguish between sensory and motor nerves and to experiment on the psychological consequences of the removal of the cerebrum. However, the state of technology still seriously hampered attempts to identify specific changes in the brain associated with particular acts of learning.

CRITICAL THINKING QUESTIONS

1 "Science is only compatible with a materialist and monist position." Do you agree?

2 Is associationism too simplistic to explain the complexities of human thought?

PIONEERING EXPERIMENTAL RESEARCH

Karl Lashley (1890–1958) was the first major researcher to take up the challenge of testing Pavlov's theory that classical conditioning involves a strengthened physical connection between centers in the brain. If this theory is correct, Lashley reasoned, cutting the connections between different parts of the brain should end or inhibit the learned behavior. Lashley trained rats on a variety of maze learning and visual discrimination learning tasks, and then made cuts in the cerebral cortexes of the rats, severing links between different parts of their cortexes. But this approach did not yield the expected results: the location of cuts was not related to performance. Rather, the extent of a cut, and the size of the section of the cortex that was removed, was related to impaired performance. This was an early indication that it is useful to view the brain as a dynamic, integrated, interdependent whole, rather than as localized, a set of specialized compartments functioning separately.

However, the dominance of reductionism in Western science continued to shape research on the memory trace. Influenced by the larger culture, researchers asked whether learning might be localized at a far more micro level. The neurosurgeon Wilder Penfield (1891–1976) noted that when electric stimulation is applied to a part of the cerebral cortex, very specific memories are evoked in patients (Penfield & Perot, 1963). Perhaps, speculated Penfield, each specific memory is stored in a different single neuron? Along the same lines, some researchers raised the possibility that each specific memory is stored in a specific RNA or protein molecule. Experiments with rather bizarre methods were conducted testing this idea, by first teaching a group of rats a task, then grinding up their brains, extracting RNA, and transferring it to untrained rats to test if the recipient rats could also perform the task. This followed earlier studies in which flatworms were taught a response, then fed to other flatworms, which apparently demonstrated the same learned response. Surely these must qualify for a TV program on "The Funniest Science Experiments." The general consensus is that these lines of research were blind alleys and that each specific memory is not stored in a single neuron or in a specific molecule (working in is not always successful). Flatworms do not become smarter by cannibalizing other flatworms who have succeeded in learning new tasks. Nor do tribe members who eat body parts of their dead ancestors gain the knowledge of the deceased. These research developments reflect conformity and groupthink among researchers (see chapter 15).

Evidence suggesting long-term potentiation

By the beginning of the twentieth century a consensus had emerged among a number of leading scholars to the effect that learning is associated with physical changes in the brain. However, the empirical basis for this view emerged slowly. Twenty-first-century views on long-term potentiation can be traced back to the Spanish neuroanatomist Ramon y Cajal (1852–1934), the English physiologist Charles Sherrington (1857–1952), and the American-born psychologist Donald Hebb (1904–85), who did his most important work in Canada.

Ramon y Cajal used newly developed methods for staining nervous tissue with silver to experimentally demonstrate two features of communication between nerve cells. First, that nerve cells are not directly joined to one another. Second, that nerve impulses pass only in one direction, from the axon of one neuron to the dendrite of the next.

An important and related discovery was made by Sherrington, who, like Pavlov, focused on behavior, rather than electrophysiology, to infer about communication between neurons. But Sherrington took as his topic of study the simple reflex, whereas Pavlov attempted the far more complex task of understanding the entire brain using behavioral indicators. Sherrington first cut all connections between the body and the brain in an animal, then studied spinal reflexes in isolation. By applying mild electric shocks to points in the animal's skin and observing the response, Sherrington came to the conclusion that conduction across and within neurons has different characteristics.

One of Sherrington's most important observations was that a single *sub-threshold stimulus*, a stimulus weaker than required to elicit a reflex response, would lead to a response if followed by a sufficient number of other sub-threshold stimuli. This suggested to him a summation effect: a buildup that would eventually be strong enough to jump across the connection between neurons. This connection or gap Sherrington and Michael Foster termed the *synapse*. Communication across the synapse has become a focal point for modern neuroscience research.

Sherrington also concluded that, when stimulated, certain neurons can have inhibitory effects (i.e. decreasing the likelihood of firing) on certain other neurons. Presumably the nature of the effect of one neuron on another depends on the kinds of communication that take place across the synapse. This picture of neurons having both stimulating and inhibiting effects on one another adds to the picture of the brain as a complex, inter-related, and dynamic whole.

The experimental research of Ramon y Cajal, Sherrington, and others suggesting communication between neurons across a synaptic gap was integrated into a biologically based explanation of behavior by Hebb in his landmark book *The Organization of Behavior* (1949). Hebb's explanation begins with the idea that when an axon of a neuron (cell A) repeatedly participates in the firing of another neuron (cell B), "some growth process or metabolic change takes place in one or both cells" (Hebb, 1949, p.62). Thus, the repeated association of the firing of two neurons brings about change in one or both of them.

Hebb went on to postulate that this "growth process or metabolic change" makes it easier for the axon of cell A to stimulate cell B in the future. Even though Hebb was not precise about the type of change, or even if it takes place in one or both cells, his idea has become very influential. The term *Hebbian synapse* is commonly used in contemporary neuroscience, referring to a synapse that increases in effectiveness because of simultaneous activity in the *presynaptic neuron*, situated on the releasing end of a synapse, and *postsynaptic neurons*, situated on the receiving end of a synapse. The "Hebbian synapse," then, is another term for the physical changes in the brain associated with learning, first postulated in the nineteenth century.

Are physical changes associated with learning just limited to connections between single cells? If so, then a simple connectionist explanation of learning seems sufficient: cell A becomes connected with cell B, cell B with cell C, cell C with cell D, and so on. But Hebb painted a more complex picture by introducing the concept of *cell assembly*, a cluster of neurons grouped together functionally as a result of being stimulated together in the past. A cell assembly can function as a closed system for a time, as a biological correlate of learning; that is, the cell assembly is the physical record of the learning taking place. Hebb was working out; he theorized and moved conceptual understanding well beyond the hard evidence available at the time. Thus, Hebb painted a picture of cell assemblies forming and re-forming, activating each other, and becoming organized as part of larger "phase sequences" or units of physical changes, as learning and unlearning take place. One of the reasons for Hebb's continuing influence is that his ideas match twenty-first-century views on brain plasticity.

DEBATE OVER LONG-TERM POTENTIATION

The idea of plasticity was discussed from at least the early twentieth century, but it was Hebb (in the 1940s) who first formulated a convincing account of behavior using this idea. However, until late in the twentieth century technological limitations hampered the empirical investigation of cell plasticity. Solid progress was first made toward overcoming these limitations in the early 1970s, with advances in electrophysiology, which allowed the exact placing of an excitatory micro-electrode in one specific brain location and a recording electrode in another. Through these new techniques, researchers identified a physical change as a result of repeated stimulation of one neuron by another (Bliss & Lomo, 1973), and the phenomenon was termed *long-term potentiation*. The term "potentiation" refers to an increase in responsiveness (to the same kind of stimulation) of cells that have been repeatedly stimulated.

In some respects the work of Sherrington using purely behavioral measures at the beginning of the twentieth century foreshadows contemporary ideas about the characteristics of LTP, particularly the following three important characteristics. First, Sherrington had discovered that when one sub-threshold stimulus is not strong enough to elicit a reflex, additional sub-threshold stimuli may do so. This links up to the *cooperativity* of LTP, whereby stimulation by just one axon produces weak or imperceptible LTP, whereas simultaneous or nearly simultaneous stimulation by several axons produces LTP. Second, Sherrington also foreshadowed the *specificity* of LTP, meaning that changes are specific to activated synapses, as well as the *associativity* of LTP, meaning that when a weak input is paired with a strong one, later response to the weak input is strengthened. Sherrington also concluded that some neurons can have an inhibitory effect, foreshadowing the contemporary concept of long-term depression (LTD), which is the opposite effect to LTP.

The cellular mechanisms for LTP are to some extent known.[1] Using single-cell recording techniques, researchers have been able to identify LTP as a correlate to learning in animals. Research with animals shows strong promise for using drugs to modify synaptic strength among neurons (e.g. Tang et al., 1999). A number of biotechnology companies are poised to take advantage of this cutting-edge research, including *Memory Pharmaceuticals*, founded in 1998 by Eric Kandel, who won the Nobel Prize in 2000 for his research on how memories are formed using the sea slug, which has a mere twenty thousand nervous system cells, compared to about 100 billion brain cells in a human. Numerous other biotechnology companies (e.g. *Helicon Therapeutics*) and major pharmaceuticals (e.g. *Merck & Co.*) are poised to make breakthroughs in developing memory-enhancing, as well as memory-inhibiting, drugs over the next decade.

Research on the role of calcium in LTP, for example, may lead to new drugs that are far more effective than currently available treatments for combating memory loss. This is particularly important for combating Alzheimer's disease, a degenerative disorder that gradually destroys the brain. Related to this are new developments in research on *stem cells*, undifferentiated cells that theoretically have the potential to become specialized to fill the specific needs of particular medical patients. For example, in the coming decades we may acquire the ability to use stem cells for cell repair and cell replacement for treating

Alzheimer's patients. These developments underline the enormous practical potential of LTP.

Continuing doubts

Although some evidence at the cellular level suggests LTP to be a real phenomenon, there are persisting doubts about various aspects of the broader idea of LTP as representing learning. First, there is more agreement about the cellular mechanisms for LTP than about whether and how potentiation is maintained through presynaptic, postsynaptic, or both presynaptic and postsynaptic mechanisms. In other words, the means by which the memory trace is maintained is still not known. Second, LTP has been demonstrated over hours and days but not over months and years. This is important, because the term "long-term" requires that *maintenance* of changes associated with learning be demonstrated.

Third, LTP is about a relatively short-term change in the responsiveness of one neuron: this is incredibly simplistic compared with the kinds of complex learning tasks humans regularly undertake, such as learning to interpret a poem or to play the piano. To use terminology introduced in chapter 1, LTP is associated with explanations of behavior with close to zero degrees of freedom, whereas much of everyday human behavior involves high degrees of freedom. Long-term potentiation as measured in a single neuron of a hippocampal slice, removed from an animal and maintained in a culture medium, may be very different in important ways from learning in everyday life. Just think of yourself learning to speak a new language or a new board game with lots of rules. To achieve this kind of complex task you need coordinated attention and problem-solving skills – not likely to be reflected in a single neuron. On the other hand, the hippocampus is known to play a particularly important role in learning and memory, and in this respect the discovery of LTP in this region of the brain matches research expectations.

Not all neuroscientists are convinced of the importance of LTP. For example, Randy Gallistel, a UCLA (University of California at Los Angeles) professor who is also a world authority on the neural basis of learning and motivation, has argued that "LTP looks like a poor candidate to be the mechanism by which the nervous system stores the values of variables" (Gazzaniga, 1997, p. 75), in large part because LTP decays continuously and rapidly. Despite the term "long-term," LTP is not long-lasting.

A broader criticism of LTP is related to reductionism, the tendency to try to explain phenomena by reference to the smallest units possible. Learning in everyday life is typically a social process, involving interactions with others. In everyday life, learning typically takes place through social interactions with others, and through individuals actively participating in the construction of meaning systems. For example, as Joe helps his father to barbeque steaks and make hamburgers outdoors, he is intentionally ascribing meaning to the activities in which he and his father are collaboratively engaged. Learning how to barbeque is integrally connected with learning gender roles. Similarly, as Myra, Joe's sister, helps their mother to prepare the salad in the kitchen, she is learning both how to make a salad and how gender roles relate to different types of cooking activities and contexts (e.g. males cook outdoors; females cook in the kitchen). All such learning is culture dependent, and meaning systems (such as those related to cooking and gender roles) tend to vary across cultures.

The role of individuals in learning is not passive. Rather, individuals both actively learn and participate in the collaborative construction of meaning. This is an ongoing process; individuals continually weave through social relationships and meaning-making activities. The source of learning, then, can be considered outside the person, in the social world shared with others. For example, Joe does not passively accept the role ascribed to him in the barbeque tradition in his family, but rather re-negotiates the role and forces his family to accept that women in the family can also barbeque, just as men can cook indoors. Such role re-negotiations involve subtle and shifting positioning on the part of family members. Obviously, when considered in relation to such complexities, LTP is still very simplistic. Long-term potentiation involves a reductionist approach, of looking to micro-level intra-personal processes and viewing learning only as it is reflected in physical changes inside the person.

CRITICAL THINKING QUESTIONS

1 In what ways could a Hebbian synapse serve as a building block in learning?

2 LTP decays fairly quickly. Why is this a shortcoming for an explanation of memory?

CONCLUDING COMMENT

The search for the physical basis of learning, starting with the memory trace or engram and culminating in the discovery of LTP, has been challenging but also very exciting and promising. This search may well lead to important applied developments, opening avenues for treating individuals with memory impairment. But we should also keep in mind the limitations: LTP probably represents one type of biological change associated with some types of learning, or at least some steps in learning. Long-term potentiation is a very simple and preliminary step toward identifying the neural basis of learning, and critics are correct to point out that the learning of complex tasks in the real world is not explained by LTP, which decays relatively rapidly and is localized in a neuron. Many questions remain. If learning depends on networks or pathways or assemblies of neurons, as Hebb and others have suggested, then how do such networks come into being, how are they maintained, how does decay take place in a network?

Thus, although LTP is considered by some as a great idea, it is more correctly described as a great idea that has yet to come to fruition. There is little doubt that in the next few decades fundamentally important developments will take place through research on LTP and stem cells, leading to a much fuller understanding of the neural basis of learning.

CRITICAL THINKING QUESTIONS

1 In what way is LTP reductionist?

2 Give an example of a practical benefit that could arise from research on LTP.

NOTE

1. Studies using slices of the hippocampus suggest a first step is the stimulation of non-NMDA (N-methyl-D-aspartate) receptors by glutamate, leading to the depolarization of the postsynaptic membrane and the removal of magnesium ions that were blocking NMDA receptors. This allows for the activation of the NMDA glutamate receptors, which in turn allow calcium to enter. The influx of calcium activates certain otherwise inactive genes, which trigger increases in the responsiveness of non-NMDA receptors in the dendrites. The resulting responsiveness or potentiation may last for hours.

FURTHER READING

Bliss, T. V. P., & Lomo, T. (1973). Long-lasting potentiation of synaptic transmission in the dentate area of the anaesthetized rabbit following stimulation of the perforant path. *Journal of Physiology, 232,* 331–356.

Baudry, M., & Davis, J. (eds.) (1991). *Long-term potentiation.* Cambridge, MA: MIT Press.

Baudry, M., & Maren, S. (1995). Properties and mechanisms for long term synaptic plasticity in the mammalian brain. *Neurobiology of Learning and Memory, 63,* 1–18.

Gazzaniga, M. S. (ed.) (1997). *Conversations in the cognitive neurosciences.* Cambridge, MA: MIT Press.

Hebb, D. (1949/1961). *The organization of behavior: A neuropsychological theory.* New York: John Wiley.

James, W. (1890/1981). *The principles of psychology.* Cambridge, MA: Harvard University Press.

Malenka, R. C., & Nicoll, R. A. (1999). Long-term potentiation – A decade of progress? *Science, 285,* 1870–1884.

Martinez, J., & Kesner, R. (eds.) (1998). *Neurobiology of learning and memory.* New York: Academic Press.

Penfield, W., & Perot, P. (1963). The brain's record of auditory and visual experience. *Brain, 86,* 595–696.

Squire, L. R., & Kandel, E. R. (1999). *Memory from mind to molecules.* New York: Scientific American.

Tang, Y. P., Shimizu, E., Dubes, G. R., Rampon, C., Kerchner, G. A., Zhuo, M., Liu, G., & Tsien, J. Z. (1999). Genetic enhancement of learning and memory in mice. *Nature, 40,* 63–69.

6

LEARNING

As I write this chapter, my six-year-old son is trying to bounce a ball on the floor one time and catch it, then bounce it two times and catch it, then bounce it three times and catch it, with the goal of winning a gold medal by bouncing it ten times before catching it. When the ball bounces out of control, not an uncommon occurrence in this high-pressure game, my son typically makes remarks about what the coach would have him do to improve his score. Each time he manages a couple of controlled bounces, he remarks on how his coach will be pleased. In the last ten minutes or so, he has not got past four bounces. However, this is a definite improvement on his performance yesterday, when he first started to play what he calls "the bounce–catch game."

At the same time that this crowd-pleasing basketball performance is going on, I can hear my thirteen-year-old daughter talking on the telephone with a girlfriend about their math homework and an upcoming algebra test they are strategizing for. Like most of my daughter's telephone conversations since she hit the teens, this is a long one, with a lot of talk about exciting social stuff mixed in with talk about dull homework. However, it is clear that by the end of the telephone conversation my daughter and her friend have together managed to work out a solution to an algebraic problem they were not able to solve when working individually. In both these situations, my son and daughter are engaged in *learning*, a relatively long-term change in behavior as a result of experience. Also, in both these situations my son and daughter are learning through the influence of others, who may or may not be immediately present. This social aspect of learning is something I shall return to later in this chapter.

Learning is at the heart of modern psychology, and research on learning played a unique role in launching psychology as a modern science. A major reason for the centrality of this role is that research on learning directly addresses a central question of concern to all psychologists: the *plasticity of behavior*, the extent to which behavior can be altered through learning. How much of human behavior is learned? How much is inbuilt? To what extent can individuals be shaped by their environments? Some researchers have claimed that if they were given a child, they could shape her or him into any kind of adult. In other words, hard-wired factors are unimportant compared with environmental ones when it comes to our behavior. We can learn to become anything. This viewpoint places the idea of learning at the heart of psychology.

Learning attained this central role through developments in the field of psychology in the nineteenth and early twentieth century, mainly through researchers trying to work in and to develop ideas strictly on the basis of empirical data. As we shall see, although the roots of these developments lie in Europe, learning evolved to be the center of a uniquely American school of psychology, behaviorism. In the latter part of the nineteenth century, the influence of Wilhelm Wundt (1832–1920) and others meant that the laboratory method was firmly established in psychology (see chapter 2). Thus, it was standard procedure for psychologists to study individual behavior under controlled conditions. However, Wundt and his followers relied heavily on the method of *introspection*, the exploration and reporting of conscious experience by individuals, and through their influence introspection came to be widely used in psychological research. In that early era, participants in studies first underwent training to introspect, then served as experimental subjects.

Edward Titchener (1867–1927), who had been one of Wundt's students in Germany, moved to Cornell University and acted as the spearhead of this new research movement in the United States. But Titchener's approach differed in fundamental ways from his teacher's. Wundt had argued that the laboratory method is only appropriate for the study of some types of behavior, such as sensations, and that complex behaviors, such as language, need to be studied outside the laboratory in the wider social context. This second psychology he referred to as "folk" or "cultural" psychology. But in part through the influence of Titchener and others who branched off from Wundt's school of structuralism and abandoned the idea of a second psychology or folk psychology, psychology in the United States became almost exclusively focused on Wundt's "first psychology."

Despite their fundamental differences, both Wundt and Titchener, as well as the numerous doctoral students researching in their respective laboratories, studied consciousness using introspective methods and interpreted their findings in support of the proposition that thought is based on mental images. They assumed that imageless thought does not exist. In the first decade of the twentieth century, a series of studies were conducted by researchers led by Oswald Külpe (1862–1915) which could be interpreted in support of the idea that imageless thought does exist. This research group soon gained fame as the "Würzburg school," and they are part of the story of how, early in the twentieth century, the focus of psychological research shifted from consciousness to learning.

The findings of the Würzburg school led to considerable controversy among leading psychologists at the start of the twentieth century. Wundt and Titchener defended the position that thought is necessarily based on images, but other researchers, including Alfred Binet, the great French pioneer in intelligence testing (see chapter 7), also reported that participants in studies using introspection had achieved thought without images. A major stumbling-block was that each group was reporting the results of studies on subjective experiences, and there seemed to be no way that introspection could determine the accuracy of different claims. For example, when Paula reports that she can have thoughts without images, how can an experimenter who believes it is impossible to have imageless thought prove Paula wrong? Paula is the only one with access to her own thoughts, so there seems no objective way to test her claims about the characteristics of her thoughts. When in 1910 Titchener published his text on psychology, this should have been a major triumph for his approach, but by that time the controversy over imageless thought had raised serious doubts about introspection as a research method and signaled the end of an era in the development of psychology as a science.

The controversy over imageless thought created fertile ground for the growth of a movement to develop a radically different approach to psychology, one strictly based on observable behavior rather than intro-spective reports of private experience. In 1913 John Watson (1878–1958) published what later became popularly referred to as the "behaviorist manifesto," in which he set out some of the basic tenets of behaviorism. This is a historically important turning-point, not because all or most psychologists immediately became behaviorists, but because through a gradual shift behaviorism became the dominant school, at least in academic psychology, over the next fifty years or so. It was not until the late 1950s that behaviorism began to be seriously challenged as the dominant school of psychology. The basic tenets of behaviorism incorporated in Watson's manifesto were:

1. Psychology is a purely experimental branch of natural science.
2. The theoretical goal of psychology is the prediction and control of behavior.
3. The science of psychology must discard all references to consciousness.
4. Both animals and humans must be studied using only objective and uniform procedures.

Although behaviorism was officially launched early in the twentieth century, with Watson's 1913 declaration traditionally considered the starting date, the behaviorist school was fundamentally influenced by two earlier developments. The first was evolutionary theory as formulated by Charles Darwin (1809–1882), which dramatically changed the scientific view of the relationship between humans and other animals. The traditional view, particularly as endorsed by conservative interpretations of Christian, Islamic, Jewish, and other religious scripture, was that humans had been created separate from other living creatures; just as the earth was the center of the universe, humans were the center of everything on earth. Galileo's ultimately persuasive arguments in support of the Copernican view of planetary movements showed the folly of assuming the earth to be the center of our universe, and Darwin's evolutionary theory convinced scientists that humans are on a continuum with other animals, that all living creatures evolved from the same source.

Evolutionary theory was used by behaviorists as a justification for studying animals as a way of better understanding human behavior. Given that humans share much of their evolutionary history with lower animals, they must share certain basic behavioral characteristics with animals. This opens up many new research avenues, because practical considerations make it much easier to study animals than humans in laboratories.

A second earlier development that fundamentally influenced behaviorism was research on animal learning, particularly by Edward Thorndike (1874–1949) and Ivan Pavlov (1849–1936). The research of Thorndike and Pavlov is part of a larger trend at the end of the nineteenth century and in the early twentieth century toward studying animal behavior. For example, the animal studies of Robert Yerkes (1876–1956) in this era paved the way for a number of animal research centers to be established in the United States. However, the animal research of Thorndike and Pavlov was highly systematic, conducted under controlled conditions, and resulted in ideas that came to have a unique role in the establishment of behaviorism.

CRITICAL THINKING QUESTIONS

1 What was the case in favor of Watson rejecting consciousness from scientific psychology?

2 Do you agree that evolutionary theory justifies the study of animals in order to better understand human behavior?

THE LAW OF EFFECT AND CLASSICAL CONDITIONING

Two sets of experiments conducted before Watson's 1913 manifesto came to fundamentally influence the new school of behaviorism. The first was conducted by Thorndike in the late 1890s as part of his doctoral research and involved training cats to escape from a "puzzle box." Thorndike made a number of puzzle boxes, which required a hungry cat placed inside to break out by pushing a latch or some other similar device. The main motivation for the hungry cat to break free was to eat the food that had been placed within its view outside the box. In the initial period after being placed inside the box, the cats would typically scramble about frantically. After some time, they would accidentally hit the latch that opened the box and then spring to freedom and food. In subsequent trials, there was a gradual improvement in performance, so that eventually the hungry cat would quickly take the correct action to open the puzzle box.

On the basis of his experiments, Thorndike proposed the *law of effect*, which postulates that the likelihood of a behavior being repeated depends on its outcome: behavior with positive outcome is more likely to be repeated, whereas behavior with negative outcome is less likely to be repeated. He also proposed the *law of exercise*, which simply put states that the more often an association is strengthened, the stronger it will become. In traditional accounts of Thorndike's research, the implication is that his major contribution is the law of effect, and the law of exercise is sometimes also highlighted as important. But neither of these laws originates with Thorndike. Less formal versions of both of these laws have been around for about twenty-five centuries. Thorndike's contribution is more the empirical justification he put forward for an exclusive focus on observable behavior.

Through repeated trials testing animals under controlled conditions, Thorndike concluded that the learning exhibited by the cats could be explained without any reference to consciousness, images, or thought. The animal did not suddenly gain insight into the problem and see the solution. If that had been the case, the learning curve would have shown a sudden shift (reflecting a "Eureka!" experience), whereas it showed a gradual slope, suggesting an incremental strengthening of an association between stimuli and response. Rather than try to imagine what might be going on in a cat's hypothetical mind, it was far better for researchers to study behavior objectively from the outside. This laid the foundation for the behaviorist movement.

Another aspect of Thorndike's research was also worthy of consideration, but it did not receive attention, at least not from radical behaviorism. A fundamental question concerning behavior is its plasticity: how much of behavior can be shaped by the environment? Just as the English philosopher John Locke (1632–1704) had argued that all knowledge comes through the senses, there being no innate ideas, radical behaviorists argued that all behavior is shaped by the environment. However, Thorndike's research using the puzzle box suggested that some behaviors are easier to shape than others, because there seem to be inbuilt tendencies for some behaviors rather than others to come to the forefront in given contexts. For example, when hungry cats are placed in the puzzle box, grooming is not a prominent behavior in this context, although in other contexts cats spend a great deal of time grooming. Consequently, in the puzzle box context it proved much easier to train hungry cats to push a lever than to groom themselves in order to gain freedom. This was an early experimental demonstration of the limits of the extent to which behavior could be shaped.

Another set of experiments started at the end of the nineteenth century proved to be historically important to our understanding of learning; these were conducted by the Russian physiologist Ivan Pavlov. He gained prominence for his research on the digestive system, but his contributions to psychology are even more famous. We need to be cautious in describing Pavlov's research as "psychological" because in his interpretations Pavlov explicitly excluded references to consciousness and focused only on observable behavior. It is too simplistic to say that he saw himself as a physiologist rather than a psychologist; a more accurate description is that Pavlov assumed all psychological phenomena could be explained biologically.

As with Thorndike, the major contribution of Pavlov to psychology was the empirical demonstration of certain long-held ideas about learning, along with new discoveries about some more detailed aspects of learning processes. At least as far back as Aristotle and other classical philosophers, the idea had been proposed that two events or ideas will more likely become associated with one another if there is, first, repetition and, second, contiguity. The role of repetition and contiguity was empirically demonstrated by Pavlov, starting with an accidental discovery in his laboratory by his assistants. Pavlov was using the inbuilt reaction, salivation, of dogs to food as part of his research on the digestive system. In this case, the food served as the unconditioned stimulus (UCS), leading to salivation, the unconditioned response (UCR). It became apparent that dogs would salivate not just when they saw food, but when they saw things associated with food, such as the dish in which food was served to them. Repeated association of food (UCS) with the dish (the conditioned stimulus, CS) now led to salivation, the conditioned response (CR). In other words, the dog had learned to make the old response (salivation) to a new stimulus (the dish). This also happens to us in our everyday lives. For example, think of yourself becoming nervous when you see the building in which your dentist has her or his office.

Starting with this basic finding, Pavlov went on to discover the detailed workings of what we now term "classical conditioning." Pavlov showed that the optimal method of conditioning is to introduce the CS (e.g. sound of bell) slightly before the UCS (e.g. meat), but the UCS should still be present when the CS is introduced. If a dog has been trained to salivate at the sound of a bell (CS), but the bell is repeatedly sounded without being accompanied by meat (UCS), then salivation will stop ("become extinguished"). However, an extinguished response can be re-learned faster the second time. For example, consider a dog that learns to salivate in response to a dish, then stops salivating in response to the dish because the dish is repeatedly introduced without meat. When the dish is again introduced with meat, it will take a smaller number of "pairings" between the dish and the meat before the dog salivates in response to the dish alone.

The same idea is used by Pavlov to explain perhaps the most complex of all human behaviors, language learning and use. The meanings of words are learned by association with signals from the environment. For example, the visual stimulus of a ball is a signal of a real ball. When the child is presented with a ball and learns to say "ball," she or he is positively reinforced by her or his parents. The word "ball" becomes associated with the visual signal of the real ball; hence words act as a "second signal system." Note that this explanation involves direct perception and excludes any reference to mental images.

Pavlov insisted that in order to explain such learning, we need only observe behavior. He did not approve of speculating about what might go on inside the brain of an animal (or human). Not surprisingly, Pavlov did approve of Watson's behaviorist manifesto and supported behaviorist efforts to develop psychology strictly as a science of (observable) behavior. In turn, Watson used classical conditioning to provide demonstrations of the new behaviorist approach. In one study, Watson first showed that infants have no innate fear of rats and some other animals traditionally assumed to be frightening. But infants did show fear in response to a sudden loud noise. Next, using a healthy eleven-month infant named Albert as the participant, Watson made a sudden loud noise by banging a steel bar with a hammer behind Albert's head each time that Albert reached for a rat. After a few pairings of the loud noise (unconditioned stimulus) with the reaching action for the rat (conditioned stimulus), the conditioned stimulus alone evoked the conditioned response (fear and crying). Along the same lines, the Chinese psychologist Zing Yang Kuo (1898–1970) demonstrated that kittens can be trained to like and play with a rat, but also to fear and kill a rat. Kuo's goal was to experimentally demonstrate that, like little Albert, kittens are malleable.

Pavlov's approach to explaining behavior is accurately described as "materialist" because his focus was primarily on physiology and he neglected references to consciousness. No doubt this materialist approach was a reason for the strong support he received from the communist regime of the USSR. Pavlov's materialist approach was in important ways in harmony with the Marxist–Leninist ideology that dominated the communist state, particularly from the 1930s to the 1950s, a period that coincided with the heyday of behaviorism in North America and Western Europe. Marxist–Leninism gave primacy to material conditions, seeing experiences of "consciousness" as arising from the material characteristics of individuals and society. It is ironic that Pavlov's research formed a foundation for behaviorism, and that behaviorism developed as a uniquely American school of psychology. Thus, the world centers of communism and capitalism both at one time endorsed behaviorism, but for very different reasons.

CRITICAL THINKING QUESTIONS

1 What is really new about the work of Thorndike?

2 Do demonstrations that animals are malleable support the behaviorist case?

THE AMERICAN CONTEXT AND INSTRUMENTAL LEARNING

Although behaviorism has its roots in the philosophy and psychology of the Old World, it developed into a peculiarly American school of thought in the early part of the twentieth century. But the relationship between behaviorism and the larger American culture has remained ambivalent. On the one hand, behaviorism affirmed that individuals could become anything. This is very much in line with the American Dream, the belief that society is open and even penniless immigrants can climb to the top in this New World. However, the American Dream assumes that individual destiny is determined by personal responsibility and self help. Individuals are assumed to benefit from free will and personal choice. This is not compatible with the behaviorist view that the only limitations on behavior are those imposed by the external environment. To use terminology introduced in chapter 1, behaviorists see limitation on degrees of freedom as exclusively determined by environmental factors rather than factors within individuals. A young girl or boy could be shaped through training to become a lawyer, a plumber, an unemployed tramp, a successful business entrepreneur, a national leader, or whatever else we want, by engineering the environmental conditions the appropriate way.

Thus, behaviorists ascribed the environment particular importance, since by changing the environment it was assumed one could change behavior. But a focus on the environment could lead to different directions in research, particularly with respect to the unit of analysis selected for study. On the one hand, the focus could be on collective social processes – such as value and belief systems, fashion trends, religious movements, and the like – that are integral to the environment. On the other hand, at the other extreme, the focus could remain on individual organisms. The individualistic culture of the United States influenced the path taken by behaviorist researchers; behaviorists focused on how individual organisms "operate on" the environment to produce particular consequences. The most influential leader of this movement was B. F. Skinner (1904–90).

During his long and productive life, Skinner took up the mantle of espousing behaviorism to a wide audience, rather as Watson had done in his time. Pavlov had focused primarily on the same response being made to a new stimulus: the dog already showed the reflex of salivation, but through classical conditioning it learned to salivate in response to a new stimulus (such as a dish in which the food was served). Skinner followed a different path, one pioneered by Thorndike using the puzzle box. Thorndike had studied how cats learned to alter or "operate" on the environment, by hitting a lever for example, in order to arrive at a desired outcome, such as gaining access to food. Thorndike's law of effect already postulated a link between a response, its outcome, and the likelihood of the response being repeated. But Thorndike's puzzle box did not allow for a systematic quantified examination of this relationship; although it did provide a measure of the time it took for the hungry cat to escape from the puzzle box, it did not provide other measures, such as the number of times a cat would press a lever in order to get a reward.

The invention of the so-called *Skinner box*, a box in which a rat could be conditioned to press a lever to receive a food pellet, allowed for a systematic examination of responses that occur spontaneously and act as operants on the environment to produce consequences. As predicted by the law of effect, such consequences determine the likelihood of a response being repeated. An important feature of research using the Skinner box was that the units of animal behavior (push on lever) and reward (pellets of food) were quantified. Also, the Skinner box does not involve a specific goal to be achieved: a rat presses or does not press a lever without limit. Thorndike's puzzle box involves discrete trails (with specific start and finish), and there is a clear goal. Each time a cat is placed in a puzzle box, the trail ends when the cat achieves the goal of getting out.

Walden II and American ideals

In a fundamental way behaviorism was in line with American ideals of open possibilities and the limited role of innate characteristics. According to the American Dream, the United States is an open society

in which any individual who works hard can move up the social hierarchy. Inherited characteristics and group membership, such as the family
into which one is born, are less important. Behaviorism as espoused by
Watson, Skinner, and others was in line with this viewpoint. However,
there were other elements of behaviorism, particularly as popularized by
Skinner, that did not match American ideals. An important example is
that of behavioral shaping and Skinner's argument that "free will" is an
illusion.

Skinner argued that the laws of learning should be used to engineer
an environment that would shape healthy behavior. Critics bristled at
the idea of "shaping behavior," but Skinner responded that behavior is
already shaped and we must discard outdated notions of freedom and
dignity. The problem with the current situation, Skinner proposed, is
that behavior is shaped by an environment that is not correctly
designed. We must overcome simplistic notions of human freedom and
act scientifically in the design of environments that shape behavior. To
achieve this goal, more data need to be gathered about learning; Skinner
claimed to be concerned with facts and not with theory building. Such
facts must be about the situation in which a behavior occurs, the behavior itself, and the consequences of the behavior. These three are directly
observable, whereas what is assumed to happen in "the mind" can be a
subject of endless speculation and theorizing, not relevant to science
according to Skinner.

Skinner's approach is captured in a novel he wrote soon after graduating from college. He titled the novel *Walden Two*, to contrast his
position with that of Henry Thoreau (1817–62), the American transcendental writer. After graduating from college, Thoreau built a small
cottage in the woods by the edge of Walden Pond, Concord,
Massachusetts, and published thoughts about his experiences under
the title *Walden*. Thoreau's adventure was a serious experiment in
living life in the raw, stripped of all non-essentials. He intended to
regain the autonomy and freedom that he believed only life within
nature could provide. His philosophy of simple-living continues to
profoundly influence the environmental movement, and his essay on
civil disobedience helped to shape the political strategies of Mahatma
Gandhi, Martin Luther King, Jr., Nelson Mandela, and other historically important leaders. Skinner was not necessarily opposed to the
political or environmental goals of Thoreau or the movements he
influenced, but he adamantly disagreed with Thoreau's assumptions
about human freedom.

Skinner argued that humans are shaped by their environments, irrespective of how "natural" such environments seem to be. By refusing to acknowledge the control that environments have over us, we risk losing the opportunity to develop control over behavior on the basis of scientific methods and the universal laws of learning. It was on this issue of the control and shaping of behavior that Skinner, and behaviorists generally, were moving in a direction contrary to American ideals, particularly in so far as American ideals emphasized self help and individual responsibility.

Behaviorism, including the radical form espoused by Skinner, was in agreement with American ideals in so far as it proposed tremendous possibilities for the progress of an individual. Watson had claimed that he could train a child to become any kind of adult that was desired. However, whereas behaviorists had a strong tradition of viewing the environment as the key factor shaping behavior, according to the American Dream anyone can make it in the United States if they have within them the necessary drive, talent, and perseverance. Thus, ultimately, the behaviorist, and particularly the Skinnerian, tradition contradicted American ideals on the important issue of the role of factors internal to the individual.

Skinner's attacks on traditional conceptions of freedom, as well as his insistence that behavior should be controlled through engineered environments, also seemed to contradict American ideals about individual freedom. In addition to exploring an imaginary society in *Walden Two* where behavior was scientifically controlled, Skinner designed an actual controlled-environment "baby-tender" and used it to raise his infant daughter, Deborah. The idea of precisely controlling the environment of infants runs against modern sentiments. As societal trends turned more liberal in the 1950s and 1960s, it seemed that behaviorism was out of step with American values.

Skinner's exclusion of thinking from psychology, and his refusal to theorize about what might happen inside the "black box" between the stimulus and response, meant that his approach to learning was in opposition to the new cognitive approach gaining influence since the 1950s. However, radical behaviorism and the new cognitive school shared the important characteristic of proposing a causal account of behavior. Whereas behaviorists assumed causes to reside in the environment (stimuli), the cognitive psychologists who attacked behaviorism and eventually won the day search for causes in cognitive processes.

CRITICAL THINKING QUESTIONS

1 In what ways does behaviorism, particularly as espoused by Watson and Skinner, match meritocratic ideals and the American Dream?

2 Do Skinner's plans for shaping behavior threaten human freedom?

THE DECLINE OF BEHAVIORISM AND THE RISE OF COGNITIVE SCIENCE

Just as imageless thought proved to be the Achilles heel of nineteenth-century structuralism, giving rise to behaviorism in the early twentieth century, the topic of language paved the way for the decline of behaviorism and the rise of the cognitive school from the 1950s. In this final section, the focus is on critical attacks on the learning model depicted by behaviorists, and also on some similarities between behaviorism and the new school of cognitive psychology that gained the upper hand in the competition for supremacy in psychology. An important point of departure for the decline of behaviorism and the rise of cognitive psychology was the debate on language between the linguist Noam Chomsky and Skinner, occasioned by Chomsky's review of Skinner's book *Verbal Learning* (1957). Chomsky's attack on Skinner's account of language had two major goals: first, to point out that language behavior is far too complex to be explained by classical and instrumental conditioning, a point expanded below; second, to propose that humans are born with certain innate capacities for language learning. After the late 1950s, more and more psychologists adopted cognitive rather than behaviorist approaches to learning, so that by the 1970s cognitive psychology had become the dominant school in academic psychology.

With respect to the complexity of language, an important point is that human language is fundamentally different from language learning in animals: humans use language in an open-ended and creative manner. Each time we speak, we may use sentences that we have never used before, and never heard or read before. We are continually constructing new sentences and using words in new ways. Also, many sentences have more than one meaning, and the interpretation of the correct meaning depends on context and subtle nuances. The creative, dynamic nature of language, and the interpretation of meaning on the basis of context, is not easily, and certainly not completely, explained by the laws of learning espoused by Pavlov, Skinner, and others in the behaviorist tradition.

Chomsky argued that, irrespective of the environmental conditions, language development in children takes place in a sequentially similar manner. Irrespective of whether a child is learning Chinese, Farsi, or English, language learning goes from crying, cooing and babbling, saying single words, using basic grammar rules, to being able to communicate using thousands of words by the age of around five. This is because humans are born programmed to learn and use language: they learn words because of an innate language acquisition device, and they speedily come to put words together correctly because of an innate universal grammar. The environment triggers innate tendencies for humans to learn language, just as the environment triggers plants to grow in spring time. There is a critical period in which language learning must take place, and if it is not triggered by environmental conditions at that critical time, it will remain dormant.

Chomsky's position in support of heredity and Skinner's position in favor of environment are extreme opposites in a long debate well known to students of human behavior. In recent centuries well-known advocates of these opposing positions have been Immanuel Kant (1724–1804), who emphasized innate universal intuitions, such as those of causation, time, and space, and John Locke (1632–1704), who insisted that at birth the mind is a blank slate, *tabula rasa*, on which experience makes marks. The consideration of extreme positions emphasizing innate characteristics (Kant, Chomsky, and so on) and environmental impact (Locke, Skinner, and so on) is useful for debate, because the arguments of the two sides lead us to more easily recognize the specific ways in which each has merit.

But Chomsky's criticisms are not necessarily applicable to all thinkers traditionally classified as in the behaviorist tradition. The idea that innate characteristics influence behavior was rejected by "radical" behaviorists, such as Skinner, but explicitly accepted by Pavlov, often considered the experimental father of modern behaviorism. Pavlov and his co-workers had the opportunity to study the same dogs in numerous experiments, sometimes over many years. They came to identify the different characteristics of individual dogs, characteristics that mediated the influence of the environment. Thus, the innate personality of each dog was seen to influence the responses dogs showed to stimuli. But this aspect of Pavlov's research did not influence behaviorists.

It was not until the 1960s that the idea of the innate returned to psychology in an important way. This took place in part through the research of ethologists such as Konrad Lorenz (1903–89), who demonstrated attachment behavior among ducklings. Ducklings are born programmed to imprint onto a moving object, usually their mother. Lorenz showed this instinct to be so strong that the newborn would become attached to any object, including Lorenz's boots, if it followed the object for about ten minutes (see chapter 11).

Another important way in which the innate returned to psychology after the 1960s is through neuroscience research, and this too was in some ways signaled by the research of early behaviorists such as Pavlov and Thorndike. Pavlov had postulated that learning, as demonstrated by his classical conditioning experiments, brought about new connections in the brain. Skinner and other behaviorists ignored the brain, but a new era of brain research was launched in the 1950s and 1960s, and this led to more detailed information about the association between specific brain locations and types of behavior. Neuroscience research demonstrated that changes take place in the brain as a result of behavioral experiences, but also that the inherent characteristics of the brain influence behavior in fundamental ways and make some types of learning easier than others for particular organisms. Thorndike's research at the end of the nineteenth century foreshadowed this idea when he demonstrated that animals are predisposed to learn some behaviors more easily than others; such as the example discussed earlier in this chapter of a cat learning more quickly to press a lever to escape a puzzle box, than learning to escape by grooming itself. This makes sense in terms of survival strategies: cats have evolved to seek food by exploratory behavior rather than by grooming themselves (although evolutionary principles suggest that a sub-group of laid-back cats who groom in contexts such as the puzzle box will also play a crucial role in the long-term survival of the species).

Re-assessing learning in cultural context

From some perspectives, then, the accounts of learning provided by behaviorists and cognitive psychologists are fundamentally different. Behaviorists focus on learning through reinforcements in the environment, whereas cognitive psychologists focus more on cognitive processes assumed to be within the individual, as well as the hard-wired characteristics of the brain that influence learning. However, from another perspective these accounts of learning from behaviorist and cognitive traditions are very similar: they are both causal, in the sense that they postulate learning to be an outcome of cause–effect relations. For behaviorists the causes are in the environment, but for cognitive psychologists the causes are more internal to individuals.

A second important shared characteristic of the approach of behaviorists and traditional cognitive psychologists to learning is the focus on independent individuals. This is most obvious in the case of cognitive psychologists, who typically study learning by isolating individual participants in controlled laboratory contexts and focusing on assumed cognitive processes within individuals. For example, a research question in this tradition might be: What cognitive strategies do young people adopt to learn a list of words as compared with cognitive strategies adopted by seniors? By aggregating data from groups of younger and older people, assumptions are made about cognitive processes within younger and older individual minds in isolation.

On the surface, it appears that behaviorists are less individualistic, in the sense that they focus on the impact of stimuli on learning behavior. The source of stimuli is necessarily the environment, which includes other people. However, since behaviorists dismiss mental life altogether, they neglect the collaborative construction of meaning that is part of learning in everyday life. In essence, learning in everyday life involves shared activities and participation in a social world.

I began the discussion on learning by relating the experiences of my two children: my six-year-old son learning to bounce a ball and continuously commenting on his own performance as his coach would see it; and my thirteen-year-old daughter talking on the telephone with a friend, mostly about social stuff but also about an algebra problem that they eventually solved together. Most of what we call learning takes place through interactions with others and through meaning making involving others. An example is what the Russian psychologist Lev Vygotsky refers to as "scaffolding," when children learn through interactions with adults and peers (see chapter 10): those who are more skilled build a "scaffold" to support the less skilled child, until the child learns to carry out the task on her or his own, and then the scaffolding support is taken away. My son's basketball coach worked with him until he could bounce the ball a few times and was able to practice basic ball control skills on his own. After that, the coach did not have to be directly present for my son to practice bouncing the ball – even though my son continued to talk about what the coach would say if he were present to watch him practice. In the case of my daughter and her friend, they mutually helped one another, each providing a form of scaffolding for the other, until they reached a correct solution.

The social, meaning making nature of learning has been neglected by behaviorists and cognitive psychologists. The growth of neuroscience research, with advances in brain-imaging technology, has tended to heighten rather than diminish this bias. This is because neuroscience research has increased the focus on brain activity and biological correlates of learning. An indirect and unintended consequence has been a further neglect of the collaborative nature of learning as tends to take place in everyday life.

CRITICAL THINKING QUESTIONS

1 What shortcomings do you see in the behaviorist account of language learning?

2 "Behavior is already shaped by the environment. All Skinner is asking us to do is to explicitly design the environment in order to improve behavior." Discuss.

CONCLUDING COMMENT

Learning is a great and central idea in psychology, for both theoretical and applied reasons. The theoretical question of the plasticity of human behavior, concerning how much is learned and how much hard-wired, has continued to engage scholars for the last few thousand years. The applied issue of how resources should be allocated to maximize learning – for example, how much support programs such as *Sesame Street* should receive – continues to challenge researching and practicing psychologists. If learning is fundamentally determined by environmental reinforcement, as behaviorists contend, then educational programs of the right sort are essential and must be amply funded. But if learning depends largely on innate characteristics, then what can be achieved with educational programs and the like is far more modest. This issue is at the heart of many debates about learning, albeit implicitly.

However, a challenge that has yet to be adequately addressed is the exploration of the social and collaborative nature of learning. Perhaps because of the individualistic cultural context in which behaviorism and cognitive psychology evolved, the focus of learning research remains the independent individual. Far too little research attention has been given to how people learn through interactions, collaborative efforts, and shared and collaboratively constructed meaning systems (see chapters 10 and 20).

CRITICAL THINKING QUESTIONS

1 Are the applied implications of theorizing a less or more important role for the environment in learning?

2 Think back to your learning experiences in recent times (such as learning your way around a new institution or neighborhood, learning a new computer software package). To what extent did these cases involve learning through interactions with others?

FURTHER READING

Barker, L. M. (1997). *Learning and behavior: Biological, psychological, and socio-cultural perspectives*, 2nd edn. Upper Saddle River, NJ: Prentice Hall.

Chance, P. (1999). *Learning and behavior*, 2nd edn. New York: Brooks/Cole.

Pavlov, I. P. (1928). *Lectures on conditioned reflexes*. New York: International Publishers.

Skinner, B. F. (1938). *The behavior of organisms: An experimental analysis*. New York: Appleton-Century-Crofts.

Skinner, B. F. (1948). *Walden Two*. New York: Macmillan.

Skinner, B. F. (1957). *Verbal behavior*. New York: Appleton-Century-Crofts.

Skinner, B. F. (1971). *Beyond freedom and dignity*. New York: Knopf.

Tarpy, R. M (1997). *Contemporary learning theory and research*. New York: McGraw Hill.

Terry, W. S. (2003). *Learning and memory: Basic principles, processes, and procedures*. 2nd edn. New York: Allyn & Bacon.

Thorndike, E. L. (1911). *Animal intelligence*. New York: Macmillan.

Watson, J. B. (1913). Psychology as a behaviorist views it. *Psychological Review*, *20*, 158–177.

7

INTELLIGENCE TESTS

Imagine you are a psychologist advising the president of a prestigious school. Student interest in the school has increased dramatically recently and this year there are two thousand applicants for only five hundred places for first-year students. The school president wants you to help her find a better way of sorting through the applications and selecting students. In theory, the best possible solution would be a time machine that could transport you four years forward in time, so you would be able to witness first-hand what would happen if you accepted particular students from the pool of applicants. Using the time machine, you could tell exactly which students would drop out, which would graduate, which students would bloom and excel in those four years. In sum, you would be able to tell what the best selections would be. But you do not have a time machine, so you need a stand-in for the time machine. The stand-in we use at present is the SAT, which used to be called the Scholastic Assessment Test but is now recognized as an achievement test rather than an aptitude test. Despite the controversy about what the SAT actually stands for, in the US it is still the most widely used measure of a person's potential for performing well at university. Intelligence tests, intended to measure a person's cognitive capabilities independent of experience, also serve as stand-ins in various educational, therapeutic, and organizational settings.

Consider, for example, the use of the most important intelligence tests, such as the *Stanford–Binet IQ test* and the *Weschler* intelligence tests, as stand-ins in the education system. ("IQ" stands for "intelligent quotient," which was once computed by dividing mental age by chronological age and multiplying by 100. For example, a ten-year-old who did as well as an average twelve-year-old would have a chronological age of ten and a mental age of twelve, resulting in an IQ of $12/10 \times 100 = 120$. Although this method is no longer used, the term "IQ" has remained with us.) Some children are extraordinarily intelligent and would benefit from fast-track education. Some other children are less intelligent and would benefit from being in special education programs that provide additional support and allow students to move at a slower pace. Because we do not have a time machine to tell us which child will benefit from each type of special education, we can use intelligence tests as stand-ins. When Jane takes an IQ test, the results are used as a stand-in to indicate how well she will do in a fast-track educational program. The stand-in role of intelligence tests is essential, and also long-standing with an extensive history in some parts of the world.

From about twelve hundred years ago there were competitive examinations for people wanting to be hired in the civil service in imperial China. Applicants took written tests that involved tasks such as composing poems. When in the nineteenth century the British Royal Navy bombarded Chinese ports and forced China to open up to trade and communications with the outside world, Westerners who entered China were surprised at the high level of efficiency of the Chinese government officials. At that time in Britain and most other Western countries, higher-level government posts, including in the military, could still be bought and were owned by the rich, but the Chinese selected their government officials through a highly competitive procedure of local, regional, and national examinations. This is one in a number of examples available of tests of ability being used before the nineteenth century to select people for specific jobs.

Modern intelligence tests attempt to measure intelligence independent of context and prior experience. In this respect, they are different from aptitude tests, such as those historically used for selection of civil servants by the Chinese, which assume (just as the SAT does) that prior training and education *will* influence the outcome of the test. Thus, modern intelligence tests attempt to measure *fluid intelligence*, the pure ability to reason and to solve problems, independent of *crystallized intelligence*: information, knowledge, and skills acquired through education and experience. There is general agreement that modern intelligence tests continue to have tremendous impact on our lives, even though there is some controversy as to how well modern intelligence tests actually do measure intelligence independent of past experience and education. As we shall see in the coming discussion, the idea of intelligence tests is great, but some of the political uses to which the tests have been put are questionable.

This chapter is organized around four main questions: Why are intelligence tests important? What are the contributions of nature and nurture to intelligence? Is intelligence singular or multiple? At what age, if ever, does intelligence become fixed? Of course, these questions are to some extent inter-related, so that the discussion of each question is connected to discussions of the other questions.

WHY ARE INTELLIGENCE TESTS IMPORTANT?

A key criterion for assessing the importance of a psychological idea, as discussed in chapter 1, is the extent to which the idea influences how we think and what we do in everyday life. On this criterion alone, the intelligence test is a great idea. Intelligence tests and the idea of IQ have popularized the notion that there is some fixed characteristic possessed by all individuals, that can be precisely measured anywhere in the world, rather like we measure height or weight, to precisely indicate cognitive ability independent of experiences.

Intelligence testing has fundamentally important implications for education, and particularly the funding of different types of educational programs. If we base public policies on the idea that intelligence is to a significant extent shaped by environmental experiences, then we are more likely to see a need to invest resources in improving nutrition, daycare services, educational programs, and life conditions for children from economically poor backgrounds. *Headstart* and other such educational programs will be expanded and receive more funding. But if we base public policies on the idea that intelligence is fundamentally inherited and there is little we can do to influence the intelligence of individuals through social programs, we are less likely to see a need to invest resources in educational and social programs to enrich the life experiences of economically disadvantaged children.

A major reason why intelligence tests are controversial, then, is because they can be used to help decide how scarce resources are allocated. This is more obvious in areas such as education and jobs, but intelligence tests have also had an impact in less obvious ways, such as on immigration policy. An example is how the results of mass intelligence testing of military recruits during World War I (1914–18) were used to shape immigration policy after the war.

During World War I millions of recruits had to be quickly assessed, trained, and placed into position in the military. Many recruits were illiterate, and many were immigrants with little knowledge of English. About 1.7 million recruits were tested using the *Army Alpha* and the *Army Beta* intelligence tests, designed for use by literate and illiterate test takers, respectively. Examinations of test results after the war demonstrated significant differences between ethnic groups of immigrants, with some groups, particularly Northern Europeans, scoring higher. This evidence was used by a coalition of forces, including some concerned with "racial purity" of the US population, to argue that immigration should be more biased in favor of those with "Nordic" blood, because other immigrants, such as the Chinese, would lower the general intelligence level of the US population. An outcome of this was changes in immigration policy in 1924, making it much more difficult for people to migrate to the United States from some non-Western European countries.

It was only later that researchers realized that the intelligence test scores of immigrants improved as they remained in the United States longer and became more fluent in English. The ethnic group differences reflected in scores on the *Army Alpha* and *Army Beta* tests were in large part a result of different levels of fluency in English (although *Army Beta* was nonverbal, test takers still needed basic English fluency to follow instructions in the testing context). In the post-1918 period Asians were considered by advocates of a notion of hereditary intelligence to be of "low intelligence stock," whereas in the twenty-first century they are considered to be "high intelligence stock." This change in itself suggests that political trends and social fashions, as well as re-conceptualizations of intelligence itself, rather than objective reality, determine how particular ethnic groups are viewed in terms of intelligence.

Thus, intelligence tests have had considerable practical influence, particularly on the way resources are distributed between groups and individuals in society. On this criterion alone intelligence tests qualify as a great idea. However, past experience suggests that the results of intelligence testing have in some cases been misused. Although research questions can be apolitical, the results of research using intelligence tests tend to become politicized because they have enormously important practical consequences. A great deal of the controversy revolves around the question of how much nature and nurture contribute to intelligence.

WHAT ARE THE CONTRIBUTIONS OF NATURE AND NURTURE TO INTELLIGENCE?

Intelligence tests took on entirely new characteristics in the nineteenth century in large part as a result of the theory of evolution put forward by Charles Darwin (1809–82). Darwin highlighted the process through which organisms that are better adapted to environmental conditions will be more successful at reproducing, and thus passing on their characteristics to the next generation. Some thinkers, often referred to as "social Darwinists," interpreted Darwin's evolutionary theory to mean that intelligence is basically inherited and that certain individuals and groups are just born more intelligent than other individuals and groups. These thinkers identified which individuals and groups were smarter on the basis of how much money they possessed. In other words, their theory of intelligence served to justify economic and political inequalities: the rich are richer because they are born smarter. The controversial debate about the contribution of heredity to intelligence continues today, both because it is a scientifically interesting question and because of its practical importance.

Given the important political consequences of intelligence tests, perhaps it is not surprising that some scholars have attempted to influence public policy through their research on intelligence. An early attempt at this was by the English scholar Francis Galton (1822–1911), who for a time dedicated his extraordinary talents to developing research methods to demonstrate that intelligence is inherited. Galton believed that his ideas on hereditary intelligence were supported by Darwin's theory of evolution. He was supremely influential with his proposition that intelligence is best indicated by reaction time and other such aspects of sensory capacity.

Galton calculated that the most eminent people in England were more likely to be related to one another by blood, and this he took as another set of evidence supporting hereditary intelligence. No doubt Galton assumed that his being related to Darwin (they were distant cousins) was another piece of evidence in support of inherited intelligence. On the other hand, critics could point out that both Galton and Darwin were from a privileged class, both were gentlemen scholars who did not have to work for a living. Perhaps they owed their intellectual achievements to their superior educational and cultural opportunities? Of course, Galton's pool of eminent people were exactly those privileged men who came from upper-class families and enjoyed the opportunities provided by such families; thus it was not surprising that they were related to one another.

Galton did make two important innovations in methodology. First, he standardized procedures for intelligence testing. He tested thousands of individuals under standard conditions in a so-called "anthropometric laboratory," measuring reaction time, auditory perception, and other aspects of sensory capacity. Second, Galton had the brilliant insight of using twins to try to tease apart the contributions of heredity and environment to intelligence. Galton did not have detailed genetic information about the differences between monozygotic (genetically identical) and dizygotic (genetically different) twins, since it was not until early in the twentieth century that genetics research gained momentum (despite Gregor Mendel's [1822–84] earlier discoveries). However, Galton was correct in thinking that a promising method for identifying the contributions of heredity and environment would be to compare twins and ordinary siblings reared apart and reared together. Those reared together were easy to find, and those reared apart he found among children who had been adopted and separated from their families at an early age.

In addition to his innovative contributions to research methods, Galton also influenced a long line of researchers who have used intelligence tests in order to try to demonstrate the hereditary nature of intelligence, from Cyril Burt in England, to Arthur Jensen in the US and Phillip Rushton in Canada. The science of this research has been tainted by controversies that were present from the very beginning, when Galton proposed the idea of *eugenics*: selective breeding of humans to increase or at least maintain the intelligence level of the human population.

It is often claimed that *eugenics* is very old and has been regularly practiced for the last few thousand years. After all, people have always carefully selected spouses for themselves and tried to find the best possible partner with whom to have children. In selecting mates, people have done what farmers and animal breeders have done for thousands of years, selectively breeding in order to pass on particular characteristics, such as size, color, and so on. Second, it is argued that classic works such as Plato's *Republic* advocate eugenic principles. This reasoning is used in order to try to justify *eugenics* as a logical and scientific solution. But rather than seeing *eugenics* as a constructive scientific solution, most people correctly see it as a dangerous idea associated with the efforts of Nazis and others to achieve "racial purity." Many Americans are unaware, however, that the eugenics movement also influenced policies in the United States and that hundreds of thousands of supposed "low intelligence individuals" were forced to participate in sterilization programs during much of the twentieth century, often without them even knowing that they were sterilized.

The claim that Plato's *Republic* advocates eugenic principles is misleading, because Plato specifically points out (in Book 3, 415b,c,d) that just because some individuals rank among the "gold" category in intelligence does not mean that their offspring will necessarily inherit the same high intelligence. Plato warns that if the rulers show favoritism to their own children irrespective of their personal qualities and give them the rights and responsibilities of the ruling class, the state will collapse. This is because the ruling class will become populated by individuals who are not of high intelligence, but the lower classes will be over-populated by individuals of high intelligence (born to parents who may themselves be of low intelligence).

Finally, discussion of the nature–nurture debate and modern intelligence tests would be incomplete without close attention to efforts to use such tests to justify existing inequalities in society. These efforts can be traced back to the social Darwinists of the late nineteenth century, who argued that intelligence is basically inherited and the brightest and best will necessarily rise to the top. In this supposedly "survival of the fittest" world, the less fit will either become extinct or will remain squashed at the bottom, begetting children who will also occupy the lowest levels of society. Thus, according to this viewpoint, the rich and powerful are rich and powerful because they are more intelligent than the rest of us, and their children become rich and powerful because they inherit higher intelligence.

A recent version of this argument was presented in *The Bell Curve* (Herrnstein & Murray, 1994). This work assumes that the United States is a meritocracy, a society in which the position of individuals on the status hierarchy is determined by personal ability and effort rather than inherited wealth and privilege. In a meritocracy, it is argued, more intelligent people rise to the top and marry others like themselves, and their children also inherit higher intelligence and succeed and remain at the top. The over-representation of ethnic minorities among the poor and in the bottom rungs of society is explained by their supposedly having inherited lower intelligence (and not because they inherit less wealth and privilege). Thus, inequalities are explained on the basis of inherited intelligence.

But critics question the idea that the United States really is a meritocracy. For example, they ask whether President George W. Bush reached the top because of his superior intelligence, and not because of his family, wealth, upbringing, connections, and so on. There is no doubt that President Bush does deserve some personal credit for his achievements, but millions of African Americans who are just as intelligent and hard-working will never get even close to becoming president of the United States, or even governor of Florida (like President Bush's brother), because they were born poor and Black. To assume that one's position in the social hierarchy depends entirely or mainly on personal intelligence is to be far too reductionist and individualistic. Of course, this assumption serves to uphold the existing social hierarchy and *status quo*.

The contribution of nature and nurture to intelligence is also further clarified by changes in the intelligence of large groups and populations. The possible decline of the "average" intelligence of the population has been a major concern for some writers. This concern goes beyond the often repeated (and comical) claim by each generation of older people that the younger people coming through just "aren't as good as they should be" or "aren't as brilliant as we were." Nourished by the eugenics movement, the concern about a decline in the intelligence of the general population is based on the ideas that (1) intelligence is largely inherited, (2) education and social status are strongly and positively associated with IQ, and (3) there is a negative correlation between the education level of women and the number of children they have. The claim is that women of lower intelligence are having a greater number of offspring, whereas those endowed with a higher level of intelligence are having fewer babies. The result of this, according to Richard Herrnstein and others, is a real danger that average population IQ is on the decline.

The truth is far more complex and suggests a much more fundamental role for culture in human behavior. Defenders of traditional tests argue that degrees of freedom in the realm of intelligence are determined in important ways by inherited factors. First, as James Flynn has demonstrated, IQ scores have been increasing and not decreasing, and this is shown by the rise in scores in the traditional intelligence tests over the last half century or so. As societies become more test oriented and people become more sophisticated test takers, they learn to do better on such tests – once again demonstrating that test results are culture dependent rather than culture independent.

Second, when results from the Human Genome Project became available in 2001, it became obvious that there are only about twenty to twenty-five thousand protein-coding genes in the human genome (this is discussed further in chapter 19). As the biologist Paul Ehrlich and others have pointed out, this is far too few genes to suggest that genes determine intelligence. Even though genes are very complex and influence one another, a key issue is that the number of genes that are unique to humans is minuscule. This leads us to also give importance to the cultural characteristics of humans. Indications are that intelligence test scores reflect a fruition of both cultural and genetic potential, but these potentials are completely interdependent; one cannot come to fruition without the other.

Third, the contribution of environmental factors is underlined by the experiences of women in Western societies over the last few centuries. Until well into the twentieth century, women and men were being instructed, often by scientists and university textbooks, that women simply do not have the kind of intelligence needed to perform well in higher education. It was only through the collective mobilization of women and the exercise of political power by feminists that this situation changed. In the twenty-first century, women are successfully competing with men at university (see chapter 17). Texts on intelligence have changed their message in line with this new reality.

Fourth, new research by Eric Turkheimer and others is showing that the *heritability of IQ*, an estimate of the IQ score variance within a population that owes to heredity, is in important ways mediated by socioeconomic status (SES), which is measured on the basis of household income, parental education, and the like. Heritability of IQ scores ranges from 0 (no genetic influence) to 1 (completely determined by genetic factors). Most of the research demonstrating that genetic factors overwhelm environmental factors in determining IQ have been conducted with middle-class children as participants. Middle-class homes typically afford good educational opportunities, through the availability of educated adults as coaches and role models, lots of books, computing resources, and the like. But when Turkheimer and his colleagues tested poor, mostly African American children as well as children from relatively affluent families, the impact of genetic factors was dramatically lower: heritability of IQ scores being 0.10 for the very poor sample, meaning there was almost no genetic influence, and 0.72 for the high SES families, meaning genetic factors had overwhelming impact. The clear implication is that the very different conditions existing in poor and affluent families determine whether genetic factors have any influence on IQ scores. Consequently, generalizations about the impact of genetic factors among the general population are likely to be misleading.

IS THERE ONE OR MULTIPLE TYPES OF INTELLIGENCE?

At the same time that modern intelligence tests have had a tremendous impact on everyday life, there has continued to be heated debate and disagreement on basic questions about such tests, such as whether intelligence is multiple or unitary.

Just as Galton achieved breakthroughs by setting a tradition of testing intelligence under controlled conditions and introducing the twins research method for identifying the contributions of hereditary and environmental factors to intelligence, the Frenchman Alfred Binet (1857–1911) revolutionized intelligence tests by designing them to assess comprehension, attention, and other aspects of "higher mental capacities." The new kind of intelligence test devised by Binet at the dawn of the twentieth century went in a completely different direction, focusing on thinking and comprehension rather than on sensory capacities. Binet devised his test in response to certain practical needs of the French education system, and in collaboration with Theodore Simon (1873–1961) produced the first modern intelligence test in 1905. This test underwent a number of revisions, and in 1916 was standardized for use in the United States as the Stanford–Binet test.

The Stanford–Binet and the Wechsler intelligence tests that were subsequently developed are the most commonly used traditional intelligence tests today. These paper and pencil tests typically involve multiple test type questions, are administered in a "one time and fixed time" manner, rather like the SAT and other school examinations. For almost a century these traditional tests have attempted to measure intelligence as a unitary characteristic of individuals, by arriving at a single index of intelligence. However, the theoretical and critical discussion about intelligence tests has proceeded in a very different direction. The outcome is that what the traditional tests measure and what most people now understand as intelligence are in important ways different.

Received wisdom tells us that intelligence is unitary and can be captured in a single indicator, the intelligence quotient, yielded by the Stanford–Binet and Wechsler intelligence tests and the like. The idea of unitary intelligence received support from the research of Charles Spearman (1863–1945), who demonstrated a tendency for there to be a positive correlation between different measures of intellectual performance. For example, children who do well in mathematics also tend to do well in history and English literature. This is akin to children who do well in the one hundred meters dash also doing well in the long jump and the hurdles. This general association between different types of abilities was interpreted by Spearman as indicating "general intelligence" (g). But the association between different types of abilities is not perfect, and individuals tend to do better in some areas than others. For example, in a class of thirty students Jane may rank second in mathematics, fourth in history, and tenth in English literature. Thus, although she does well in all three subjects, her rank is particularly high in mathematics. In Spearman's terminology, her specific (s) rank for mathematics is higher than for history or English literature. However, despite the acknowledgment that scores for specific intelligences vary, the primary emphasis remains on general intelligence. Also, the focus of the traditional intelligence tests has remained on academic, paper and pencil tasks, mostly or exclusively through multiple choice tests familiar to students in school contexts. This contrasts with the issues raised by critics about the need for a much broader definition of intelligence and the advantages of testing in more naturalistic settings, meaning situations that are more similar to those we experience in everyday life.

The critics and the idea of "multiple" intelligence tests

Traditional intelligence tests, including the Stanford–Binet and the Wechsler tests, have been the target of harsh criticism almost since their inception. Such criticism intensified during the political activism of the 1960s, when a great deal of attention was given to possible cultural biases in traditional intelligence tests, biases that apparently discriminate against African Americans and other minorities. A few tentative efforts were made to develop alternative intelligence tests that were biased in favor of African Americans rather than middle- and upper-class Whites. An example of items included in alternative tests is street slang used by some lower-class, streetwise, African American youngsters but less familiar to middle-class Whites. However, such alternative tests were not well developed and remained little more than symbols of a dissatisfaction with traditional tests of intelligence. It is only since the 1980s that there have emerged a number of concrete, relatively well-developed alternative approaches to the issue of intelligence testing. Although these alternative approaches have had tremendous influence on how we think about intelligence, particularly in schools, it remains to be seen whether they lead to practical alternative intelligence tests that actually replace the Stanford–Binet and Wechsler type tests.

The alternative approaches have adopted a broader conception of intelligence than the traditional tests, which are criticized for conceiving intelligence as far too narrow. The traditional tests have resembled academic paper and pencil examinations and assume that all the important aspects of intelligence are highly associated with one another. This is not surprising, given that Spearman's original research on general and specific intelligences was conducted with schoolchildren and their scores in school examinations, in subjects such as mathematics, English, and history. Critics have sought to re-define intelligence in much broader terms.

Howard Gardner has spearheaded a movement that proposes there are "multiple" intelligences, not necessarily related to one another. Among these multiple intelligences are some that are easily recognizable from traditional school examinations and intelligence tests, such as logic, spacial and mathematical reasoning, and language abilities. But also included among multiple intelligences are bodily-movement skills, musical ability, sensitivity to other people, sensitivity to similarities and differences among nonhuman living things, ability to deal with the biological world, self-understanding, and self-control. It is argued that these types of intelligence are not necessarily related, so that, for example, a person could be high on logic but low on sensitivity to communications from others; or low on mathematical reasoning but high on bodily-movement skills. The theory of multiple intelligences is an example of researchers "working out," because the idea came ahead of the empirical data to support it. Indeed, critics argue that there is still a lack of empirical evidence in support of Gardner's multiple intelligence theory.

Two other points warrant highlighting. First, whereas traditional tests measure intelligence by taking individuals out of their everyday contexts and by conducting testing in brief sessions, the multiple intelligences approach is associated with more attention to cultural diver∨∿∿∿∾ ᴧ᷈ᴨᴧ᷈ᴧᴧᴧᴧᴧᴧᴧ attention to styles of intelligence among individuals. The theory of multiple intelligences gives considerable importance to the particular intelligences of each individual, and thus corresponds more closely to the mood of the twenty-first century and the philosophy of "everyone is intelligent in their own way" and "everyone is a star." Perhaps because the theory of multiple intelligences is in harmony with the prevailing political ethos, it has been particularly influential in educational settings and among the general public.

Alongside the research on the theory of multiple intelligences, the definition of intelligence has also been expanded through explorations of *emotional intelligence*, the ability to effectively regulate one's own emotions and interpret the emotions of other, *Machiavellian intelligence*, strategies for manipulating others for personal gain, even at times against the other's self interest, and *practical intelligence*, problem-solving common-sense strategies that are not taught but are based on tacit knowledge. The so-called "triarchic theory" of intelligence put forward by Robert Sternberg focuses on practical intelligence, as well as the thought processes involved in what we recognize as "intelligence" and the situations that require intelligence from us. Discussions of these various types of intelligence, particularly emotional intelligence, has expanded to the popular media, so that the lay public is now incorporating the new language of a much expanded conception of intelligence. At the same time, researchers are learning more about different conceptions of intelligence around the world, and this is feeding into the idea of multiple intelligences (Sternberg, 2004).

What of the traditional intelligence tests? Is their role diminished by the growing popularity of an expanded conception of intelligence and the adoption of terms such as "emotional intelligence" in everyday language? In some ways, yes, traditional tests are at least being given more *critical* attention. There are even signs that there may be less reliance on traditional tests in some domains. For example, some universities, including the University of California State System, is giving less importance to SAT results when evaluating applicants. However, major challenges remain, because the theory of multiple intelligences and other alternative approaches have not given rise to alternative tests that are as easy to use and economical as traditional Stanford–Binet-type tests.

The lack of functional alternative intelligence tests has contributed to alternative approaches to intelligence remaining a theoretical rather than practical alternative. Most people, experts included, agree that it is a good idea to expand the definition of intelligence, but so far there is very little agreement on the success of intelligence tests based on expanded definitions and multiple intelligences. Adding to this complexity is the controversy about the limits to multiple intelligences. For example, why not include *transcendental intelligence*, the ability to have transcendental experiences, *humorous intelligence*, the ability to see the funny side of life, *risk-taking intelligence*, the ability to recognize and to take promising risks, among many other additional possibilities? What exactly are the limits to the expanded conception of intelligence?

Finally, with respect to cultural biases, in defense of traditional intelligence tests it could be argued that such tests should be biased to reflect the culture of the world in which people have to work and compete. Mainstream Western society, it could be argued, has certain distinct characteristics and makes particular demands on those who want to succeed. For example, to do well on Wall Street individuals have to adapt to the local culture and learn the local rules. Because power and money are concentrated in such places, traditional tests are biased in favor of those who can go on to do well in the jungle of Wall Street, rather than the Amazon jungle. This is a powerful argument, but we should also keep in mind that mainstream culture, including Wall Street, is continually changing. The "mainstream" today is different from the "mainstream" one hundred years ago, and tests to identify intelligence for the "mainstream" context should also change.

AT WHAT AGE, IF EVER, DOES INTELLIGENCE BECOME FIXED?

Another theoretical question that has important applied implications concerns assumptions one might make about intelligence "leveling out" or becoming "fixed" at a particular age. Should we assume that intelligence becomes fixed when a person reaches the age of five? Ten? Twenty-one? Forty-five? Sixty-five? Ninety-nine? Or, perhaps never? The answer has sometimes had a tremendous impact on everyday life, at least for some people. Imagine, for example, that we assume intelligence peaks and becomes fixed at the age of eleven, rather like a person reaching their maximum height at a certain age and remaining the same height after that point irrespective of where they are and what they do. An applied implication is that we can test the intelligence of children at the age of eleven and place them in educational systems appropriate for their particular level of intelligence, knowing that their intelligence level will after that point always remain the same. Those eleven-year-olds who score high on intelligence tests can be placed in schools that prepare students for university and higher education, and those who achieve lower scores can be placed in schools that prepare students for technical or manual jobs. In other words, the kinds of jobs people end up being trained to do will be determined by how they score on intelligence tests at the age of eleven.

Well, just such a system was established in England after World War II, and is still in place in parts of the country, despite the controversy and criticisms associated with the so-called "eleven-plus test" and the policy of deciding the educational fate of individuals at such an early stage in their lives. This policy took shape largely through the influence of the psychologist Cyril Burt (1883–1971), who conducted much of his empirical research on intelligence in the period between the two world wars. Burt's research has attracted a great deal of criticism, in part because of its implications for educational policy, but also in part because it seems he was so eager to prove his views on heredity and intelligence that he fabricated some of the data he reports on this topic. The so-called "Burt affair" underlines the strong and direct link between research on intelligence and political ideology and policy.

The claim that the intelligence test is a great idea rests in part on the proposition that through testing we will arrive at an accurate picture of changes in intelligence over time. For example, by testing individuals we will be able to chart the course of intelligence during development. This would presumably indicate when, and if, intelligence growth takes place, or if intelligence reaches a peak at a certain age, or goes into decline at any time. Traditional tests do provide a rough profile of the course of development of some major types of intelligence. For example, mathematical intelligence peaks much earlier than verbal intelligence. Also, verbal intelligence often does not decline until the very last years of life. In terms of the distinction between fluid and crystallized intelligence, fluid intelligence seems to peak first, perhaps by the age of twenty. Crystallized intelligence peaks much later, possibly not until mid-life.

However, traditional intelligence tests fail to reflect how context impacts on the development of intelligence. For example, studies focused on seniors and intellectual functioning in advanced age clearly demonstrate a "use it or lose it" phenomenon. In contexts where seniors have the opportunity to remain mentally and physically active, they demonstrate "higher intelligence." Steven Sabat's research suggests that this trend is also present among Alzheimer's disease (AD) sufferers: AD sufferers who are supported to perform better actually do perform better.

A substantial body of social psychological research, including studies by Robert Ronsenthal, suggest that how well individuals perform on both academic tests and intelligence tests can be influenced by the expectations of teachers. When teachers expect higher performance on the part of particular students, those particular students do perform better. The research of Claud Steele and others suggests that lower societal expectations, as reflected by negative stereotypes, can lead individuals to perform less well on objective tests. For example, when African American test takers are reminded of negative stereotypes about African Americans, they score lower on objective tests.

Thus, the question of "what is the course of development of intelligence" can only be addressed accurately by attending to the context of behavior, and what kind of intelligent behavior is supported by the context.

CRITICAL THINKING QUESTIONS

1 List in order of importance the types of intelligence that you value.

2 What are some consequences of assuming that intelligence becomes fixed at an early age?

CONCLUDING COMMENT

Intelligence tests have had great impact on modern life, because they serve to screen people, to select for advancement in education and jobs, and to influence how scarce resources are allocated. Moreover, intelligence tests have influenced how we perceive and assess ourselves and others. But major questions persist, perhaps the most important being: Do intelligence tests measure ability independent of past training? The best answer we can give at present is: "intelligence test scores are very dependent on past experience." Although impressive advances have been made in constructing intelligence tests, these tests to some extent still measure how well individuals have been trained to take intelligence tests.

CRITICAL THINKING QUESTIONS

1 Why is the nature vs. nurture debate on the issue of intelligence important for public policy?

2 Do you believe it is possible to measure intelligence independent of past experience?

FURTHER READING

Flynn, J. R. (1999). Searching for justice: The discovery of IQ gains over time. *American Psychologist, 54*, 5–20.

Gardner, H. (1999). *Intelligence reframed: Multiple intelligence in the 21st century*. New York: Basic Books.

Goleman, D. (1995). *Emotional intelligence*. New York: Bantam Books.

Gould, S. J. (1996). *The mismeasure of man*. 2nd edn. New York: Norton.

Greenfield, P. M. (1997). You can't take it with you: Why ability tests don't cross cultures. *American Psychologist, 52*, 1115–1124.

Herrnstein, R. J., & Morray, C. (1994). *The bell curve: Intelligence and class in American life*. New York: Free Press.

Premack, D., & Premack, A. (2003). *Original intelligence: Unlocking the mystery of who we are*. New York: McGraw-Hill.

Schaie, K. W. (1996). *Intellectual development in adulthood: The Seattle Longitudinal Study*. Cambridge, England: Cambridge University Press.

Sternberg, R. J. (ed.) (1999). *The handbook of intelligence*. Cambridge, England: Cambridge University Press.

Sternberg, R. J. (2004) Culture and intelligence. *American Psychologist, 59*, 325–338.

Sternberg, R. J., Grigorenko, E. L., & Kidd, K. K. (2005). Intelligence, race and genetics. *American Psychologist, 60*, 46–59.

Turkheimer, E., Haley, A., Waldron, M., D'Onofrio, B., & Gottesman, I. I. (2003). Socioeconomic status modifies heritability of IQ in young children. *Psychological Science, 14*, 623–628.

8

ARTIFICIAL INTELLIGENCE

Imagine you are seated at the back of a dark room, with a large screen situated at the front. On this screen appear words typed by a person or a machine positioned behind the screen, "Hello, I am a human being. Is there anything you would like to ask me?" You have five minutes to ask any questions you want, then without leaving your seat you have to guess whether there is a machine or a human hidden behind the screen. In 1950 the English philosopher and mathematician Alan Turing (1912–54) proposed that computers will become so efficient that in this kind of situation an average interrogator will most of the time fail to detect whether it is a person or a machine behind the screen. This so-called *Turing test*, in which machines attempt to *simulate*, that is to imitate, human thinking, seems to present a practical solution to a fundamentally important question: Can machines think?

Such questions are at the heart of *artificial intelligence* (AI), the science of designing machines to simulate human thinking. Artificial intelligence is a truly multi-disciplinary domain, involving computer scientists, engineers, linguists, philosophers, psychologists, among others. Artificial intelligence uses computers as its instruments. Moreover, artificial intelligence adopts a computer metaphor, whereby mental states are computational processes, and vice versa. There have been many different metaphors for human thinking. For example, Robert Sternberg has described questions raised by, among others, a *geographical metaphor*, what form does a map of the mind take? And *biological metaphor*, how does the anatomy and physiology of the brain and the central nervous system account for intelligence? Metaphors that more specifically derive from technology include human thinking as a telegraph network and as a telephone switchboard. But the computer metaphor has proved to be the most influential, both among researchers and among the lay public. This is perhaps because of the enormously important and wide-ranging application of computers, from machines that play chess and other games, to those that recognize speech, help in medical screening, security checks, and countless other essential tasks.

In the terminology introduced in chapter 1, researchers in artificial intelligence have both worked in and worked out. On the one hand, these researchers have worked in with a focus on hard data and precise practical problems to be solved. They have tried to adjust their computer programs in line with empirical feedback from problem-solving tests. On the other hand, some researchers have started with grand theories about how the brain functions, or how human thinking can be simulated, and only later given attention to hard data.

The theories of artificial intelligence are expressed as computer programs and run on computers, as tests to see if the outcomes are the same as reached through human thinking. This process is highly useful, first because it forces researchers to specify in considerable detail the steps they assume are involved in human thinking, and second because it makes us realize just how much is involved in even simple, everyday human activities. Because human activity is so complex and involves multiple steps that often remain unnoticed by the actors themselves, many people assume that machines cannot simulate human thinking. A challenge has been to arrive at a test with clear-cut criteria for deciding whether or not machines can think as humans do.

The Turing test proposes that if an average interrogator is unable after five minutes to tell whether a respondent is a machine or a person, then we must accept that computers "can think." The Turing test is at one level very simple: it adopts a strictly behavioral criterion of whether machines can simulate human thinking. According to the Turing test, then, we need not be concerned with what goes on inside a human mind or inside a computer, just the output (not unlike the behaviorists' approach; see chapter 6). At the same time, the Turing test side-steps fundamental questions about the nature of thinking, the kinds of characteristics required for anything or anyone to engage in thinking, and what may be distinctly human features of human thinking that are not revealed in one-to-one interrogation. After all, humans live in groups, so tests to differentiate between humans and machines should, some argue, be designed with this in mind.

Artificial intelligence is a new and fast-expanding field associated with the cognitive psychology movement. In the next section I discuss the broader context and historical background of this new field. Finally, I examine some ways in which artificial intelligence is leading to new approaches for tackling timeless puzzles, such as what makes humans distinct.

THE CONTEXT OF ARTIFICIAL INTELLIGENCE

The industrial revolution, which gained momentum in late eighteenth-century Western Europe and was in full swing by the nineteenth century in Europe and North America, set the stage for the development of modern computers. The increased power of machinery, and the rapidly improved precision of machines in completing all kinds of tasks previously undertaken solely by human effort at work and at home, set a number of scholars to speculate about possibilities for "thinking machines." The English mathematician and inventor Charles Babbage (1792–1871) worked out in the 1830s some basic features of calculating machines, conceptualized in mechanical terms. A theme evident in the work of Babbage and later researchers is the tension between conceptual plans and practical means to implement plans: we can draw up plans for all kinds of thinking machines that work in theory, but building such machines is a different and often more difficult challenge.

Just as Babbage's ideas for an "analytical engine" were too advanced to be implemented through the engineering of the first half of the nineteenth century, so too the Turing machine proposed in 1937 took some years to come to fruition. The Turing machine incorporated the basics of modern digital computers. Turing conceived of his machine as involving a device to carry information and a device for reading information. Information would be carried on an indefinitely long tape of squares, each square having on it "0" or "1" or nothing (i.e. blank). Information would be read by a "head" that could also wipe out and register information on the tape. The head could move anywhere up and down the tape. Turing worked out a basic set of rules according to which this machine could carry out an enormous range of computations.

Turing is often thought of as the most important theoretician behind modern computers, but he also made enormously important contributions to solving a huge practical problem facing the free world in his lifetime: breaking the top-secret codes used by Germany during World War II (1939–45). In order to break the German code, Turing helped design what is probably the first programmable computer, nicknamed the Colossus. This work would remain a secret for decades after the war.

While Turing is generally recognized for his contributions to the theoretical design of computers, von Neumann (1903–57) is recognized as the greatest contributor to the realization of computer hardware design. Von Neumann led a team that in 1946 constructed the first digital computer. Almost all modern computers are descendants of von Neumann's design. The key feature of the von Neumann type machine, for the purposes of this discussion, is the material representation of both data and the rules of computation. Thus, physically represented in the machinery are both the information used to solve problems and the rules according to which problem solving is attempted. Later in this discussion, we shall see a link between this issue of physical representation in machines and memory trace or long-term potentiation in humans (as discussed in chapter 5).

Preparing the ground for the cognitive revolution

The impressive progress made in computer technology through the contributions of Turing, von Neumann, and others coincided with a number of important developments in psychology in the 1950s. These developments culminated in a move away from behaviorism, with its exclusive focus on overt behavior, and a return to thinking and mental life as a proper topic for psychological science. This shift proved essential and fortuitous for the future of artificial intelligence, because only through a return of "mental life" to psychology, a move opposed by behaviorists such as B. F. Skinner (1904–90), could there be serious psychological studies simulating human thinking using machines.

From the 1930s and 1940s a series of events helped prepare the ground for the first cognitive revolution (as well as the field of artificial intelligence) that took shape in the 1950s and 1960s. An important early development was the research of the English psychologist Frederick Bartlett (1896–1969), and particularly the ideas discussed in his seminal book *Remembering* (1932). Bartlett conceived the memory process as dynamic and involving "effort after meaning." That is, individuals reconstruct the past in a way that makes their experiences meaningful. He introduced the concept of *schema*, an active organization of past experiences giving rise to a broad cognitive structure that represents multiple specific instances of those experiences. Schemas orient people, giving direction to future behavior. Because of the dominance of behaviorism in the United States, it was several decades after their publication that Bartlett's ideas started to have impact in North America. In the United States, it was not until George Miller's famous 1956 paper on the "magic number seven, plus or minus two," that the thread of Bartlett's argument was taken up again. Miller argued that people remember better when they "chunk" items; thus Miller highlighted a mental organization strategy akin to Bartlett's "schema."

Another development in the 1930s and 1940s that helped prepare the ground for the cognitive revolution, as well as artificial intelligence, was the research of Edward Tolman (1886–1959) and others on *latent learning*, learning that takes place without being currently evident in performance. Latent learning contradicted the behaviorist idea that learning takes place through classical and instrumental conditioning because both procedures alter action (see chapter 6). Tolman championed an alternative interpretation of learning, one proposing that learning involves the acquisition of new knowledge. According to Tolman, it is possible for knowledge to be acquired but not immediately manifested. He demonstrated this in studies with rats and other animals, in which the animals were not allowed to learn by doing, but were instead expected to learn by being in a context and observing. For example, animals who were transported through a route on trolley cars still learned about the route even though they did not physically transport themselves. Tolman proposed that animals and humans develop "cognitive maps" of their environments; an idea far more in line with the cognitive rather than the behaviorist school of psychology.

Thus, Bartlett's research on the concept of schema and Tolman's idea of cognitive maps were early harbingers of a historic shift in psychological research in the 1950s. Below I identify five related research developments that were integral to the launching of the cognitive revolution.

Bruner and the "new look" research

Jerome Bruner became a leading voice in the new 'cognitive' movement in psychology in the 1950s and has remained in the vanguard of revolutions in psychology ever since (see chapter 20). Bruner conducted a series of highly influential experiments that demonstrated subjective biases in the way people perceive the world. For example, when estimating the size of coins, children were found to over-estimate the size of the more valuable coins, and this over-estimation was greater among the poorer children. Thus, perceptions of the world were shown to be related to socioeconomic experiences. The demonstration of the important role of subjective interpretations went against the aversion of behaviorism to everything mentalistic and subjective.

The turn to cognition was reflected by a seminal 1956 book by Bruner and his colleagues, *A Study of Thinking*. This text turned its back on behaviorism and took thinking to be the main topic of study in psychological science. Through categorization and other cognitive processes (such as Bartlett's "schema" and Miller's "chunking"), people are able to manage and impose meaning on the infinite amount of information around them. For example, there are millions of discernible colors, but humans use a relatively very small number of color categories and ignore differences within categories. English speakers, for instance, use the color category "blue" without distinguishing between the thousands of discernible types of blue. Through such examples, Bruner and others were able to identify some of the active, dynamic processes through which the human mind filters information and imposes meaning on the world. In a later book that was also very influential, *Beyond the Information Given* (1973), Bruner explored how people construct their world views on the basis of limited, often incomplete, and subjectively perceived information. This contradicted behaviorism and gave greater momentum to the cognitive revolution.

Planned behavior

A second development in the 1950s that helped launch the cognitive revolution was increased communications and exchange between psychologists, linguists, and computer scientists, best reflected in the ground-breaking book *Plans and the Structure of Behavior* (Miller et al., 1960). The authors gave central importance to the role of plans in human behavior, a "plan" being a temporary and changeable ordered sequence of operations used to carry out a task. A key feature of a plan is that it allows for feedback, so that behavior can be adjusted on the basis of new information. This is rather similar to Bartlett's "schema," which changes with experience. Moreover, a plan, like a schema, is clearly a part of mental life.

George Miller and his colleagues used examples of simple planned behavior, such as a plan for hammering a nail into a board, to illustrate their ideas. A plan is analogous to a computer program, and simple plans, such as one for hammering a nail into a board, were feasible for machines in the 1950s. Miller and his colleagues turned their backs on the behaviorist stimulus–response unit and, instead, conceptualized a plan as a hierarchy of *test–operate–test–exit* or TOTE units. In this example, a test is made to determine if the head of the nail is flush. If the nail still sticks up, then the position of the hammer determines whether the hammer should be lifted up or struck down. If the nail is flush, the plan is completed and one can exit. This cycle is continued until the plan is implemented according to the set criterion of correctness. This seemingly simple idea of "planned behavior" represented an enormous leap forward from the behaviorist position.

Chomsky and the link with linguistics

Developments in linguistics, particularly through the influence of Noam Chomsky, served as a third factor helping to launch the cognitive revolution in the 1950s. To appreciate the importance of Chomsky's influence, we must remind ourselves of behaviorist assertions about language learning. According to the behaviorist account, language learning can be explained in the same way that all learning can be explained, by way of stimulus–response associations and the laws of learning (see chapter 6). For example, two-year-old George is shown a grape by his mother at the same time as she says "grape" and smiles. When George repeats the word "grape," his mother positively reinforces his behavior by gleefully exclaiming, "What a clever boy!" giving him a kiss, and putting some grapes in front of him. The next day, George says the word "grape" again and his mother presents him with more grapes.

Because of the essential and unique role of language in human life, the challenge of explaining language learning was seen as strategically important for the behaviorist movement. All human societies have languages, and language is generally seen as the most complex feature of human behavior. If behaviorists could adequately explain language learning, then their dominant position in psychology would be further strengthened. However, Chomsky's attack on the behaviorist account of language learning proved to be a very serious blow.

Chomsky's ideas fundamentally changed the study of language, and at the same time severely weakened behaviorism and strengthened the cognitive movement in psychology. First, Chomsky argued convincingly that behaviorist explanations of language learning are inadequate. Most importantly, language is creative and limitless in the variations of sentences that can be formed. We use words, phrases, and sentences in ways we have never heard before to create new sentences and to communicate new meanings in ways that could not be explained by stimulus–response-based accounts. At the same time, language is structured and rule bound. Chomsky's emphasis on the rules that regulate language is reflected in his revolutionary 1957 book *Syntactic Structures*, and his idea that important aspects of cognitive behavior are built into the brain is more fully reflected in *Language and Mind* (1972) and other later works. Inherited human characteristics allow people to learn the rules of their particular heritage languages, then apply them to generate sentences creatively. As with Bartlett's concept of schema, Bruner's discussions on thinking, and Miller and colleagues' emphasis on planning, Chomsky's theory of rule-following in language strengthened psychology as a science of mental life.

Cell assemblies, neural networks, and parallel distributed processing

By the 1960s cognitive psychology was emerging as the dominant school in academic psychology. At the same time, advances in computer technology rapidly led to more powerful and more manageable computers (particularly in terms of size). These two developments merged to produce a flourishing of research in artificial intelligence, and *neural networks* as a sub-field, a neural network being a large number of usually simple components wired together so they can function as one unit. Research on neural networks was influenced by Donald Hebb's ideas, put forward in *The Organization of Behavior* (1949), of how memory could be encoded through changes at what has become termed the "Hebbian synapse," the point at which one nerve cell communicates with another (see chapter 4).

Hebb proposed that, through modifications of connections between them, neurons become organized in *cell assemblies*, temporary networks of nerve cells that are the material embodiment of transient cognitions. As the individual has different thoughts, cell assemblies form, dissolve as connections between a temporary network weaken, and come into being in new networks. Hebb's ideas became particularly influential among researchers exploring neural networks and *parallel distributed processing* (PDP), computer processing models in which information is evaluated in parallel (rather than serially by one processor) and distributed throughout the network. To appreciate possible advantages of parallel distributed processing models, it is useful to contrast them with the traditional (*good old-fashioned AI*, GOFAI) models I referred to earlier in this chapter.

From a psychological perspective there are several important reasons why parallel distributed network models could be advantageous over serial models of problem solving. First, the general consensus among researchers is that the human brain works in a way that is closer to parallel distributed processing models than to serial models. That is, humans solve problems by simultaneously taking and assessing information from different sources to reach a solution. Second, parallel distributed processing models afford more opportunities to incorporate and test learning in the model. This can be done by manipulating the different connections and paths in a neural network, for example simulating the kinds of changes that may come about in a Hebbian cell assembly.

More specifically, a first way that neural networks can be manipulated is by setting different levels of activation for *nodes*, the formats (features, letters, words, and so on) for representing concepts in a semantic network. Other examples are: connections between nodes can be manipulated; connections can be cut and new connections can be set up. Perhaps most importantly, each node has excitatory and inhibitory input, and rules have to be specified according to which this input is combined with current excitation. The rules by which nodes incorporate input can be changed.

Information-processing theory

A fifth development that helped launch and give shape to the cognitive revolution was an explosion of research and theoretical development in the area of information processing, a springboard for which was a seminal 1958 paper on human problem solving. This paper initiated a very productive period of collaboration between Alan Newell and Herbert Simon, who articulated the framework for information-processing theory in their 1972 book *Human Problem Solving*. The authors discussed a project for not only programming a computer to solve problems but also using the computer to better understand human problem solving. This was the start of a long series of interactive research projects involving: programming computers to solve problems, with feedback from studies of how humans solve the same problems.

In order to better understand how people solve problems, researchers worked out detailed procedures for collecting *verbal protocols*, spoken self-reports of thought processes. This involved the use of introspective techniques in some ways similar to those used by Wilhelm Wundt and his students a century earlier (see chapter 6). Twentieth-century researchers were faced with some of the same challenges as faced by Wundt and his students. For example, because of the relatively high investment in time and effort needed for collecting verbal reports, only a small number (often less than ten, and sometimes only two or three) of participants were studied – small relative to the hundreds or even thousands of participants involved in some research studies. This has meant that the reported thought processes of a very small number of people, usually college students, are taken as representative of thought processes among all humankind. But this possible methodological weakness in research methods was overshadowed by the revolutionary nature of information-processing theory.

The approach advocated by Newell and Simon treats all psychological experiences – including intimate desires, personal motives, and feelings – as information. As such, psychological experiences can be treated like all other information, as symbols that are actual physical states of material entities. An intriguing way to think about this is to assume that all psychological experiences must have a physical basis or "trace" in the nervous system, and thus we will one day be able to discover the physical representations of all psychological experiences at the biological level. Of course, this materialist assumption is at the heart of neuroscience (see chapter 4).

It is important to clarify that in the context of machines the term "symbol" means not "standing in for a type" of something, but actually acting as a one-to-one token for something. In computers, the symbols are organized to *causally* act on one another. Exactly which symbols act on which other symbols is determined by the rules set out in the computer program. To use a simplified example, a rule could stipulate that symbol X triggers Y, in a case where X is a token for "joy" and Y is a token for "dance." (This example is very simplified, because presumably it would be configurations of symbols that stand for things as complex as joy and dance.)

Thus, artificial intelligence evolved through the coming together of researchers from many different disciplines to address issues such as machine problem solving. Artificial intelligence helped popularize the computer metaphor and the idea of thinking as computer processing. Behaviorist psychologists rejected such ideas, because they excluded thinking and mental life generally from the realm of scientific psychology.

But the cognitive revolution launched in the 1950s paved the way for the very active participation of psychologists in artificial intelligence.

CRITICAL THINKING QUESTIONS

1 What is the Turing test and what two questions would you ask if you were assigned the role of interrogator in the Turing test?

2 Do you see the cognitive revolution as an improvement on behaviorism?

THE LONG DEBATE AND ARTIFICIAL INTELLIGENCE

From at least as far back as the era of classical Greek scholarship, led by Aristotle, Plato, and others twenty-five centuries ago, humans have grappled with a number of questions central to a "long debate" of critical thinking. What is human nature? What does it mean to think? What makes humans unique? Artificial intelligence is contributing to this long debate, particularly by leading scholars to address these long-standing questions in new ways. This contribution will become clearer in the following discussions, in which I address the question of human nature and the meaning of thinking. We shall see that artificial intelligence has important limitations, not because of the quantitative characteristics of individual computers and humans but because of the qualitative characteristics of "computer societies" and human societies.

Is human cognition shaped by nature or nurture?

Are human beings born with most or all of their important characteristics fixed, "hard-wired," or are they born with few or no important inherited characteristics and are shaped by the environment in which they grow up? The debate between those who emphasize the importance of inherited characteristics and those who give more importance to environmental influences in shaping human behavior is vibrant and ongoing in many research areas central to psychology, such as intelligence and personality (see chapters 7 and 13). Almost all researchers agree that both heredity and environment have a role, but there are fundamental disagreements about how much of a role each has. This heredity–environment question is part of the "long debate" in scholarship. In recent history, it has been contested under the banners of "nativists" versus "empiricists."

The nativist position is represented by historic figures such as Emmanuel Kant (1724–1804), who argued that we are born with certain fundamental characteristics, such as our inherited perceptual systems for experiencing space, time, and causation. For example, the argument is that we naturally have an understanding of cause–effect relations without being taught about such relations through environmental influences. Our perceptions of the world certainly depend to some degree on the sensations reaching us from the environment, but they also depend in important ways on the inbuilt apparatus we use to perceive. This apparatus consists of hard-wired categories that filter and give shape to information. Today, in the domains most relevant to artificial intelligence, the nativist position is represented by Noam Chomsky and his followers. This is reflected in Chomsky's argument that there are innate universal cognitive structures that give rise to language.

The nativist view was opposed by empiricists, such as John Locke (1632–1704). Locke was among the most prominent of the British associationists, who argued that thoughts, feelings, and other psychological phenomena become associated through similarity and frequency of contiguity. That is, ideas that resemble one another become associated (similarity), as do ideas that are regularly experienced together (contiguity). Thus, it is environmental influences that shape thought and action. Locke's famous metaphor for the mind of the newborn was *tabula rasa* (blank slate). As the infant grows up, experience makes marks on the slate, and gradually the personality, intelligence, tastes, and general characteristics of the person takes shape.

Steven Pinker is among researchers who believe that artificial intelligence, and neural networks more specifically, offer a unique avenue for testing the claims of associationists. This is because in neural networks, he argues, conditions can be set up so that symbols that physically represent thoughts and other psychological experiences become associated through similarity and frequency of contiguity. Thus, computers can be programed to begin as blank slates, and we can assess the kinds of things that the computers can learn to do and whether they are able to solve the kinds of problems that humans can solve. Through this strategy, Pinker argues, we find that the raw associationist approach, the absolute dominance of environment over heredity, is flawed.

Among the everyday tasks that blank slate computers have problems with is dealing with the idea of an individual. For human beings, the properties of two objects may appear identical, but each can still be seen as distinct and independent. I may not be able to tell the difference between the identical twins Bruce and Oscar, but I still know they are different individuals. When I walk into a lecture room with one hundred chairs that look exactly the same to me, I still recognize each chair as distinct. Pinker points out that at present neural networks are unable to achieve this feat. What they can do is to treat each individual as an extremely specific sub-class.

A second feat that is problematic for associationists is *compositionality*, the ability to have a representation that is made out of different parts, and imparts meanings both from its parts and its totality. This reminds us of the Gestalt dictum, "The whole is more than the sum of its parts." Pinker's argument implies that the Gestalt dictum can work only for humans, not for neural networks, because only humans can derive different meaning both from parts and wholes. Through these and other examples, Pinker attempts to demonstrate that "raw connectionism" is not viable and that to achieve many of the mental feats we often take for granted, such as dealing with the concept of an individual, cognition has to have certain inbuilt structures. This is very much in line with Chomsky's arguments about language and cognition generally.

Unfortunately the idea that computers can be used to test the validity of associationism, and to shed light on the broader empiricism vs. nativism debate, has a fatal flaw. This becomes obvious when we consider the enormous advances made in computer technology and programing since the 1940s: just because neural networks are unable to achieve a particular feat now does not mean they will not be successful in the future. The response to arguments made by Pinker and others could simply be: you may be correct about current limitations of neural networks, but in another fifty years your arguments will have become obsolete and incorrect because of advances in both hardware and software. Given the rapid advances being made in computer technology, this kind of "wait and see" argument is difficult to disregard.

Can computers think?

We saw that, according to the Turing test, if, after cross-examining a computer and a person situated behind a screen for about five minutes, we have a low success rate in telling which responder is the computer, then we should accept that computers can think. Given the high level of sophistication of twenty-first-century computers and their ability to provide answers to questions, the application of the Turing test would probably lead to the conclusion that, indeed, computers can think.

However, some scholars have argued that the Turing test is inadequate and the application of more rigorous tests demonstrates that computers are unable to think. As will become clear in the following discussion, a great deal in this debate depends on what we mean by "think."

An important implication of "thinking" in the human context is consciousness of meaning. For example, when Catherine is asked, "I know you are perfectly bilingual, but do you find it easier to think in French or English?" the assumption is that Catherine is conscious of the meaning of words she is using, in both French and English. But is a machine that uses language conscious of the meaning of words? Intuitively, many people feel there is something special about human consciousness that is not present in machines.

A number of attacks on the idea that computers can think have come from scholars who argue, in one way or another, that there is something special about human consciousness and insight that is not true for computers. For example, in his widely read book *The Emperor's New Mind* (1989), Roger Penrose argued that a computer program can have as output statements that are true but the program is unable to demonstrate to be true. Penrose seems to attribute to human programmers/mathematicians extraordinary powers that enables them to recognize true statements through the special characteristics of consciousness. Though Penrose has been severely criticized, his underlying assumption that there is something special about human consciousness that is not achieved in computer problem solving is widely accepted, particularly among the lay public. We humans intuitively feel our consciousness is unique, separating us from both machines and animals; but at the same time our intuitions can lead us down blind alleys (Myers, 2003).

A far more powerful and influential attack on the idea that computers can think, as well as on the kinds of criteria put forward by the Turing test, was launched by the philosopher John Searle in 1980 through a thought experiment popularized under the title of the *Chinese room*. Imagine that Karl is placed in a sealed room that has only two outlets, one for receiving bits of paper with scribbles on it, and another for passing out bits of paper that Karl writes scribbles on according to instructions. In the room are piles of manuals with detailed rules about when to pass out pieces of paper and what kinds of scribbles to put on them. After some time, Karl gets skilled at using the rules and he can fairly quickly accept incoming papers, write scribbles according to the rules, and pass papers out when he should.

Unbeknown to Karl, the scribbles on the papers he is taking in and passing out are Chinese characters. The rules he is applying are a computer program for processing questions in Chinese. As far as the person outside the Chinese room is concerned, Karl is fluent in Chinese, even though in actual fact Karl does not know a word of Chinese. A key point is that even though Karl is successful at manipulating symbols, so that he appears to "speak Chinese" perfectly, he does not *understand* Chinese. He does not even know he is writing Chinese characters. The conclusion we must reach, according to Searle, is that running a program does not imply understanding; symbol manipulation does not involve thinking. Thus, the Chinese room points to a fundamental flaw in the Turing test: a computer could answer questions in Chinese without understanding Chinese.

The Chinese room thought experiment has generated an enormous amount of critical debate and an ingenious set of counter-attacks by Searle and his defenders. For example, one criticism has been that the thought experiment does not reflect the kind of parallel processing the whole brain does. In response, defenders of Searle's position have asked us to think about a gigantic *Chinese gym*, involving multitudes of people communicating with one another as neurons do in a brain, with lines of communication similar to a neural network. Even though the answers that exit from the *Chinese gym* are in perfect Chinese, the gym does not understand even a word of Chinese.

The numerous attacks and counter-attacks by defenders and support-ers of Searle's position have for the most part been hampered by a common flaw: individualism. The unit to be considered and assessed has almost always been taken to be the isolated individual, both the indi-vidual human and the individual machine. In the final section, I turn to consider thinking in context as it actually takes place in everyday human life. This shift from the individual to the collective level helps us better understand how human thinking is different from computer thinking; in essence, why computers cannot think as we humans do.

The collective Turing test

In exploring such questions as "Can computers think?" the individualism of Western culture has led researchers to adopt reductionist approaches (that is, to consider smaller rather than larger units of analysis). In everyday life, most people most of the time interact with others and live a social life. Very few human beings spend much time in isolation. Indeed, we find isolation painful and isolate people as punishment, such as by sending a child to spend some time alone in his room or placing a prisoner in solitary confinement. The normal state of affairs is for people to be with others, and to carry out remembering, perceiving, and other cognitive functions in the company of others. Even when they want to study for final exams, students often prefer to study in groups or with study partners.

Through social interactions and life in groups, people collectively construct and collaboratively uphold particular views of the world. For example, Abe and his friends see themselves as the coolest, sharpest gang in the neighborhood. They have their own special names for everything and their own style of doing things – so much so that outsiders find it hard to understand them. What is special about their gang is the sub-culture that has arisen as a result of their interactions; a sub-culture that is influenced by each individual gang member, but is more than the sum of the individual members. It is a sub-culture that will not be replicated when the gang disbands.

A fundamentally important feature of Abe's gang is the *normative system*, the rules, norms, values, and so on that regulate the behavior of group members (see chapter 15). For example, one of the rules regulating relations between Abe, the gang leader, and his followers is that he rides at the head of the gang when they are out on their mountain bikes. However, this rule is sometimes violated, because of various reasons and circumstances that are difficult to predict. Another rule is that all the gang wear blue or black shirts when they meet up. However, this rule is never strictly adhered to, often because mom or dad has put the only blue or black shirts a gang member has in the laundry and only shirts of other colors are available for a gang member to wear. There have even been times when a gang member simply says, "I didn't feel like wearing my blue or black shirt today. So what?"

A first distinct feature of rules and other aspects of normative systems in human societies is that they are collectively shared and collaboratively upheld; they depend on the collectivity. Even the gang leader, Abe, needs the participation of others if a rule is going to regulate behavior among group members. If the other members refuse to cooperate, then Abe cannot lead. A second distinctive feature is that rules and other aspects of the normative system act as guides for behavior; they *do not cause behavior* (for example, gang members can fail to wear the correct color shirt). This is not the case in computer programs, where a rule causes certain outcomes with one hundred percent certainty. To make the distinction using terminology introduced in chapter 1, rule following in human societies allows for some degrees of freedom, but rule following in computer programs involves zero degrees of freedom.

It is possible to introduce randomness in the application of rules in computer programs, or even to insert a second layer of rules stipulating when a first rule does not apply, but these do not simulate human rule-following behavior. This is because what is still missing is the shared, social nature of human normative systems. In the human sphere, the rules and so on that regulate behavior emerge through social interactions and are upheld or transformed through social interactions. Consequently, the key comparison to be made is not between a computer and a brain, or even a single computer and a single person in isolation, but between a group of computers in interaction and a group of human beings in interaction.

Thus, the Turing test becomes far more effective if it is revised as a collective test. Rather than cross-examining an individual person and an individual computer, one should cross-examine a group of computers in interaction and a group of humans in interaction. After each question, the machines should talk among themselves and arrive at an answer, and the humans should talk among themselves and arrive at an answer. If interactions continue, the human group will develop a distinct human subculture, involving leadership, nicknames, special jokes, and so on. The machines may well develop something akin to a distinct style of interaction, but, whatever it becomes, it will be recognizably nonhuman. It is at the collective level and in the sphere of culture that human uniqueness is most striking, and different from any machine culture that emerges.

CRITICAL THINKING QUESTIONS

1 How convincing is associationism?

2 In what ways might the Turing test be reductionist?

CONCLUDING COMMENT

The realm of artificial intelligence is extremely fast paced and still highly unpredictable. One hundred years ago, only H. G. Wells (1866–1946) and other science fiction visionaries came close to imagining machines with the kinds of abilities possessed by twenty-first-century computers. No doubt progress over the next century will be even faster and more impressive, in ways that we cannot predict. But though computers may develop much better abilities to simulate human thinking as it takes place in isolated individuals, we should keep in mind that human cognition and action is first and foremost social and arises out of collective processes. It is the collectively constructed world "out there" that supports human uniqueness, and not necessarily the billions of neurons inside us.

CRITICAL THINKING QUESTIONS

1 How has the Chinese room been used to attack the idea that machines can think?

2 "Individual computers can become very like individual humans, but groups of computers in interaction will have a different culture from groups of humans in interaction." Do you agree? Give reasons to support your answer.

FURTHER READING

Dennett, D. (1998). *Brainchild: Essays on designing minds*. Cambridge, MA: MIT Press.

Boden, M. A. (ed.) (1996). *Artificial intelligence*. New York: Academic Press.

Bruner, J. S., Goodnow, J. J., & Austin, G. A. (1956). *A study of thinking*. New York: Wiley.

Bruner, J. S. (1973). *Beyond the information given*. New York: Norton.

Chomsky, N. (1957). *Syntactic structures*. The Hague: Mouton.

Chomsky, N. (1959). Review of *Verbal Behavior* by B. F. Skinner. *Language, 35*, 26–58.

Chomsky, N. (1972). *Language and mind*. New York: Harcourt Brace Jovanovich.

Clark, A., & Millican, P. J. R. (eds.) (1996). *Machines and thought: The legacy of Alan Turing* Vol. 1. Oxford: Clarenden Press.

Göranzon, B., & Florin, M. (eds.) (1990). *Artificial intelligence, culture and language: On education and work*. London: Springer-Verlag.

McCorduck, P. (1979). *Machines who think: A personal inquiry into the history and prospects of artificial intelligence*. New York: Freeman.

Miller, G. A. (1956). The magic number seven, plus or minus two. *Psychological Review, 63*, 81–97.

Miller, G. A., Galanter, E., & Pribram, K. (1960). *Plans and the structure of behavior*. New York: Holt, Rinehart & Winston.

Millican, P. J. R., & Clark, A. (eds.) (1996). *Connectionism, concepts, and folk psychology: The legacy of Alan Turing*, Vol. 2. Oxford: Clarendon Press.

Mitchell, T. (1997). *Machine learning*. New York: McGraw Hill.

Myers, D. (2003). *Intuition*. New Haven: Yale University Press.

Newell, A., & Simon, H. A. (1972). *Human problem solving*. Englewood Cliffs, NJ: Prentice Hall.

Pinker, S. (1997). *How the mind works*. New York: Norton.

Penrose, R. (1989). *The emperor's new mind*. New York: Oxford University Press.

Poole, D., Mackworth, A., & Goebel, R. (1998). *Computational intelligence*. Oxford: Oxford University Press.

Rumelhart, D., McClelland, J., & PDP Research Group (eds.) (1986). *Parallel distributed processing: Explorations of the microstructures of cognition*, Vols. 1–2. Cambridge, MA: MIT Press.

Russell, S. J., & Norvig, P. (2002). *Artificial intelligence: A modern approach*, 2nd edn. Upper Saddle River, NJ: Prentice Hall.

Searle, J. R. (1980). Minds, brains, and programs. *Behavioral and Brain Sciences*, 3, 417–424.

Sternberg, R. (1990). *Metaphors of mind: Conceptions of the nature of intelligence*. Cambridge, England: Cambridge University Press.

Tolman, E. C. (1948). Cognitive maps in rats and men. *Psychological Review*, 55, 189–208.

Turing, A. A. (1950). Computing machinery and intelligence. *Mind*, 59, 433–460.

The following organizations are resource centers for artificial intelligence:

American Association for Artificial Intelligence (AAAI)
European Coordinating Committee for Artificial Intelligence (ECCAI)
Society for Artificial Intelligence and Simulation of Behavior (AISB)

9
STAGE MODELS OF DEVELOPMENT

"There are four distinct stages in the life of a butterfly or moth – egg, caterpillar, pupa, and adult." This quotation is from Barbara Taylor's (1996) book on butterflies and moths, which I must have read dozens of times to my two children. There is something very appealing about the idea of such stages in development. Perhaps part of the appeal is that it makes life predictable: we know what is going to happen as the organism moves through the life stages. There are no real surprises, no unexpected turns. The caterpillar never turns back into an egg; it always moves through the predictable stages, into a pupa, then an adult. Similarly, the growth of plants is characterized by predictable stages, from seed, to sprout, to plant. The same kind of stage-wise progression seems to characterize at least some kinds of human development. For example, infants learn to crawl, to walk, and then to run, typically in that order; they generally do not learn to run first, then go back and learn to crawl.

The tendency to view human development as being in stages is reflected in the belief systems of many different cultures. Examples from Chinese, French, Greek, Indian, and Italian cultures, among others, are provided in the first part of *The Oxford Book of Aging* under the title "Stages/Journey" (Cole & Winkler, 1996). For example, the Chinese sage Confucius (c. 551–479 BCE) described six developmental stages, ending with a positive depiction of old age: "At seventy I could follow my heart's desire without transgressing the boundaries of right." Perhaps the most well-known example in the English language is found in William Shakespeare's *As You Like It* (II, vii, 139): "And one man in his time plays many parts/His acts being seven ages," which puts forward the following stages in life-span development: (1) infancy, (2) early childhood, (3) adolescence, (4) young adult, (5) middle age, (6) old age, (7) senility.

But such discussions of stages by Shakespeare and other writers in the Western tradition, as well as in the Eastern, are explicitly accepted as reflecting cultural biases and having limited applicability. For example, Shakespeare's depiction of the teenager as preoccupied with romantic love and "Sighing like furnace" would be rejected as inappropriate for teenagers in at least some cultures, such as conservative religious ones. The challenge taken up by psychologists has been to go beyond such cultural limitations and to establish stages in development that are universal. The most influential psychological stage models are those proposed by Sigmund Freud (1856–1939) on psychosexual development, Erik Erikson (1902–94) on life-span development, Jean Piaget (1896–1980) on cognitive development, and Lawrence Kohlberg (1927–87) on moral development. Among these, Piaget and then Kohlberg were the ones who worked in more, keeping their ideas closer to the results of empirical evidence. But all four researchers shared a single vision: degrees of freedom being limited by inbuilt developmental stages. Such stage models contrast with linear models that assume development to be continuous, such as behaviorist models (see chapter 6) and social constructionist approaches (see chapter 20). The objective of this chapter, then, is to critically assess the idea of stage models of development. I begin by briefly describing the main stage models in turn. In the main part of the discussion I highlight the core assumptions common to stage models, then critically assess the idea of stage-wise development.

THE MAJOR STAGE MODELS

Some of the ideas and terminology of the *major stage models*, theories about universal, inbuilt, uni-directional, hierarchical, stages of development, are now very much part of our everyday conversation. We use terms like "ego" and "egocentric," for example, without necessarily thinking about their theoretical origins. Perhaps Freud's stage model has had the greatest impact on the wider culture, but Erikson's is also very influential, particularly because Erikson's model gives more attention to the later stages of life and this corresponds with the interests of the aging population. The stage models proposed by Piaget and Kohlberg have had greater impact on academic research and in educational settings.

Freud's model of psychosexual stages and personality development

Freud continues to be the most influential psychologist in history, and his proposed psychosexual stage model, which is closely associated with his model of personality development, is among the most important of his contributions. Freud depicts individuals as being in a continuous struggle, pulled in different directions by conflicting forces, throughout the development process. Freud's approach is integrative, proposing that personality development takes place in association with psychosexual development. Infants come into this world screaming out their needs and demanding to be satisfied instantly. Their personality at this stage is dominated by the id, which is driven by the pleasure principle. The id is the irrational, impulsive component of personality. "I want milk and I want it now!" screams the infant, oblivious to the fact that it is four o'clock in the morning and mother and father were sound asleep. Gradually parents and other caretakers begin to impose limits, and the infant begins to sense external pressures, particularly in the form of a moral order that specifies good and bad, right and wrong, as well as ideals. The moral order and the ideals of society begin to be internalized, to form a superego. The task of balancing the irrational, impulsive, pleasure-seeking id with the superego, reflecting morality and ideals, falls to the ego, a rational, realistic mediator that constitutes the third component of personality. The psychological health of the adult depends in important ways on how well the balance between the id and the superego is achieved.

The struggles of individuals are centered on a different part of the body during each distinct stage of development. During the oral stage, the first eighteen months of life, the mouth is the center of experience. Infants at this age try to put everything they grasp into their mouths, as a way of knowing and feeling the world. During the anal stage, the third and fourth years of life, individuals are gaining control over their bodies, particularly through toilet training. But toilet training also gives little boys and girls an opportunity to exert control vis-à-vis caretakers, by not always doing what adults want (anyone who has attempted to toilet-train kids can testify that they sometimes do the opposite of what adults want, perhaps in some cases intentionally). From around the age of three to six is the phallic stage, during which children learn about their own body and the bodies of other girls and boys. They learn about how the two sexes are different, and how certain parts of the body must not be shown or touched in public. Words like "dirty" and "private" come to be associated with certain body parts, and feelings of guilt and shame are experienced according to societal norms. The latency period follows, starting around the age of seven and coming to completion at puberty. Sexuality is repressed and strong preference is shown for same-sex peers. Sexual identity re-emerges in the genital stage, after puberty. This is associated with the growth of a strong interest in the opposite sex.

As depicted by Freud, then, human development is fundamentally about how the pleasure-seeking, impulsive, irrational urges within the individual are harnessed and brought under control, so that the young are eventually shaped into "civilized" adults. At each psychosexual stage, the individual faces new challenges brought about by the growth of the body and changing desires, on the one hand, and societal expectations and ideals about "correct" behavior on the part of individuals at different stages, on the other hand. For example, Jean, Kathy, Bill, and Jack play in a pool and splash water at each other with no clothes on when they are two years old, but refrain from doing the same when they are married thirty-year-olds. Clearly, they may still enjoy playing and splashing in a pool with each other in the nude when they are adults, so why do they not do it? The answer is that they have now developed strong superegos; they have consciences that keep them, like most other people much of the time, on the straight and narrow according to societal norms about correct behavior.

Thus, underlying Freud's discussion of id, ego, and superego is the idea that at an initial stage the id is dominant, but at a second stage the superego comes to exert more control as the person conforms to the demands of civilization. Becoming civilized has a price. The desires and wishes that are condemned by society do not vanish; they are repressed into the unconscious. This means that such desires and wishes can influence behavior and be the real motives for why a person behaves a particular way, but remain altogether hidden from the person. Sometimes, societal pressures are too great, or not applied in a healthy way, and as a consequence the individual experiences psychological problems as an adult.

Freud's stage model is based in large part on insights gained through therapeutic practice, and this is also a characteristic shared by Erikson's stage model. But one way in which Erikson's stage model is different from Freud's is that it covers the entire life-span rather than being focused on the early part of life.

Erikson's model of life-span development

In contrast with Freud's emphasis on psychosexual development, Erikson focuses on psychosocial development, particularly highlighting social roles and relationships. Erikson proposed that each of eight distinct life stages, supposedly experienced by all humans in the same order, is characterized by particular struggles that must reach a successful conclusion for an individual to grow into a healthy adult. That is, the resolution of each stage affects personality. These struggles are not just internal to the individual, but involve relationships with others.

The struggles of infants center on trust and arise out of a strong need for a dependable, supportive social environment; infants learn to trust or mistrust others. During stage two, ages two and three, the main struggle is between autonomy and doubt; infants desire independence, but find that the help of others is in practice indispensable. If infants fail to gain confidence to do things by themselves, they may be crippled by self doubts. Stage three, ages three to six, is characterized by the struggle between initiative versus guilt; children who are not allowed to follow their own initiative experience guilt for their attempts to gain independence. The struggle between industry and inferiority characterizes ages seven through puberty. Children tackle activities valued by adults, and if they consistently fail they feel inferior. During adolescence the main struggle is between identity and role confusion; success comes with developing a positive identity as part of a group, and failure is associated with confusion about self identity and life goals. Stage six is young adulthood, when individuals struggle between intimacy and isolation, searching for a partner who will help them feel fulfilled. During adult years, people struggle between generativity and stagnation, striving to be productive at work and to build a family at home, or risk stagnation. Finally, the senior years see a struggle between integrity and despair; coming to see their past life as meaningful or feeling it was in vain. Individuals can revisit particular stages.

The stage models of Erikson and Freud have arisen from, and been particularly influential in, the clinical arena. For example, the "abnormal" behavior of some individuals is interpreted as involving regressing or a revisiting of earlier stages that a person has already passed through. The next two stage models we consider have closer ties with education.

Piaget and the stages of cognitive development

Piaget's stage model of cognitive development has monopolized academic research on infants and children for almost half a century and been particularly influential in modern schools and curriculum development. Whereas many original and productive European theorists, such as Vygotsky (see chapter 10) have been relatively neglected by the US academic world, Piaget had been enormously influential in North America. One reason may be that Piaget's stage model so closely matches the emphasis on individualism and rationality in the wider American culture. Another important reason for his widespread influence in North America is his empirical approach and the research he conducted and stimulated.

Whereas Freud and Erikson focus mainly on personality development and irrational processes, Piaget is more concerned with cognitive development and rational processes. Piaget is particularly concerned with how well particular cognitive tasks are tackled by isolated individuals at each developmental stage. He called his research approach *genetic epistomology*, the search for how humans develop an understanding of the world, particularly causality, quantity, and space. He took the position that development takes place through the interaction of factors internal and external to the individual.

In Piaget's model, the building block of development is the *schema*, a pattern of cognition (e.g. "dogs are furry") or action (e.g. grabbing the fur of a dog) that guides interactions with the environment. Most of the research focus has been on cognitive schemas, but it is important to keep in mind that in Piaget's view cognitive and motor schemas are interdependent. The interaction between cognitive and motor schemas runs through all of development and involves continual *adaptation*, the process by which individuals change their cognition and actions in order to function effectively in an environment. This emphasis on adaptation reflects Piaget's biological approach to understanding human cognitive and physical growth.

Consider, for example, an infant who develops a schema for how to grab hold of objects, such as a nipple. Not all objects can be held. For example, a table leg is too large for the infant to grab. Consequently, through encountering such large objects the infant learns adaptation, a process involving both *assimilation*, how new experiences are incorporated into existing schemas, and *accommodation*, how existing schemas are altered to incorporate new experiences. In this way, development involves the individual both being changed by experiences and also actively changing their interface with the outside world through their experiences.

Development, then, progresses in dialectical fashion, with assimilation and accommodation moving forward with one another, but not in perfect tandem. At times, assimilation and accommodation reach equilibrium. However, this balanced state does not persist, as the individual or the environment or both change and assimilation or accommodation temporarily dominates. For example, the infant is placed in a new daycare facility and is suddenly faced with adapting to a novel environment that entails many unfamiliar physical and social phenomena. The initial period of stay in the daycare will no doubt require a great deal of accommodation by the infant as she or he adapts to the unfamiliar surroundings. However, after sufficient adaptation, the infant will be able to assimilate some experiences in the new environment to existing patterns of thought and action. Gradually, equilibrium will be achieved between assimilation and accommodation. But as the infant becomes more confident in the new surroundings, she or he will explore further and once again have new experiences that will require more accommodation. In this way, equilibrium will temporarily come to an end again.

Piaget proposes that cognitive development takes places through a series of stages. The first or *sensorimotor stage* is from birth to eighteen months, when experience is gained through motor responses to sensory stimuli. The world is experienced as it is immediately present, in an "out of sight, out of mind" manner; infants are unaware of things not directly visible. Thus, infants are assumed to lack an awareness of *object permanence*, the understanding that an object is present somewhere even if it cannot be sensed directly. This lack of awareness is assumed because infants tend not to look for objects that are out of sight.

From around eighteen months to the seventh year, the young are in the pre-operational stage. The pre-operational child lacks *operations*, the ability to reverse mental processes. For example, four-year-old Samantha can describe the dolls and the dollhouse on the table from where she is sitting, but cannot describe them from the perspective of her sister sitting on the other side of the doll table. The pre-operational child also lacks *conservation*, the ability to recognize that the weight, volume, and other such properties of objects can remain the same even when they change shape. For example, the same amount of water poured into containers of different shapes will still have the same volume and weight.

Understanding of the conservation of physical properties is achieved at the stage of *concrete operations*, from age seven to eleven. Progress is gradual and faster with respect to the conservation of some properties than others. For example, a child may come to understand the conservation of the volume of water, that the same amount of water poured into containers of different shapes will still have the same volume and weight, but not yet understand that a block of plaster will not change its weight when it is rolled flat. By the end of this stage the child can perform such mental operations on physical or "concrete" objects, but still cannot manage to deal with abstract ideas and theoretical concepts. The ability to manipulate concepts and ideas and to make plans about hypothetical situations comes at the stage of *formal operations*, which begins at eleven and continues to adulthood. At this stage, the individual can plan ahead and tackle problems with foresight. Thus, Piaget sees the child's thinking as growing less and less *egocentric*, seeing the world only from her or his point of view and unable to take on the viewpoint of others, and less based on the concrete experiences of the here and now. This progression results in the ability to symbolically manipulate the world and to conceptualize hypothetical situations.

Kohlberg's stage model of moral development

The main focus of Kohlberg's stage model is moral development, but his theoretical approach is similar to Piaget's in that he highlights cognitive processes. Kohlberg is specifically interested in the reasoning behind moral decisions, in *how* people come to certain decisions on moral issues. But whereas Piaget studied cognitive development by direct observations of children's behavior (particularly his own) in real life settings, Kohlberg studied moral reasoning by asking participants in his studies to provide solutions to hypothetical moral dilemmas. He presented participants with scenarios depicting such moral dilemmas. For example, consider the case of a husband who does not have the money to buy the medication needed to save his wife's life. Should he break into the pharmacy and steal the medication, or should he obey the law? Kohlberg was interested in the reasons given for a moral decision, rather than the decision itself. In this instance, of interest to him was the question of *why* the husband should break into or not break into the pharmacy, rather than whether or not he should commit the robbery.

Kohlberg proposed that people move through six stages, with two stages at each of three levels. The lowest level (stages 1 and 2) is characterized by pre-conventional thinking, avoiding punishment, and seeking reward: "I am not going to steal the medication from the pharmacy, because I will end up in jail" (the implication being that if I could get away with it, I would steal the medication). The middle level (stages 3 and 4) is characterized by conventional thinking, doing what societal norms and laws require: "I am not going to steal the medication from the pharmacy, because it is against the law" (the implication being that if the law allowed it, I would steal the medication). The highest level (stages 5 and 6) involves post-conventional thinking, acting according to internalized principles: "I am not going to steal the medication from the pharmacy because it is wrong to steal" (implying that even if I can get away with it, and even if the law allows it, I will not steal because I believe it is wrong). An alternative solution could be: "I will steal the medication from the pharmacy, because I must save a life."

CRITICAL THINKING QUESTIONS

1   What do you think are the two most important common characteristics of the major stage models?

2   The models of Piaget and Kohlberg have been criticized for giving priority to abstract thinking by independent individuals, rather than to people working out problems through interacting with one another. Do you agree with this criticism?

CORE ASSUMPTIONS

The major stage models of human development share a number of core assumptions, eight of which are highlighted below.

Development is stage-wise

The first and most important assumption is that development is stage-wise rather than continuous. Individuals are assumed to experience long periods of relatively slow change, followed by periods of faster, more dramatic change. The stages of development are characterized by qualitative differences; each stage brings something fundamentally different in nature, rather than simply quantitative increases in what there was before. In the domain of individual development, debates between researchers who depict development as continuous versus those who view it as stage-wise parallel debates in the domain of human evolution. Charles Darwin argued that evolution is basically a continuous process, there being gradual quantitative differences between different species. A number of modern biologists have disagreed and argued for discontinuous evolution. Perhaps the most well-known concept put forward by Stephen Jay Gould and others arguing for continuously gradual evolution is "punctuated equilibrium," suggesting evolution is characterized by long periods of "steady state" or relative constancy, broken or "punctuated" by sudden leaps forward.

Developmental stages are in fixed hierarchy

A second common assumption of the stage models is that development is stepwise: progress to a higher stage is only possible after successfully passing through the lower stages, in the set order. This is like a person climbing up a ladder having to take each step in turn and not being able to skip a step or move down a step. Thus, for example, in one's moral development an individual is not able to move from pre-conventional to post-conventional reasoning, but must move from pre-conventional to conventional, and then on to post-conventional reasoning. Also, having achieved post-conventional moral reasoning, it is assumed the individual will now remain at this level and (under normal circumstances, and in the case of healthy individuals) not descend to conventional or pre-conventional thinking again.

Stages of development are universal

The stage models share the characteristic of assuming universality; all human beings are assumed to pass through the same developmental stages in the same sequence. Irrespective of whether a person grows up in Brazil, or Saudi Arabia, or Canada, or South Africa, or anywhere else, the supremacy of the stages and their sequences holds. Thus, the healthy route to development is the same for all human beings; it is not altered by context, although context can create deviations. For example, very high levels of environmental deprivation can lead to an individual progressing through a stage more slowly or even not succeeding to progress through a stage at all; whereas environmental enrichment can lead an individual to progress through a stage more quickly.

Developmental stages are determined

A fourth assumption is that future development is determined. Freud viewed internal pre-set mechanisms, that control what will happen and in what order, as the more important in determining development. Piaget, Kohlberg, and Erikson gave more balanced attention to environmental factors. However, in all stage models it is assumed that, though the environment can prevent an individual from successfully passing through a stage of development, or can facilitate progress through a stage, it cannot determine what the stages are and in what sequence an individual makes progress through them. This is rather like a person climbing up a ladder under different environmental conditions. Rain, snow, wind, tornado, sunshine, clouds, and other features of the changing environment can influence the person climbing up the ladder (for example, influence her or him to climb slower or faster or not at all) but cannot change the sequence of steps that have to be taken to get from the bottom to the top of the ladder.

Integrated development

The major psychological models of stage-wise development assume that development takes place in an integrated manner, biological and psychological development being strongly linked. Indeed, biological changes, often accompanied by physical growth (e.g. a child growing taller, stronger, faster) are taken to be the visible indicator of the way in which psychological growth takes place in stages. For example, just as an infant is seen to progress physically in stages – such as lift head, roll over, sit up, pull self to stand, walk with support, walk independently, walk up steps, run – it is assumed that integrated with these physical changes are psychological developments taking place in stages in the brain.

The integrated approach to development has not viewed biological and psychological processes as having equal priority and importance; although these are psychological models, advocates of the integrated approach have assumed that biological processes are dominant and foundational. Even Freud, the founder of psychoanalysis and the most important pioneer in depth psychology, assumed that ultimately behavior will be reducible to biochemical processes.

Healthy development is uni-directional

Sixth, the stage models assume that normal, healthy development always moves from the "lower" to the "higher" stages in a set sequence. For example, Piaget is concerned with improved cognitive abilities, from thinking that can deal only with the here and now to thinking that can manipulate symbols and abstract concepts, such as "duties" and "rights." Kohlberg is concerned with moral thinking based on rewards and punishments to moral decision making based on universal principles, such as "free speech." In cases where individuals move in a downward rather than an upward direction, experiencing "regression" from a higher to a lower stage of development, such behavior is interpreted as problematic and indicative of psychological pathologies.

Universals in healthy development

A seventh interesting common feature of stage models is that they are not relativistic; rather, they claim that certain paths of development are healthier and better than others. The stage models assume that the most healthy adult behavior is an outcome of the successful transition of a person through all the stages of development, in order from the lowest to the highest. The higher stages are better than the lower ones, so absolute criteria may be used when assessing progress in development. The relativistic "everyone is a star" attitude is rejected, and a more universalist "some people are psychologically better developed than others" approach is preferred.

Self-regulating individualism

Finally and perhaps most importantly, the major stage models are all individualistic. Although these models, particularly Piaget's, emphasize the active way in which individuals construct the world, rather than passively "receive" it, the "construction" they consider is by isolated minds. Piaget's model, for example, is claimed to incorporate "active" individuals giving meaning to the world (particularly through adaptation, assimilation, and accommodation), but the "activity" considered is not enmeshed in a social network of collective activities. Rather, the individual is viewed as an independent, "self-regulating" system. Even when Piaget considers the role of social interactions in moral development, the focus remains on processes within the individual child rather than processes between children. The traditional stage models, then, fail to take into consideration the *collaborative* construction of social worlds, and the mutual upholding of certain world views by people in interaction. For example, how the mother and child interact to construct an idea of "good food" together.

Although the stage models, and particularly Piaget's model, could be interpreted as giving importance to both individual and context, to intra-individual processes and social processes, the dominant Western interpretation has been individualistic rather than interactional. Those aspects of the stage models that emphasize self-regulating individualism have been highlighted. This fits in with the reductionism of modern Western psychology. Reductionism moves researchers to try to find explanations for behavior within individuals, and at a more micro level. In particular, the idea of biological factors controlling developmental processes fits well with this reductionism, biological factors being more micro and fixed relative to external social and political conditions.

The wider ideological implications of reductionism in the realm of development is similar to the case of intelligence (see chapter 7). In both cases, the implication is that the achievements of individuals, their power, wealth, and status in particular, are determined by factors within themselves. By implication, the reason that Joe is a low-paid factory worker and Jack is the chief executive officer (CEO) of the company is that their development took different paths, directed by inbuilt factors. External factors, from parental support to educational programs, played a secondary role in this development. The primary role was played by factors within Joe and Jack themselves. Consequently, the primary responsibility for their very different fates lies within each of them. In fundamental ways, then, the stage models reflect Western ideals of individualism, each person being viewed as responsible for her or his own outcomes.

In conclusion, then, the stage models emphasize uni-directional development from lower to higher stages, with higher stages representing "better." This development is viewed as characteristic of all human beings, irrespective of context. The implication is that factors within individuals shape developmental paths.

Criticisms of the stage models

The most important criticisms of the stage models revolve around a central question: Do the developmental stages reflect social constructions or objective universals? On one side are defenders of the traditional stage models, who claim that such models are objective and reflect universals in human behavior. This group would defend the assumptions underlying the stage models as valid. On the other hand, critics argue that the stage models are social constructions, reflecting changing cultural practices and norms. Such critics argue that the assumptions underlying the stage models are false.

In order to assess the case made by critics, let us consider the very basic proposition that there are universal life stages. The evidence in support of the stage models varies from weak to fairly strong, the strongest evidence being in support of Piaget's model. Despite the various criticisms (as listed above), there is general agreement among traditional researchers that cross-cultural evidence supports Piaget's basic model. Cross-cultural research shows that children who are at the same chronological age have basic similarities in the way they tackle cognitive tasks. Thus, on the basis of traditional empirical evidence, we must conclude that Piaget's model is well supported.

But critics contend that cross-cultural similarities in how children solve cognitive tasks do not demonstrate there are fixed universal stages in development. The issue of how children at each particular age think is different from the question of whether cognitive development is stage-wise. In other words, according to critics, although there is evidence for similarity in thinking at different ages, evidence for discontinuous developmental stages in thinking is questionable. Also, critics of traditional research still contend that the evidence supporting Piaget is flawed because this evidence comes from research that shares Piaget's main reductionist assumption about the role of inbuilt characteristics within the individual.

The research consensus is less strong in support of the universality of the developmental models put forward by Freud and Erikson. These stage models provide stimulating viewpoints, but alternative viewpoints may be just as valid. Freud's claims about an "anal stage" or "oral stage," for example, are intriguing but hardly factual. Erikson's claims are similarly problematic. For example, the claim that between the ages of three and six growth is characterized by a struggle between initiative and guilt might lead to the question: Why not between action and inaction, or pride and shame, or any other combination? The stage models of Freud and Erikson are useful constructions in some (mostly Western and Westernized) contexts, but far from universally valid.

Kohlberg's model of moral development has also received critical research attention, not always supportive. A first criticism arises from research showing that the level of reasoning individuals use, whether it is pre-conventional, conventional, or post-conventional, depends a great deal on what suits their interests in a given context. Participants have been shown to use conventional reasoning in one situation and post-conventional reasoning in a second situation, depending on what suits their particular personal needs. Examples of this abound in the real world: during the 1980s right-wing Western politicians, such as Margaret Thatcher and Ronald Reagan, supported the rights of labor movements in communist societies as a way of weakening communist states, but at the same time the same leaders opposed the rights of labor movements in their own countries. Similarly, the leaders in communist states (such as Cuba and China) have persistently supported the rights and freedoms of workers abroad, but not in their own countries.

A second criticism concerns the rift between theory and practice: how people solve moral dilemmas on paper, and how they actually behave in practice. In defense of Kohlberg I must add that his model of moral reasoning is about cognitive problem solving, and not actual behavior. Thus, Kohlberg would argue that his model is not designed to explain what people do, only how they think. However, this has not prevented critics from pointing out that individuals can be trained to solve abstract moral dilemmas using post-conventional reasoning, but in practice this may have no impact on how they actually behave. The business leaders who in the 1990s and early 2000s cheated investors and got away with billions of dollars no doubt took ethics courses at prestigious business schools and achieved high grades, but in practice they behaved unethically.

Flexibility of stages: the example of "old age"

One of the constructive lessons gained from the critical discussions about the stage models of development concerns the possibility that some "stages" of development are malleable and change over time. An important example is the stage of "old age." On the surface, this seems non-problematic. Surely everyone would agree that old age exists. After all, aging is a universal phenomenon. Irrespective of whether one lives in the era of Shakespeare or in the twenty-first century, or whether one is in the United States or India, all humans age. Thus, there seems little controversy in claiming that a stage of old age exists.

But on closer inspection, the validity of this claim falls apart. First, if stages are defined by chronological age (as they are), then when does "old age" begin? Do we mark the beginning of old age as sixty-five years old, or seventy-five, or sixty, or eighty, or perhaps sixty-seven? If we select any of these ages, we immediately reveal a strong cultural bias, influenced by Western society in the twenty-first century. It is estimated that in the year A.D. 1000, life expectancy at birth was still under twenty-five years for people around the world. For the next nine hundred years or so, from around 1000 to 1900, life expectancy crept up very slowly until it reached close to fifty years (Moore & Simon, 1999). Thus, until the twentieth century a definition of "old age" based on chronological markers such as sixty-five years would include a very small number of exceptional individuals, because most would die at half that age.

It is during the twentieth century that we have witnessed the most dramatic rise in life expectancy, at least in the United States and other Western societies. Life expectancy in the United States went up from around fifty years in 1900, to about sixty-eight years in 1950, to approximately seventy-seven years in 2000 (Statistics.com and United Nations data). But this is far from a universal trend; there are important variations even within the United States population. For example, in the last decade or so life expectancy for African American males has been about fourteen years less than for White females, and when we look specifically at economically poor African American males compared with affluent white females, the difference in life expectancy jumps up again: affluent white women live a quarter of a century longer. Thus, even within the United States smaller percentages of the membership of some groups experience "old age," if we define old age by a chronological marker such as sixty-five years.

When we look at the world context, a smaller percentage of the people of some countries tend to reach "old age" if this category is defined by a chronological marker such as sixty-five or seventy years (see <http://www.un.org/Depts/unsd/social/health.htm>). For example, the life expectancy of males and females in Afghanistan is forty-three and forty-four years respectively; in Angola forty-five and forty-seven years; in Burundi forty and forty-one years; in Central African Republic forty-three and forty-six years; in Lesotho forty-one and forty years; in Malawi forty and thirty-nine years; in Mozambique thirty-seven and thirty-nine years; in Niger forty-six and forty-seven years; in Sierra Leone thirty-nine and forty-two years; in Swaziland thirty-eight and thirty-eight years; in Uganda forty-five and forty-seven years; in Zambia forty-three and forty-two years; and in Zimbabwe forty-three and forty-two years. Thus, most people in all these countries would never reach "old age," according to our definition of "old age" as starting at sixty-five or seventy years.

Of course, life expectancies are averages and we need to be cautious about how we interpret such information. In general, in countries with low life expectancy there is also high infant mortality. However, even when we only consider those who live past infancy, life expectancy has increased in industrialized societies over the past century, and life expectancy in countries such as Swaziland and Zambia is far lower than in Switzerland and Japan.

Perhaps the best definition of "old age" is not chronological, but behavioral. Can we agree that in old age people become inactive, slow of body and mind, uninterested in excitement, detached from the world, and so on? Anyone who interacts with seniors in the twenty-first century will quickly see this is an inaccurate stereotype. People are living much longer, but they are also remaining active in the senior years. In Western societies, where life expectancy has increased most dramatically compared with the rest of the world, the stereotype of senior life is changing in major ways. Seniors are now far more active in sports, in sex life, travel, and other domains. Anyone doubting this new trend should contact organizations such as the Grey Panthers or the National Institute on Aging, or review the current popular guides to aging, such as *The Practical Guide to Aging* (1999).

By examining the malleability of particular stages, such as the "stage of old age," we come to realize that some of our assumptions about "inbuilt stages" may actually reflect historical and cultural characteristics. In other times and other places, the stage in question may be thought of rather differently, just as "old age" now has different characteristics.

CRITICAL THINKING QUESTIONS

1 Which of the assumptions underlying the stage models do you think is most central to the models?

2 If definitions of stages, such as "teenager" and "senior," change over time and across cultures, give an example of why it is still useful for scientists to use stage models.

CONCLUDING COMMENT

In everyday life we find it convenient to think about life being in stages. Great writers, including Shakespeare, have provided descriptions of such stages, and more recently psychologists have formalized stage models of human development. The stage models of Freud and Erikson are influential in clinical therapy and among the lay public; the stage models of Piaget and Kohlberg have been more influential in academic research and in schools. The most important value of stage models may prove to be their ability to stimulate research. Piaget's model has stimulated an enormous body of international research, most of which supports his basic ideas. Despite criticisms and possible flaws, Piaget's model is a great idea because it has served an invaluable purpose by stimulating a great deal of international research. Also, despite a lack of empirical evidence in support of their universality, Freud's model and, to an increasing extent, Erikson's also have been hugely influential among the arts, the mass media, and the larger public.

CRITICAL THINKING QUESTIONS

1 Stage models propose that human behavior is in important ways predictable, and directed by factors internal to the individual. How does this match the traditional goals of psychology?

2 In what ways do stage models reflect Western ideals of individualism?

FURTHER READING

Bremner, G., & Fogel, A. (eds.) (2001). *Blackwell handbook of infant development*. Oxford: Blackwell.

Cassell, C. K. (ed.) (1999). *The practical guide to aging*. New York: New York University Press.

Cole, T. R., & Cole, S. R. (1996). *The development of children*, 3rd edn. New York: Freeman Press.

Erikson, E. H. (1968). Life cycle. In D. L. Sills (ed.), *International encyclopedia of the social sciences*, Vol. 9. New York: Crowell, Collier.

Freud, S. (1930). Civilization and its discontents. In J. Strachey (ed. & trans.), *The standard edition of the complete psychological works of Sigmund Freud*, Vol. 21. London: Hogarth Press.

Gilligan, C. (1982). *In a different voice: Psychological theory and women's development*. Cambridge, MA: Harvard University Press.

Kitchener, R. F. (1986). *Piaget's theory of knowledge: Genetic epistemology and* ıı ıı ıı⁄ıı ıı.ıı.ıı, New havon: Yale University Press

Kohlberg, L. (1963). Development of children's orientations toward a moral order. *Vita Humana, 6,* 11–36.

Lamb, M. E. (1999). *Parenting and child development in nontraditional families.* Mahwah, NJ: Erlbaum.

Moore, S., & Simon, J. L. (1999). The greatest century that ever was: 25 miraculous trends in the last 200 years. *Policy Analysis, 364,* 1–32.

Piaget, J. (1977). *The development of thought: Equilibration of cognitive structure.* New York: Viking.

Piaget, J., & Inhelder, B. (1969). *The psychology of the child.* New York: Basic Books.

Shonkoff, J. P., & Phillips, D. A. (2000). *From neurons to neighborhoods: The science of early childhood development.* Washington: National Academy Press.

Taylor, B. (1996). *Butterflies & Moths.* New York: Dorling Kindersley.

10

THE ZONE OF PROXIMAL DEVELOPMENT

It is already late August and the schoolchildren and their parents are going shopping with their "back to school" lists, and asking questions about the new teacher. What is the new teacher like? they wonder. You, the new teacher, are wondering about the kinds of children who will sit in your class. The school principal has let you know that there will be twenty-six of them. You feel confident you can handle a class that size and are happy to have been assigned a third-grade class in an elementary school. But you have only just graduated from university and this is your first year of participation in the *Teach for America* program. You feel inexperienced and there is one particular issue that continues to puzzle you: how advanced a subject-matter should you teach? How hard or easy should the class material be for the children?

You have studied the traditional stage models of development, which suggest that each child moves stepwise through a series of fixed stages. Inherent in the traditional approach is the assumption that at each stage of development the child has certain cognitive limitations, and these limit the mental tasks the child is able to carry out. Should you try to make the kids in your class feel more comfortable and at ease by teaching material that is below their developmental level? That way, you reason, you could hammer home the basics by repetition, so that by the end of the year you could be sure that the class has a firm foundation of learning. It is true that they would not be pushed to move ahead, but at least they would all feel comfortable with the material presented. It would be an easy class, one they would feel confident about. A major shortcoming of this approach might be that a lot of the children, or perhaps all of them, would not feel challenged, and may even become bored.

Instead, perhaps you should teach not below but at the developmental level of the kids in your class. That way, you reason, the kids would be taking up tasks that correspond to their stage of development. Presumably, each child is moving through the stages of development step by step, and one idea is that the level of development of each child should correspond to the material being taught in class. In this way, the kids in your class would not find the material too easy or too difficult, because the tasks presented to them would fit nicely with their individual capabilities.

But perhaps instead of teaching below or at the developmental level of the kids in your class, you should teach to a degree ahead of this level. In this way, you would set high standards for students. Also, you as the teacher would not continuously be playing a waiting game, putting off introducing material to the kids in your class until and unless they reach a developmental level that matches the material.

The traditional approach to the above questions would begin by testing each child individually to determine her or his present developmental level. Next, guided by the developmental model of the highly influential Swiss psychologist Jean Piaget, the traditional approach would involve teaching at, rather than below or above, the level of the child as determined by individual testing. Thus, you would have to wait until the child reached a level of developmental readiness before you could begin teaching material corresponding to that particular level.

There are a number of very good reasons why you should be critical of the traditional approach and seriously consider a vibrant alternative influenced by the Russian psychologist Lev Vygotsky (1896–1934). In the next section, I briefly point out a number of characteristics of the traditional approach, some of them related to the discussion in chapter 9 of the stage models of development. Finally, in the main body of the chapter, the alternative approach is discussed in greater detail, with specific reference to concepts and ideas introduced by Vygotsky.

Before launching on the main discussion, I want to highlight that there is a vitally important similarity between the topic of this chapter and the chapter on intelligence (chapter 7): at the heart of both is the issue of scarce resources, and political decisions about how resources are allocated. The key issue concerns the role of the environment in cognitive performance: to use terminology introduced in chapter 1, what do we assume to be the role of the environment in determining degrees of freedom in behavior? If we give greater importance to the environment (as did Vygotsky), then it implies that inequalities in resources are a cause of differences in cognitive performance. Children growing up in disadvantaged conditions, including dysfunctional families, poorly educated siblings, and poorly funded schools, will do less well because they have less constructive support or "scaffolding" holding them up and launching them off. Children growing up in advantageous conditions, including highly educated and affluent families and well-funded schools, will do better because they receive much better support. On the other hand, if we give less importance to the role of the environment, the implication is that the cognitive performance of children is dependent on their individual characteristics, independent of their surroundings. From this perspective, resource inequalities – the fact that some children grow up in impoverished family, school, and neighborhood conditions – are not relevant to their individual performance on cognitive tests. The following discussion, then, is subtly but importantly related to political decisions about how to allocate scarce resources among different school districts and other competing groups.

ASSUMPTIONS OF THE TRADITIONAL APPROACH

The traditional approach to human development (see chapter 9), as represented by Piaget in particular, has been highly influential in stimulating research internationally. The traditional approach does give some attention to the interaction of the individual with the environment, but at the same time it places even greater emphasis on the individual as an independent biological entity, self-regulated through pre-set internal mechanisms. It is assumed that there is something akin to a biological master plan, with a built-in clock, to a large degree regulating the development of the individual stage by stage. Individual development is thus self-regulated, in the sense that it is to a significant degree independent of instruction. It is "pre-set," in the sense that the stages are largely determined by biological factors, and the order of the stages is fixed.

The traditional approach makes two important assumptions about testing. First, that the unit of concern in testing is the individual, and only the individual. What else could it be? If a teacher wants to know the level of instruction that is appropriate for Jane, then surely the only way forward is to test Jane under controlled conditions. As part of these conditions Jane should be tested on her own, without being able to communicate with others who might guide her to the correct answers or tell them to her directly. If Jane is found to have received help from others, then the results of the test must be considered invalid, meaning that the test did not measure what it was supposed to measure: Jane's individual level of cognitive development.

Second, the traditional approach assumes that aptitude and training are independent. That is, the stage of development and the cognitive readiness of the child are not in important ways influenced by training and instruction. Thus, it is cognitive processes and not their contents that are of interest. This links up to the traditional idea (discussed in chapter 7) that intelligence tests measure some hypothetical entity, the intelligence quotient, that stands independent of education and past experience. There is, therefore, an assumption that there is a split-level experience: at the highest level there is continuity in cognitive processes, such as assimilation (interpretation of the environment in terms of the schemas the child has at the time) and accommodation (changes in schemas as the child interacts with the environment) as discussed in Piaget's model (see chapter 9); at a lower level there is the content of thought, and this changes over time.

Defenders of the traditional stage models of development would contend that these models do give importance to the role of the environment. For example, Piaget attempts to incorporate this role through concepts such as accommodation, which proposes that the child's cognitive schemas will change as a result of environmental influences. In some limited ways, then, the traditional approach is "interactionist," taking into consideration person–environment interactions. However, in at least three fundamentally important ways the traditional approach is not interactionist: first, in conceiving development to be primarily driven and directed by pre-set biological factors; second, in proposing that there are processes, such as assimilation and accommodation, that are independent of the content of thinking; third, in assuming that the developmental level of the child should be measured by assessing the child in isolation, under exam conditions.

CRITICAL THINKING QUESTIONS

1 Think about what you would prefer to do if you were put in charge of an elementary school class: teach below, at, or above the developmental level of the children?

2 What are some of the implications for education of assuming that aptitude and instruction are independent (i.e. that tests of aptitude are not influenced by teaching)?

A VYGOTSKIAN APPROACH TO CHILD DEVELOPMENT

Students of psychology early in their studies become familiar with the historic and continuing debate about the contributions of heredity and environment to human behavior, particularly in areas such as intelligence. Traditional tests discuss this debate by emphasizing the importance of both heredity and environment, and the advantages of an "interactional" approach. However, in practice it is extremely difficult to implement an interactional approach and to maintain focus on what uniquely arises out of person–environment interactions. This is because in research it is far easier to isolate smaller aspects of the subject of study and examine an isolated aspect under controlled conditions (see the discussions in chapter 2). For example, behaviorists studied the effect of the environment by isolating one or a small number of stimuli and recording responses to the stimuli presented (see chapter 6). Vygotsky is considered by many critics, particularly in Europe, as having been particularly successful in putting forward a more dynamic view of the environment and identifying important new behaviors that arise out of person–environment interactions. Vygotsky tried to work in, by developing ideas on the basis of empirical evidence; but he also worked out and pushed forward the theoretical boundaries.

Although Vygotsky conducted his research in the 1920s and 1930s, it is only since the 1980s that his ideas have become influential. From around the mid 1930s until the late 1950s, Vygotsky's publications were banned in the Soviet Union, because they were seen by the Soviet authorities as ideologically unsound. However, by the 1960s Vygotsky's writings had begun to become known again in his own society, and in the decades that followed his influence spread to the West. In the twenty-first century, Vygotsky has experienced a reversal of fortunes, becoming increasingly influential upon both developmental theory and educational practice in the West. No doubt the collapse of the Soviet empire, the end of the Cold War, and improved international communications have facilitated this trend. Since the changed environment helped to spread Vygotsky's ideas, it is fitting that we next discuss his view of the role of the environment in development.

From a Vygotskian perspective, the environment is not just out there as something the individual interacts with, but becomes integrally part of the behavior that researchers attempt to assess. An important feature of the environment as conceived by Vygotsky are "ideal forms" represented by adults; the child draws on such environmental resources particularly through imitation and play. This subtle change of emphasis, from testing isolated individuals to testing individuals and environmental support, has important applied implications that I discuss later in this chapter.

The environment

A first point about Vygotsky's particular approach to the environment is that it assumes children will interact with the environment differently, according to their individual meaningful experiences. The same environment will be experienced differently by different individuals. For example, two sisters aged six and sixteen will experience the environment of the family differently. The younger sister interacts with this environment in terms of her role as "family baby" and the older sister interacts in terms of her role as "oldest sibling/stand-in mother." The same event, such as a fight between the parents, will have different meanings for the six- and sixteen-year-old daughters. The six-year-old becomes frightened and confused, whereas the sixteen-year-old becomes protective of her younger siblings and takes on a mature role. This emphasis on subjective experience from the perspective of the particular individual contrasts with the exclusive emphasis of behaviorists on external stimuli (see chapter 6). On the other hand, this emphasis is in agreement with the Gestalt idea of *psychological field*, the particular social space that a person is subjectively aware of and interacting with at any one time. For example, George is sitting in his early morning calculus class, but he is looking out of the window and daydreaming about his trip to Europe next summer. The psychological field for George is very different from the psychological field for Guy, who is focused on the calculus professor.

A second feature of Vygotsky's approach to the environment is the importance given to ideal forms, these being the fruition of development as found in the behavior of adults. Ideal forms provide examples of the "correct" way to do things, such as to greet strangers, to eat politely, to ask questions, to solve practical problems, and so on. Through interactions with others, children acquire the skills to identify ideal forms as well as to change their own behavior toward ideal forms. Children do not passively accept ideal forms as given. On the contrary, children actively select and interpret ideal forms. The interactions of children with others play a particularly important role in their development.

A third facet of Vygotsky's approach to the environment is the priority he gives to social experience. In explaining this social aspect of Vygotsky's approach, it is important to clarify the meaning he gives to "social," a meaning that is very different from how "social" is interpreted in traditional psychology. For example, in traditional social psychology the focus remains on the individual, and testing often involves an isolated individual in a laboratory setting. "Social" in this context typically refers to the attitudes, values, prejudices, attributions, and so on that an individual holds regarding other persons or groups or other social phenomena. Another meaning of "social" in traditional research concerns how others influence an individual, such as when a group places pressure on an individual to conform to group norms, or when an authority figure influences an individual to do harm to others. In these cases, the "social" element is the influence others have on the individual's behavior. The "social others" are assumed to act as a cause, affecting specific changes in the behavior of the target person.

The Vygotskian interpretation of "social" focuses on the new behaviors that emerge when an individual interacts with the social world; it is neither of the interpretations of "social" described above. The interaction does not involve a one-way causal process, as in "an authority figure causing a person to do harm to others." Rather, in a Vygotskian sense the interaction involves the individuals collaboratively constructing a new behavior. The emphasis here is on the *collaborative* construction, so that all parties exert some influence and help shape the outcome. Thus, the outcome is dependent on the characteristics of all those involved in the interaction and is not just a result of one-way cause–effect relations. For example, even in the case of a mother–infant interaction, where the infant has very little power relative to the mother, the infant still influences the behavior of the mother. How the mother feeds the infant, her timing and speed of feeding for instance, is influenced by the infant's feeding behavior.

Ideal forms and imitation

A central feature of the environment, according to Vygotsky, are the ideal forms that are represented in the behavior of adults. These ideal forms can guide the developing child toward particular "correct" ways to behave. The absence of ideal forms deprives the child of guides that are essential to healthy development. Thus, ideal forms are not additional luxuries but are necessary: children deprived of ideal forms become developmentally deprived.

Children benefit from ideal forms through imitation; the child learns to use longer and more complex sentences by imitating the speech of adults. Imitation is not treated by Vygotsky as something automatic and mundane, but as a fundamentally important process involving insight. Imitation involves not just changes in overt behavior, so that the child can now do something she or he could not do before, but also changes in thinking and understanding, so that the child has new insight into something and can think through something she or he could not think through before. This contrasts sharply with the behaviorist view of learning, where the focus is exclusively on overt behavior (see chapter 6). Thus, imitation also involves changes in how the child will think through problems in the future.

Play has a similarly important role in the life of children. Through play, children create imaginary situations in which they can practice imitating ideal forms. The six-year-old can pretend to be a doctor or a police officer or a pirate and in these roles imitate the kinds of longer sentences and more complicated words that parents, teachers, and other adults use. Play is in this sense a kind of practice ground, in which there are unfolding and endless opportunities for children to test and extend their skills. They can try things out in play, with support from others, but without facing the consequences that such experimentation would lead to in "real life." Another fundamentally important aspect of play among children is that it involves collaborative construction of an imaginary social world. A group of eight-year-olds playing at pirates collaborate to create the imaginary pirate ship and treasure island. The children create a story and mutually uphold the imagined fiction. Thus, the eight-year-old playing the role of pirate captain is supported in this role by the rest of the pirate crew of children. In their role playing, the children are individually extending themselves and behaving above their current level of development, the performance of each being supported by others. The importance of play, particularly when it involves others, is that it allows children to extend themselves developmentally, to act above their age, to do things as part of a collectivity which they are individually too young to do.

The zone of proximal development

Vygotsky's understanding of the environment, the importance he gave to ideal forms, to imitation, to play, and to mutually upheld social activities, all were associated with a re-assessment of how the cognitive abilities of children should be tested and how teaching in schools should be organized. This re-assessment has had important theoretical and applied implications and has been particularly influential in Western societies since the 1980s.

Since the pioneering work of Alfred Binet (1857–1911), through which modern intelligence testing was launched (see chapter 7), intelligence testing has involved individuals being tested on their own and under controlled conditions. Considerable care has been taken to ensure that testing gets at the performance of the isolated individual. If a child solves a problem through hints or direct help received from a teacher or another adult, it has been assumed that this does not represent a useful or "true" indication of the developmental level of the child. Any outside influence would distort what a child can really do alone.

The approach adopted by Binet and others was that tests should establish the cognitive level of the child. This strategy tested the *zone of actual development*, meaning the level of development of the isolated individual. But it did not test what the child could do through collaboration with others. For example, consider a five-year-old child, Jane, who has a mental age of five years when tested alone in accordance with the traditional exam procedures, but has a mental age of eight years when provided with hints and guides by an adult. Another five-year-old, Samantha, has a mental age of six years according to the traditional testing procedures, but manages a mental age of seven years when provided with the same quality of hints and guides as was Jane. Whereas adult support added three years to Jane's mental age, it only added one year to Samantha's mental age. Thus, Jane gained more from interaction with adults than did Samantha.

A fundamentally important point is that the gain achieved by Jane and Samantha arises uniquely out of interactions with others (in this case an adult providing hints and guides). The improvement made by each girl would not be identified if the girls were tested in isolation. In this light, there is clearly a need for a measure that gets at more than the zone of actual development; it is also necessary to measure the *zone of proximal development*, the difference between the score achieved by an individual when tested alone and the score achieved when tested in interaction with a supportive adult. The zone of proximal development is not the same for all individuals, as suggested by the case of Jane and Samantha above. Some individuals benefit less from interactions with others, perhaps because they are less skilled and perceptive at picking up and using the hints and prompts provided them. Other individuals benefit more and tend to bloom in a collective context where they can be guided by the information and suggestions others provide.

Such variations are no doubt present among schoolchildren, even in a single classroom. You, the teacher, give the same information, suggestions, and hints to all of the twenty-six children in your class, but some of them gain more through interactions with you. The support you provide allows some of them to perform two years above their mental age, others to perform less than one year above their mental age. However, all the children benefit to some degree.

An important applied implication of the zone of proximal development is that teachers do not have to wait for children to reach a developmental level before they start teaching at that level. Most and perhaps all children can perform above their zone of actual development when they are provided with supportive hints and suggestions by skilled adults. The support adults provide acts rather like scaffolding around a building under construction. As the workers build up from the foundations, they use scaffolding to support the building. When the work is complete and the building is finished, the scaffolding is dismantled and the building is now able to stand on its own. Similarly, when a child is learning to write in small letters, for example, the teacher provides suggestions and a helping hand that act like a scaffolding in support of the child's efforts. When the child has made sufficient improvement, the teacher removes the scaffolding and allows the child to complete the task alone. Later, the child can perform the task without assistance.

Although Vygotsky's approach has a different applied emphasis than the traditional stage models, such as Jean Piaget's, Vygotsky was not dismissive of "sensitive periods" in development; for example, the idea that there is a sensitive period for language learning. Thus, in Vygotsky's psychology as in Piaget's psychology we find the idea that if environmental conditions are not supportive, certain developments will not take place in the child, or will remain under-developed. However, in Vygotsky we find not just a greater emphasis on the role of the environment, but a richer and more complex understanding of the social in supporting the child through sensitive periods.

CRITICAL THINKING QUESTIONS

1 In what way is the environment of your present classroom subjective and based on personal meaning?

2 Give an example of the zone of proximal development in a classroom setting.

CONCLUDING COMMENT

In his interpretation of the environment, Vygotsky gave importance to personal meaning, and in interpreting the "social" he highlighted collaborative constructions, such as involving a teacher and a child. The relationship between teacher and child is not symmetrical, but nevertheless the child contributes and benefits. The level of benefit is highlighted by the concept of the zone of proximal development. This concept leads to a more forward-looking approach to education, one that places emphasis on the performance level the child can achieve when supported by scaffolding constructed by peers or adults. The highlighting of scaffolding inevitably leads to a focus on resources, and the politics of how resources are allocated among schools and the children they serve.

CRITICAL THINKING QUESTIONS

1 What kinds of implications does the zone of proximal development have for the training of teachers and for the teaching style of teachers?

2 How can the concept of zone of proximal development help us better understand our performance levels in our everyday life and work activities?

FURTHER READING

Kozulin, A. (1990). *Vygotsky's psychology: A biography of ideas*. Cambridge, MA: Harvard University Press.

Van Tiel vvvr, R., & Valsiner, J. (1991). *Understanding Vygotsky: A quest for synthesis*. Oxford: Blackwell.

Vygotsky, L. S. (1962). *Thought and language*. Cambridge, MA: MIT Press.

Vygotsky, L. S. (1978). *Mind in society*. Cambridge, MA: Harvard University Press.

11

ATTACHMENT

There is a long history, going back at least to Plato's writings in the *Republic* and the *Laws* some twenty-five centuries ago, to the view that how infants are cared for and socialized will in important ways influence their later psychological development and life as adults. In modern psychology, this general idea has evolved into a more focused empirical exploration of the relationship between a primary caregiver, usually the mother, and the infant. A core organizing idea behind this modern research is *attachment*, an observed bonding between the young of many species and their primary caregivers. In human populations, attachment typically involves uniquely strong emotional ties between infants and their mothers.

Considered in the context of modern psychology, the idea of attachment is rather special in a subtle and important way: attachment is focused on relationships, on the world "out there," on what is collaboratively constructed and collectively upheld between the infant and the caregiver. Attachment is an outcome of what the caregiver and the infant do together, rather than being solely dependent on the characteristics and actions of either one of them. Attachment is about the shared world outside, rather than just the private world inside; it is about the characteristics of the larger social world, rather than dispositional characteristics within individuals. Thus, attachment moves us away from the individualism and reductionism pervading traditional Western psychology and provides a fruitful link with some alternative psychological ideas derived from other, more critical and social traditions, such as the idea of the zone of proximal development (see chapter 10). However, this does not mean that efforts have not been made to interpret attachment in individualistic and reductionist ways, such as explaining attachment in terms of the temperament of the child or the personality of the mother.

We begin by considering the context in which the idea of attachment arose, including some cultural and intellectual movements that influenced attachment research. Next, we assess the seminal idea of attachment itself, as well as the empirical research that has followed.

THE HISTORICAL CONTEXT OF THE IDEA

The idea of attachment is special because it provides an unusually strong focus and point of discussion, and sometimes surprising agreement, for scholars from very different orientations to psychology. The infant–caregiver bond is evident across many species, so it is of interest to researchers who, following Charles Darwin's (1809–82) elaboration of the theory of evolution, view humans and other living organisms as lying on different points of the same evolutionary continuum. This includes behaviorists, who dominated psychology for much of the early twentieth century and did most of their experimental research on rats, pigeons, dogs, and other animals (see chapter 6).

Behaviorists explained the mother–infant bond by reference to the laws of learning. In classical conditioning, food serves as the primary reinforcer, meaning that the dog instinctively salivates in response to food. Sufficient pairings of food with the sound of a bell, for example, will result in the dog salivating in response to the bell. Similarly, food serves as a primary reinforcer for the infant, and sufficient pairings of the mother with food lead to the mother becoming a secondary reinforcer. The baby reacts positively to the presence of the mother and negatively to separation from the mother.

Psychoanalysts are in rare agreement with behaviorists on the key role of food in mother–infant bonding. Central to Freud's explanation of human infant behavior is the concept of homeostasis. For example, homeostasis is achieved when an infant feels adequately fed. When an infant has not had enough food or drink, basic biological needs create deficiencies, so the infant feels thirst and hunger. More and more pressure will build up as the infant experiences moving away from a set point that represents balance. Infants are driven to compensate for deficiencies, until they reach an adequate level of satisfaction.

Infants feel displeasure as deficiencies arise, and pleasure as they are satisfied. During the first eighteen months or so of life, according to Freud's psychosexual model of development, the primary focus of pleasure is the mouth, and the main source of pleasure is food. Infants become attached to others who feed them, and typically the most important other in this regard is the mother. For Freud, the relationship between the infant and the mother, and the successful transition of the infant from the oral to subsequent stages of psychosexual development, has fundamental implications for adult life. Thus, in terms of the importance of food for mother–infant bonding, behaviorists and psychoanalysts are in rare agreement.

Yet another surprising agreement is found in that at least some aspects of humanistic psychology can also be interpreted as endorsing the unique importance of food in mother–infant bonding. For example, according to Abraham Maslow's hierarchical model of human needs, the first level is physiological needs and those make eating and drinking imperative. If this first basic need is not satisfied, the infant will not be motivated to satisfy other, "higher" needs, such as needs for social interactions and intimacy. According to Maslow, physiological needs are the first of the "deficiency needs," meaning that if they are not adequately satisfied, there will be deficiencies in later development. Thus, Maslow's model, although in the humanistic tradition, is similar to behaviorist and psychoanalytic interpretations in endorsing the central role of feeding not only in mother–infant interactions but in later adult behavior.

Not all developmental explanations of the mother–infant bond place direct emphasis on the role of food; some do so only indirectly. For example, perhaps the most influential model of life-span development is that of Erik Erikson (see chapter 9). Each of the eight stages in Erikson's model is characterized by a conflict; failure to resolve a conflict at each stage results in problems for the individual with that conflict in later development. For example, conflict over trust is at the center of Erikson's first stage, corresponding to the first year of life. Because human infants are utterly dependent on caregivers, the issue of trust is supremely important. The infant must develop a strong sense of trust in the reliability of the caregiver to feed, protect, comfort, and support in all the ways necessary for successful survival. In cases where the infant successfully bonds with the mother, typically the primary caregiver, and develops a healthy sense of trust, it is possible to move on and build a sense of independence in the second stage of Erikson's developmental model. The infant now feels that she or he will not be abandoned, and this sense of security is a platform for exploring the world with more autonomy. Thus, in Erikson's model, healthy attachment provides an essential basis for later development.

Freud, Maslow, and Erikson all focused on assumed universals in human behavior. Universals and continuities in human and animal behavior are emphasized in *ethology*, the study of animals in natural settings. The research of ethologists, particularly Konrad Lorenz (1903–89), has demonstrated the importance of *imprinting*, a learned and stable attachment formed at a critical period in early development (Hess, 1973). Starting in the mid 1930s, Lorenz's studies showed that during a critical early period a newly hatched duckling that is able to walk (about ten hours after birth) will follow a moving stimulus and after about ten minutes become imprinted. This behavior is adaptive, because in natural settings the first moving stimulus that a newly hatched duckling encounters is most likely to be its mother. Ducklings that are effective at keeping close to their mothers are more likely to survive. Bowlby, who was the main pioneer in modern attachment theory and is discussed later in this chapter, was in important ways influenced by ethological research and gave considerable weight to adaptive aspects of attachment. However, Bowlby was also influenced by research conducted by Harry Harlow (1905–81), showing that the adaptive function of mother–infant attachment involves much more than the reinforcing role of food.

Harlow used newborn rhesus monkeys in an experiment to test directly the hypothesis that the basis of attachment is the role of the mother in providing food, against the hypothesis that the basis of attachment is the role of the mother in providing comfort and security. The newborn rhesus monkeys were separated from their mothers and raised in isolation. Each monkey had the company of two surrogate stationary mothers: one wire figure, the other a softer figure covered with cloth. Irrespective of whether the milk bottle was attached to the wire figure or the soft cloth figure, the monkeys spent more time in contact with the soft cloth figure. The preference of the moneys for the soft cloth figure was most clear when they were frightened, such as when unfamiliar objects approached or strange noises were heard. The clear implication of Harlow's research is that attachment arises out of a need for comfort and security, rather than food. Harlow's research had wide impact in many different areas of psychology, including clinical psychology, because it demonstrated that monkeys that experienced social isolation and inadequate attachment were more likely to grow up to be dysfunctional adults. Thus, we see that research has shown that attachment strongly influences degrees of freedom (as discussed in chapter 1), limiting the range of behavioral options during infancy (and some, such as Freud, would argue well beyond infancy).

Another debate in psychology that has influenced thinking on attachment concerns *intersubjectivity*, how individuals come to understand one another and to some extent share an understanding of the world. At least some accounts of attachment assume, sometimes explicitly, that mothers and infants come to share understandings, and communicate with one another on the basis of mutual understandings. Behaviorists do not endorse the view that attachment involves the development of shared understanding, because they reject the very idea that concepts such as mind and thought can have a useful role in scientific psychology. But most psychologists now reject the behaviorist position, and view the growth of intersubjectivity as an essential aspect of infant development. Infants develop ideas about other minds, with "mother" typically being the most important other in their lives. This takes place even before the infant is able to use complex language, and mother–infant communications involve what Bateson and others have termed "protoconversations," responsive mother–infant interactions.

Intersubjectivity arises out of what I have termed "interobjectivity," the understandings about the world that are shared within and between cultures. Attachment takes place within a cultural context, and the understanding of other minds is not just based on individual characteristics; it is contextually based on group characteristics. For example, shared mother–infant understandings arising in Beijing are in some respects different from shared mother–infant understandings arising in New York. As one example, in much of Africa, Asia, and Latin America, infants sleep with one (usually the mother) or both parents even when separate rooms are available, whereas in the US and other Western societies infants sleep in a separate room when this possibility is available. Such cultural differences, which range from ideas about how to feed, teach, and communicate with the infant, eventually result in cultural differences in adult behavior.

In summary, there is a long history of thinkers giving importance to the mother–infant bond. In the twentieth century a number of research movements formulated more specific ideas and/or provided more detailed empirical evidence about this bond. A number of schools of thought, including behaviorism and psychoanalysis, agreed on the important role of feeding in bringing about the mother–infant bond. Ethologists demonstrated the pervasive and hard-wired nature of at least some aspects of the mother–infant bond through demonstrations of imprinting in animals. But Harlow's research provided a dramatic demonstration of how the mother–infant bond is not simply dependent on the nourishment needs of the infant. Next, we turn to the development of the idea of attachment itself.

CRITICAL THINKING QUESTIONS

1 Is it surprising that there was agreement between several important schools of psychology regarding mother–infant bonding?

2 How were the contributions of Lorenz and Harlow really different with respect to our understanding of attachment?

BOWLBY'S FOUR-PHASE MODEL

The modern idea of attachment was given shape by John Bowlby (1907–90), a British psychiatrist with training in psychoanalysis and also a serious interest in ethology. Bowlby's views were shaped by his practical experiences of working with children who had serious problems, such as children separated from their parents because of the Second World War, and children who got into trouble with the law and were placed in juvenile homes. During the war years, hundreds of thousands of young children were sent out of London and other major cities to live in rural areas away from the most intense enemy bombing. Also, many children, both in Britain and elsewhere, lost one or both parents in the war. There was an urgent need for a better understanding of the consequences of the separation of children from their parents. Bowlby recognized this need and through his work with children he came to see the context of development, as well as relationship between the child and the primary caregiver, as fundamentally important. In his earliest writings from the 1940s and 1950s, it is clear that he saw children as vulnerable and dependent on a special relationship with the primary caregiver, usually the mother. Thus, Bowlby was working out, in the sense that he was developing theoretical ideas ahead of his time, but he was also to some extent working in, in the sense that he used his practical experiences to formulate theoretical ideas.

Bowlby gave children a lot more credit than other researchers had done, particularly in terms of their cognitive and emotional experiences. He came to believe that through their early attachment experiences infants develop working models, rather like cognitive templates, of how future attachment figures will act toward them. These working models are used by children to guide future behavior: how much to trust and rely on others, for example. In the emotional arena, he came to see children as capable of experiencing grief as a result of rejection and abandonment by caregivers. Moreover, he saw the attachment that takes place between a mother and infant at a critical period as unique, in that the mother could not simply be replaced by somebody else who could feed the infant. Just as Harlow's research implied, for Bowlby the mother–infant relationship is founded on emotional ties of comfort and support, rather than physiological needs that could simply be satisfied by food. Bowlby's main long-term contribution may be that he systematically explored the emotional sense of loss (for example, as associated with low confidence and self worth) experienced by children as a result of rejection or abandonment by caregivers.

The psychological consequences of a lack of adequate support from caregivers he saw as having evolutionary roots. Infants have evolved to show anxiety and distress when separated from caregivers, because infants who stay in close proximity to caregivers are more likely to be fed, protected, and trained to survive. Thus, the negative reactions of infants to separation from caregivers have the same adaptive roots as the negative reactions of newborn ducklings or other young animals when separated from their mothers.

But attachment is only one adaptive behavior that has evolved to enhance survival chances; the young must also venture out, explore the world, and learn to become independent. Bowlby saw a need for a balance between dependence and independence, between remaining close to caregivers and venturing out to get to know the world and gain independence. This balance is arrived at gradually, the level of dependence and independence shifting as the infant grows older.

Bowlby's model of attachment, like the developmental models of Erikson, Piaget, and Kohlberg (see chapter 9), is hierarchical, stepwise, and universal. It is assumed that all human mother–infant attachments pass through the same four stages, irrespective of the culture in which they live. The process of attachment in humans is akin to imprinting in birds, in the sense that certain hard-wired factors move infants along a set path.

Preattachment (birth to about 6–8 weeks)

For the first eight weeks or so of life infants do not show strong reactions when they are left alone with an unfamiliar caregiver. As long as they receive adequate care, nourishment, warmth, and comfort, infants at this stage do not show strong preferences between caregivers. This is not because they are non-social or because they are unable to differentiate between other people. Even at this early stage infants do engage in social communications. They do so, for example, by joining another person to attend to an action or thing (often by looking to the same place that another person is looking). Another example of infant social communication is simple forms of behavior that can be interpreted as imitation, such as poking out their tongue at adults who poke their tongue out at them. Also, infants can differentiate between other people. Research by Aidan Macfarlane has shown that ten-day-old infants show a preference for the smell of their mother's milk over the smell of the milk of another woman.

Beginnings of attachment (6–8 weeks to about 6–8 months)

There is a slow, gradual, but definite increase in the infant's tendency not only to differentiate between other persons but to show preferences for familiar faces. Infants at this stage tend to be more cautious and wary when confronted by strangers.

Clear-cut attachment (6–8 months to 2–3 years)

At the start of this phase the infant is able to crawl, and by the end of the phase the toddler is able to run around with some speed. Thus, now it is not just the mother who can move away and cause a mother–infant separation, but the infant also. But the new increased mobility of the infant is kept in check by separation anxiety, experienced markedly by the infant when separated from the mother, but also experienced by the mother when she senses that her child has wandered too far away. The movement of the mother and infant seems to take place within the boundary of an invisible sphere; if either of them steps outside the boundary, separation anxiety arises. To avoid separation anxiety, the infant uses the mother as a secure base and continually checks back with her before venturing out to explore.

Mother–infant partnership (2–3 years and older)

The toddler is now able to move around fairly well, and the challenge is to coordinate with the mother to arrive at a satisfactory equilibrium between dependence and independence. Separation anxiety gradually declines. A secure relationship between the mother and infant is precious, because it can serve as the working model for later relationships experienced by the maturing individual.

Thus, Bowlby highlighted the sensitivity of children to parental rejection and abandonment, and he gave particular importance to the bonding of the mother with the infant at a critical stage. Bowlby developed his idea of attachment on the basis of his practical experiences rather than controlled research. But his ideas did serve as a springboard for detailed empirical studies by the next generation of researchers.

CRITICAL THINKING QUESTIONS

1 What role did Bowlby give to cognition in his discussion of attachment?

2 In what way is Bowlby's model similar to those of Erikson and Piaget?

VARIATIONS ON THE ATTACHMENT THEME

Bowlby's original idea of attachment was holistic in so far as it incorporated both biological and social aspects of the mother–infant interaction, it gave importance to cognition and overt behavior, and it gave the infant credit for both acting upon the world and being sensitive to surroundings, most importantly the mother. Following Bowlby's seminal contribution, three main developments have taken place in attachment research: first, empirical research using the strange situation; second, research on temperament and other "individual difference" characteristics that might influence attachment behavior; third, critical reassessment of Bowlby's emphasis on the mother–infant bond in light of cultural changes and variations.

The strange situation

The most influential research method used to study attachment is the *strange situation*, where a mother temporarily leaves an infant in the company of a stranger, and the researcher studies the infant's reactions to the exit of the mother, to being alone with the stranger, and particularly to the return of the mother. The strange situation was developed by Mary Ainsworth on the basis of her cross-cultural studies of mother–infant interactions, such as her detailed case study of infancy in Uganda. The basic procedure for the strange situation is as follows: a mother and infant are introduced to a room where the infant has the opportunity to play with toys. No other person is present. A stranger enters the room. The stranger tries to keep the infant's attention while the mother leaves the room. After a few moments, the mother returns to the room. Throughout these steps, the behavior of the infant is closely observed.

On the basis of observations of infants and mothers in the strange situation, Ainsworth and her colleagues came to two main conclusions. First, the most important indicator of the type of attachment achieved is the behavior of the infant when the mother returns after having left the infant in the company of a stranger. Second, the reaction of the infant to the mother's return falls into three basic categories: secure attachment, anxious/avoidant attachment, and anxious/resistant attachment. About two-thirds of middle-class US infants fall in the secure-attachment category. These children play confidently in the presence of the mother and even interact with the stranger, but react negatively when they notice the exit of the mother. The key point is that they respond positively to the mother returning and quickly become calm and resume play. The other third of middle-class US infants are mostly in the anxious/avoidant category. These infants behave in a way that has traditionally been interpreted as indifference, and they do not always react strongly when the mother leaves or returns. Instead of seeking to be close to the mother after her return, they sometimes look away. A small group of the infants, about 10–12 percent of the total, fall in the anxious/resistant category. These infants show a high level of anxiety even in the company of their mothers, get very upset when the mother leaves, and, most importantly, show resistance to the mother's efforts to comfort them when she returns.

The criteria used to categorize infants on the basis of their behavior in the strange situation are supposed to be universally valid. However, this assumption seems implausible. Takahashi and others have questioned the universality of assumptions underlying the strange situation. Labels such as "anxious," "resistant," "avoidance," and "secure" are not neutral, but have evaluative connotations that vary across cultures. For example, instead of "avoidant," one could label an infant as "independent." It is not surprising that when the strange situation procedure is used across different cultures, some variations arise in the percentage of infants who fall into the three main categories of secure attachment, anxious/ avoidant attachment, and anxious/resistant attachment. However, the question of how such differences should be interpreted does not have easy answers, particularly if we return to Bowlby's original position that emphasizes the adaptive aspect of attachment.

From an evolutionary perspective, behavior is more adaptive when it enables individuals to survive better in their particular environmental conditions. This implies that different environmental conditions, such as the different cultures in which infants grow up, require adaptations in behavior that are at least to some degree different. For example, in the Japanese context, it may well be more adaptive for infants to develop a more dependent style of behavior, and it may be more adaptive for US infants to become more independent more quickly because that is what their environment rewards. But presumably as cultures change, the behavior of infants will also eventually change. In past research, the proportion of Japanese infants falling into the anxious/resistant category has been shown to be higher compared with US infants. As the structure of Japanese and US families changes, we can expect changes in the adaptive behavior of infants in these cultures. This underlines the need to view attachment in the larger cultural context.

Some qualifications

The central idea that is stable across individuals, cultures, and situations is that infants starting around 6–8 months old consistently experience distress and anxiety when separated from their mothers. The percentage of infants experiencing separation anxiety increases for the next eight months or so, then there is a gradual decline in the intensity of distress manifested as a result of mother–infant separation. This trend is found among many populations, with some variations as a result of the characteristics of the infant, the characteristics of the mother, and the cultural context (including family and child care arrangements). Although it is useful to explore the contribution of each of these to the attachment process, it is misleading and reductionist to view any one factor as a single cause of behavior independent of other factors.

In terms of the characteristics of the infant, a great deal has been made of *temperament*, a style of reacting to the environment as well as a characteristic level of energy, and *resilience*, the ability to overcome quickly adverse environmental conditions and negative experiences. The two concepts are different, since temperament is assumed to be inborn, whereas resilience is supposed to be something individuals can learn, at least to some degree and with the appropriate training. But they are similar in that they are supposed to determine how well an individual copes in different, and particularly adverse, environmental conditions. For example, something about the temperament and the resilience of some individuals is assumed to help them get through even terrible experiences relatively unscathed, whereas individuals with different temperament and lower resilience are affected profoundly.

Similarly, the characteristics of the mother, particularly her style of interacting with the infant, have been a research focus. The sensitivity of the mother and her responsiveness to the needs of the infant have been highlighted as particularly important. Infants with more responsive and more sensitive mothers have a higher probability of falling in the secure-attachment category. This is in line with research in other domains where the characteristics of parenting, particularly the mother, are thought to lead to problems in later development for the child. For example, in the same post-1945 years that Bowlby was developing his model of attachment, a group of researchers led by Theodor Adorno were studying the authoritarian personality, characterized by being submissive and obedient to authority but vindictive toward minorities and non-conformists. Authoritarians are more likely to support anti-democratic leaders and movements. Adorno and his colleagues concluded that authoritarians are more likely to be raised by mothers who are withdrawn, less responsive, and aloof from the child (see Moghaddam, 1998).

The cultural context

Perhaps the most blatant weakness in Bowlby's idea of attachment is his almost exclusive focus on mother–infant interaction, to the exclusion of father–infant and other variations of caregiver–infant interaction. The model developed by Bowlby reflected the particular characteristics of his culture and time, mid twentieth-century Western society. The expectation was that the mother would be by far the most important caregiver, and the father and others would play a relatively minor role. But this is a rather limited viewpoint when considered in historical and cross-cultural context.

Historically, the structure of the family has changed dramatically, and gender roles continue to shift (see chapter 17). Women are now competing successfully with men in education and many employment domains, as reflected most dramatically by trends in higher education. For example, fifty-seven percent of bachelor's degrees from US colleges were awarded to women in 2002. In most Western societies, the majority of women with children work outside the home. To compensate, men are participating more fully in child care, including looking after infants. When fathers spend enough time with infants, secure attachment to fathers can take place as it can to mothers. In cultures where infants are cared for mainly by older siblings or other relatives, secure attachment to these other caregivers can take place.

We should not be surprised at the flexibility of infants in terms of whom they form attachments with. It is useful to remind ourselves of the evolutionary function of attachment: at a critical time in development, infants become attached to particular others who seem most likely, in terms of proximity and availability, to provide them with warmth, comfort, and food. Lorenz showed that ducklings can even become attached to a moving object such as his booted legs, if the ducklings are exposed to the object at the critical time in their development. Such flexibility has adaptive functions, because only a substitute mother might be available in some cases. From an evolutionary perspective, it makes sense for human infants also to show some level of flexibility in terms of whom they become attached to, because circumstances might lead particular others to become unavailable.

The history of families across societies shows that mothers have typically had multiple responsibilities and the challenge of finding suitable care for the young has always existed. This challenge was traditionally met through support from the extended family (grandparents, aunts, cousins, and so on), but in modern societies this challenge is more often met through paid professional help. The key factor seems to be the quality of care provided for the infant, rather than the specific persons who provide the care. This point is particularly relevant to the controversy about the effects of child care centers, where infants of working parents are placed for care.

The "child care controversy" is too simplistic, particularly when the question is raised "Should parents send infants to child care?" This question assumes working parents have a real choice about whether or not to use child care centers. Most middle- and lower-class families in the United States (and increasingly in other Western societies) are forced by economic pressures to have both parents work full-time outside the home; thus child care is a necessity rather than a choice for such families. The "welfare reform" legislation of 1996 has meant that state authorities can require single parents to be engaged in work or work-related activities (e.g. job training) outside the home even before the infant is one year old. As a consequence of these legislative changes and strong economic pressures, by 2000 almost half of all infants under the age of one and almost sixty percent of two-year-old infants regularly attended child care in the United States.

Second, the question of whether child care centers have good or bad effects is too simplistic. The answer lies in the quality of care provided: just as some mothers are insensitive and unresponsive, some child care centers provide insensitive and unresponsive care. Good child care centers nurture securely attached infants. The quality of child care centers depends a great deal on the resources available to appropriately train child care teachers and provide well-designed programs, housed in well-maintained facilities. Not surprisingly, well-funded child care centers with well-trained teachers tend to provide better care.

CRITICAL THINKING QUESTIONS

1 In some cultures, infants are cared for by multiple providers. How would this influence the strange situation?

2 What does reductionism mean in explanations of attachment?

CONCLUDING COMMENT

The idea of attachment as developed by Bowlby has proved to be robust and fruitful in terms of the research it has stimulated. Through Ainsworth's strange situation, an enormous research literature now exists on different aspects of attachment, including the influence of the characteristics of the infant, the mother, and the context. Moreover, the high number of infants attending child care centers suggests that it is now normal for infants to interact with strangers in strange new situations (i.e. professional instructors in child care centers), and that the strange situation research method developed by Mary Ainsworth is in this respect appropriate. However, it may be that human behavior is actually in some ways more flexible than Bowlby envisaged. The infant can become securely attached to people other than the mother, as long as they provide the necessary support and comfort at the critical time. The crucial factor seems to be the quality of care, rather than whether it is provided by the mother, the father, or others, such as siblings or paid professionals.

CRITICAL THINKING QUESTIONS

1 There are many cross-cultural variations in care arrangements for infants. What does this imply for the traditional view that infants become attached to mothers?

2 What are the key characteristics of quality care?

FURTHER READING

Ainsworth, M. D. S. (1967). *Infancy in Uganda*. Baltimore: Johns Hopkins University Press.

Bateson, M. C. (1979). "The epigenesis of conversational interaction": A personal account of research development. In M. Bullowa (ed.), *Before speech: The beginning of human communication*. New York: Cambridge University Press.

Belsky, J. (1999). Infant–parent attachment. In L. Balter & C. S. Tamis-LeMonda (eds.), *Child psychology: A handbook of contemporary issues*. Philadelphia: Psychology Press.

Bowlby, J. (1940). The influence of early environment in the development of neurosis and neurotic characters. International Journal of Psycho-analysis, 21, 1–25.

Bowlby, J. (1951). *Maternal care and mental health*. Geneva: World Health Organization.

Bowlby, J. (1960). Grief and mourning in infancy and child development. *Psychoanalytic Study of the Child, 15,* 9–52.

Bowlby, J. (1969). *Attachment and loss: Vol. 1. Attachment*. New York: Basic Books.

Bowlby, J. (1973). *Attachment and loss: Vol. 2. Separation: Anxiety and anger*. New York: Basic Books.

Bowlby, J. (1980). *Attachment and loss: Vol. 3. Loss: Sadness and depression*. New York: Basic Books.

Cassidy, J., & Shaver, P. (eds.) (1999). *Handbook of attachment theory and research*. New York: Guildford Press.

Greenberg, M. T., Cicchetti, D., & Cummings, E. M. (eds.) (1990). *Attachment in the preschool years*. Chicago: University of Chicago Press.

Harlow, H. F., Harlow, M. K., & Soumi, S. J. (1971). From thought to therapy: Lessons from a primate laboratory. *American Scientist, 59,* 538–549.

Hess, E. H. (1973). *Imprinting: Early experience and the developmental psychobiology of attachment.* New York: Van Nostrand

Koops, W., Hoeksma, J. B., & Van den Boom, D. C. (eds.) (1997). *Development of interaction and attachment: Traditional and non-traditional approaches.* Amsterdam: North-Holland/Elsevier.

MacFarlane, A. (1975). Olfaction in the development of social preferences in the human neonate. *Parent–infant interaction.* New York: Elsevier.

Main, M., & Weston, D. (1981). The quality of the toddler's relationship to mother and father: Related to conflict behavior and the readiness to establish new relationships. *Child Development, 52,* 932–940.

Mikulineer, M., Shaver, P. R., & Pereg, D. (2003). Attachment theory and affect regulation: The dynamics, development, and cognitive consequences of attachment-related strategies. *Motivation and Emotion, 27,* 77–102.

Moghaddam, F. M. (1998). *Social psychology: Exploring universals across cultures.* New York: Freeman.

Moghaddam, F. M. (2003). Interobjectivity and culture. *Culture & Psychology, 9,* 221–232.

Moore, C., & Dunham, P. (eds.) (1995). *Joint attention: Its origins and role in development.* Hillsdate, NJ: Erlbaum.

Shonkoff, J. P., & Phillips, D. A. (2000). *From neurons to neighborhoods: The science of early child development.* Washington: National Academy Press.

Shweder, R. A., Jensen, L. A., & Golstein, W. M. (1995). Who sleeps by whom revisited: A method for extracting the moral goods implicit in practice. *New Directions for Child Development, 67,* 21–39.

Takahashi, K. (1990). Are the key assumptions of the "strange situation" procedure universal? *Human Development, 33,* 23–30.

Van den Boom, D. C. (2001). First attachments: Theory and research. In G. Bremner & A. Fogel (eds.), *Blackwell handbook of infant development.* Oxford: Blackwell.

12

DISPLACED AGGRESSION

> Scott had a terrible day at the meat-packing plant where he has been working for the last six years. After arriving at work late because of a mechanical problem with his car, he got shouted at by his boss and was wrongly blamed for the contamination of several thousand pounds of meat. Scott was forced to put in four hours of back-breaking unpaid overtime to clean up the contamination. When he finally arrived back home that night, he was exhausted, starving, and very angry. He slammed the front door, screamed at his wife, and walloped his eight-year-old boy for "being in the way."

The above scenario describes an instance of *displaced aggression*, action intended to harm others by a person who feels provoked against a third-party target who is not responsible for the provocation. In the scenario, Scott is provoked by his boss, but he displaces aggression onto his wife and child, soft targets. The idea of displaced aggression was first formally developed by Sigmund Freud (1856–1939). Since then, three groups of researchers have further examined displaced aggression and refined the idea: John Dollard and colleagues in the 1930s and 1940s, Leonard Berkowitz and others in the 1960s and 1970s, and Norman Miller and his associates since the 1990s. While Freud for the most part worked out and developed his theoretical ideas on the basis of creative insight rather than experimental evidence, the more recently active groups of researchers have relied more on working in and developing explanations tied to experimental studies. As we shall see, Freud's theoretical account of displaced aggression is expansive and covers both inter-personal and inter-group aggression. The more recent experimental research on displaced aggression, on the other hand, has remained almost exclusively limited to inter-personal aggression.

Although displaced aggression is only one part of the general topic of aggression, displaced aggression is a great idea because it provides a convincing and profoundly new explanation of a wide variety of inter-personal and inter-group situations. Common to all these situations is provocation by a source that is too powerful to be attacked directly, for fear of retaliation (such as a boss, as in the case of Scott in the scenario above), and a weaker third party that eventually becomes the soft target of attack (such as Scott's wife and child). The scenario about Scott concerns an inter-personal situation. Now, consider an inter-group example involving a *minority*, those with less power, and a *majority*, those who enjoy greater power: a dictator turning his army against minority groups, as in the case of Saddam Hussein attacking minorities in the 1980s and 1990s. One interpretation of Hussein's actions is as follows: frustrated by his lack of success fighting against more powerful foes, including the United States, the dictator unleashed his military forces against weaker third parties, such as the small nation of Kuwait, as well as the Kurdish ethnic minority and the Shi'a religious minority in Iraq. This is an instance of inter-group displaced aggression, and Freud's account of displaced aggression is particularly creative and innovative at the inter-group level.

Displaced aggression is a great idea in part because it seems to apply to human behavior across many different cultures. Although there are fundamental differences across cultures with respect to the source and the target of aggression, the phenomenon of displaced aggression is consistently found in most cultural settings. An example of this is found among religious fundamentalists across cultures. While some Christian fundamentalist leaders have described other religions as "Satanic" and guided their followers to displace aggression onto the members of other religions (the most obvious target since the tragedy of 9/11 being Muslims), Islamic fundamentalists have targeted the United States as the "Great Satan" and maneuvered all hostilities among their populations onto this target. Displaced aggression is central to both situations, but the source and target are different, depending on whether the context is the United States or a country such as Iran.

In the first section below, I critically discuss the general characteristics of Freud's idea, displaced aggression, as well as more recent elaborations by other scholars. In the second section, I re-assess the assumed relationship between frustration and aggression.

THE IDEA OF DISPLACED AGGRESSION IN WIDER CONTEXT

Theories of conflict can be usefully categorized into two groups: first, rational theories, such as *realistic conflict theory*, based on materialism and balance. These theories assume that aggression has an instrumental or "realistic" basis and that it is driven by competition for resources. For example, X and Y are fighting in order to gain control of oil reserves in a region. When X attacks the material interests of Y, conflict arises and escalates in a tit-for-tat way: for example, Y strikes at X, then X strikes back at Y to gain access to scarce oil reserves. Each side in the conflict is behaving "rationally" in the sense that each side knows what they are doing and why. The conflict is "balanced" in the sense that each aggressive act by one party receives an aggressive response from the opposing party; action brings about reaction directed at the original source of action.

A second group of theories, such as displaced aggression, propose that conflict is not rational, materialist, or balanced. Displaced aggression is not rational because the aggressors generally are not aware of why they are attacking a third-party target: for example, Scott is not consciously aware that he is displacing aggression onto his own wife and child because he is too afraid to attack his boss. Displaced aggression is not materialist, because it is feelings, emotions, and psychological experiences, and not the material conditions, that fundamentally shape behavior in this realm. Scott hits his child in a moment of anger, rather than with any idea of making material gain. Third, displaced aggression is not balanced, because it does not follow the tit-for-tat pattern of violence: the source of the frustration (e.g. Scott's boss) does not receive reciprocal treatment; rather, a soft third party (e.g. Scott's wife and child) becomes the target of aggression. In general, then, displaced aggression gives priority to psychological factors rather than to material conditions.

Some critics contend that displaced aggression is limited in that it deals with emotional or *angry aggression*, such as an act of violence arising out of momentary passion, but not *instrumental aggression*, a premeditated, planned attack designed to gain material benefit for the aggressor. However, from a Freudian perspective the deeper roots of both types of aggression are the same (as explained below), and the distinction between angry and instrumental aggression does not hold up. Although in theory we can distinguish between the two types of aggression, in practice it seems impossible to find instances of instrumental aggression that do not involve angry aggression, or cases of angry aggression that do not involve instrumental aggression. Besides, people often use emotions in instrumental ways. It is not uncommon for individuals to make themselves feel angry in order to achieve instrumental goals: Bob throws a temper tantrum because experience tells him this will persuade his parents to let him stay out later at night. In practice, then, displaced aggression deals with both instrumental and angry aggression, because the two are intertwined.

Displaced aggression and Freud's psychology

Displaced aggression is best considered in the context of Freud's broader understanding of the role and nature of the unconscious (discussed in chapter 5). A cost of becoming civilized is that the individual learns to repress basic instincts and motives, particularly in the realm of sexuality and aggression, that are taboo according to societal norms. Wishes, desires, and so on based on taboo instincts and motives become associated with anxiety, and by pushing them into the unconscious individuals avoid the negative experience of anxiety. In this sense, the repression of psychological experiences into the unconscious serves a useful function.

Freud's model can be described as "hydraulic," meaning that basic instincts and motives, particularly related to sex and aggression, can be pushed down into the unconscious through various defense mechanisms, but they do not completely disappear. Rather like water pushed back by a dam, the water (repressed phenomena) always finds a way to seep through the cracks and crevices. It is as if a powerful pump is continually pushing the water (repressed phenomena) upward, into the path of least resistance. When one set of paths are blocked, alternative possibilities are tested to find a way through. But when the water (repressed phenomena) does seep through, individuals experience anxiety and fear, sometimes intense enough to disable them. It is in order to avoid disabling anxiety that individuals employ various *defense mechanisms*, behavioral and cognitive strategies intended to reduce anxiety.

In Freud's psychology, displaced aggression is one of a number of secondary defense mechanisms, the primary one being repression. Other important examples include *projection*, whereby what are actually one's own wishes, motives, and thoughts are attributed to another person or group rather than oneself. Projection plays a particularly important role in inter-group relations. For example, instead of correctly recognizing their own fear and hatred of the Greens, the Blue group proclaim that "the Greens hate and want to destroy us. We must attack them first." Another secondary defense mechanism is *rationalization*, whereby individuals reinterpret their own thoughts and feelings to make them more acceptable. For example, the day after Scott (in the scenario above) beat his child, he explained his behavior by saying, "It's a tough world out there and the kid has to suffer knocks to grow into a man. He should be grateful for the lessons I'm learning him." Rationalization also plays an important role at the inter-group level. For example, throughout history those who have waged war and invaded other countries have often claimed that they are "liberators," just as groups of terrorists often claim to be "freedom fighters."

Freud's ideas on displaced aggression are associated with his therapy experiences with *transference*, a process through which patients transfer feelings and experiences from earlier experiences onto the therapist. For example, a patient who had a particularly difficult relationship with a hard-to-please father transfers her hostility to the new authority figure of the therapist and says to the therapist, "Don't tell me what to do." The idea of displaced aggression incorporates similar transference of feelings, thoughts, and experiences, but from one (usually powerful) source of discomfort to an alternative (usually less powerful or threatening) target. An implication of Freud's hydraulic model is that transference and displacement have a common basis: built-up pressure or frustration that inevitably manifests itself through the path of least resistance. The assumed inevitability of outcome means that low degrees of freedom are envisaged for this behavior.

CRITICAL THINKING QUESTIONS

1 Describe an example of displaced aggression you have experienced or witnessed.

2 Describe how an instance of displaced aggression could also involve projection.

DISPLACED AGGRESSION AND FREUD'S INTER-GROUP PSYCHOLOGY

Freud made monumental contributions to our understanding of inter-group relations, not by conducting empirical research but by using his personal experiences to construct theoretical explanations. He was a member of a small but highly progressive and productive Jewish intellectual community living in Vienna in the late nineteenth and early twentieth century. He experienced anti-Semitism and knew first-hand the life of a minority group member. He also witnessed the beginnings of modern warfare from the end of the nineteenth century, culminating in the First World War (1914–18). The rise of the Nazis from the 1920s and the invasion of Austria by Hitler's armies resulted in Freud taking refuge in England, where he died in 1939 at the dawn of the Second World War (1939–1945). Thus, although he achieved great professional success and worldwide fame, he also suffered through a terrible, violent time in human history – albeit in some respects perhaps no more terrible or violent than our own time.

Displaced aggression played a central part in Freud's inter-group psychology, adding to the pessimistic (some would claim "realistic") outlook Freud provides. To better understand the role of displaced aggression in Freud's inter-group relations, the following discussion is organized around four topics: libidinal ties, group leadership, displacement and cohesion, and displacement targets.

Libidinal ties

At both the inter-personal and inter-group levels Freud postulated a central role for *libido*, consisting of the energy of instincts that come under the broad label "love," and *libidinal ties* consisting of "love relations" that are sexual but also other types of love relations such as between parents and children, or between close friends, or the love of citizens for their national leaders. All love relations arise out of the same instinctual emotions and are characterized by complexity and ambivalence.

Individuals in libidinal ties experience psychological ambivalence because such ties involve feelings of both love and hostility. In Freud's writings about intense emotional relationships between people, it is proposed that repulsion and attraction, love and hate, are always interwoven. Lovers who feel pain when they are apart always have bittersweet experiences, because their feelings are a mixture of attraction and aversion. Even children who love their parents experience psychological ambivalence, sensing both dependency and repulsion, a need for security and a need to break free.

A major challenge is how to cope with the ambivalent feelings when individuals desire to maintain love relationships. At the inter-personal level, the primary defense mechanism of repression is used to push negative feelings below the surface into the unconscious. Other, secondary defense mechanisms are also used. For example, Angela is intensely jealous and unconsciously wishes some calamity would befall her talented and popular older sister. However, Angela manages her negative feelings through the secondary defense mechanism of *reaction formation*, which means she displays emotions exactly opposite to what she really feels. She smothers and overwhelms her older sister with affection and admiration, thus warding off the anxiety she would experience if her real feelings came to the surface.

But even in the most loving inter-personal relationships, the negative feelings associated with libidinal ties are only managed and pushed outside consciousness; they do not disappear altogether and are never far from the surface. The negative feelings, the hostilities, are always lurking, always ready to push out into the open. That is why, Freud would argue, a couple who have lived a loving married life for twenty years can suddenly turn against one another in a divorce court, with all the malice of old enemies ready to do as much harm as possible to the opposition.

At the group and inter-group levels, the psychological ambivalence associated with libidinal ties is managed particularly through the secondary defense mechanism of displaced aggression. However, this is only possible through the influence of effective group leadership, which we turn to next.

Group leadership

Freud limited his discussions of groups to groups with leaders, because he believed that only through the influence of leaders can groups become cohesive and take effective action. His position could be criticized by pointing to examples of some traditional tribes without leaders, as well as some small groups in modern societies which function well without leaders, such as orchestras without conductors. However, in defense of Freud's position, one could argue that such exceptions do not involve large groups functioning in technologically advanced societies: they either involve technologically simple, traditional societies, or small groups in modern societies. To achieve the high level of organization necessary for effective functioning in large and technologically advanced societies, according to Freud, effective leadership is necessary.

Group members, "followers," develop bonds with the group through *identification with the leader,* a process through which followers form emotional ties with the leader and act as if they are the person with whom the tie exists. Thus, group members have a deeply significant commonality. they all share strong emotional ties with the leader, and the leader is now an integral part of their ego (for a discussion of the ego and consciousness, see chapter 5). This shared love for the same object, the leader, moves group members to identify with one another and to cooperate toward common goals. Their energies become channeled in the same direction through identification with the leader.

Freud uses the examples of the Catholic Church and the army to illustrate his points concerning the identification of followers and leaders. Despite their differences, Freud argues, the Church and the army both function on the basis of the same illusion of there being a leader, in the Catholic Church, Christ and in the army the commander-in-chief, who loves all the followers equally. The leader is like a father, and he treats all followers as brothers and sisters in the same family. Through libidinal ties, the family members are bonded to one another and to the leader. But it is the leader–follower bond that enables the bonds between followers to exist: when a leader is eliminated and not replaced, there is also a disappearance of ties between followers. It is the father figure who keeps the group intact and cohesive: the Catholic Church without Christ or an army without a commander-in-chief is not functional. The vitally important role of the leader becomes clearer when we consider the negative feelings involved in libidinal ties.

Libidinal ties not only involve love and positive emotions; they also involve hostility and negative emotions. Perhaps the most important role of the group leader is to manage the negative feelings that surge up inside the group, the jealousy, hatred, vengefulness, and so on that group members feel. Leaders achieve this through displaced aggression and the re-directing of negative feelings outside the group.

Displacement and cohesion

The genius of Freud's model of inter-group relations is most clearly apparent in his treatment of displaced aggression and the role it has in the achievement of group cohesion. The negative side of libidinal ties does not just disappear in the group setting; it remains present and persistent. The leader manages feelings of aversion and hostility by directing all such feelings onto targets outside the group. Freud contends that it is always possible to "bind together a considerable number of people in love so long as there are other people left over to receive the manifestations of their aggressiveness" (1930, p. 114). This seemingly pessimistic view of inter-group relations explains inter-group conflicts and their various manifestations, from subtle and indirect discrimination to outright warfare involving hundreds of millions of people, that continue to plague human societies.

The displacement of aggression from *in-groups*, groups to which a person belongs, onto *out-groups*, groups to which a person does not belong, is one of the most effective strategies through which leaders can strengthen in-group cohesion. The effectiveness of this strategy is demonstrated by experiments conducted both in the field and in the laboratory. For example, the field studies of Muzafer Sherif in the 1950s and 1960s demonstrated that threat from an out-group leads in-group members to band together and to be more supportive of aggressive leaders. In turn, aggressive leaders further solidify the rift between groups and nurture in-group cohesion and inter-group hostility. In line with this, the experimental laboratory research of Henri Tajfel and his associates in the 1970s and 1980s suggests that as soon as individuals become aware of the presence of an out-group, they tend to show bias in favor of their in-group. The clear implication is that potential out-group competition increases in-group cohesion; leaders can maneuver to get their followers to focus on the out-group threat and in this way minimize in-group strife and maximize in-group solidarity.

But what about evidence from everyday life; does displaced aggression lead to increased in-group cohesion in the real world? The case of national leaders suggests this to be the case. There are numerous examples of an external threat leading to increased in-group cohesion and rallying around the flag. The most important recent case of this followed the tragedy of the 9/11 terrorist attacks. The approval ratings of President George W. Bush surged up following the terrorist attacks, as US citizens rallied around the flag and patriotic sentiments soared; just as the US public had shown very strong support for his father, President Bush, Sr., during the Gulf War of 1991, when the US and its allies ended the Iraqi occupation of Kuwait. While the perceived threat from terrorism and "rogue states" leads to stronger support for US presidents within the US, the leadership in some other countries, such as Iran and North Korea, uses the "international threat" posed by the US, described by some of its enemies as the "Great Satan," to rally support, strengthen their own power positions, and minimize internal dissent.

Perhaps the most unfortunate feature of displaced aggression onto an external threat is its association with increased conformity and obedience within the in-group. This comes about in two main ways. First, external threat is used to justify a more authoritarian leadership style and the use of harsher measures to try to minimize dissent and minimize individual freedoms. Under such conditions, opposition to government policy is more readily labeled "unpatriotic." This is a form of censorship from above. Second, there is also censorship from below, whereby many people become less tolerant of dissenting voices. The presence of an enemy at the gate means that many people are more inclined to want to speak in one voice, the leader's voice. The presence of diverse voices is seen as unhelpful, at best, and even as unpatriotic and traitorous in some cases; those who are different become targets in such situations.

Displacement targets

In his analysis of different groups, including major religions, Freud lays great stress on the idea that in-group love is associated with hostility toward out-groups: "every religion… is a religion of love for all those whom it embraces; while cruelty and intolerance toward those who do not belong to it are natural to every religion" (1921, p. 98). But he also formulated more precise predictions about the characteristics of those out-groups which are more likely to become the targets of displaced aggression. Freud argued that the more dissimilar the out-group, the more likely it will be selected as the target of displaced aggression.

Thus, Freud formulated an early version of what became known as the *similarity-attraction hypothesis*, that individuals will be positively disposed toward others who are more similar to them and negatively inclined toward those who are less similar to them. An enormous variety of research evidence was gathered by Don Byrne in support of this proposition; a study by Lisa Osbeck and others is among a number that find strong support for similarity-attraction at the inter-group level in North America. A visit to the lunch room of any large high school or college will confirm the same trend: people like to be with others who are similar to them; students typically sit in clusters of those who are similar to themselves. Dissimilarity-attraction is a big theme in some Hollywood movies, but in real life similarity-attraction is a more repeated pattern.

Although similarity-attraction seems to be a universal relationship, the criteria selected for defining similarity are highly influenced by local culture. In the North American context, ethnicity is a widely used criterion for defining similarity; consequently, our visit to college lunch rooms is likely to reveal seating patterns based on ethnic similarity. In the Middle East, religion is a very important criterion, so that Christians, Jews, and Muslims tend to interact more with other religious in-group members. In some traditional religious societies, including Islamic ones (e.g. Iran, Saudi Arabia), gender is highly important, so that a lot of activities are carried out exclusively with members of one's own gender, women and men being excluded from the realm of the opposite gender (for example, in sports). In most societies power is a hidden criterion, the elite (those who enjoy more power) interacting more with other members of the elite, and the non-elite (those who have relatively little power) interacting with other members of the non-elite. Through their greater power, the elite have more influence on how aggression is displaced.

From a Freudian perspective, prejudice and discrimination against African Americans and other minorities represent instances of displaced aggression. Such biases against minorities tend to increase during times of economic depression, and this too is in line with Freud's predictions: as the White majority feel that paths to their goals are blocked in poorer economic times, their rising negative feelings are displaced onto dissimilar out-groups. This can be a two-way process: minorities can also displace aggression onto the majority group and blame the majority when they are blocked from reaching goals. A fundamental difference is that the majority group has the power to seriously harm the minority through displaced aggression (particularly through control of economic, political, and legal systems), whereas the minority has far less power.

CRITICAL THINKING QUESTIONS

1 What is an example of displaced aggression in relationships between nation states?

2 Give an example of how similarity influences the selection of the target of displaced aggression.

RE-THINKING THE ASSUMED ASSOCIATION BETWEEN FRUSTRATION AND AGGRESSION

Freud's writings provided important insights and served as a launching pad for more precise theoretical formulations in the area of aggression. Among the most important of these was the frustration–aggression hypothesis put forward by John Dollard and his associates working in the 1930s and 1940s, which postulated that frustration always leads to some form of aggression. We can relate this back to the idea of a hydraulic model: frustration arises when a goal is blocked, just like when a dam blocks water. But the motor pumping the water keeps working and creating more and more pressure, until a way opens up through the path of least resistance. Thus, aggression in some form or other always arises from frustration, just as water under pressure breaks through some path or other.

But further research by Leonard Berkowitz and others revealed that the frustration–aggression hypothesis assumed too few degrees of freedom: frustration does not always result in aggression. In other words, the range of possible outcomes is greater than Dollard and others had assumed. For example, an individual may repress feelings of hostility toward another person rather than overtly act on them. The new research showed there to be greater degrees of freedom: frustration brings about anger and a greater potential for aggression, but this potential is only realized under certain conditions. Examples of such conditions are when a person frustrates others by doing something he or she could have avoided (such as deliberately trashing another person's car), and when there are triggers to violence (such as guns) available in the context.

Another important factor explored more recently is the sequential order of frustrating events. If a first frustrating event is following by a second, then some of the excess anger from the first incident could transfer to the second and increase its likelihood of leading to aggression. For example, if Mark is still angry about having his wallet stolen, and then Lee trashes his car, the spillover of anger from the first incident added to anger arising from the second incident might be enough to push his anger level high enough for him to take aggressive action – even though each incident by itself would not trigger aggressive action. This kind of transference of anger from a first frustrating incident to a second implies that the link between frustration and aggression is more complex and indirect than initially proposed by Dollard and his associates, part of the complication being associated with the characteristics of the individuals involved, particularly those individuals experiencing frustration.

The traditional view has been that displaced aggression will be shown toward a soft third-party target, rather than a powerful authority figure who is the original source of frustration (such as Scott's boss). For example, Scott (in the example above) does not show aggression toward his boss, because if he did he would be punished and perhaps be fired from his job. Consequently, Scott displaces aggression onto his wife and child. But is this traditional view of displaced aggression fully accurate? Does this traditional view reflect the complexity of displaced aggression in everyday life? Probably not, because there are many different, particularly indirect, ways that minorities can be aggressive toward majorities.

For example, returning to the case of Scott, the traditional view is that he will displace aggression onto soft targets such as his wife and child. However, it is also possible that Scott will displace aggression, through sabotage, work disruptions, sneak attacks on the machinery, calling in sick, and other indirect means, onto an authority even more powerful than his boss, the company manager who hired his boss and backs up the latter in any kind of disagreement. The company manager could face many unexpected obstacles to meeting production goals as a result of displaced aggression. However, in such cases the source and means of displaced aggression may remain hidden; for example, the company management may not discover Scott's role and his motives for creating work disruptions.

This viewpoint provides an intriguing perspective for better understanding terrorism, such as the tragic attacks of 9/11. One interpretation of the 9/11 attacks is that they arose out of frustration with the situation in the Islamic world. Rather than attacking the corrupt and despotic rulers of Saudi Arabia and other such regimes, the terrorists targeted the US mainland. Thus, it could be argued that the terrorists displaced aggression onto a highly powerful foe, but did so in a sneaky way that involved subterfuge rather than open warfare. There are other important examples of displacement onto powerful out-groups, but they can only be understood through the consideration of power and the minority/majority status of groups, topics we further explore below.

Power and displaced aggression

Discussions of displaced aggression – from Freud, Dollard and his associates, to modern researchers – have given some attention to the power status of the target of displaced aggression and generally assumed the target to have less power, as in the case of Scott's wife and child (in the opening scenario). However, researchers have given less attention to the power status of the person or group who actually show displaced aggression (as Scott did). This neglect needs to be rectified, because the power of the person/group has important implications for the ways in which they can and do displace aggression.

Individuals and groups who have more power can displace aggression more directly, more openly, and in a more controlled manner. For example, when Scott returns home, he has the power to directly and openly displace aggression onto his wife and child. However, when his wife is frustrated by her life conditions and she wants to displace aggression onto Scott, she has fewer options. Since Scott is physically stronger than her, she can only take indirect action, such as socializing her son to disrespect his father and turning other relatives against Scott through gossip, innuendo, and other such tactics (of course, she can also call the police and try to get legal authorities involved on behalf of herself and her child).

But, as suggested by our discussion of Freud's inter-group psychology earlier in this chapter, there is also a subtle but important similarity between the displaced aggression manifested by majority and minority groups. In the case of both majority and minority groups, displaced aggression functions to increase group cohesion and solidify support behind the leadership. Numerous leaders have applied this idea to increase support for themselves and to silence internal critics: after all, when an enemy is threatening from the outside, it seems unpatriotic to criticize and weaken the leadership on the inside.

CRITICAL THINKING QUESTIONS

1 Can you think of a situation in which you have experienced frustration and anger but not become aggressive?

2 What are some of the ways in which a minority could displace aggression onto a majority?

CONCLUDING COMMENT

Freud conceived of displaced aggression as one of a number of defense mechanisms that could be used to ward off anxiety and to manage the negative emotions associated with libidinal ties. He viewed displaced aggression as a particularly powerful force at the inter-group level, in large part because group leaders can use displacement to strengthen in-group cohesion and get followers to rally around the flag. In Freud's psychology, displaced aggression is only one possible consequence of a goal being blocked, because he also envisages a role for other defense mechanisms in the management of negative feelings. Thus, in this sense Freud was not as mechanistic or deterministic as Dollard and his associates, who postulated that frustration always leads to some form of aggression. However, Freud was deterministic in that he believed repressed experiences would find an outlet, one way or another. The challenge, as Freud saw it, is to try to provide more constructive outlets (such as sports) for potentially destructive energies.

CRITICAL THINKING QUESTIONS

1 What role could the Olympics and other such international sporting events play in ending war?

2 Give an example of how the idea of displaced aggression could be used to explain a recent event in the news.

FURTHER READING

Berkowitz, L. (1965). The concept of aggressive drive: Some additional considerations. In L. Berkowitz (ed.), *Advances in Experimental Social Psychology*, Vol. 2. New York: Academic Press.

Berkowitz, L. (ed.) (1969). *Roots of aggression*. New York: Atherton Press.

Bushman, B. J., & Baumeister, R. F. (1998). Threatened egotism, narcissism, self-esteem, and direct and displaced aggression: Does self-love or self-hate lead to violence? *Journal of Personality and Social Psychology, 75*, 219–229.

Byrne, D. (1971). *The attraction paradigm*. New York: Academic Press.

Dollard, J., Bood, L., Miller, N., Mowrer, O., & Sears, R. (1939). *Frustration and aggression*. New Haven: Yale University Press.

Freud, S. (1921). Group psychology and the analysis of the ego. In J. Strachey (ed. and trans.), *The standard edition of the complete psychological works*, Vol. 18. London: Hogarth Press.

Freud, S. (1930). Civilization and its discontents. In J. Strachey (ed. and trans.), *The standard edition of the complete psychological works*, Vol. 21. London: Hogarth Press.

Marcus-Newhall, A., Pederson, W. C., Carlson, M., & Miller, N. (2000). Displaced aggression is alive and well: A meta-analytic review. *Journal of Personality and Social Psychology*, *78*, 670–689.

Melburg, V., & Tedeschi, J. T. (1989). Displaced aggression: Frustration or impression management? *European Journal of Social Psychology*, *19*, 139–145.

Miller, N., Pederson, W. C., Earlywine, M., & Pollock, V. E. (2003). A theoretical model of triggered displaced aggression. *Personality and Social Psychology Review*, *7*, 75–97.

Osbeck, L., Moghaddam, F. M., & Perreault, S. (1997). Similarity and attraction among majority and minority groups in a multicultural context. *International Journal of Intercultural Relations*, *21*, 113–123.

Pederson, W. C., Gonzales, C., & Miller, N. (2000). The moderating effect of trivial triggering provocation on displaced aggression. *Journal of Personality and Social Psychology*, *78*, 913–927.

Sherif, M. (1966). *Group conflict and cooperation: Their social psychology*. London: Routledge & Kegan Paul.

Tajfel, H. (ed.) (1982). *Social identity and intergroup relations*. Cambridge, England: Cambridge University Press.

Taylor, D. M., & Moghaddam, F. M. (1994). *Theories of intergroup relations: International social psychological perspectives*, 2nd edn. Westport, CT: Praeger.

13

PERSONALITY TRAITS

The science of psychology has at its center the concept of *personality*, the consistencies in behavior that characterize an individual. No concept is more central than is personality to the discipline of psychology, or more important in the research of the major psychologists. All of the most influential psychologists, including Sigmund Freud, Carl Jung, B. F. Skinner, Carl Rogers, Hans Eysenck, and Karen Horney, have contributed to the debate about the nature of personality. The concern with personality bridges the divide between practicing and researching psychologists, as well as between the major schools of psychology. The centrality of personality is also reflected in its impact on the wider public: among lay people, psychology is in many ways synonymous with ideas about personality, as reflected by the widespread use among the public, as well as in the popular media, of terms such as "ego," "extroversion," and "neuroticism."

Just as personality is central, it can also seem overwhelming. After all, personality encompasses the potentially infinite variety of ways in which individuals do things, how they think and solve problems, how they experience emotions, the style in which they interact with others, and their particular ways of self-reflection. How can we possibly deal with this vast array of information? And then there is the issue of change: in everyday life people do so many different things each day, and what they do tomorrow can differ in so many ways from what they did today and yesterday. How can we incorporate so much information in a way that will both help us arrive at a better theoretical understanding and lead to more effective practical interventions?

Modern psychology has arrived at a great idea for dealing with these challenges: reducing the complexity of behavior to a small number of traits, each trait encompassing long-lasting consistency in behavior. Many psychologists have concluded that human personality is captured in just five traits; an example of the five traits is *openness to experience*, the tendency to enjoy encountering new ideas, people, places, and so on (we discuss the details of the "Big Five" trait model later in this chapter). This means that, instead of being overwhelmed by the enormous variety and complexity of behavior that can come under the umbrella of "personality," psychologists now only need to deal with just five traits. Obviously, this makes the task of measuring and assessing personality far more manageable.

The reduction of personality to a small number of traits is a great achievement, but it is not without controversy. To explore this controversy is not to detract from the achievement of the trait approach to personality; rather, it is to recognize the many complex challenges that researchers face in the area of personality assessment. Trait research is a young endeavor within the young science of psychology, so although much has been achieved, in some respects we still have a long way to go. This discussion, then, is a report of work in progress on a great idea.

HISTORICAL BACKGROUND TO MODERN TRAIT THEORY

Historically, personality researchers have worked out and theorized about personality without limiting themselves to empirical evidence. As we discuss later in this chapter, however, a turn toward working in characterizes most of the recent psychological research. The challenge of reducing the complexity of personality was first systematically addressed in the classical era of Greek scholarship some twenty-five centuries ago. The main solution adopted by early researchers was to simplify and arrive at a classification of personality types, often linking personality with physical characteristics. Early examples of this approach are found in the classification system of Hippocrates (c. 400 B.C.) and its adaptation by Galen (c. A.D. 200). The resulting proposition is that the relative amounts of four bodily fluids determine the temperament of an individual. Too much black bile produces the melancholic (depressive) type; too much yellow bile produces the choleric (quickly angered, aggressive) type; excess of blood produces the sanguine (active and cheerful) type; and excess of phlegm results in the phlegmatic (easy-going and calm) type. The Hippocratic "Big Four" system remained influential even around the time of the Renaissance, but lost influence through advancements in science in the seventeenth and eighteenth centuries. After the industrial revolution, other classification systems evolved, attempting to link personality types with physiological differences.

In the nineteenth century, *phrenology*, the study of relations between the shape and contour of the skull and personality, gained influence, particularly through the work of Franz Gall (1758–1828). The basic assumption of phrenology was that different aspects of personality are located in different parts of the brain. The growth in size of brain parts indicates the extent to which a particular personality aspect has developed, and this will be reflected in the bumps and dips on the skull. For example, a person who is highly combative will have a bump in that part of the skull beneath which is the brain center for combativeness. Today students in psychology research methods courses learn that phrenology uses a method that is reliable (measurement of the bumps and dips gets the same results consistently) but not valid (the inferences made on the basis of the bumps and dips on the skull are incorrect). Phrenology represents an example of an approach to personality that gained influence for a time, but in hindsight is judged to be worthless.

Since the 1940s William Sheldon's "Big Three" classification of body types and their hypothesized associated temperaments has received more attention: the endomorphic (soft and round) body type is easy-going and sociable; the ectomorphic (tall, thin, sensitive nervous system) is introspective and creative; the mesomorphic (powerfully built, rectangular) is assertive and energetic. Although neither the four humors classification nor Sheldon's body type classification is used in psychology today, some of the underlying assumptions of their general approach are still with us. First, that inherited biological processes causally determine personality type. Second, that underlying factors cause long-lasting stability of behavior across situations.

In modern psychology, classification of "types" is based on personality *trait*, long-lasting consistency of behavior. Whereas historically the most influential classification systems had used physiological type to make assumptions about psychological type, as in the Hippocratic humors and Sheldon's body types, in the last few decades there has been a trend to use psychological typologies to make assumptions about physiological typologies. An example of this, influential since the 1970s, is the "Big Two" distinction between Type A and Type B personalities, which is used to try to predict coronary disease. Type As are more competitive, combative, impatient, striving, and driven to set and to meet tight deadlines. Type Bs are more relaxed and carefree, less likely to

multi-task, and less prone to coronary disease. In this case, then, personality traits serve as a basis for predictions about physiological outcomes.
To use terminology introduced in chapter 1, traits are assumed to reduce
degrees of freedom, so that the range of behavioral options for each
individual become reduced by traits.

Attempts to achieve effective predictions incorporating traits are
hampered by ambiguity about the nature of traits. In a sense, a trait is in
the eye of the beholder, and there are as many traits as there are ways to
describe behavior. The gradual trend since the early twentieth century has
been to reduce the number of traits from thousands to a handful, the most
agreed-upon number in contemporary research being five (although
researchers have not agreed about the particular five traits that should be
included). In the process of reviewing how this downsizing came about, it
is useful to highlight a number of dilemmas that have characterized
empirical research on personality traits. Each dilemma reflects different
possible research paths for exploring traits, and in each case there continues to be controversy about the path taken in traditional psychology.
These dilemmas are discussed below in two categories concerning: category 1, methodological issues; category 2, conceptual issues.

CATEGORY 1. METHODOLOGICAL DILEMMAS

The first three dilemmas more directly concern research methods:
whether to focus on words or actions, self-reports or other-reports, and
a fewer or greater number of traits.

There are a variety of possible methods that could be used to identify
and study traits. These include, first, the study of observable behavior
and the interpretation of traits based on direct observations; second, the
inference of traits based on observations made by those (e.g. family
members) who interact with the person included in the sample being
studied; third, the inference of traits based on self-reports. Only the
third possible method has been used extensively, with the consequence
that a number of dilemmas characterize the research on personality
traits.

Words vs. actions

Among the important questions faced by researchers are: Should
researchers studying traits focus on what people say, or on their

observable actions, or on both? What should be given priority when words and actions contradict one another?

The main method for studying personality traits has been to ask participants to rate the extent to which they see themselves accurately described by terms such as "reserved," "outgoing," "emotional," "shy," "suspicious," "shrewd," "assertive," "imaginative," and the like. Thus, the raw data of research on personality traits are derived overwhelmingly from verbal reports rather than from direct observation of behavior. After a researcher has been informed by Bob that Bob is assertive, for example, typically the researcher does not assess Bob's behavior to verify that Bob actually does act in an assertive way during interactions with others. The entire research project moves forward solely on the basis of Bob's word, and the self-reports of all other participants, about their own behavior. Some trait researchers have attempted to deal with this over-reliance on words. For example, Cattell in addition to using self-ratings did incorporate some ratings from observations of the participant in both everyday situations and more controlled, structured situations. However, the overall trend in trait research is the predominance of self-ratings.

Personality researchers face particular challenges that are also faced by researchers interested in the relationship between attitudes and behavior, because both groups of researchers have to deal with the complex and seemingly contradictory relationship between words and actions. Both personality researchers and attitude researchers rely on what people report about their behavior (words) to predict what they will do in the future (actions). Both attitude and personality research rely on participants completing self-report questionnaires about themselves. Consequently, we can learn about the relationship between words and actions in the realm of personality by looking at the relationship between words and actions in the realm of attitudes.

There is a long line of research on attitudes and behavior, suggesting that what people say does not always predict actual behavior (and, by implication, that self-reports of personality are not always accurate). For example, since the 1930s research has suggested that individuals who express negative attitudes toward minorities do not necessarily behave in a prejudiced manner when interacting with minorities (the reverse is also sometimes true, where individuals verbally report that they are not prejudiced against minorities, but nevertheless they do discriminate against minorities in practice). Although the early research of Robert LaPiere showing a weak link between words and action has rightly been faulted for methodological weaknesses, by the 1960s and 1970s a series of methodologically stronger studies had made the same basic point: what people say is not a reliable predictor of what they do. This critical literature was used by Walter Mischel and others in the late 1960s to argue that behavioral consistency is an illusion and a product of research methods, and later I discuss this issue further under the topic of "stability vs. change." For now, our focus remains on the relationship between words and actions.

In the 1970s and 1980s Icek Ajzen and Martin Fishbein spearheaded a spirited defense of the idea that expressed attitudes (a form of verbal self-report) do predict behavior. These researchers argued that in order to predict behavior on the basis of attitudes, certain methodological requirements have to be met. First, the measures of attitudes and behavior must be at the same level of specificity. For example, in order to predict the actual use of contraceptives by young people, measures must be taken of attitudes toward contraceptive use specifically (rather than attitudes toward general topics such as sexual behavior, religion, family life, and the like). Second, multiple measures of attitudes and behavior should be used, rather than single measures (as a general rule, single measures are less reliable than multiple measures in any kind of psychological testing). For example, if researchers are attempting to predict future condom use on the basis of attitudes, they should not just ask a single attitudinal question such as "Do you believe men should use condoms when they engage in sexual intercourse?" because it is likely to prove unreliable. Individuals may endorse this statement about condom use by people in general, but not endorse other statements about condom use by themselves personally, or condom use with partners who use other forms of contraceptives, for example.

Throughout the 1980s and 1990s, research accumulated to suggest that several other factors also improve the accuracy with which attitudes predict behavior. These include attitudes based on direct experience, attitudes attended to, and attitudes based on knowledge. For example, when Bob's attitudes toward condom use is arrived at through his personal experiences, when he is consciously thinking about his attitudes toward condom use, and when he has based his attitude on more information about condom use and safety in the age of AIDS, then his attitudes will better predict his actual condom use. Thus, there is now greater confidence among researchers that under certain methodological conditions, expressed attitudes can effectively predict behavior. The new optimism is based on a rationalist view of behavior, that assumes humans form attitudes in a thoughtful way, and such attitudes lead to predictable behavior. In essence, the nature of behavior is assumed to be a logical consequence of the nature of attitudes.

But the rationalist approach to understanding the association between self-reports and behavior is culturally limited, partly because it is shaped by the distinct ideals of the Western societies out of which it evolved. The assumption that there is a direct rational link between what people say about themselves and their actions reflects a Western ideal, "a man is as good as his word," popularized in cowboy movies starring the likes of John Wayne and Clint Eastwood. The heroes in such movies say what they mean and do what they say. They do not tolerate contradictions within themselves and they fight to wipe away contradictions in the wider society. The same assumption of harmony between words and actions underlies a number of major psychological theories, such as cognitive dissonance theory (which assumes that individuals experience discomfort when they become aware of having incongruent cognitions, and are motivated to end the discomfort by changing their thoughts and/or actions to end the perceived incongruity) that have evolved as part of Western psychology.

The Russian psychologist Alexander Luria has provided fascinating examples of thinking among unschooled people in Central Asia, and how they work through issues in a way that seems to Westerners to be contradictory. For example, from a Western perspective, the question "Which is the odd item from the following: a hammer, a saw, a log, and a hatchet?" has an obvious answer: the log, because the other three are tools. But an answer Luria received from his Central Asian participants is that none of these is the odd one out, because the saw has to saw the log, the hammer to hammer it, the hatchet to chop it. From this perspective, it is logical to think of each tool in relation to the log.

The exploration of apparent contradictions in thinking among non-Western people leads us to reflect back on behavior in Western societies. In a Western context, also, there are many instances where people live with apparent contradictions between words and actions. They often deal with contradictions by keeping them in separate spheres. For example, some tough-minded scientists who demand hard evidence before they believe a scientific theory put aside such demands and criteria in the realm of spirituality. They are ready to have faith in spirituality without hard evidence. But there are numerous more blatant and explicit examples of words contradicting actions: in some situations participants describe themselves in one way and behave in a different way either because they do not have an accurate picture of their own behavior, or because they prefer to describe themselves in a way that they see as more positive. Both of these are elaborated in discussions below

Self-reports vs. other-reports

Among other questions central to modern personality research are: Should researchers rely on self-reports? After all, are people not the best judge of their own characteristics? Or, alternatively, are individuals fundamentally biased in their self-perceptions, and a poor guide to their own psychological characteristics?

Since the 1970s a series of theories and studies have challenged the idea that we know ourselves better than other people know us. The implication is that research on personality traits has been misdirected in relying on self-reports rather than reports by others. The idea that we are strangers to ourselves seems counter-intuitive but is supported by some intriguing theories and studies. First, there is the notion that our information about ourselves comes from the same source as our information about others. Daryl Bem has argued that we know both ourselves and other people by observing behavior. The professor returns home by bus from campus, forgetting that he drove his car to work in the morning. When his wife suggests he is forgetful, the professor thinks about his behavior and agrees that he fits the stereotype. He walks back to campus to collect his car, drinks a lot of water on the way, and concludes that he must have been very thirsty. In each case, his view of himself is based directly on his behavior. While Bem's theory is in line with behaviorism (see chapter 6) and rejects the idea that we need to incorporate cognitive processes in an adequate explanation of how we understand ourselves, another body of research does incorporate cognition and explores how we mis-perceive ourselves when we look within our own minds.

Also directly relevant to the self-report method used in personality research is the argument that even though we have privileged access to information about ourselves that is not available to us about others, our perceptions of ourselves are often inaccurate. For example, in a classic study Richard Nisbett and Timothy Wilson asked participants to select one of four nightgowns, as part of what was purportedly a survey of consumer preferences. Participants showed a preference for items placed on the right to those placed on the left, and this is in line with research showing that people manifest this bias in these kinds of choices. The clear implication is that people are affected by the position of the item. However, when asked to explain their choices, participants gave all kinds of other reasons for their choices and dismissed the notion that their choice may actually have been influenced by serial position.

Since the 1970s the research of Nobel Prize winner Daniel Kahneman and colleague Amos Tversky has shown the many ways in which people make biased, typically over-confident estimations of their own accuracy in perceiving the world. It seems that how confident we feel about the accuracy of our perceptions does not correlate highly with how accurate we actually are. The same seems to apply to our own perceptions of our own behavior, as suggested by the research of Robert Vallone and others. For example, how confident we are about whether we shall complete a course, live off campus, or declare a major does not correlate highly with our accuracy in predicting our behavior. We are, then, forced to question our ability to report accurately on ourselves.

Fewer vs. greater number of traits

Among other questions central to modern personality research are the following: How many traits are sufficient to capture the essentials of human personality? Should we try to arrive at a list that has as few traits as possible, or should we include as many traits as possible?

In theory, one could identify as many personality traits as there are words to describe behavior. One way to identify all such words is to examine a standard dictionary, such as Webster's. This is exactly what Gordon Allport (1897–1967) did with help of colleagues, compiling a list of over eighteen thousand words. Allport is considered the major pioneer of research on personality traits, but, as we shall see in the next section, research on traits took a direction that was very different from his original intentions. Whereas Allport believed research should focus on individuals, traditional psychological research has concentrated on general trends.

After the identification of thousands of trait words, a major challenge was to reduce the number on the assumption that this was the best way to make research on traits more practical and meaningful. One strategy was to categorize the traits; for example, Allport distinguished between three types of traits, from most to least pervasive and foundational in personality: cardinal traits, central traits, and secondary traits. Allport's approach was in large part intuitive and based on individual case studies rather than psychometric and based on research with large samples. The psychometric tradition of research on traits was spearheaded in the twentieth century by Raymond Cattell and Hans Eysenck.

Cattell was born in England and studied for his doctorate in psychology at University College, London, where he became influenced by two research traditions established by Francis Galton (1822–1911), Cyril Burt (1883–1971), and Karl Pearson (1857–1936). The first tradition involved a heavy reliance on statistical procedures to explore relationships between personality traits. Galton and Pearson had pioneered correlation techniques, and for a while Cattell worked directly with Pearson. A second tradition involved heavy emphasis on inherited characteristics. This has led to the accumulation of evidence showing that monozygotic (identical) twins are more similar to one another than are dizygotic (fraternal) twins with respect to a number of traits, particularly extraversion. Also, evidence suggests that personality characteristics are not learned by children imitating their parents.

Cattell relied heavily on powerful statistical procedures, particularly factor analysis, to try to identify the common themes he assumed underlie human personality. He reduced the thousands of trait words Allport had started with to just sixteen factors or "themes." The resulting list forms the basis of Cattell's widely used Sixteen Personality Factor Test (16 PF). Examples of important themes in this test are "reserved–outgoing," "less intelligent – more intelligent," and "emotional–stable." Although Cattell emphasized inherited characteristics, he argued that the 16 PF could be used to assess how much patients have been changed through therapy.

A further step toward further reducing personality traits was taken by Eysenck, who worked in the same psychometric tradition as Cattell; a tradition heavily reliant on data gathering using self-report questionnaires, and placing primary emphasis on inherited characteristics. Eysenck's approach in personality assessment is particularly interesting because he not only attempts to develop a more succinct picture of personality structure but also proposes a hierarchy of elements in the structure. The elements are, from bottom up: habits, traits, and types. The starting-point, the "ground level," for this hierarchy is observable responses, such as occasions when a person declines an offer to attend a party, eats alone, spends time reading rather than socializing with others, and the like. Correlations between habitual responses form the basis of traits, such as being withdrawn, low on sociability, reserved, and quiet. In turn, traits act as the basis for types. In this example, traits such as "withdrawn, low on sociability, reserved, and quiet" would suggest an introverted type.

On the basis of extensive research Eysenck concluded that personality is characterized by three dimensions: introversion/extroversion, stability/neuroticism, and impulse-control/psychoticism. The first of these, introversion/extroversion, had been pioneered by the Swiss psychoanalyst Carl Jung, but Eysenck claimed that his own use of introversion/extroversion was not only different in content but also based on empirical evidence, whereas Jung had remained an "armchair psychologist." In modern personality research, introverts are seen as reserved and introspective, whereas extroverts are outgoing and sociable. The second dimension, stability/neuroticism, is primarily related to heightened and often exaggerated anxiety in the minds of neurotic individuals. The third dimension, impulse-control/psychoticism, is largely concerned with impulsivity and sensitivity in relationships with others. Eysenck's most important research instrument, the Eysenck Personality Questionnaire (EPQ), has been translated and used in research in many different cultures, and largely on this basis it is proposed that the three dimensions of personality identified by Eysenck are universal.

On the matter of universal traits, since the research of Warren Norman in the 1960s there has gradually emerged an even more influential view than Eysenck's; the new view being encapsulated by the slogan "Big Five." There has been some disagreement over the years as to which particular traits should be included in the Big Five, but since the 1990s the consensus seems to be on the following: agreeableness (the extent to which a person is gentle/rough, good-natured/irritable, and so on), consciousness (the extent to which a person is responsible/irresponsible, carefree/careless, and so on), introversion/extroversion (the degree to which a person is outgoing, sociable, and so on), neuroticism (the degree to which a person is calm/anxious, composed/excitable, and so on), and openness to experience (the extent to which a person is imaginative/simple, intellectual/unreflective, and so on).

Although personality traits is a great idea, we should be cautious in assuming that the Big Five is the final word with respect to the number of universal traits. To assume that the Big Five is the final word would be to disregard historical and cultural experience. Even when researchers in other cultures use basically the same traditional psychometric methods as used to arrive at the Big Five, the results can be different. For example, using traditional Western psychometric procedures, Fanny Cheung and others developed the *Chinese Personality Assessment Inventory* (CPAI), and found an 'inter-personal relatedness' dimension not identified by researchers starting with a research instrument developed in Western societies. Looking back at the history of traits, the clear trend is for researchers to reduce the number of traits used to assess personality, but it is not clear how many traits are necessary to capture the essence of personality. Is it sixteen? Two? Six? Ten? The past suggests that the numbers and nature of the traits identified will continue to vary as a result of changing cultural and historical circumstances.

CRITICAL THINKING QUESTIONS

1 In what ways are the classical typologies of personality (e.g. Hippocrates' four humors) similar to modern trait models (such as the Big Five), and how are they different?

2 The assessment of personality traits has been heavily dependent on self-reports. Discuss the most important advantage, as well as the most serious disadvantage, of this approach.

CATEGORY 2. CONCEPTUAL DILEMMAS

The second set of dilemmas concern more abstract, conceptual decisions about interpretations of: cause and effect, stability and change, and individual uniqueness versus group averages.

Causes vs. effects

A first question is: Are traits causes or effects? For example, if a person is described as "aggressive," is aggressiveness a cause of certain types of behavior, or an effect of some underlying characteristic?

In everyday life we often attribute a trait to a person, then use the same trait to explain that person's behavior. For example, we describe Mary as "shy" in her manner of interacting with other people. Later, when someone asks why Mary has moved away from the dance floor and is standing in a corner, we respond "because Mary is shy." In essence, we use "shyness" as both cause and effect in our explanations. The challenge of avoiding this circularity extends to the research arena.

A fundamental dilemma underlies all research on personality traits: on the one hand a trait directly or indirectly depends on words used to describe observable behavior, but on the other hand a trait is also explicitly assumed to be an underlying cause of behavior. One way to try to overcome circularity is to develop a conceptual scheme that distances overt or "surface" behavior from assumed underlying causes or "sources." This is the approach Cattell adopted, distinguishing between *surface traits*, clusters of observable actions that are associated with one another, and *source traits*, the underlying causes of surface traits. Eysenck's distinction between habits, traits, and types attempts to achieve the same goal, of avoiding the circularity of identifying the same trait as both cause and effect.

Unfortunately trait research is mired in confusions about cause and effect. Critics have pointed out that constructs such as Cattell's surface and source traits and Eysenck's habits, traits, and types are simply different ways of describing behavior. Consistencies in behavior descriptions, across contexts and/or across situations, do not necessarily signify causes. This criticism is particularly damning when we consider that the consistencies in question are largely based on self-reports, which involve self-presentation. An important point in this regard is that self-presentation is explained by normative accounts rather than causal ones. That is, what people say about themselves is explained by their interpretations of what is appropriate for them to say about themselves in a given circumstance.

Stability vs. change

Other questions that need to be addressed are: Should researchers focus on behavioral stability or change? The concept of personality traits emphasizes stability in behavior, but should we ignore behavioral changes across situations and over time?

In our everyday lives, although we may view each person as unique, we typically view personality as consistent across contexts. This may in part be because we tend to interact with others in the same kinds of contexts and roles over and over again. For example, Ms. Rothgerber meets with her students in class each day at 10:30–11:30. The students notice that Ms. Rothgerber behaves in a consistent way each day in class, and the behavior of the students seems consistent to Ms. Rothgerber. Even when they meet Ms. Rothgerber outside class, they still view her as "teacher" and Ms. Rothgerber sees them as "students." Their expectations of one another are to some extent responsible for behavioral consistency, according to prescribed roles. But our general tendency is to explain behavior through reference to the characteristics of the person rather than the situation. We expect people to behave consistently, because of the generally held cultural assumption that individuals are responsible for their own behavior. Research by Joan Miller and others suggests that in some traditional Eastern cultures, the causes of behavior are ascribed more to the situation and circumstances of events, and less to factors within the individual.

The search for a causal account and for stability in personality is undoubtedly influenced by *bodily individualism*, the physical separateness of each person across situations. We see Martha as she arrives at work, then while she is having lunch, and later as she steps into a train to go home. She is a separate entity, moving from one situation to another. Physically she is the same person, separate from others, from one situation to the next. It makes sense for us to assume that, just as physically there is stability in her characteristics from one situation to another, there is also stability in what we call "personality." Traits as "causes" lead her to behave consistently across situations, so it is assumed.

But the assumption that personality is causally shaped to be stable runs counter to some important movements in both theoretical and applied psychology. For example, in humanistic psychology considerable emphasis is placed on "personality growth" and "self-actualization" throughout the life-span. This alternative perspective emphasizing change in personality is in agreement with some Eastern perspectives, such as the Hindu and Buddhist traditions. A number of leading personality texts now reflect this "growth" and "change" perspective (e.g. Fadiman & Frager, 2002).

In the applied domain, it is instructive to ask: What is the goal of therapy? Although there are many different schools of therapy, supporters of all schools surely would agree on one point: therapy is an attempt to change behavior patterns, so that patients/clients come consistently to behave in ways that differ from how they were behaving. A major way to assess the effectiveness of therapy is to examine how much desirable change has taken place in patient/client behavior. Of course, effective therapy brings about long-term rather than short-term change. In short, therapy is intended to change people, so that we would expect them to complete self-report personality questionnaires differently after therapy compared with before therapy.

This raises a thorny issue concerning how we should interpret the results of the standard structured personality assessment tests, such as the Minnesota Multiphasic Personality Inventory (MMPI) and the

California Personality Inventory (CPI), and the most commonly used projective tests, such as the Rorschach and the Thematic Apperception Test (TAT). Structured tests ask specific, closed-ended questions and require specific answers (e.g. "Do you sleep well at nights?" Answer: yes/no); projective tests require open-ended answers to ambiguous stimuli or questions. For example, a participant is shown an ambiguous picture of several people interacting and asked to interpret the situation through questions such as: "What led to this scene? What is going on now? What will happen next?" If we begin with the assumption that personality is stable and causally determined by underlying traits, then changes in test scores on structured tests from one test session to the next presumably indicate low reliability of the test instrument.

Received wisdom tells us that projective tests are less reliable than structured tests, because scores on projective tests tend to vary more than do scores on structured tests from one test session to the next. However, an alternative interpretation is that projective tests are more sensitive to identifying changes in personality. If we start with the assumption that personality changes over time and across contexts, then when they are administered multiple times structured tests may lead to more similar scores than projective tests because structured tests fail to identify changes in personality.

The idea that change is normal and healthy in personality development is central not only to humanistic psychology but also to psychoanalysis as pioneered by Freud. From these perspectives, changes in personality come about as part of healthy growth, which is arrested only when relationships and psychological experiences go wrong. The clear implication is that healthy individuals should register change when they take personality tests at different times in their lives.

Idiographic vs. nomothetic

A final question concerns individuality: should each person be studied as a unique individual, or should psychologists ignore uniqueness and focus exclusively on trends in populations?

Each of us tends to think of ourself as a unique individual, as being different from other people. Typically, we do not like our individuality to be ignored or dismissed. In the legal arena, each individual is judged as a separate case, without regard to group membership. For example, racial profiling is now banned, because it is seen as treating individuals as category members rather than as independent persons. Thus, both in terms of our informal everyday experiences of how we would like to be treated by others and in terms of formal law, the correct approach is to treat each person as a separate and independent case.

This is in line with the idiographic approach to studying personality, whereby each individual in studied on a unique case. Allport was among the prominent psychologists who supported this approach and provided examples of how idiographic studies could be conducted. For example, Allport analyzed the letters of a single individual and had independent judges assess her personality in terms of traits. Allport adopted a first typology of traits based on breadth: cardinal traits are the most extensive in how much of a person's behavior they cover; central traits are less extensive; and secondary traits are the least extensive. For example, a person may be power-hungry (cardinal trait), be interested in politics as a way of gaining power (central trait), and prefer to use TV rather than direct face-to-face meetings to get his or her message across (secondary trait). Allport also made a distinction between common traits, shared more or less by everyone, and personal dispositions, which are unique to individuals. His argument was that psychologists should focus on personal dispositions, because only in this way can we arrive at an adequate understanding of individual personality. This is because individual uniqueness is reflected more in personal dispositions.

Despite the efforts of Allport and others, the nomothetic approach, based in general trends of populations, has become the dominant one in psychology. Defenders of the nomothetic approach contend that it is only by exploring personality traits among large samples of people that we can arrive at universals. The idiographic approach, they argue, leads to in-depth understanding of individuals, but fails to inform about universals and consequently fails to meet a key criterion for a science of psychology. A further criticism is that the idiographic method is so labor intensive that only a small number of case studies can be completed, whereas the nomothetic approach can incorporate data from much larger populations.

But what of the claim that the nomothetic approach has led to the identification of universals, such as the supposedly universal Big Five traits? A first point is that when considered historically, the Big Five follows a tradition of researchers in each age claiming that their system of categorizing and systematizing personality is universal, from the Hippocratic Big Four to more recent variations, such as the Big Two of Type A and Type B. A second point, more specific and concerning methodology, is that the so-called Big Five has emerged in the context of

Western societies and is culturally limited. Claims that the Big Five have been tested cross-culturally should be considered very critically, because typically such "cross-cultural validation" has involved including samples of Westernized students from the affluent modern sector of non-Western societies. These students typically have a life-style that is very similar to that of Western students (they wear the same clothes, read the same books, listen to the same music, watch the same films, and so on) but is very different from the traditional sectors of their own non-Western societies. In the traditional sector, people tend to be rural dwelling, illiterate, poorer, more religious, living in extended families, and unlike Westerners in self-presentation. For most people in the traditional sector, an MMPI form would represent a cultural shock and be unlikely to yield to a confirmation of the Big Five. The nomothetic approach would, at the least, yield different results in traditional sectors of non-Western societies.

Perhaps one solution to the idiographic vs. nomothetic debate is to adopt both approaches, but to emphasize one or the other depending on the questions that need to be addressed. Questions about population trends could be more appropriately addressed through a nomothetic approach, whereas questions about the personality of specific individuals could better be addressed through an idiographic approach.

CRITICAL THINKING QUESTIONS

1 From your everyday experiences can you give examples of how your behavior changes across contexts?

2 What do you see as the most important advantage and disadvantage of the nomothetic approach?

CONCLUDING COMMENT

The search for universal classifications of personality is not new. What is new is the great idea that personality can be reduced to traits, and the powerful statistical treatments given to large data sets from different samples, in order to arrive at a small number of traits. A widely popular model proposes that five major traits are universal and sufficient to characterize personality. The nomothetic approach that has led to the Big Five traits model emphasizes characteristics common to many

people. The alternative idiographic approach emphasizes the uniqueness of each individual but has received relatively little attention, except
in the practical everyday work of therapists and counselors. Future
research may show that a fusion of the nomothetic and idiographic
approaches represents the best path forward.

CRITICAL THINKING QUESTIONS

1 What kinds of questions can be better answered through an idiographic
rather than a nomothetic approach?

2 What implications does the idea of "personality growth" have for the
measurement of personality, and particularly the reliability of
personality tests?

FURTHER READING

Ajzen, I. (1988). *Attitudes, personality, and behavior.* Chicago: Dorsey Press.

Allport, G. W. (1961). *Patterns and growth in personality.* New York: Holt,
Rinehart & Winston.

Allport, G. W. (1965). *Letters from Jenny.* New York: Harcourt, Brace & World.

Cheung, F. M., Cheung, S. F., Leung, K., Ward, C., & Leung, F. (2003). The
English version of the Chinese Personality Assessment Inventory. *Journal of
Cross-Cultural Psychology, 34,* 433–452.

Eysenck, H. J. (ed.) (1982). *Personality, genetics, and behavior: Selected papers.*
New York: Praeger.

Eysenck, H. J. (1990). Biological dimensions of personality. In L. A. Pervin (ed.),
Handbook of personality: Theory and research. New York: Guilford Press.

Jung, C. G. (1976). *Psychological types,* ed. R. F. C. Hull and trans. H. G. Baynes.
Princeton: Princeton University Press.

Fadiman, J., & Frager, R. (2002). *Personality & personal growth,* 5th edn. Upper
Saddle River, NJ: Prentice Hall.

Fishbein, M., & Ajzen, I. (1975). *Belief, attitude, intention, and behavior: An
introduction to theory and research.* Reading, MA: Addison-Wesley.

Kahneman, D., & Tversky, A. (1979). Intuitive prediction: Biases and corrective
procedures. *Management Science, 12,* 313–327.

Loehlin, J. C. (1992). *Genes and environment in personality development.*
Newbury Park, CA: Sage.

Lake, R. I. E., Eaves, L. J., Maes, H. H. M., Heath, A. C., & Martin, N. G. (2000). Further evidence against the environmental transmission of individual differences in neuroticism from a collaborative study of 45,850 twins and relatives on two continents. *Behavior Genetics, 30*, 223–233.

Luria, A. R. (1974/1976). *Cognitive development: Its cultural and social foundations*, trans. M. Lopez-Morillas & L. Solotaroff. Cambridge, MA: Harvard University Press.

Miller, J. G., Bersoff, D. M., & Harwood, R. L. (1990). Perceptions of social responsibility in India and the United States: Moral imperatives or personal decisions? *Journal of Personality and Social Psychology, 58*, 33–47.

Mischel, W. (1986). *Introduction to personality*. New York: Holt, Rinehart & Winston.

Nisbett, R. E., & Wilson, T. D. (1977). Telling more than we know: Verbal reports on mental processes. *Psychological Review, 84*, 231–259.

Norman, W. T. (1963). Toward an adequate taxonomy of personality attributes: Replicated factor structure in peer nomination personality ratings. *Journal of Abnormal and Social Psychology, 66*, 574–583.

Ryckman, R. M. (1997). *Theories of personality*, 6th edn. Pacific Grove, CA: Brooks/Cole.

Vallone, R. P., Griffin, D. W., Lin, S., & Ross, L. (1990). Overconfident prediction of future actions and outcomes by self and others. *Journal of Personality and Social Psychology, 58*, 582–592.

14
THE SELF

As you read this chapter, you can think about yourself reading this chapter. As you think about each idea you encounter, you can think about yourself thinking about the ideas you encounter. How is it possible for you to think about yourself reading and reflecting? Does this imply you have two selves, one looking over the shoulder of the other?

Questions such as these concern the nature of the *self*, the totality of personal experiences. Given the centrality of the self to human experience, one might imagine that the study of the self has always been integral to psychology. But this is far from the case. The self has had a very uneven history in modern psychology, despite the pioneering work of William James (1842–1910). In his monumental text *Principles of Psychology* (1890), James discussed different facets of the self extensively. But the attention given directly to the self by James was the exception rather than the rule. Although the self was not often the direct subject of study in the nineteenth century, the introspective methods adopted by Wundt (1832–1920) and his students in the second half of the nineteenth century at least indirectly explored aspects of the self, such as images and memory. Moreover, in his "second psychology," the folk or cultural psychology that took place outside the laboratory, Wundt examined social processes that help to shape the self.

While Wundt and his students, particularly Tichener (1868–1927), strongly influenced academic psychology, Freud (1856–1939) influenced academics, practitioners, and society in general, first in Europe and then in North America, particularly after his 1909 journey to the United States and the increased availability of his work in English. Freud's psychology can be considered an exploration of the inner self, with emphasis on those parts of the self, the unconscious, that remain hidden but can be brought to light through psychoanalysis (see chapter 5). Freud's psychoanalytic methods can be seen as designed to help individuals to discover their "true selves" more fully, by becoming aware of the unconscious motives, wishes, and so on that actually influence their behavior. According to Freud, the discovery of the true self proves to be extremely difficult in practice, because during early development individuals come to suppress wishes, feelings, motives, and other experiences that conflict with the moral order of their societies. One of the costs of "becoming civilized," then, is that aspects of the self are repressed.

A number of influential scholars who branched off from Freudian psychology placed greater emphasis than did Freud on the role of social interactions in the development of a self. Particularly influential was the work of Harry Sullivan (1892–1949), who highlighted the role of inter-personal relations in shaping personality and the self. Sullivan saw maladaptive behavior as being rooted in anxiety-arousing aspects of inter-personal relations, such as insufficient love and support for a young child. Karen Horney (1885–1952) also gave particular importance to the role of social relationships in the formation of the self, arguing that feminine and masculine selves arise out of cultural processes. She explicitly rejected Freud's views on male–female characteristics, which depict women as being deficient in various ways, such as their supposed "penis envy."

While Freud's psychology had tremendous influence on most aspects of societies, eventually even in the lower-income and less literate regions of the world, academic psychology took a dramatically different turn starting from the second decade of the twentieth century (see chapter 6). The emergence of behaviorism as the dominant force in academic psychology, after the 1913 launch of this school by J. B. Watson, meant a dramatic decline in interest in the self in the psychology departments of major universities. As the influence of behaviorism increased, research on the self decreased. This is because of the insistence on the part of behaviorists that in order to become a true science psychology must focus only on behavior that can directly be observed, objectively measured, and publicly verified. All references to "mind," "thinking," "self," and other supposed characteristics of an "inner world," the subjective and the private within persons, must be discarded because, the behaviorists argued, it is not possible to objectively verify and measure such characteristics. The self became an outcast, shunned by most research psychologists for about half a century. It was not until the 1960s, with the decline of behaviorism, that the spotlight once again was cast on the self in academic psychology.

The re-emergence of the self owed, to some extent, to the influence of humanistic psychology, and particularly the pioneers Abraham Maslow (1908–70) and Carl Rogers (1902–87). Maslow has been particularly influential through his ideas on a "hierarchy of needs," arguing that individuals are motivated to satisfy needs in a stepwise fashion: from basic physiological (e.g. food and water), safety, and love needs, to acquiring positive esteem, and finally self-actualization, which is the flowering of a person's full potential. Self-actualization is not achieved by everyone. The theme of growth and "becoming" of the self was also central to the psychology of Gordon Allport (1897–1968). This emphasis on the growth of a self to its full potential as the ultimate goal of development is also reflected in the work of Carl Rogers. Each individual, Rogers argued, is a unique being, inclined toward growth, rationality, and wholeness. The Rogerian therapeutic technique, so-called "client-centered therapy," uses the concept of self as a unifying theme and has the growth of self as its goal. Thus, humanistic psychologists working in the first half of the twentieth century were also instrumental in re-introducing the self to psychology.

Since the 1960s research on the self has been influenced by a number of important trends in international psychology. First, the rise of cognitive psychology as the dominant school of psychology has been associated with the "return of the mind" and renewed interest in cognitive processes. The "cognitive revolution" meant that it was once again respectable for academic psychologists to examine topics such as the self. Second, the social constructionist movement (see chapter 20) led to an interest in the construction of the self and questions concerning the relationship between the self and context, as well as narratives about the self. This includes questions about how the self may vary across cultures. Third, feminist, ethnic, gay, and other minority movements since the 1960s have been associated with a concern with "esteem," both personal and collective. The issue of self esteem has been at the forefront of political, educational, and social debates. Various applied programs have been developed to try to protect or "save" individuals from assumed low self esteem. These movements have led to an enormous psychological literature on the self, including hundreds of books and thousands of papers, in addition to dozens of psychological scales designed to measure different aspects of the self, including self and collective esteem.

More broadly, the return of the self to mainstream psychology owes to complex cultural movements. For example, baby-boomers have been known as the "me generation" and it is not coincidental that the focus on the self arose at a time when baby-boomers in Western academia reached middle age and became particularly influential as researchers and professors. Another factor influencing the increased focus on the self has been the widespread political debate about the self-esteem of women, ethnic minorities, seniors, and other power minorities. Associated with these trends has been a rise in interest not only in the self in psychology but also in autobiography in literature. Since the 1980s in particular the bestseller lists on both sides of the Atlantic have been amply populated by autobiographies in which individuals self-reflect and self-analyze in a "tell all" fashion. There are no signs of the interest in the self abating. Indeed, the idea of the self remains important and central to psychology, and surely this is how it should be. One important reason is that the self is the reference point of all our experiences, and this is important for cognition. For example, we remember things better when we relate them back to the self – as students well know, because a lot of them use this "self-referencing" strategy to remember material in tests. New brain-imaging technologies may well lead to even greater focus on the self, as researchers explore the parts of the brain that are activated in association with different types of self-reflection.

But is the self a great idea, or were the behaviorists right in insisting that the self (and other such topics) be excluded from the science of psychology? Is it possible for researchers studying the self to work in, or must they always rely on working out and developing ideas independent of empirical evidence? Are there restrictions on how the self can be constructed, or are there limits to the degrees of freedom in this realm? Let us begin by considering the sense of self, then discuss self-perception and self-presentation. At each step it becomes apparent that, although some very innovative experimental studies have been conducted regarding the self, major conceptual puzzles remain.

THE SENSE OF SELF

Are we born with a sense of self, or does a sense of self develop within us over time? In exploring the developmental aspects of the sense of self, an intriguing discovery was made when researchers placed a red dot on the noses of infants and then placed mirrors in front of the infants. Human infants eighteen months and older touched the red spot on their noses (the only other creatures capable of this feat are the great apes), and this was taken as a sign that these infants recognized themselves in the mirror. Received wisdom informs us that this research shows the sense of self develops at around eighteen months in humans. When they are younger than this age, infants fail to touch the red dot on their noses when they look into the mirror, and this is taken to mean that they fail to see that "it is me with the red dot on my nose in the mirror." But there are reasons why one might question this interpretation.

In the debate about the development of a sense of self, a great deal hinges on what we accept as a valid indicator of a sense of self. When an infant learns to cry out for attention, must there not already be a sense of "this is me crying out, and it is me who is soon going to receive attention"? When the mother comes to the infant with milk and the infant begins to feed, must there not already be a sense of self at least as a being existing in a specific location in space and time? However, it could be argued that crying, feeling hungry, and the like are inborn behaviors that do not require a sense of self. Thus, the infant who learns to cry to get attention need not necessarily have a sense of self.

But another type of infant behavior seems to provide more solid evidence of the early appearance of a sense of self. Research on infants only a few minutes old shows they can repeat an act carried out by another human, such as poking their tongues out in response to watching an adult poke her or his tongue out. This type of behavior may be described as mere "reactivity," but it can also be interpreted as indicating true imitation behavior. In order for imitation to take place, it could be argued that the infant has to have a sense of "another" and a "self." Imitation implies that the infant has a sense of "this is me, imitating that other." However, we need to be careful with this line of argument because animals can mimic, but this does not necessarily mean that they have a sense of self in the same way that humans do.

If, as I am suggesting, the sense of self is present much earlier than eighteen months of age, then why do infants who have a red spot placed on their noses not touch their noses when placed in front of mirrors? One possibility is that the so-called "rouge test," of whether or not an infant touches the red spot, is not a sensitive enough test of the infant's sense of self. It may also be that the rouge test tells us more about the way infants interact with mirrors, and their limited understanding of the physics of mirrors, than about an infant's sense of self. Perhaps a sense of self may manifest itself in other, more subtle ways before it becomes apparent through cruder indicators such as the rouge test.

Beyond the question of when a sense of self first emerges, fundamental questions arise concerning possible universals with respect to a sense of self. A key universal characteristic of the sense of self seems to be that the self resides in one body. The belief of "one body, one self" is taken to be normal across societies, so that in most or perhaps all societies a person reporting more than one self in a single body would be judged to be mentally ill. Indeed, according to the "demonic" interpretation of insanity, highly influential in most Western societies well into the nineteenth century, a person becomes mad when evil powers enter his or her body and take control. In order to drive the demons away, a cure was to make the body so uncomfortable – through beatings, submersion in water, and the like – that the evil powers would leave. A cured person would once again have a single self in a single body. In some cultural contexts particular individuals are thought to be possessed or "visited" by good spirits (e.g. Christian saints visited and guided by angels). But all these are exceptional cases to the general rule of a single self in a single body.

On the other hand, the idea of a single self in a single body seems to be challenged by our everyday experiences. As indicated at the start of this chapter, each of us is capable of reflecting back on our own self. As I sit thinking about the sentences I write, I can reflect back on "me," the "myself" doing the writing. This I/me distinction, with the "I" as the narrator and the "me" as the subject of narration, seems to suggest that there indeed are two selves within my body. However, this is an example of how the language we use can mislead us. The fact there are two terms in English, "I" and "me," that can refer to the self does not mean that there are multiple selves. In Farsi, the same term, *khod,* can at times refer to both "me" and "you," but that does not mean we are the same self. Rather, it is another example of how the language we use can mislead us.

It becomes clear that the 'I' and the 'me' are referring to the same unitary self when we consider that it is impossible to focus on both at the same time. This is sometimes referred to as the problem of the "fleeting I": as soon as one focuses on the "I" it becomes the "me." This is akin to seeing Venus in the eastern sky at sunrise and calling it the "morning star," then seeing Venus in the western sky at sunset and calling it the "evening star," and concluding that there must be two different stars, a morning star and an evening star.

Another probable universal with respect to the sense of self is continuity. When you woke up this morning, you did not ask yourself, "Who am I?" You assumed you were the same person who went to bed last night in the same body. When other people meet you in the morning, they too assume that your body has the same self within it; that there is continuity in your self. In some languages, such as Kawi (old Javanese), the idea of temporal contiguity is more explicitly introduced (e.g. "The I who is in class today is happy that the I of yesterday remembered mother's birthday," as opposed to saying in English, "I am happy I remembered mother's birthday yesterday").

The sense of self no doubt has social origins, but the essential feeling "that I exist" is a requirement for human social life. A person may experience doubt, and even misgivings and forgetfulness, about *who* they are, but not *that* they are. Even people experiencing memory loss know that they exist.

CRITICAL THINKING QUESTIONS

1 Give an example of how language can mislead in our understanding of the self.

2 Why is it important that continuity of the self be a human universal?

SELF-PERCEPTION

How do we come to see ourselves? In the realm of self-perception some of our most comfortable assumptions have been challenged by psychologists. For example, we generally assume that we know ourselves better than anyone else knows us, in large part because we have privileged access to ourselves. After all, I am the only person who can experience my private thoughts and feelings, so presumably I know my mind better than anyone else. But even this simple assumption is challenged by psychological research.

Self-perception theory (discussed in chapter 13) argues that we know ourselves the same way as we know others, by observation of behavior. When we are asked to watch a cartoon with a smile on our face, we later report the cartoon to be funnier – presumably recalling how we were smiling the entire time we watched the cartoon. Self-perception theory is in the behaviorist tradition (see chapter 6) and proposes that there is no need for explanations of the self based on introspection: we simply know ourselves by observing our own behavior. But another line of research suggests that when we observe our own behavior, we can give explanations that are misleading. For example, research has established that when people are presented with a set of items, such as four night-gowns, they tend to prefer the item on the right to those on the left. However, when participants are asked to explain why they prefer a particular item, such as a nightgown on the right, they tend to offer various explanations such as quality and color, but are dismissive of the idea that serial position might have influenced their choice. In other words, when they look at their own behavior they tend to explain it in misleading ways. This suggests that in at least some situations we do not see ourselves accurately (for divergent views on this theme of self-perception, see Martin & Tesser, 1992).

Another approach to explaining how we see ourselves is associated with the term "looking-glass self," coined by Charles Cooley (1864–1929) over a century ago to propose that how we see ourselves depends largely on how others see us. This suggests that our perception of ourselves is context dependent, that we change our views of ourselves when there is a change of feedback about ourselves. Everyday experiences suggest the same idea. In families, schools, and other places most people attempt to provide the young with positive feedback and support, on the assumption that positive self-perceptions will arise among the young as a result. George Herbert Mead (1863–1931) further developed the idea that self-perceptions arise out of social interactions, by focusing on *significant symbols*, actions and words children learn to use in order to elicit the desired behavior from others. Through participation in symbolic interaction, children learn *role taking*, imagining oneself in the place of others, and to arrive at a clearer perception of both others and themselves.

The idea that how we see ourselves arises out of reflections of how others see us is intuitively appealing, but I have argued that this is a warped mirror and the image that we see tends to be distorted. In other words, our self-perceptions are based not so much on how others see us, but on how we come to believe that others see us. This is a subtle but fundamentally important difference, because "how we come to believe that others see us" leaves a lot of room for distortions. This may not be as important for members of majority groups, who are relatively privileged, as it is for members of minority group, who enjoy fewer privileges and may come to see themselves even more discriminated against and excluded than they actually are. My own research among some minority groups in North America suggests this does sometimes take place. For example, among high school students in Montreal, I found that ethnic minority immigrants tended to see themselves as less accepted by majority groups than majority groups actually saw them, whereas immigrants from Western Europe saw themselves as more accepted than they actually were. Thus, ethnic minority immigrants looking into the mirror of society saw a distorted negative image, whereas Western European immigrants saw a distorted positive image.

Another way in which distortions arise concerns the boundaries we see between ourselves and others. Since the 1970s a number of concepts (such as independent/interdependent and individualism/collectivism) have been used in psychological research to suggest that the boundaries of the self are more rigid and clear in some cultures than they are in others. Individuals in more interdependent and collectivist societies are seen as having less clearly bounded and less autonomous selves. Such individuals typically describe their responsibilities less in terms of individual effort and self help and more in terms of collective responsibility and group effort. Similarly, individuals in such cultures describe behavior as arising more from the characteristics of the context than from the assumed stable characteristics of personality (they would say "he obeys when his parents are around" rather than "he is obedient").

Given that our self-perceptions are often biased, are there patterns to such biases? A possible universal in the realm of self-perception is the motivation to see oneself, and to be seen by others, in a positive light. Of course, these others whom one cares to be seen by in a positive light may be only a small in-group. For example, an avant-garde painter may only care about how a handful of other avant-garde painters see her. If she is favorably evaluated by this tiny peer group, she may care far less that the general public finds her paintings incomprehensible (and even reprehensible!). Similarly, rebellious teenagers may only care that their close group of friends like their clothes. When their parents and other adults react negatively to their clothes, they may be pleased because it represents another endorsement of their view of themselves as rebels.

But we should be careful not to portray too simplistic a view of the motivation to achieve a positively evaluated self. If people are motivated to achieve a positively evaluated self, then what is the explanation for minorities who seem to adopt negative stereotypes of themselves, such as African American children who show bias in favor of whites, or the ethnic minority group members who see themselves rejected by the majority even more than they really are? One possibility is that such negative self-perceptions hinder a group from developing a distinct and positive collective identity. This is highly detrimental for group members; a distinct and positive collective identity has been viewed by various researchers as essential for the healthy functioning of group members (see Taylor, 2002).

The idea of the "looking-glass self" implies that our self-perceptions have social origins and that they are arrived at in relativistic terms. That is, we see ourselves in the reflections of others and we make social comparisons to determine how favorable such reflections are. Leon Festinger (1919–89) originally proposed that we make social comparisons to determine our self worth particularly in domains where there are no objective measures. For example, Joe looks around at the opinions of others in order to get a better idea of the worth of his own opinions. But is it really necessary for Joe to compare his own opinions with those of others to determine their worth? If Mike and Jack have different opinions from Joe, does this make Joe's opinions worth any less or more? Well, it should not in the ideal, but it may well be that in practice social comparisons do intrude in this kind of self-assessment.

CRITICAL THINKING QUESTIONS

1 Think of some examples in your everyday life that illustrate the "warped looking-glass."

2 Does self-perception theory completely put aside the mind and thinking?

SELF-PRESENTATION

On the one hand, concern with self-presentation would seem to be a rather shallow and perhaps frivolous occupation. After all, "self-presentation" implicitly at least gives importance to how one appears to others, rather than the inner self; to the surface and the observable rather than the deep, personal, and private. On the other hand, concern with how we present ourselves could be argued to be important and serious, because how we look to others actually is very influential in their evaluations of us. From the moment we are born, how our personality and looks appear to others influences how others behave toward us.

Self-presentation depends in part on physical appearance. Even when we are babies in hospitals, how much attention we receive depends to

some degree on how attractive we are. Also, as infants we show a preference for looking at more attractive faces. Later as adults, how much
attention we are paid at work depends in part on how attractive we are.
It really does seem to be an unfair world! But physical attractiveness is
only one factor influencing how others see us. We all know physically
attractive individuals who are not seen as attractive personalities. In
practice, how attractive we are seen to be depends in part on our particular style of self-presentation.

There are two main types of variations in the ways individuals
present themselves. First, there are "awareness" variations, to do with
how much attention a person gives to the self and to the context. This is
reflected in the concept of "self-monitoring." High self-monitors are
exquisitely aware of themselves and the characteristics of the context,
high self-monitors being individuals who try to change themselves to
say and do what others will like. They are inclined to even switch dating
partners to suit the activity. For example, Mary, a high self-monitor,
does not take her current boyfriend David, an environmental activist,
to the wedding of some ultra-conservative friends because she thinks
David would not be a good match for the event. This is particularly
because David is a low self-monitor, meaning he would not try to fit in
with the ultra-conservative wedding crowd.

A second variation in the ways individuals present themselves
concerns "strategy," the particular means by which a person tries to
develop self-presentation. Edward Jones (1990) has identified the main
strategies as ingratiation (e.g. flatter), intimidation (e.g. threaten), self-
promotion (e.g. boast), exemplification (e.g. self-sacrifice), and suppli-
cation (e.g. beseech help). But each strategy involves risks and requires a
good performer in order to be carried out effectively. For example, an
employee who adopts ingratiation in order to get his boss to see him
more positively may not be able to play the part convincingly, with the
negative result that he comes to be seen as a bootlicker. Clearly, there are
enormous variations across cultures as to what strategies are most
appropriate. For example, at least some strategies, such as nepotism,
seen as appropriate in a traditional authoritarian society where advancement depends for the most part on family relations, would be less
appropriate in a merit-based, democratic society.

The discussion of self-presentation brings us back to the fundamental
question about the unitary or multiple nature of the self. William
James (1890) discussed how each of us has multiple social selves. I am a
father, a professor, an occasional soccer player, a neighbor, a job search

committee member, and so on. In each of these different roles, I present a different self, and it is often important for these selves not to overlap. For example, it would be a big mistake to present myself as a professor when I play soccer. Also, when I coach children in soccer, I should not present myself as a coach to the adults I play soccer with. But how is it that each of us is able to present ourself in so many different ways? Does it mean that there is a kind of core or stable self in the background, monitoring as the various different social selves are presented in differ-ent contexts? For example, is there a core or stable self within me, moni-toring as I present myself as a professor, a soccer player, and so on? If so, the implication is that the self is multiple.

As we saw in the earlier discussion of the I/me distinction, we can sometimes be misled by language. There are multiple terms we can use to describe the social roles of any one individual, such as "mother," "sister," "engineer," "cook," and so on. Each social role is akin to a self-presentation. But it would be a mistake to conclude from this that there really are multiple social selves, behind which is a monitoring core or stable self. It is useful to return to William James's notion of a stream of consciousness and the idea that at any one time a person can only occupy one particular point in the stream. Each of us has many different self-presentations over time and across contexts, but at any one moment in time we only have one self.

Similarly, I can reflect back on the self-presentation I made a minute ago, and think ahead to a different self-presentation I will make in another minute, but this is simply looking backward and forward along the stream. It does not change the limitation that at any one time my self occupies one point in the stream.

The dramaturgical model and its limitations

All the world's a stage,
And all the men and women merely players:
They have their exits and their entrances,
And one man in his time plays many parts.

(Shakespeare, *As You Like It*, II, vii)

As suggested by the above quotation from Shakespeare, the idea that "all the world is a stage" is not new, but modern social scientists have devel-oped it in new ways. In particular, Erving Goffman (1922–82) explored the ways in which all of us are performers on the giant stage of everyday life. It is instructive to explore self-presentation through the work of Goffman in particular, first because Goffman has been extremely influential, and second because Goffman changed his mind about the *dramaturgical model*, the view that all of us are performers. In his later writings Goffman came to the conclusion that all the world is not a stage, and it is informative for us to see why he came to this conclusion.

In *The Presentation of the Self in Everyday Life* (1959) and particularly the earlier edition of this book, Goffman adopts the dramaturgical model. Among the main concepts of this model are *a performance*, the activities of a person that influence others in the situation; *a team*, a group of people who collaborate to sustain a set of performances; *a region*, the "back-stage" and "front-stage" spaces available for performances; and *impression management*, the art of maintaining a performance in accordance with the intended or desired presented self. For example, consider the hectic scene at a five-star restaurant when it is packed with clients. The kitchen is the "back-stage" where performances are rehearsed by the waiters and other staff, while the restaurant area where clients are served is the "front-stage."

In the "back-stage" of the restaurant, there may be a great deal of chaos and confusion, as the head chef directs the various cooking staff, waiters and waitresses rush around collecting their orders and shout complaints about late orders, wine waiters check and juggle wine bottles, and other staff rush around trying to keep the kitchen clean and safe. The head wine waiter may have just engaged in a fierce fight with the head chef back-stage, but when he steps out onto front-stage, he is suddenly transformed into a calm, refined, super-caring being whose only concern in the world is the clients' enjoyment. The clients also put on a performance, playing their parts as characters who belong in a five-star restaurant. Each performer on front-stage supports or "colludes in" the performances of the others. For example, when the head wine waiter slips up and spills some wine on the floor, the clients pretend not to notice. Similarly, if a client slips up and uses the wrong utensils, the serving staff pretend not to notice.

The dramaturgical model, the "world as a stage," is a very interesting way of viewing self-presentation. However, limitations in this viewpoint led Goffman to conclude in later writings that all the world is not a stage. A first reason for this change in orientation concerns the many ways in which performing on stage and performing in real life actually differ. For example, actors on stage follow a script and know exactly what will happen at the end of the story. The actors who play Romeo and Juliet know that both characters die a tragic death at the end of Shakespeare's play of the same name, and that the two feuding families finally make peace after the deaths of the hero and heroine. But in real life individuals do not know what will happen at the end of their performances. Also, on stage the actions of the other characters are completely predictable, because they are following a set script. Again, this is very different from real life, where the behavior of others with whom one is interacting is not completely predictable.

A second reason why Goffman decided that all the world is not a stage concerns his rejection of the "two selves" thesis, the idea that the self is an entity "half concealed," standing back and presenting different fronts to the world. Performance in real life involves the self as a "changeable formula," so that the self becomes, for example, a student in one context, a daughter or son in another, and a boyfriend or girlfriend in a third context. This is different from performances on stage, Goffman argues, where, for example, the actor playing Romeo has an identity and personal history different from Romeo's and at the end of the play the actor stops playing Romeo and resumes his own identity and personal history. Despite such differences between performances on stage and performances in real life, the dramaturgical model is an interesting way of viewing self-presentation in everyday life.

The "self esteem movement"

An important question concerning the self and self-presentation in particular is: What motivates individuals? Received wisdom informs us that individuals are motivated by a concern to achieve positive *self esteem*, a sense of self worth, as well as positive *collective esteem*, a sense of worth of one's in-group (the group to which one belongs). Since the 1980s particularly, a great many programs in schools and elsewhere have been designed to help individuals, particularly children, to achieve positive self esteem. These efforts have expanded to such a degree throughout society that one can accurately describe them as comprising a self esteem movement. An example of the influence of this movement is the belief that "every child is a star," as declared by countless posters and announcements in contemporary schools.

The basic premise of the self esteem movement is that the problem experienced by numerous children, particularly the members of minority groups, is that of low self esteem. The problems that are assumed to arise from low self esteem seem to be countless, from apathy toward schoolwork to aggression and even homicide. Consequently, the challenge is seen to be to raise the self esteem of children and avoid the problems associated with low self esteem.

The basic premise of the self esteem movement came under critical attack in the 1990s. Roy Baumeister and others argued that the problem of self esteem is not so much low self esteem as it is inflated and unstable self esteem. For example, Jack has an inflated self esteem in the sense that he exaggerates his tennis skills. His self esteem is unstable in the sense that when he is challenged by a tennis player who really is talented he feels extremely threatened and vulnerable because he feels he will lose. The combination of having an unstable and inflated self esteem makes Jack potentially aggressive.

A more general point concerns the assumption that in schools and other institutions, priority should be given to boosting the self esteem of students. How should such boosting be tied with the actual performance of individuals? For example, if I am not doing well in basic writing or reading or mathematics, should I be given feedback designed to boost my self esteem, with the hope that boosting my self esteem will eventually lead to better performance on my part? Or, will boosting my self esteem under such conditions lead me to be poorly prepared for the competition I will face outside school? Such questions are leading to a re-evaluation of assumptions underlying the self esteem movement.

CRITICAL THINKING QUESTIONS

1 How does our concern with fashion and clothes reflect our concern to present ourselves positively to others?

2 Give examples of how you present yourself differently in different contexts.

CONCLUDING COMMENT

Since the decline of behaviorism, the self has made a welcome return to psychology. Scores of books and hundreds of papers are now published annually by psychologists on different aspects of the self. While the sense of a unitary and continuous self is almost universal, there also seem to be some universals in how we see ourselves and in self-presentation style. We seem to be biased to see ourselves, as well as to try to present ourselves, so as to achieve a positive self image. Integral to the self esteem movement is the idea that low self esteem is the root of many personal and social ills. Consequently, numerous programs have been developed in order to try to boost self esteem, particularly in schools with large numbers of ethnic minority students. More recently, key assumptions underlying the self esteem movement have been challenged and it has been proposed that the real problem lies in unstable and inflated self esteem.

CRITICAL THINKING QUESTIONS

1 Why has interest in the self been uneven in psychology?

2 What in your view is the most important universal characteristic of the self?

FURTHER READING

Baumeister, R. F. (ed.) (1999). *Self in social psychology*. New York: Psychology Press.

Dweck, C. S. (2000). *Self-theories: Their role in motivation, personality, and development*. New York: Psychology Press.

Festinger, L. (1954). A theory of social comparison processes. *Human Relations*, 7, 117–140.

Forgas, J. P. & Williams, K. D. (eds.) (2003). *The social self: Cognitive, interpersonal and intergroup perspectives*. New York: Psychology Press.

Gallup, G. G. Jr., (1977). Chimpanzees: Self recognition. *Science, 167*, 86–87.

Goffman, E. (1959). *The presentation of the self in everyday life*. Harmondsworth, England: Penguin.

Goffman, E. (1974). *Frame analysis: An essay on the organization of experience*. New York: Harper & Row.

Harré, R. (1998). *The singular self: An introduction to the psychology of personhood*. London: Sage.

Harré, R., & Moghaddam, F. M. (2003). *The self and others: Positioning individuals and groups in personal, political, and cultural contexts*. Westport, CT: Praeger.

James, A. (1890). *Principles of psychology*. New York: Henry Holt.

Jones, E. E. (1990). *Interpersonal perception*. New York: W. H. Freeman.

Markus, H. R., & Kitayama, S. (1991). Culture and the self: Implications for cognition, emotion, and motivation. *Psychological Review, 98*, 224–253.

Martin, L., & Tesser, A. (eds.) (1992). *The construction of social judgment.* Hillsdale, NJ: Lawrence Erlbaum.

Moghaddam, F. M., Taylor, D. M., Ditto, P. T., & Shepanek, M. (1994). The warped looking glass: How minorities perceive themselves, believe they are perceived, and are actually perceived by majority group members. *Canadian Ethnic Studies, 26*, 112–123.

Mruk, C. (1999). *Self esteem: Research, theory, and practice.* New York: Springer.

Rogers, T. B. (1981) A model of the self as an aspect of the human information processing system. In N. Cantor & J. Kihlstrom (eds.), *Personality, cognition, and social interaction.* Hillsdale, NJ: Lawrence Erlbaum.

Sedikides, C., & Brewer, M. B. (eds.) (2000). *Individual self, relational self, and collective self.* New York: Psychology Press.

Taylor, D. M. (2002). *The quest for identity.* Newport, CT: Praeger.

Twenge, J., & Crocker, J. (2002). Race and self-esteem. *Psychological Bulletin, 128*, 371–408.

Wicklund, R. A., & Eckert, M. (1992). *The self as knower: A hero under control.* New York: Plenum.

15

CONFORMITY TO GROUP NORMS

Conformity, changes in behavior that arise from real or imagined group pressure, is the glue that holds society together. Each of us in our everyday life is repeatedly influenced by real or imagined group pressure. We listen without interrupting and speak only when we are called on by the teacher in a classroom; we wait in line until it gets to our turn to purchase concert tickets; we act respectfully in a house of worship; we search for a particular style of fashionable shoe in a particular fashionable color; we keep our hair long or short depending on the prevailing tastes of our times; we sometimes even nod agreement with views expressed by friends despite actually feeling differently on an issue. All such behaviors show that conformity to group norms is part and parcel of our everyday lives. Put another way, group norms decrease the degrees of freedom (as discussed in chapter 1) in a situation, so that people have a smaller range of behavioral options.

There is good reason for the centrality of conformity in our everyday lives, since conformity has important practical advantages. Because most of us behave "correctly" most of the time, and generally "do the right thing," we have a fairly good idea of what to expect from each other. That is, we mostly behave as others expect us to behave. As a consequence, we do not have continuously to spend energy trying to understand and predict every move others make. When we invite guests to our house for the first time, we are fairly certain they will enter only those parts of the house that are generally known to be open to guests. For example, such guests would typically not enter bedrooms uninvited. Conformity facilitates understanding and communication between people and allows individuals to interact and collaborate smoothly in groups, such as when hosts and guests interact at a party. Conformity helps to explain how separate individuals, each with private thoughts and experiences, tend to fit into regular and to some extent predictable patterns of interactions in the larger society.

But conformity also has negative connotations, particularly in the popular culture of the United States. The hero in popular movies, plays, and songs tends to be a rebel, a non-conformist rather than a conformist. To be called a "conformist" is not a compliment in most contexts in Western societies, whereas the label "non-conformist" has a positive ring to it. We think of artists, writers, revolutionary leaders, explorers, and other inspired individuals as being non-conformists rather than conformists. Those who "blaze trails" and show the way ahead are hailed because they took the path less taken rather than the common road traveled by most others. They are non-conformists; they reject restrictions on the degrees of freedom in any situation.

A major cultural reason for the negative connotations of conformity in some societies, such as the United States, is that by implication conformity seems to negate individual choice and responsibility. If Jack gets involved in petty crime and drugs, it is his choice and he should be considered responsible for his own actions when the police catch up with him. From this "individual responsibility" perspective, it is unacceptable to claim that Jack's criminal behavior is conformity to group norms, and unacceptable to argue that, just as in affluent neighborhoods young people conform to group norms by going to college and embarking on professional careers, Jack has conformed to the norms of his neighborhood by dropping out of school and getting involved in crime and drugs and this is the "normal" path for him to follow. On the other hand, if Jack conforms to family norms and gains entrance to a good school, the ethos of individual responsibility suggests that Jack, rather than his family norms, should get the credit. One reason, then, that conformity is viewed negatively is that it goes against "self help" and "individual responsibility," ideals so central to US culture. Despite being viewed negatively, however, conformity is central to all our everyday lives.

Given the fundamental importance and pervasiveness of conformity, it is not surprising that researchers from different disciplines, including sociology, anthropology, and economics, have shown interest in this topic. For example, sociologists have examined the role of schools and other institutions and mechanisms of socialization in training individuals to conform to *norms*, guides to correct behavior in a given setting, and *rules*, prescriptions of how individuals in particular role relationships (e.g. parent–child, professor–student, doctor–patient) should behave. Anthropologists have explored how conformity leads to similarities and differences across cultures, for example in relationships between men and women. Economists have been interested in the choices individuals make in the marketplace, and how shifts take place in consumer preferences. What, then, is the particular contribution of psychologists to our understanding of conformity? We will see that this contribution has been made for the most part by working in and linking theory closely to empirical evidence.

There are at least four areas in which psychologists have made fundamental contributions to our understanding of conformity. First, psychologists have experimentally demonstrated the arbitrary nature of norms. Second, psychologists have shown that, despite being arbitrary, violation of norms comes at a psychological cost for the individual. Third, the power of the majority to enforce conformity to majority-established norms, despite the arbitrary nature of norms, is underlined by psychological research. Finally, psychologists have also uncovered features of the conditions in which a minority influences a majority to conform to minority-established norms.

CONFORMITY TO ARBITRARY NORMS

The claim that norms are arbitrary is based on the lack of objective criteria for most norms, including those norms considered sacred in particular societies. For example, consider the norm in fundamentalist Islamic societies that, in public, women should cover all of their body except their hands and face. The covering of hair is given particular importance. Why does this norm apply to women but not to men? Why should there not be a norm for men to cover their hair? One idea might be that men are particularly attracted to the long hair of women, but what objective evidence do we have that women are any less attracted to the hair of men? Examples of arbitrary norms also abound in Western societies. For example, why do women wear skirts and not men? In some societies it has in the past been the norm for men to wear skirts (e.g. the kilt worn in Scotland), but according to modern fashion men should wear pants and not skirts. Why at the turn of the twenty-first century do women wear their hair long and men wear their hair short? During the 1960s, and in certain other past eras (e.g. sixteenth-century England), the fashion for men was also to have long hair. Examples of such arbitrary norms abound.

We should not imagine that science is immune from having arbitrary norms. For example, a number of detailed studies have documented how researchers negotiate interpretations of scientific research and arrive at norms about how facts should be presented (for example, Latour & Woolgar, 1979). Closer to home for psychologists, a number of such norms regulate the behavior of researchers in psychology and are particularly evident in psychology journals, journal editors acting to enforce conformity among researchers. An example is the setting of the criterion for statistical significance at $p < 0.05$ and $p < 0.01$. It has become the norm in psychology journals to report findings as "significant" if the probability of the findings being arrived at by chance is computed to be less than 0.05, and to report the findings as "highly significant" if it is less than 0.01. These cut-off points are completely arbitrary. Instead of 0.05 and 0.01, the cut-off points could have been 0.02 and 0.03, or 0.0002 and 0.0003, or countless other possibilities. There is nothing objectively better about the magic cut-off points of 0.05 and 0.01. Despite the arbitrary nature of this norm, it is enforced through group pressure. If a researcher submits a paper to a psychology journal and uses the cut-offs 0.029 and 0.019 to report "significant" findings, the journal editors would object. Objections would also be raised if instead of the terms "significant" or "highly significant," a researcher reported $p = 0.019$ as "extraordinarily significant" or "tremendously significant." This is despite the fact that descriptive terms such as "significant" and "highly significant" are merely cultural constructions, with no objective basis.

This is just one of many possible examples of arbitrary norms enforced in science. A contribution of psychologists is to demonstrate experimentally the power of arbitrary group norms.

The experimental demonstration of conformity to arbitrary group norms

All of us have at some time or another stared up at the stars. There is something magical about the night sky when it is cloudless and we can gaze up and imagine what might be out there. If you focus on a single star, something strange seems to happen: the star dances around. This perception of movement (the star only seems to move; it does not actually move) is called the *autokinetic effect* and is well known among astronomers. The amount of movement seen varies among individuals;

some people see less movement and others see relatively more movement. This perceptual phenomenon was used in a highly creative way by
Mozafer Sherif (1906–88) to demonstrate conformity to arbitrary group
norms, in a series of classic studies first conducted in the 1930s.

Sherif placed participants in a darkened room and asked them to estimate the amount of movement they see in a single tiny light. Sherif
started with individual participants making one hundred estimates each
session for four sessions. He found that over the course of four hundred
estimates, each participant arrives at a "personal norm." Next, Sherif
brought the participants together and asked them to give estimates in a
group. He discovered that in the group setting there is a convergence of
individual estimates, to create a group norm.

Two additional findings are particularly noteworthy. First, when individuals are taken out of the group and asked to make estimates by themselves, the group norm still influences what they see. Thus, the group
does not need to be physically present for it to have an impact on the
individual through the group norm. Even when the individual is no
longer with the group, the group norm is present inside the individual.
Second, the group norm does not have as much impact on participants
who were previously alone participants as it does on participants who
start by making estimates as part of a group and only after that make
estimates alone. This suggests that the formation of a personal norm
before being placed in a group to some extent inoculates a person
against group pressure to conform with group norms.

Sherif's original studies focused on *spontaneous norms*, norms that
evolve naturally within groups without any effort to manipulate norm
formation. Subsequent research using *manipulated norms*, norms
explicitly brought about by design, demonstrated that group norms
could be influenced, for example by planting "extremists" in the midst of
the group. Of course, these extremists were confederates of the experimenters, and their job was to give exaggerated estimates of how much
they saw the light move. The exaggerated estimates of such confederates
had an impact on the group norm, even after the confederates left the
group and were replaced by naive participants. Indeed, several generations of naive participants continued to be influenced by the extremist
estimates planted earlier by confederates of the experimenters.

The most crucial feature of Sherif's study is that the group members
are always wrong in their estimate of movement, because the light never
moves. Irrespective of the specific amount of movement a group arrives
at as its norm, as long as it perceives some movement in the light, the

group norm is wrong. Despite being wrong, the group norm continues to influence individuals after they leave the group and make estimates on their own.

The power of arbitrary norms, demonstrated so effectively by Sherif in a laboratory experiment has also been extended to real life also through field research by Irving Janis, among others. Janis examined a number of major decision-making fiascos, such as the failure of the US military to be prepared for the Japanese attack at Pearl Harbor, the Bay of Pigs invasion in 1961 during which US-backed forces invading Cuba were routed, and the escalation of the war in Vietnam by Lyndon Johnson in the 1960s. In each of these cases, highly intelligent individuals came together and made terrible decisions as part of a group. The explanation for such *groupthink*, the tendency for people in groups to converge on unwise courses of action they would have avoided if they were making the decision individually, is in part that individuals were conforming to incorrect and to some extent arbitrary group norms, such as wildly exaggerated estimates of the effectiveness of counter-revolutionary groups intending to overthrow Fidel Castro in Cuba.

The same tendency is probably involved in more recent intelligence failures, such as those prior to the 9/11 tragedies, and both before and after the invasion of Iraq by the United States and coalition forces. We now know that the different US security agencies had information that, if brought together in a coordinated way, could have increased the probability of preventing 9/11. However, each agency remained within its own closed system, and information was not shared with outsiders. We now also know that intelligence estimates were mistaken about an "imminent threat" from weapons of mass destruction supposedly amassed in Iraq during the 1990s. Adherence to arbitrary and incorrect norms probably also influenced the poor management of events in Iraq after the invasion. In all of these cases, groups of decision makers were influenced by arbitrary and incorrect internal group norms. However, because of secrecy, the problematic nature of such norms only became evident after it was too late.

The shared nature of norms and the cost of non-conformity

Why do individuals conform? There is plenty of evidence to show that the group norms with which we conform are arbitrary, and sometimes even wrong. What power induces us to conform to such norms? A possible answer is that the more intelligent we are, the less we conform. But this explanation is too simplistic. The research of Janis and others confirms what we observe in everyday life: even highly intelligent individuals, such as elite presidential advisors, can under certain conditions conform to incorrect group norms.

The answer to why we conform becomes clearer when we consider the shared nature of group norms. The origin of Sherif's ideas for the classic norm formation studies using the *autokinetic effect* lie in the concept of *collective representations*, shared views of the world prevalent in a group, discussed by the sociologist Emile Durkheim (1858–1917). The shared, collective nature of norms means that they are not dependent on any individual; norms are present before we arrive in society and they persist after we have left. But irrespective of whether they are brief or more long-term, norms are in the collective culture and are taught to individuals as they are socialized to become part of the larger society.

Norms act as signposts for correct behavior, informing individuals of what to do in order to be readily accepted and positively evaluated by the group. We may not like particular norms, but in not conforming to a norm we also have to consider the typically negative reactions (e.g. rejecting, boycotting, or labeling us as "stupid") on the part of other group members. Perhaps another reason why the non-conformist is sometimes regarded as a hero, in Hollywood movies and in some cases even in real life, is because we realize the enormous power of the group norm and the sometimes very heavy costs to being a non-conformist. Because of their shared nature, norms hover above the heads and beyond the control of individuals.

In situations that are ambiguous, where individuals are unsure how to behave, they look to others for guides. For example, in Sherif's norm formation studies using the *autokinetic effect*, the stimulus was ambiguous, meaning the spot of light seemed to move to some extent but the participants could not be certain, so each participant in the group situation looked to others for guidance and came under the influence of the group norm. The important role of ambiguity was highlighted by Bibb Latane and John Darley, who showed that in situations of uncertainty, bystanders who see a person apparently in trouble look to one another and if other bystanders are not helping, they too are likely to refrain from helping. That is, a norm emerges for all bystanders to simply walk past the person in need without offering help.

On the more positive side, norms arising out of ambiguous situations can also be pro-social. For example, in one of his innovative studies on social norms, Stanley Milgram (1933–84) explored what happens when a person asks a complete stranger in the New York City subway system for his or her seat. Seats in the subway are filled on a first come, first served basis, and although people are often crushed together they rarely speak to fellow passengers. Thus, the request for another person's seat was very unexpected, because it violates at least two norms for the New York subway context, particularly when it is *not* accompanied by any kind of explanation (such as "because I'm feeling ill"). This unexpected request created an ambiguous situation, and resulted in fifty-six percent of the participants giving up their seats to the person making the request – perhaps because the participants simply did not know *how not to* comply. Thus, in a sense they were being pro-social because it was the less uncomfortable way to behave.

An important aspect of this study is that those making the requests for seats, graduate students who acted as Milgram's collaborators, also reported feeling very uncomfortable during the interaction with participants. This was probably because they recognized that their request for a seat violated several norms for subway passengers. The heavy cost of non-conformity is underlined by these findings.

CRITICAL THINKING QUESTIONS

1 What are three arbitrary norms with which you conformed recently?

2 Give an example of a situation in which you became particularly aware of the cost of non-conformity.

POWER, NORMS, AND CONFORMITY

The power to influence norms and to bring about conformity is not equally distributed among individuals and groups. Majority groups, those who command more power, have more influence, and minority groups, who by definition possess less power, have less influence (in the psychology literature, majority/minority status is defined in terms of power and not the number of people in a group; a numerical minority can be, and often is, a power majority).

In everyday life there are many examples of the superior power of majority groups and their extraordinary capability to shape norms and influence conformity, particularly to further majority group interests. Consider the norms (in addition to the formal laws) developed by White

Americans to regulate the everyday behavior of Whites and African Americans, during and after the institution of slavery in the United States. Such norms are now not as explicit or rigidly enforced as they once were, but still influence dating and marriage, among other areas of behavior. Whites and African Americans who enter mixed-race marriages still face some level of prejudice.

It is important to remember that conformity is often, far more often, enforced by informal norms and rules than by the formal legal system, or "black-letter law." For example, legal reforms in formal black-letter law in the United States have banned discrimination on the basis of race, gender, religion, national origin, and so on (but not sexual orientation). However, in some social contexts informal norms and rules still sustain racial discrimination, so that a White person and a Black person might feel pressured to stop dating one another even though they are attracted to each other and mixed-race dating is no longer against formal black-letter law. In such circumstances, the two individuals involved may clearly see that they are in the right, but through sheer pressure the majority can still influence them to make a different decision and to conform to established norms.

Conformity to majority-established norms

Imagine you have volunteered to be a participant in a psychology experiment. As a first step, you are tested to ensure that you have normal eyesight. When you step into the laboratory, you discover that five other participants arrived before you and are ready to begin. You sit down in the only chair left vacant. The experimenter shows you three lines of different lengths, and then a standard line that is the same length as one of the three other lines. You and the other participants have to say which of the three lines is the same length as the standard line.

The other participants call out their answers, and you are the last to give your answer. Everything proceeds smoothly, with all of you in full agreement as to which of the three lines is the same length as the standard line being shown on each trial. You are just starting to relax, because the answers seem obvious, when something unexpected happens: the others call out an answer that looks wrong to you. The line they say is the same length as the standard line is obviously not the correct one, so you think. You rub your eyes, look again, blink a few times, and still do not see what the others report. What exactly is going on? You feel anxious and uneasy.

The objective of Solomon Asch was to place individuals in a situation where they could clearly see they were correct and the majority was wrong, but felt pressure to conform to the incorrect majority-established norm. An important feature of this situation is that the stimulus is unambiguous, unlike the context created by Sherif in his norm formation study using the autokinetic effect, where the movement of the spot of light was ambiguous. In the Asch study, then, individuals who know they are correct are under pressure to give incorrect answers. Surprisingly, about a third of all the estimates made by all of the participants were conforming, and seventy-two percent of the participants conformed at least once during the experimental trials.

Replications of this study in numerous different Western and non-Western cultures show that it is not just in the United States that such conformity takes place. The main trend of the finding remains intact in cross-cultural studies: something between twenty and fifty percent of participants show conformity to majority-established norms in Asch-type studies with diverse populations. This experimental finding matches our everyday experiences, showing that the basic phenomenon of minority conformity to arbitrary majority norms is evident in many societies and is probably universal.

Those who do not conform to majority-established norms, those who reject traditional ways and insist on moving in new directions, also open up possibilities for innovation and better adaptation to changed environmental conditions. For example, consider a majority-established norm that regulates eating: food should be collected and hunted during daylight, never at night time. Most people in the group conform to this norm, but a small minority are non-conformists; they gather and hunt food at night-time. Imagine if ecological conditions change and food gathering and hunting become very difficult during the day, so difficult that there is no longer enough food for all of the young in the group. The minority who hunt and gather food at night find they have plenty to eat, and the numbers of their offspring increases. Consequently, the minority way of doing things ensures the survival of the group, and soon the minority become the majority (of course, a norm to hunt only at night might have been established to protect against over-hunting, in which case breaking the norm could, under certain conditions, deplete the environment and diminish rather than enhance a group's survival chances). The implication is that an open society that leaves room for, and even supports, non-conformity increases its own chances of surviving and thriving.

But are we justified in taking such leaps of faith to draw inferences from estimations of lengths of lines to conformity in everyday life? The foundational studies of Asch and other influential psychologists have been carried out in the laboratory. As discussed in chapter 2, the psychological laboratory has a number of shortcomings. I argue that in the realm of conformity we are justified in interpreting from laboratory studies, in large part because laboratory studies are supplemented by both field research and everyday experiences of conformity, such as in the context of institutions.

Conformity to majority-established norms has been explored with great insight by Erving Goffman (1922–82) and a number of other researchers in the context of *total institutions* (such as asylums and prisons), where all activities are regimented by a single authority and conducted as part of the collectivity. Goffman argued that the main basis for individuals being labeled "insane" and placed in asylums, often against their will, is their refusal to conform with the norms for acceptable behavior, as defined by authorities. Because of non-conformity by "patients," within asylums "patients" are robbed of their identities and new identities are constructed for them. In order to cope with this pressure on them to conform, "patients" develop a number of different strategies, such as situational withdrawal, literally escaping from the situation by fantasizing. Second, they may try to set limits, an intransigent line, to how much they conform within the institution, and when this limit is broken they rebel, sometimes violently. Third, "patients" may change their own perceptions, so that the world in the institutions is seen as more favorable than the outside world, so they behave as if they do not want to leave. Finally, "patients" may conform to seeing the world as do the "authorities," so as to get out of the institution as quickly as possible. In effect, they try to become "model patients," to accept labels such as "insane" and "sane," and to conform to majority-established norms.

Whereas Goffman's study was in the context of a real total institution, Philip Zimbardo explored conformity to majority-established norms through a simulation of a prison. Zimbardo first screened potential participants and selected about two dozen intelligent young people with normal personality profiles. Next, he randomly assigned them to take on the roles of prison guard and prisoner in a simulated prison, which had locked doors and bars and was designed to look as much as possible like a real prison. Both groups had on uniforms appropriate for their roles; the guards were given clubs and instructed to keep order. The simulation had to be ended after only six days, well short of the planned two weeks, because the guards mistreated the prisoners to a dangerous degree. Both prisoners and guards conformed to what they assumed were the norms of a real prison, and as a consequence exhibited high levels of hostility, aggression, and mistreatment of others.

However, it is also important to remember that conformity rarely, if ever, involves the entire group behaving in the same way. Some non-conformists always seem to be present as well. Not all guards mistreat prisoners, and not all prisoners become passive or devious. In the Asch experiments, about two-thirds of the participants did not conform; rather, they insisted on calling out the correct answer in the face of perceived majority group pressure. This is important to keep in mind, because the non-conformists play an essential role in open societies, in terms of both political freedom and economic enterprise. It is these individuals – who refuse to conform, who will not follow the lead of the majority group – who despite costs to themselves will help prevent the danger of dictatorship and the loss of basic freedoms. In some circumstances it is a minority that brings about change in the majority.

There is also a more subtle relationship between conformity and non-conformity: in important respects non-conformity helps construct conformity. It is through non-conformity that we come to understand conformity. If everyone conformed, behavior would remain the same. But the thoughts and actions of some individuals do change, and this allows us to recognize what remains relatively stable.

Under what conditions can a minority influence a majority?

Imagine what it must have been like for the early Christians about two thousand years ago. There were so few of them, with so little resources, facing the might of the Roman Empire and all the other enormous forces intent on wiping out this weird new sect, Christianity. The same situation, of the few confronting the overwhelming might of the many, characterized the beginnings of all the other major religions, including Judaism and Islam.

How did Mahatma Gandhi (1869–1948) and his small band of nonviolent activists manage to turn the tide and win independence for India in the face of opposition from the British Empire? Gandhi and his followers were a very small group initially, and India was a fragmented British colony. How did the change come about for the Indian independence movement, from insignificant to unstoppable power? Martin

Luther King, Jr. (1929–68) also began with a small band of supporters and with little resources. How did they bring about such monumental change in the United States? How did they overcome the enormous obstacles confronting them? How did they spread and become so successful, starting from so little?

When we look back in history, again and again we find that many of the most monumental changes were brought about through movements that began as minority movements. Instead of the minorities always conforming to majority-established norms, they sometimes cling to their own radically new norms and create a completely new movement, which eventually engulfs the majority group. How does a minority influence a majority to conform to minority-established norms?

This way of asking the question, of putting the minority group first, is associated with European research on conformity, as opposed to US research that traditionally put the majority first and focused on conformity to majority-established norms. Serge Moscovici and other European researchers have put the Asch paradigm on its head and examined conditions in which a minority can influence a majority to conform to minority-established norms. The general consensus is that a minority that is seen as taking a consistent position, but not one that is rigid or dogmatic, is more likely to influence the majority. For example, both Gandhi and King succeeded in presenting their movements as principled, open to dialogue, and not dogmatic.

The more controversial claim of Moscovici and his associates is that minority influence leads to *conversion*, conformity (changing of one's mind) arising out of persuasive argument, rather than *compliance*, conformity (changing of one's behavior) arising through forceful pressure, whereas majority influence is more likely to lead to compliance rather than conversion. The logic of this proposition seems sound. The majority have more power and enjoy more opportunities to force minorities to comply. For example, Whites in the United States enjoy greater power and have greater opportunities to force minorities to comply to their norms. Minorities do not have enough power to force compliance by a majority, so they have to resort to persuasion. An implication of this argument is that minority influence is morally superior, because to be persuasive minorities have to rely on the power of their arguments, whereas majorities can simply rely on brute force.

Although this distinction between the nature of majority and minority influence seems appealing in theory, it has two drawbacks. First, it has not been clearly and strongly supported by research studies; this is an instance of working out rather than working in. Second, just because minorities lack the raw power to force a majority to comply with minority-established norms, it does not follow that they will persuade by reason as Moscovici claims. There are other avenues open to them, such as appeals to feelings (rather than logic), cunning, trickery, and even terrorism. Thus, it is not necessarily the case that minority influence will be achieved through means that are morally superior.

CRITICAL THINKING QUESTIONS

1 Which in your opinion is more important for change and innovation: majority influence or minority influence?

2 Is minority influence better than, or just different from, majority influence?

CONCLUDING COMMENT

The fundamental importance of conformity in the evolution of human societies should not prevent us from also recognizing the central role of non-conformity. Conformity enables social life to proceed smoothly and with efficient use of resources: people know what they and others will most likely do in given situations, so a lot can be taken for granted during interactions with others. But in order to improve human survival chances, social life has to be dynamic and adaptive, rather than static and unchanging. The potential must be present for different and new forms of behavior to emerge, to meet the changing challenges of an evolving environment. In this regard, we can see why the presence of some non-conformity proves to be adaptive.

CRITICAL THINKING QUESTIONS

1 In what ways have you been a conformist today?

2 If conformity has benefits, why does the label "conformist" have negative connotations in the United States and some other societies?

FURTHER READING

Asch, S. E. (1955). Opinions and social pressure. *Scientific American*, *193*, 21–35.

Asch, S. E. (1956). Studies of independence and conformity: A minority of one against a unanimous majority. *Psychological Monographs*, *70* (9, Whole No. 416).

Goffman, E. (1961). *Asylums*. Harmondsworth, England: Penguin.

Latané, B., & Darley, J. M. (1970). *The unresponsive bystander: Why doesn't he help?* Englewood Cliffs, NJ: Prentice Hall.

Latour, B., & Woolgar, S. (1979). *Laboratory life: The social construction of scientific facts*. Beverly Hills, CA: Sage.

Milgram, S. (1992). *The individual in a social world: Essays and experiments*, 2nd edn. New York: McGraw Hill.

Moghaddam, F. M. (1998). *Social psychology: Exploring universals across cultures*. New York: Freeman.

Sherif, M. (1936). *The psychology of group norms*. New York: Harper.

Stangor, C. (2003). *Social groups in action and interaction*. New York: Psychology Press.

Zimbardo, P. (1972). Pathology of imprisonment. *Transactional/Society*, 4–8(a).

16

OBEDIENCE TO AUTHORITY

Obedience, changes in behavior that arise when people follow the instructions of persons in authority, cements and regulates social relationships, and in this respect serves a function similar to conformity (discussed in chapter 15). But there is even more controversy associated with obedience than there is with conformity, probably because obedience is more explicitly associated with major tragedies in human societies, such as the acts of genocide and atrocities committed by different groups of people throughout human history, and more recently the terrorist attacks of 9/11. Obedience is at the heart of such events. For example, the 9/11 attacks apparently were carried out through "blind obedience" to the orders of fundamentalist leaders. Most of the 9/11 attackers did not seem to have known the nature of their mission until the final stage; they simply followed orders irrespective of the consequences for others and even for themselves. This is an example of a situation where the degrees of freedom are minimal; reduced by the power of authority.

Although unquestioning obedience has negative associations, it is important to keep in mind that obedience also serves vital positive functions. Indeed, it is difficult to conceive of a complex society surviving without obedience being practiced in some important ways, in this case toward positive ends. In any complex organization, whether governmental or non-governmental, the efficient implementation of tasks requires obedience to the directives of those higher up in the organization. For example, imagine if the orders of the chief executive officer of an organization were ignored by managers and employees. When the CEO instructs managers to hire more sales personnel and to increase the sales force, instead they fire the existing sales personnel and reduce the sales force. Such an organization would not function effectively and would probably go out of business. Consider a classroom context in which the students refuse to follow the instructions of the teacher and each student does as she or he likes while the teacher is trying to explain how to solve a particular problem. Chaos would ensue and little learning would take place. Clearly, some types of obedience in some contexts are essential for the proper functioning of complex societies, at least as we presently know them.

In distinguishing between obedience and conformity, we can benefit from the insights of Stanley Milgram (1933–84), who has contributed more than any other psychologist to our understanding of obedience to authority and who for the most part worked in, proving empirical evidence for his theoretical account. The following four differences between obedience and conformity identified by Milgram are particularly noteworthy:

1. *Hierarchy*. Obedience regulates relations between individuals of unequal status (e.g. soldiers obey their commanding officer), whereas conformity regulates relations between individuals of equal status (when soldiers gather together, they conform to norms of behavior for their group).
2. *Imitation*. Obedience involves compliance with orders, whereas conformity involves imitation and the adoption of similar behavior. Military officers issue orders that they do not have to follow themselves but that their subordinates have to comply with, whereas the soldier conforming with a group norm in a group of soldiers does so by imitating other group members.
3. *Explicitness*. Obedience involves compliance with explicit commands; we readily acknowledge acting under orders. But norms are generally implicit and lead to conformity to implied and tacit requirements that are seldom acknowledged.
4. *Voluntarism*. In explaining their behavior, those who obey attribute responsibility to authority figures ("I was ordered to do this"), whereas those who conform typically claim to be doing what they do on a voluntary basis ("I dress the way I like, irrespective of how my group dresses").

THE HISTORICAL AND CULTURAL CONTEXT LEADING TO PSYCHOLOGICAL RESEARCH ON OBEDIENCE

There is a continuing and long-running debate about the optimum level of obedience necessary for the proper functioning of an open society. Much of this discussion, going back several thousand years to Plato, has been concerned with the challenge of how there can be obedience to authority without that authority becoming corrupt. In more recent history, republics such as France, but most of all the United States, were strongly influenced by the ideas of the Roman scholar Cicero (106–43 BCE) to introduce a system of checks and balances to control executive power, even or particularly when the president has popular appeal. Theorists have argued in favor of both the extreme position that "obedience is essential and must be achieved by cunning" and the position that "obedience as we know it is unnecessary." Regarding "obedience as essential," Niccolo Machiavelli (1469–1527) explored, in *The Prince* particularly, artful ways in which those in positions of authority could get others to obey them. Regarding the second view, Karl Marx's (1818–83) vision of an idealized "classless society" envisages a situation where the central authority dissolves away because it is not needed, and obedience to authority as we know it disappears, to be replaced by individuals behaving in the interests of the larger community because of their conscience.

There seem to be some historical trends in the styles of obedience practiced in different societies. This is reflected in the changing balance between rights and duties. A *right* is a demand placed on others by the person who possesses it; a *duty* is a demand placed by others on the person who owes it. Historically, it was the duties of subordinates that were given the highest and sometimes exclusive priority. For example, within the family, women and children were expected to show unquestioning obedience to the "man of the house." In the larger context, individuals were expected to show unquestioning obedience to the monarch, the head of the church, and their local representatives.

A series of changes over the last thousand years or so very gradually gave rise to a greater emphasis on rights. An early indication of this trend is the *Magna Carta* (1215), which placed limitations on the powers of the English monarch and gave more rights to at least some citizens, such as the right to trial by one's peers. Greater individual rights also arose out of reforms in the Church, particularly through the teachings of Martin Luther (1483–1546), and the increased influence of science after the Renaissance. Perhaps the two most important shifts in perspective were brought about when the Copernican view of planetary movements was proved correct by Galileo Galilei (1564–1642) and the theory of evolution was put forward with strong evidentiary support by Charles Darwin (1809–82): the earth was no longer seen as the center of the universe, and humankind was no longer seen as created separate from other creatures. These and other scientific changes were associated with the decline of religious orthodoxy and increased emphasis on individual rights.

The gradual shift toward greater emphasis on individual rights was also influenced by political and economic changes in Western societies, particularly the industrial revolution and political revolutions in Europe and America in the eighteenth and nineteenth centuries. The new middle class turned against duties to the traditional landed aristocracy and the traditional church, and instead emphasized the rights of the individual. This is reflected in a series of declarations that highlight individual rights, including the *English Bill of Rights* (1688), the *United States Constitution* (1787), the *Declaration of the Rights of Man and Citizen* from the French National Assembly (1789), and more recently the *Universal Declaration of Human Rights* (1948). The importance given to rights has continued, and in some ways increased, in more recent times. For example, the great social and political movements of the past century have placed rights at the forefront, as reflected in slogans such as "women's rights," "Black rights," "gay rights," and so on. The decline of the authority of traditional churches also continues, as indicated by a turning away from the traditional tendency to "pay, pray, and obey" by members of the Catholic Church, particularly in most Western societies.

The shift toward rights and the rejection of duties to traditional authorities has been slower outside Western societies. For example, in much of the Islamic world religious authorities still wield absolute power. Indeed, in most Islamic societies the religious authorities are also the political authorities. After the overthrow of the dictatorship of the Shah in Iran in 1979, there emerged a religious dictatorship wherein a supreme religious leader has absolute power in all domains. Despite the continued tradition of obedience to authority in Iran and many other parts of the Islamic world, the idea of individual rights is also gaining influence in such societies, particularly among the young. As democracy takes tentative steps forward, the rights of citizens become highlighted.

But change is not always in one direction or predictable: in some cases enshrined rights have been threatened or even lost. For example, the threat to individual rights was evident during the anti-communist "witch hunts" of the 1950s in the United States, and some would say during attacks on United States citizens deemed "unpatriotic" by the G. W. Bush administration after the tragedy of 9/11. A far more extreme example is the loss of rights in Germany during the 1940s with the rise to power of the Nazis. The rights of German citizens were systematically replaced by duties to obey Hitler and his representatives. The Nazis gradually transformed a democracy into a terrible, destructive dictatorship. Individuals lost rights and had to obey orders in support of a war of aggression and genocide. But how did this come about? Why did so many ordinary people obey orders to harm, directly or indirectly, so many others? To what extent should we hold individual citizens responsible for their actions in such a context?

Modern psychology has added to our understanding of obedience in unique and valuable ways. The exact nature of this contribution can be best appreciated in relation to a question that arises whenever individuals have to defend their involvement in organized acts of aggression: who should be blamed, the individuals involved in carrying out the actions or the authorities who ordered the actions, or perhaps neither, or both? For example, when genocide is committed, should we blame the individual soldiers who followed orders to carry out the genocide? Surely the soldiers were just following orders, as good citizens following the instructions of authority figures? Imagine you are a soldier during a time of war and your army commander orders you to fire on civilians belonging to the enemy side; is it not your patriotic duty to carry out such orders? If you disobey in a time of war, surely you deserve to be court-martialed?

In the war crimes trials at The Hague following World War II, at the trial of Lt. William Calley in 1971 following the murder of Vietnamese civilians during the Vietnam War, at the trial of war criminals following attempts at "ethnic cleansing" in Bosnia, among numerous other instances, those accused of war crimes put forward a common defense: "I was following orders, just doing what my superiors ordered me to do. As a good citizen, you would have done the same. After all, chaos would come about if citizens disobey the authorities." This kind of explanation asserts that the context was more powerful in determining the outcome than individual characteristics; that whichever particular individual was placed in this particular context, the outcome would have been the same. Thus, obedience is explained here by giving highest importance to context and the authority figure, and no importance to the individual person taking orders.

One of the greatest achievements of modern psychologists is experi-mentally to test the question of how much responsibility should be attributed to the context and how much to the individual taking orders. This experimentation has resulted in a picture of obedience that is unex-pected but also highly controversial.

CRITICAL THINKING QUESTIONS

1 Think of three examples of how you have recently obeyed authority figures. How difficult would it be for you to disobey in these three instances?

2 Imagine living in the seventeenth century rather than the twenty-first century. What are some ways in which you would experience less individual rights and be expected to show greater obedience to authority?

THE EXPERIMENTAL STUDY OF OBEDIENCE

Before 1960, two ground-breaking series of studies on conformity were conducted by psychologists, the first initiated by Muzafer Sherif in the 1930s and the second by Solomon Asch in the 1950s. Both of these series of studies were conducted in contexts involving issues that had little real-world significance: estimating the movement of a spot of light (in the case of Sherif's studies) and estimating lengths of lines (in the case of Asch's studies). During 1959–60 Stanley Milgram was working in Asch's laboratory and thinking about what would happen if instead of the movement of a spot of light, judgments of line lengths, or the like, issues of greater human significance were introduced into the laboratory. Would the individual still bend to the will of the majority? This question was the point of departure for Milgram's studies on obedience to authority, and it eventually led to the question of how far individuals would obey an authority figure.

Milgram recruited participants by advertising for volunteers aged 20–50 to take part in a study on the effect of punishment on learning. Participants were told that a goal of the research was to discover how much punishment is good for learning, how much difference it makes whether an older or younger person is giving the punishment, and similar such questions. From the pool of applicants he was able to select a sample of participants with varied ages and backgrounds. In each experiment, the participants were forty percent skilled and unskilled workers, forty percent white-collar, sales, and business, and twenty percent professionals. All those selected had been screened to ensure that they had a normal psychological profile. When the selected participants arrived at Milgram's laboratory, they were introduced to another person who was supposedly also a participant but was actually a middle-aged accountant selected to act as Milgram's confederate. It was explained to the participants that this learning experiment required a teacher and a student. The two participants drew lots to decide who would play the role of the teacher and who would play the role of the student, but the outcome was pre-arranged so that the confederate would always play the role of student. There was also a scientist in a white laboratory coat in the room, purportedly in charge of the "learning study."

The task of the teacher (the real participant) was to teach the student (the confederate) word associations. The teacher read out a series of word pairs, following each pair with four terms. The task of the student was to identify which of the four terms had been originally paired with the first word of each pair. For example, the word pair "road–lamp" would be followed with the terms "summer," "red," "lamp," "deer," and the student had to identity "lamp" as the correct answer.

The teacher was instructed that each time the student got the answer wrong, a punishment would have to be administered (because the experiment was ostensibly about the effects of punishment on learning, there was strong justification for introducing punishment). A device labeled "Shock Generator" was introduced, with marked switches that went up in fifteen-volt increments from zero to 450 volts. There were clear labels on each group of four switches, increasing from "slight shock," to "moderate shock," "strong shock," "very strong shock," "intense shock," "extreme intense shock," "danger," "danger: severe shock," and finally several switches marked "XXX." The teachers were given detailed instructions on how to use this "Shock Generator," and also given a taste of punishment by being subjected to a shock of forty-five volts. Thus, before the start of the actual experiment the teachers knew both how to work the "Shock Generator" and also how it felt to receive a shock generated by this machine.

The task of the teachers was to instruct the students, but also to administer punishment at an increased voltage level each time the student gave an incorrect answer. As a way of ensuring that the teacher was aware of the severity of shock being administered, at each step the teacher had to call out the voltage level. If the teacher became unsure about what to do, the scientist in the white laboratory coat provided a series of prods, starting from a mild "Please continue" but becoming more firm ("You have no other choice; you must go on") if the teacher disobeyed. The scientist also provided assurance that the electric shocks would not leave permanent tissue damage – even though when the shock level reached 150 volts the student cried out that he wanted to be freed, and at 300 volts the student called out in agony and let it be known that he would no longer provide answers to the memory test. Those teachers who continued and eventually reached the maximum shock level of 450 volts were instructed to continue to give shocks at that level.

An important feature of the experimental procedures is that the participants are not suddenly placed in a situation in which they are asked to take extraordinary action, but are eased into such a situation step by step from a rather uneventful start. In the initial stage, the level of shock administered is mild and the response of the student to being punished is also mild. Nothing is happening to worry the teacher. It is only later, through a very gradual process of increasing shock levels and more extreme reactions from the student, that participants find themselves in a conflict. This gradual step-by-step process is critical to bringing about the unexpected results.

The results of the Milgram studies showed that about sixty-five percent of the participants were fully obedient, meaning that they continued to give shocks until they reached the highest voltage level marked "XXX." Subsequent replications and variations of this basic obedience experiment, in the United States and various other Western and non-Western countries, revealed obedience rates ranging between forty and ninety percent. The participants in the first series of experiments were all males, selected because males are more physically aggressive than females, and because cross-cultural research shows a near universal trend: combatants, torturers, and the like are invariably males. However, Milgram did replicate the experiment using female participants and discovered the same unexpectedly high level of obedience among female participants as among males. These results came as a complete surprise and the Milgram study has continued to be at the center of heated controversy. Are the results of these experiments really important? Should these experiments have been conducted at all? How exactly should we interpret the results of the Milgram experiments?

WHY ARE MILGRAM'S OBEDIENCE STUDIES IMPORTANT?

A first response to the results of Milgram's obedience experiments might be dismissive: "I could have told you so; the results are so obvious." This is a valid reaction to the findings of some psychological research, but certainly not this one. The results of Milgram's obedience experiments were not obvious or predictable. We have empirical knowledge of this because before conducting his research, Milgram took the precaution of describing his study in detail to a group of lay people and a group of scientists and asking them to make predictions. The almost unanimous predictions of both groups was that participants would refuse to administer shocks of more than minimal voltage. Thus, the results of the Milgram obedience experiments were truly unexpected, and enormously controversial.

Another possible weakness of Milgram's obedience experiments concerns the possibility that they are unethical because of the way in which the participants were treated. First, participants are deceived. They are told a fake story in order to hide the real purpose of the experiment. Second, and perhaps more seriously, participants are put through a series of situations in which they might experience harmful levels of stress. For example, stress may be experienced when the scientist instructs participants to continue to administer shocks at higher and higher levels, and at the same time the student calls out for help and to be allowed to leave the study. This tug of war may create a harmful psychological conflict within the participant. Given this and other possibilities, were the participants in Milgram's experiments actually harmed by the experience?

Evidence shows no harm done, based on extensive follow-up research conducted by Milgram and his associates. There was thorough debriefing, as well as friendly reconciliation with the student "victim." The participants became fully aware that no shock was actually administered to the student. A sample of the participants were also interviewed by an experienced university psychiatrist, and no negative effects resulting from participation were discovered. About eighty-one percent of participants reported they were glad to have taken part, and seventy-four percent reported they had learned something of personal importance by having taken part.

Some critics have not been satisfied with this follow-up and still insist that Milgram's research was unethical. The climate of opinion has become less accepting toward such risky studies since the 1980s. At the dawn of the twenty-first century it would be extremely difficult, and perhaps impossible, to get institutional approval at a major university to conduct research involving the kinds of deception and potential stress entailed in the Milgram obedience experiments. This is unfortunate, because the immense value of Milgram's experiments on obedience far outweighs the possible risks involved, which have been exaggerated. First, Milgram did check for harmful effects and found none. Second, in their everyday lives many people, particularly minorities, experience far greater stress and deception than anything encountered in the Milgram obedience experiments. Ultimately, the justification for this kind of research rests on the contributions made to understanding human behavior, and the potential for using such understanding to better the human condition. Let me add that I do not see this as a "the ends justify the means" argument, because I believe that the means were ethical and are justified in themselves.

Milgram's experiments on obedience make an invaluable contribution because of the great idea behind them: obedience arises out of certain characteristics of the context, most importantly the presence of an authority figure giving orders in a clear and unequivocal voice. An unavoidable conclusion from these experiments is that the power of the context can be overwhelming. In the terminology introduced in chapter 1, the degrees of freedom in some contexts are so low that obedience becomes highly probable. This finding forces us to re-think how we attribute responsibility in such contexts, and to re-assess the issue of choice in situations involving subordinates and authority figures.

The participants in Milgram's obedience experiments were selected as "ordinary people," so how they behaved does raise the question of how we ourselves might behave in such a situation where an authority figure orders us to behave in a manner that is harmful to others. Would we have done the same? A first point is that not everyone in Milgram's obedience experiments showed complete obedience. About one-third of the US participants refused to obey the authority figure, and in some cultures about two-thirds disobeyed. Thus, it is **not** inevitable that we would have obeyed, because we might have been among those who refused to administer high levels of shock. Not surprisingly, those who obeyed were also more likely to score higher on a measure of authoritarian personality (Adorno et al., 1950). According to this measure, individuals are identified as "High Authoritarians" when they endorse statements such as "No insult to our honor should ever go unpunished,"

"It is only natural and right that women be restricted in certain ways in which men have more freedom," and "Too many people today are living in an unnatural, soft way; we should return to the fundamentals, to a more red-blooded, active way of life." Those high on Authoritarianism tend to be punitive toward subordinates and minorities, and respectful and obedient toward authorities.

Should individuals be held responsible for their actions in such contexts? This is an extremely difficult question to answer, but Milgram's studies allow us to identify certain characteristics of the context that decrease the degrees of freedom and thus lower the range of behavioral options open to participants. The most important factor influencing degrees of freedom was the physical presence of the authority figure. When Milgram introduced a second authority figure and there was disagreement between the two authority figures, the participants were far less obedient. When the authority figure was giving orders from another room, obedience levels declined again. Another factor influencing degrees of freedom was the distance between the teacher (the real participant) and the student: when the teacher was forced to stand next to the student, there was less likelihood of him obeying and administering high levels of shock. When the teacher was administering shock from another room and could only hear the student's calls through a wall, obedience increased. Thus, greater distance of the teacher from the authority figure decreased obedience, but great distance of the teacher from the student increased obedience. Given these kinds of systematic relationships, the claim could be made that the characteristics of the context determined the degrees of freedom and the behavioral options open to the teacher. According to this line of argument, the teacher should not be held responsible for obeying, because obedience was caused by characteristics of the context and the very limited degrees of freedom.

Further, it could be claimed that a number of personality characteristics, such as authoritarianism, that are also outside the control of the individual also decreased the degrees of freedom for some teachers, so that they became more likely to obey. A person's personality characteristics, it could be argued, are no more in their control than is their height or other such characteristics. Just as individuals cannot control how tall they grow, they are not able to control how authoritarian they become. Consequently, according to this view, teachers who were completely obedient in the Milgram experiments cannot be held personally responsible for their actions because the cause of their obedience, high authoritarianism, is not in their control. The same goes for those who commit war crimes by carrying out the orders of authorities.

If we follow the logic of this line of reasoning, in Milgram-type contexts we should hold individuals responsible for their actions only under conditions with high degrees of freedom, in which obedience has been shown to be low rather than high. That is, individuals should be held responsible for the consequences of their obedience if they score low on authoritarianism, were standing close to the student "victim" and positioned at some distance from the authority figure, and if there were several authorities present and they were in disagreement with one another. Under these conditions the degrees of freedom are higher, and thus presumably the teacher has more real choice of what course of action to take. If the teacher is completely obedient under this condition of higher choice, then presumably he or she should be held personally responsible.

But a critical look at the Milgram experiments suggests perhaps even more important lessons.

CRITICAL THINKING QUESTIONS

1 Milgram discovered that the further the teacher was from the student, the more likelihood there was of higher shock levels being administered. What does that imply about the role of modern high-tech weapons in human aggression?

2 When there were two authority figures and they disagreed, obedience declined. What does this imply about the kind of obedience there might be in an open, democratic society as opposed to a less democratic society in which leadership decisions are not openly questioned?

LESSONS FROM PSYCHOLOGICAL RESEARCH ON OBEDIENCE

The first important lesson to be learned from Milgram's experiments on obedience to authority, as well as related studies, is that the characteristics of the context play the key role in obedience. Under certain circumstances, many and perhaps most of us would obey authority figures to behave in a manner that would have harmful consequences for others. This means that we must pay very close attention to the characteristics of the context in which relations with authority figures take place, and shape such contexts to try to minimize blind obedience. In both governmental and non-governmental sectors, there must be safeguards to try to ensure that harmful orders are not carried out.

With respect to police and military authorities, in many democratic countries there are now well-established mechanisms through which both uniformed subordinates and private citizens can complain against the behavior of authority figures when and if such behavior is unjust. The protection of whistle blowers is essential as part of democracy, and such protection has been strengthened recently. This is a much needed step in the right direction, although there remains considerable need for reform. Psychological research by Leonard Bickman and others has shown that simply by wearing a uniform, individuals acquire an extraordinary ability to command others and to have their orders carried out. When people in the street were asked by an individual dressed as a guard, as a milkman, and as a civilian to pick up a bag, give a dime to a stranger, or move away from a bus stop, the individual dressed as a guard was obeyed more than the individuals dressed as a milkman and a civilian. Even when the order given has nothing to do with the authority role in question (for example, as in the case of a person dressed as a fireman telling a passer-by, "Give him a dime"), a person in uniform is more likely to be obeyed than a civilian. The special power that individuals acquire when they put on a uniform needs to be checked through efficient and effective civilian oversight.

The power of the uniformed authority figure is magnified in the context of institutions, such as the prison. Philip Zimbardo's simulation of a prison dramatically illustrates this point. Zimbardo randomly assigned healthy young research participants to play the roles of prison guards and prisoners in the context of a simulated prison. The simulation developed in very unexpected directions, both because of the harsh and aggressive behavior of the prison guards and because of the submissive and passive behavior of the prisoners. The context of the prison, and particularly the uniformed guards, overwhelmed the prisoners. This adds to a large body of evidence strongly suggesting a need to safeguard against abuses of power by those in positions of authority, particularly in total institutions.

The second important lesson we can learn from psychological research on obedience is the vital role of those who refuse to obey authority figures when obedience will result in harm to others. This disobedient group is sometimes numerically a minority, and it may be no more than a handful in some cases, but it can help prevent disasters.

From this perspective, the Milgram experiments are as much about disobedience as they are about obedience. In the United States, about one-third of the participants disobeyed, despite being put under intense pressure by the authority figure, the scientist. In some replications as many as sixty percent of the participants proved to be disobedient.

This disobedient group is vitally important, because if the wrong types of individuals manage to get to positions of high authority, then the survival of democracy may depend on individuals who *refuse* to carry out orders that could be harmful to democracy. Examples from recent US history are those who disobeyed and finally brought down President Richard Nixon during the Watergate scandals of the early 1970s and those who brought an end to the paranoia created by Senator Joseph McCarthy's anti-communism crusade in the 1950s.

There is a third and more subtle lesson to be learned from the Milgram experiments: obedience to authority comes about particularly when the demands to obey are incrementally increased. The participants in Milgram's studies experienced a gradual, step-by-step increase in demands: they were expected to increase the electric shocks by steps of fifteen volts, starting from an apparently harmless low voltage. Related to this is research on the so-called "foot-in-the-door" phenomenon, demonstrating that people are more likely to comply with a large request if they have earlier complied with a smaller request. Obedience to orders to carry out small acts makes it more likely that individuals will obey orders to carry out more serious actions. This step-by-step process reflects how dictatorships often come into being through incrementally increased demands of obedience.

CONCLUDING COMMENT

Psychological research on obedience underlines the need to have in place checks and balances, to ensure effective oversight in all contexts in which authorities wield power. From Cicero writing in the first century BCE to Karl Popper writing in the twentieth century AD, a long line of eminent thinkers have warned us about the dangers that unchecked power represents for an open society. As education levels improve and societies around the world move toward greater democracy, the hope is that more and more formal mechanisms will be put into place through which ordinary citizens can influence the decisions of authority figures. Through these processes, hopefully, unquestioning obedience will also decline. Lord Acton in 1887, and William Pitt before him, popularized the idea that "Power corrupts and absolute power corrupts absolutely." Both power and obedience to authority are essential for the smooth working of complex societies; the challenge is to put into practice an effective set of checks and balances so that civil liberties are safeguarded and democracy has a greater chance of long-term survival.

CRITICAL THINKING QUESTIONS

1 Milgram used a scientist as the authority figure in his experiments; what other authority figures could be used, and in what kinds of scenarios or cover stories could they be placed, to experimentally study obedience to authority?

2 Have you ever experienced a situation in which you had to obey an authority figure even though you thought the consequences of your obedience would not be positive?

FURTHER READING

Adorno, T. W., Frenkel-Brunswik, E., Levinson, D. J., & Sanford, B. W. (1950). *The authoritarian personality.* New York: Harper & Row.

Baumrind, D. (1964). Some thoughts on ethics of research after reading Milgram's "Behavioral study of obedience." *American Psychologist, 19,* 421–423.

Gibson, D. (2003). *The coming Catholic Church: How the faithful are shaping a new American Catholicism.* New York: HarperSanFransisco.

Milgram, S. (1964). Issues in the study of obedience: A reply to Baumrind. *American Psychologist, 19,* 848–852.

Milgram, S. (1974). *Obedience to authority: An experimental view.* New York: Harper & Row.

Milgram, S. (1997). *The individual in a social world: Essays and experiments,* 2nd edn. New York: McGraw Hill.

Moghaddam, F. M. (1998). *Social psychology: Exploring universals across cultures.* New York: Freeman.

Moghaddam, F. M., Slocum, N. R., Finkel, N., Mor, T., & Harré, R. (2000). Toward a cultural theory of duties. *Culture & Psychology, 6,* 275–302.

Moghaddam, F. M., & Marsella, A. J. (eds.) (2003). *Understanding terrorism: Roots, consequences, and interventions.* Washington: American Psychological Association Press.

Persico, J. (1994). *Nuremberg: Infamy on trial.* New York: Viking Press.

Pratkanis, A. R., & Aronson, E. (1991). *The age of propaganda: The everyday use and abuse of persuasion.* New York: W. H. Freeman.

17
FEMINIST PSYCHOLOGY

Feminist psychology attempts to harness the power of psychology to improve the status of women. But in order to be able to use psychology to bring about change in the wider world, feminist psychologists believe they must also bring about change in psychology. This is because, feminist psychologists argue, traditional psychology still reflects many of the gender biases of the larger society, albeit in subtle and implicit ways. By changing the theories, methods, and practices of psychological science, feminist psychology aims to influence how society understands the behavior of females and males, as well as the policies that emerge from such understandings. Feminist psychology is explicitly political and nourished by the feminist movement.

Toward the goal of improving the status of women, feminist psychology has challenged traditional psychology particularly on the interpretation of gender roles and gender differences, and this is reflected in major collections of feminist psychology writings, such as *Representing the Other: A Feminism and Psychology Reader* (Wilkinson & Kitzinger, 1996) and *Deconstructing Feminist Psychology* (Burman, 1998). For example, in the domain of intelligence, feminist psychologists emphasize that there is almost complete overlap between the distribution of scores for females and males on measures of intelligence (i.e. any differences that arise involve only a very small section of the population), and the main source of differences is environmental and not hereditary. However, in other domains feminist psychologists have emphasized rather than diminished the extent and role of female–male differences. For example, as discussed later in this chapter, some feminist psychologists have argued that in the moral domain females speak "in a different voice." Irrespective of whether feminist psychologists have argued for or against female–male differences, they have been **consistent in trying to improve the status of women.**

Feminist psychology is a great idea because it has helped transform the way psychologists conceptually approach the study of females and males. It is no longer acceptable for researchers to adopt the male as the norm according to which the female must be judged, or to work on the general assumption of male superiority. Moreover, there is greater interest in studying females in and for themselves, rather than just in comparison with males. However, the impact of feminist psychology remains at the broad conceptual and political level, rather than with respect to specific empirical findings. Indeed, as we discuss below, the major propositions of feminist psychologists in domains such as moral thinking have not been supported by empirical evidence. Moreover, feminist psychologists have had very little impact on the research methods, or even the main research topics, of traditional psychology. The general ideology underlying feminist psychology has also received severe criticism, particularly in popular literature such as *Professing Feminism* (Patai & Koertge, 1994).

In the following discussion it is useful to keep in mind a distinction between the term *sex*, the biological category people belong to, and *gender*, the social role ascribed to people who fall in either the female or male sex category. In the terminology introduced in chapter 1, sex allows for lower and gender allows for higher degrees of freedom. This categorization of the social world actually glosses over some complications. Each year some infants are born sex ambiguous, but in the Western context, at least, they are speedily placed in the female or male category. This category determination is sometimes completed through surgical operations to help better demarcate the sex of the infant. Even so, the female/male categories are made more complicated by *hermaphrodites*, individuals born with some organs of both sexes; *transvestites*, those who take on the dress and appearance of the opposite sex; and *transsexuals*, those anatomically born of one sex and socialized as such but who feel they belong to the other sex.

THE CULTURAL AND HISTORICAL CONTEXT

Feminist psychology is fundamentally shaped by the political movement known as feminism. While this movement has important intellectual precursors in earlier centuries, such as Mary Wollstonecraft's *Vindication of the Rights of Women* (1792), modern feminism is a broad-based, policy-oriented as well as an intellectual movement that gained considerable momentum in the 1960s. The main focus of the modern feminist movement has been to transform society so that women can fully develop their talents and achieve equality in power, inside and outside the home. Feminism involves both theoretical accounts of the present state of society, and practical guides to how society should be re-organized. Feminist psychology shares this commitment to reform and societal change: feminist psychologists not only want to understand human behavior; they want to change it in fundamental ways. This has important implications for their position on relativism.

The most influential feminist psychologists are not relativistic, if by "relativism" is meant that all values have equal merit. Feminist psychologists believe that some values should have priority, because they are better than other values. For example, different kinds of gender relations do not have equal merit. It is better for women to gain freedom and equality than to remain shackled by traditional gender roles. Interestingly, this anti-relativist position is shared by religious fundamentalists and traditionalists who typically oppose feminism. Such groups also believe that some values are inherently better than others, but of course they disagree with feminists about the merit of various values. For example, *the Promise Keepers* and other similar right-wing Christian organizations believe that the Bible, literally interpreted, should be used as the guide for gender relations, and that the Bible explicitly sets out the leadership role of men in the family.

This kind of anti-relativist position is fundamentally opposed to cultural relativism, whereby the values of each culture can be assessed only within the context of the cultural group itself, and universal criteria for evaluating behavior are rejected. For example, in societies governed by Islamic fundamentalists, such as the Islamic Republic of Iran, men are permitted to have up to four "permanent" wives (most Iranians are Shi'a Muslims, permitted additionally to have any number of "temporary" wives). According to cultural relativism, the merit of such marriage practices can only be evaluated from within the value system of Shi'a Islam as practiced in Iran. This would mean that the same behavior might be judged very differently in different cultures. For example, according to US law it is illegal for a man to have more than one wife. Thus, within the United States a man who practices polygamy would be condemned, but the same does not apply in Iran. In this and many other cases, according to cultural relativism, what is "wrong" behavior in one culture could be "correct" behavior in another. Feminist psychologists and their traditionalist opponents both reject such relativism, although each group puts forward "universals" that are fundamentally opposed to "universals" put forward by the other group.

Feminist psychologists also face criticism from left-wing opponents. Interpreted strictly, Marxism leads to an exclusive focus on social class. Historical development is depicted as an inevitable progression whereby repeated clashes between *capitalists,* those who own the means of production, and the *proletariat,* the labor on sale in the marketplace, eventually lead to the polarization of society into two major classes. Through this process develops *class consciousness,* whereby each class (particularly the proletariat) comes to see itself correctly as a distinct class with interests opposed to the other class. This progression results in class warfare, leading to the downfall of capitalism and the eventual emergence of a classless society.

However, the path to the classless society is very difficult to follow, because many distracting factors serve to perpetuate *false consciousness,* the incorrect perceptions by people about their true social class membership and interests. Among the distracting factors are feminism and other such movements (including those based on ethnicity, race, religion, and so on) that turn attention away from social class. Although some feminists do attend to the intersection between social class and gender (as well as ethnicity, class, and gender), they are still considered by some left-wing critics to be distractions. Just as such critics see religion as the "opium of the people," they view feminism as misleading and as a factor that delays the emergence of class consciousness.

Finally, feminist psychologist have attempted to both work out and work in, to theoretically explain gender relations and to provide empirical bases for their theories. For example, feminist psychologists have proposed that gender identities are constructed and women and men are "positioned" through everyday conversations, and they have empirically studied everyday discourse to examine this idea (see examples in Harré & Moghaddam, 2003, particularly chapter 10). However, in most areas of discussion, theory and ideology help shape feminist debates, empirical research efforts taking a back seat. This situation may change in the future, as increasing numbers of women become engaged in empirical research and take up academic and research positions.

A great idea in action: the changing role of women in psychology

Feminist psychology has helped bring about change in the role of women in psychology. This process is part of a larger change in the role of women in society more broadly. The history of psychology before the 1960s is the history of research predominantly conducted by White males in Western Europe and North America. A handful of women and non-White psychologists do make an appearance in this history but, as is evident from the contents of psychology history texts, they do not gain much prominence. Even less visible are psychologists from outside Western societies.

Just as the characteristics of psychologists were very limited, so were the characteristics of the participants in psychological studies. In many studies, most or all of the participants were young White Western European or North American males. This is because the participants in the vast majority of psychology studies were students in Western European and North American universities, and most students in these locations happened to be White and male.

In recent decades, at least some aspects of this situation have changed, in the context of major changes taking place in Western societies and the rest of the world. Since the 1960s, equal rights legislation in the US and many other Western societies has created new educational and employment opportunities for women and ethnic minorities. Discrimination on the basis of sex, race, and religion (as well as sexual orientation, in some instances) has become illegal. Whereas in 1899–1900 there were rarely any women on the faculty of psychology departments at major US universities, by 1984 at least twenty-two percent of the faculty were women and this figure had increased to thirty-six percent in 1999–2000. Correspondingly, between 1984 and 2000 there was a fourteen percent decrease in the number of male faculty at US institutions. In the same period there has been a smaller increase in the number of ethnic minority faculty to about ten percent in 2000.

The participation of female students in psychology programs has increased even more dramatically. In 1899–1900 very few US institutions of higher learning admitted female students, but in 1999–2000 three out of every four full-time enrollees in graduate psychology programs were females. In some important specialties, such as developmental psychology, since the mid 1990s over eighty percent of new Ph.D. degrees have been earned by females. Increasingly, as senior male faculty retire, the new faculty hired to replace them are female. If current trends continue, by 2020 probably at least sixty percent and perhaps as much as eighty percent (compared with the current thirty-six percent) of full-time psychology faculty at major US universities will be female. Also, psychological research continues to rely heavily on psychology students as participants. Given that at most major institutions at least seventy-five percent of psychology majors are female, a consequence is that the behavior of females is no longer neglected by psychologists. The science of psychology used to involve White males studying White males and generalizing the results to all humankind, but increasingly both researchers and the subjects of study are female.

These trends may lead us to conclude that females are already well represented in psychology. Since 1973 the American Psychological Association has had a division (number 35) devoted to the psychology of women (the equivalent was established in the UK in 1991), and about half a dozen journals are exclusively devoted to psychology of women, with titles such as *Psychology of Women Quarterly* (published since 1977), *Women & Therapy* (published since 1982), and *Feminism & Psychology* (published since 1991). There are also numerous major texts on feminist psychology and the psychology of women.

These changes are in line with the success of women in academia more generally. By 2000, young women in North America and much of Western Europe were having at least as much, and in some areas more, success as young men in gaining entrance to competitive university programs, including graduate programs in important fields such as law and medicine. *In 2002 more American women than men earned doctorates in US universities.* Perhaps inevitably, the changed role of women in psychology, and society more generally, tends to be taken for granted now, with the result that the important role played by feminist psychology in bringing about this change is often neglected.

Feminist psychology or psychology of women?

The main idea we are assessing in this chapter is "feminist psychology," but this involves an influential but numerically small group within the broader movement of research on "gender relations" and "psychology of women." Why has there been a preference for the label "psychology of women" over "feminist psychology?" Why is it that rather than a "Society for Feminist Psychology," there is within the American Psychological Association a division (established 1973) titled "Society for the Psychology of Women," and sections with similar titles are now established as part of national psychology associations in many other Western countries? One major reason is that "feminist psychology" is explicitly political and advocacy oriented, and this contradicts the political neutrality that traditional psychology attempts to portray.

A major challenge taken up by traditional psychology is to establish psychology as the "science of behavior." According to the traditional view, science is supposed to be a politically neutral enterprise. Thus, traditional psychology has made efforts to distance itself from political movements and labels, including "feminist psychology." Of course, critics argue that traditional psychology is not politically neutral, particularly in research areas such as intelligence (see chapter 7). Despite such criticisms, traditional psychology has shown a strong preference for "psychology of women" over "feminist psychology," on the grounds that "psychology of women" is a better fit with "scientific neutrality."

Another reason for a preference for "psychology of women" over "feminist psychology" is that in the view of some segments of the general public, the term "feminism" has become associated with "radicalism." For this reason, some scholars who describe themselves as researching in the domain of "psychology of women" actually approve of feminist goals and values but for reasons of political positioning prefer to avoid being labeled as "feminists."

Above and beyond the particular labels used, there is no denying that a wide range of views are represented in research on the behavior of women and men.

CRITICAL THINKING QUESTIONS

1 What are the relative merits of the terms "psychology of women" and "feminist psychology?"

2 Feminist psychologists tend to be against relativism. Do you believe they are correct in taking this stand?

DISCOVERING AND INTERPRETING GENDER DIFFERENCES

Feminist psychologists have challenged traditional psychology particularly with respect to the interpretation of gender differences. Feminist psychologists have consistently interpreted gender differences to enhance the role and status of women. For example, traditional psychology, influenced by evolutionary psychology (see chapter 19), has depicted the tendency for males to report being more sexually promiscuous than females as inherited and arising out of long-term adaptation strategies, the implication being that we should just accept it as something "natural." In contrast, feminist psychologists argue that in many Western and non-Western societies, a double standard guides the sexual behavior of females and males, keeping females under control and giving males far more freedom. This double standard, feminist psychologists argue, is part of a male-dominated culture, but is not "natural" or universal. In support of this position, feminist psychologists point to cross-cultural research in societies where females enjoy at least equal sexual freedom and are sexually active with multiple partners (including *polyandry*, where a wife has multiple husbands at the same time, as practiced among the Nyinba of Nepal). By identifying the variety of sexual and marriage practices (e.g. see Stockard, 2002), then, feminist psychologists have undermined the idea that there is one "natural" way for females and males to interact, as well as the "natural" differences between females and males.

However, different groups of feminist psychologists have taken different positions on the existence of gender differences, or whether gender differences should be a subject of study at all. Four different positions with illustrative research examples are elaborated below: (1) women and men are worthy of study in and by themselves, without reference to any differences that may exist between them; (2) gender differences reflect male superiority; (3) gender differences reflect female superiority; (4) gender differences do not exist.

Women are worthy of study in and by themselves

Two related lines of argument underlie this position. First, the value of studying *differences* between women and men is questioned. Second, it is argued that, irrespective of male characteristics, females should be studied in their own right.

The psychological characteristics of women do not change because men have certain psychological characteristics. For example, if men are shown to be at level X on aggression, or empathy, or any other characteristic, and women are at level Y, the level Y at which women are located does not change in any way because men are at level X. Moreover, the difference between women and men tells us nothing about the actual characteristics of either group; it only tells us about the extent of the gap between the two groups. According to this argument, then, we should not study gender differences, because irrespective of whether such differences are large or small, or exist at all, the particular characteristics of women do not change.

A central proposition of feminist psychology is that women are worthy of study in their own right. Starting from this point of departure, one could argue that the psychological characteristics of women should be studied in order to arrive at a scientific understanding of women; not in comparison with men, but as a group in and of themselves. For example, there are certain life experiences, including menstrual cycles, pregnancy, childbirth, motherhood, and menopause, together with their associative psychological experiences that are particular to women. Associated with some such experiences are hormonal changes and mood swings, sometimes leading to depression. An example is postpartum depression, experienced by some women (but no men) shortly after giving birth.

The contention is that experiences such as postpartum depression can be understood better by focusing on the experiences of women, and not by making comparisons with men. We must ask: What are the factors in the lives of women that lead to this kind of depression? In everyday life and in the mass media, hormonal changes are often depicted as the source of depression among women. This seems to make intuitive sense, because life events such as pregnancy involve hormonal changes. However, if hormones do play a role, they do so in subtle and complicated ways, because simple measures of hormone levels do not distinguish between depressed and non-depressed women. Another possible source is the particular coping style many women tend to adopt. Depression may well be exacerbated by dwelling on one's own feelings, focusing on one's problematic experiences, and constantly talking with others about being depressed (Nolen-Hoeksema & Morrow, 1991).

But, despite the call for more studies on the psychological experiences of women in and of themselves, the research on gender differences continues to grow. Studies on gender published in the major psychology journals tend to focus almost exclusively on differences between women and men, rather than just on women studied for their own sake. The view that women and men are fundamentally different in terms of their psychology remains extremely pervasive, as reflected by the success of such popular books as *You Just Don't Understand: Men and Women in Conversations* (Tannen, 1990). An argument in favor of this "gender differences" approach is that information about both males and females is essential because it provides invaluable context: scores on psychological tests, such as those pertaining to intelligence, personality traits, and so on, are only meaningful in relative terms. The information arrived at about women is best understood in comparison with information about men, and vice versa.

A number of different arguments could be made in favor of making comparisons across female and male groups. One argument is that psychological tests do not stand on their own objective feet, but simply provide means of making comparisons between people. Thus, for example, if Jane scores Y and John scores X, the values Y and X are not situated on objective ratio scales (with a true zero and equal intervals between values on the scale), but simply provide points of comparison on some kind of an ordinal scale, which only allows for judgments of one value being lower or higher than another. This assumption is not accepted by defenders of traditional psychology, who view psychological measures, such as intelligence tests and personality scales, as objective and of merit as stand-alone indicators. For these thinkers, who present a different argument in favor of making comparisons across gender groups, such comparisons are of value, not because psychological tests are not objective, but because gender differences are worth studying in themselves. On the one hand, then, feminist psychologists argue that women (and men) are worthy of study in and of themselves without making comparisons with the opposite sex. On the other hand, defenders of gender differences research argue that such differences are worthy of study in and of themselves.

Gender differences reflect male superiority

Until very recently, and some would claim even now, the domain of "gender differences" has been dominated by studies that purportedly demonstrate the inferiority of women. The point has been emphasized by feminist psychologists that gender differences have been highlighted and publicized when the results of psychological research confirm traditional stereotypes about women and men. According to this argument, in the nineteenth century the pioneering studies of Francis Galton (1822–1911) became influential in thinking about women and men, because Galton depicted women as intellectually inferior to men, and a similar bias has been noted in the first extensive psychological discussions of differences between women and men, such as Ellis's (1894) book *Man and Woman*. The main thrust of this kind of research, critics argue, is to, first, show that women are psychologically less than men and, second, to position the male profile as the norm or even the ideal that women should be aspiring to emulate.

In support of the proposition that men are superior in important areas such as intelligence, advocates referred to Darwin's theory of evolution and also produced evidence of differences between the brains of men and women, in terms of size, function, laterality, and so on. As Shields (1975) and others have pointed out, scientific evidence was interpreted in line with traditional gender stereotypes. The main issue was and remains the claim that intelligence is largely inherited, that certain people (that is, men of White European ancestry, and more recently men of Asian ancestry) are born more intelligent and that environmental conditions have relatively little bearing on the matter (see chapter 7).

Evidence for the superiority of men was gathered through studies in many different psychological domains, including leadership. Both in everyday life (particularly in the realm of politics) and in research studies, men seemed to come out more as the natural leaders. However, a closer look at studies of leadership reveals that traditional gender stereotypes have a powerful impact on the performance of females and males. For example, in studies where women and men interact with one another for a short time (e.g. less than thirty minutes), so that they do not have the opportunity to get to know the personality of other group members, then males are more likely to be selected as leaders. However, the likelihood of females emerging as leaders increases when people have more information about one another, and by implication when gender stereotypes are not the only basis for perceptions and action.

The detrimental impact of traditional gender stereotypes on the status of women has also been demonstrated in another context where males are assumed to be superior: mathematical ability. When females and males were tested on mathematical ability, the scores achieved by females decreased after verbal reference was made to the traditional stereotype of females not being good in maths. This suggests that traditional gender stereotypes can serve as an important source of gender differences on mathematics, among other domains.

Gender differences reflect female superiority

A third, more recent approach to the study of femininity–masculinity is to return to the idea that there are gender differences but to argue that at least in some important domains females have the preferable character-istics. The major academic influence on this third perspective, highlight-ing the superiority of women in some domains, was the research of Carol Gilligan, who challenged the account of moral reasoning provided by Lawrence Kohlberg. Kohlberg's stepwise stage model has dominated the traditional view of moral thinking (see chapter 9). Kohlberg conducted a longitudinal study of boys growing up to become adults. He identified a stage-wise progression in moral thinking among the boys, moving from pre-conventional (avoid punishment, seek reward), to conventional (abide by the law of the land, irrespective of what it condones), and post-conventional thinking (abide by principles of right and wrong that are above and beyond local mores).

Kohlberg developed a series of scenarios involving moral dilemmas. In the famous "Heinz Dilemma," for example, Heinz needs a certain drug to save his wife's life, but the only pharmacist who sells the drug is asking a price Heinz is unable to pay. Should or should not Heinz steal the drug, and why? Kohlberg judged the level of moral reasoning attained by the participant through the reasoning put forward for the decision of whether or nor Heinz should steal the drug (and not through the decision itself). Based on the moral reasoning displayed, a participant could be assessed as being at a certain level of moral reason-ing according to Kohlberg's hierarchy. It was discovered that females generally score lower on Kohlberg's hierarchy.

Carol Gilligan argued that Kohlberg's test of moral reasoning was developed with a male-centric bias, and it fails to incorporate the differ-ent voice of females (the general consensus now is that Gilligan's criti-cisms of Kohlberg are not supported by evidence, and Kohlberg's procedures do not undervalue women's moral reasoning). She inter-viewed women about real-life moral reasoning dilemmas they face, including women faced with the dilemma of whether or not to have an abortion, and discovered they have a more communal way of solving moral dilemmas. Gilligan claimed that whereas men tend to emphasize rights and individual justice issues, women emphasize responsibility and relationships. From this difference the claim arose that women have a more caring approach to moral reasoning, one that benefits the larger society and is less self-centered. In the decades that followed these origi-nal claims, research has shown that there are, indeed, different styles of thinking through moral dilemmas, but the overlap between women and men is considerable. The fundamental difference is not so much between men and women, but between women and men who think through moral issues in a more communal manner with an emphasis on duties to the larger group, and those women and men who think through such issues with an emphasis on individual rights and universal justice rules. The tradition has been to assess women and men on paper and pencil moral reasoning tasks, what women and men actually do can and often does differ from how they solve problems on paper. Many business executives who follow unethical business operating practices (in the manner of the ENRON executives) are clever enough to solve paper and pencil moral dilemmas in a "principled" manner.

More recently, the particular merits of female psychological characteristics have been highlighted by research from an unexpected quarter: the study of *autism*, a condition characterized by an individual's lack of ability to relate and interact with others, compulsive actions, and retarded language development. An idea being explored at Cambridge University's *Autism Research Center* is that autism represents an extreme version of the male brain. According to this theory, the essential difference between females and males is the capacity for *empathy*, the drive to discover the emotions and thoughts of others and to respond to them with appropriate emotions and thoughts. The hard-wiring of females gives them greater capacity for empathy and the understanding of other people (whereas the hard-wiring of males gives them more capacity for understanding systems). An implication of this viewpoint is that the high female capacity for empathy serves as protection against autism and explains why a far greater number of boys than girls are autistic.

Gender differences do not exist

Given that for much of the history of modern psychology gender differences were interpreted as demonstrating female inferiority, it is perhaps not surprising that the emergence of women in larger numbers as research and practicing psychologists was accompanied by the publication of research reports apparently showing no gender differences. Associated with these new findings was the assumption that more egalitarian environmental conditions would wipe away major gender differences. There had been a few earlier publications by men reporting minimal gender difference, but the major change of direction came in the 1960s with the research of a new generation of feminist psychologists, particularly Eleanor Maccoby, Sandra Bem, Janet Spence, and Alice Eagly.

The first step in this new movement involved reviews of the sex differ-ences literature, a tradition strengthened by the scholarship of Eleanor Maccoby since the 1960s, with the conclusion that there were actually only a few areas in which sex differences of note existed. Since the 1980s Alice Eagly and others have made extensive use of *meta-analysis*, a method for computing trends based on statistics from multiple studies, to survey gender differences. Although there is disagreement as to how the results of meta-analysis on gender differences should be interpreted, there is more agreement on some areas of gender differences. These areas are: higher physical aggressivity among men, higher verbal ability among women (although there is weaker support for this among adult samples since the 1990s), higher spatial and mathematical ability among men. An impor-tant point is that the distribution of scores for the vast majority of females and males overlap, and the non-overlapping scores of only a very small number of females and males account for these gender differences.

But a more fundamental step was taken when researchers rejected the tradition set by the first masculinity–femininity scale (Terman & Miles, 1936) to use a unidimensional measure, which placed "male" and "female" at opposite ends of the single dimension. For example, imagine you are a participant in a study and are asked the following question:

Rate the extent to which you see yourself as masculine or feminine:
I see myself as…
Completely masculine 1   2   3   4   5   6   7 Completely feminine

Using this kind of rating scale, the more a respondent endorses one gender category, the less the respondent endorses the alternative. For example, a person who strongly endorses "completely masculine" must necessarily reject "completely feminine."

This kind of unidimensional scale was eventually replaced with a multidimensional view of femininity–masculinity when Sandra Bem and Janet Spence published their alternative measures in 1974. An important step in the move away from unidimensional measures of masculinity–femininity was the conceptual argument that femininity and masculinity can be measured *independently* of one another. In theory, an individual (male or female) could be low on both femininity and masculinity, or high on both, or medium on both, or low on one and high on the other. That these different possibilities actually do come about was confirmed through the measures introduced by Bem and Spence, which allowed femininity and masculinity to be measured independently from one another. To illustrate this approach, imagine you are a participant in a study and are asked the following question:

Rate the extent to which you see yourself as masculine or feminine:
I see myself as...
Not at all feminine 1   2   3   4   5   6   7 Completely feminine
Not at all masculine 1   2   3   4   5   6   7 Completely masculine

The multidimensional approach allows for the same person to rate herself or himself as "7" on both femininity and masculinity, or "1" on both, or "4" on both, or any other combination.

The new multidimensional research instruments allowed for a measure of *androgyny*, the extent to which a person has both feminine and masculine characteristics. The more equal the scores on feminine and masculine characteristics, the more androgynous a person is judged to be. Perhaps the most dramatic shift away from the traditional way of thinking was the proposition that more androgynous individuals are better adjusted and healthier (although this claim is not supported by empirical evidence). This was a complete reversal from the traditional view that men and women who are a closer fit with the profile of the masculine male and the feminine female are also better adjusted and psychologically healthier.

The concept of androgyny does not so much argue for or against the existence of sex differences as it negates the concept of sex differences altogether. Every individual, it is argued, to some extent has both feminine and masculine characteristics. If attention is given only to a person's masculine characteristics, then his feminine characteristics are ignored. Similarly, if attention is given only to a person's feminine characteristics, then her masculine characteristics are ignored. The most useful and accurate strategy is to measure both femininity and masculinity as characteristics of the same individual, and look at the balance between the two.

Gender differences: looking to the future

Advances in technology since the 1980s have allowed for far more accurate and detailed studies of brain functioning, with the result that gender differences are now more clearly identified in hemispheric specialization. The available evidence suggests that hemispheric asymmetry is less pronounced in females, meaning that females rely more on both sides of the brain. A number of other, more specific differences are suggested by studies, such as women having a higher proportion of gray matter than men do. While research on gender and brain functioning is leading to intriguing results, the implications of such results for actual thought and action are unclear. Differences between females and males in thought and action do not have a clear link with any female–male differences in brain functioning. For now, it may be useful to think of biological factors as constituting a framework for the development of gender roles and relations.

Biological sources undoubtedly play a part in gender roles and relations, probably by demarcating limits to the "plasticity" or changeability of females and males. That is, biological factors place a boundary beyond which we are unable to transform females and males. This is suggested by the case of John, an infant boy who in 1963 was left without a penis after a botched circumcision when he was eight months old. It was decided that the best strategy was to raise him as a girl, and John's testicles were removed and an artificial vagina was created for the infant, re-named "Joan." Years of continuous medical monitoring and treatment followed, with Joan eventually growing breasts through hormone therapy. This case was discussed by researchers as an illustrative example of the plasticity of sex: biological factors had been overpowered by social and psychological ones; a male had been re-shaped to become a woman. But in practice Joan was never happy as a female and she eventually asked to return to being a male. Through additional medical treatment and after decades of suffering, "Joan" did become "John" again, and he married a woman who (fortunately) already had children.

CRITICAL THINKING QUESTIONS

1 Do you believe that female-male differences should be studied?

2 What implications does the measurement of androgyny have for the way we think about female and male roles in society?

CONCLUDING COMMENT: QUESTIONS FOR THE FUTURE

From one perspective, feminist psychology may melt away as women gain equal status and power in the most important sectors of society. The prejudices that gave impetus to this movement will be gone and will hold only historical interest, and so will the justification for the movement itself. It could be argued that the first part of this change is already taking place to some degree, as reflected by the dated evidence frequently cited to show prejudices against women. An example is the ꜰꜱꜱꜱꜱꜱꜱꜱꜱꜱꜱ ꜱꜱꜱꜱ ꜱꜱꜱꜱꜱꜱꜱ ꜱꜱ ꜱꜱꜱꜱꜱꜱ ꜱ ꜱꜱꜱꜱ ꜱꜱꜱꜱ displaced from the labor force when men came back from the Second World War. To many young people today, this seems like ancient history and does not correspond with their personal experiences of relations between females and males. It could be argued that the most important examples of prejudice against women cited in feminist books, such as women not being allowed to enter prestigious professions (law, medicine, and so on), are from past eras. From a different perspective, however, it could be argued that feminist psychology will continue even when women have achieved their political goals, because women are worthy of study irrespective of their particular societal situation and status in relation to men.

CRITICAL THINKING QUESTIONS

1 Given the success of women in academic competition, what do you see to be the future of feminist psychology?

2 The position of research psychologists on the nature and extent of female–male differences has shifted back and forth over the last century or so, depending on social and political trends. What does this imply about the relationship between psychological research and societal forces?

FURTHER READING

American Psychological Association Research Office. (2003). Analysis of data from graduate study in psychology 1999–2000. <http: research.apa.org/ grad00contents.html>.

Baron-Cohen, S. (2003). *The essential difference: The truth about the male and female brain.* Cambridge, MA: Perseus.

Becker, S. W., & Eagly, A. H. (2004). The heroism of men and women. *American Psychologist, 59,* 163–178.

Bem, S. L. (1974). The measurement of psychological androgyny. *Journal of Consulting and Clinical Psychology, 42,* 155–162.

Brettell, C. B., & Sargent, C. F. (eds.) (1997). *Gender in cross-cultural perspective*, 2nd edn. Upper Saddle River, NJ: Prentice Hall.

Burman, E. (ed.) (1998). *Deconstructing feminist psychology*. London: Sage.

Burn, S. M. (1996). *The social psychology of gender*. New York: McGraw Hill.

Cahill, L., Haier, R. J., & White, N. S. (2001). Sex related differences in amygdala activity during emotionally influenced memory storage. *Neurobiology of Learning and Memory*, 75, 1–9.

Eagly, A. H., & Karau, S. J. (1991). Gender and the emergence of leaders: A meta-analysis. *Journal of Personality and Social Psychology*, 60, 685–710.

Ellis, H. (1894). *Man and woman*. London: Scott.

Harré, R., & Moghaddam, F. M. (eds.) (2003). *The self and others: Positioning individuals and groups in personal, political, and cultural contexts*. Westport, CT: Praeger.

Helgeson, V. S. (2002). *The psychology of gender*. Upper Saddle River, NJ: Prentice Hall.

Lauer, R. H., & Lauer, J. C. (2004). *Marriage and family: The quest for intimacy*, 5th edn. New York: McGraw Hill.

Lips, H. M. (1993). *Sex & gender*, 2nd edn. Mountain View, CA: Mayfield.

Maccoby, E. E. (1998). *The two sexes: Growing up apart, coming together*. Cambridge. MA: Harvard University Press.

Maccoby, E. E., & Jacklin, C. N. (1974). *The psychology of sex differences*. Stanford, CA: Stanford University Press.

Nolen-Hoeksema, S., & Morrow, J. (1991). A prospective study of depression and posttraumatic stress symptoms after a natural disaster: The Loma Prieta earthquake. *Journal of Personality and Social Psychology*, 61, 115–121.

Patai, D., & Koertge, N. (1994). *Professing feminism: Cautionary tales from the strange world of women's studies*. New York: Basic Books.

Smallwood, S. (2003). American women surpass men in earning doctorates. *Chronicle of Higher Education*, 12 December, A10.

Spence, J. T., Helmreich, R., & Stapp, J. (1974). *The Personal Attributes Questionnaire: A measure of sex-role stereotypes and masculinity–femininity*. *JSAS Catalog of Selected Documents in Psychology*, 4, 43–44.

Steele, C. (1997). A threat in the air: How stereotypes shape intellectual identity and performance. *American Psychologist*, 52, 613–629.

Stockard, J. E. (2002). *Marriage in culture: Practices and meanings across diverse societies*. New York: Harcourt College Publishers.

Tannen, D. (1990). *You Just Don't Understand: Men and Women in Conversations*. New York: Morrow.

Terman, L. M., & Miles, C. C. (1936). Sex and personality. New York: McGraw-Hill.

Wilkinson, S. (ed.) (1996). *Feminist social psychologies: International perspectives*. Buckingham, England: Open University Press.

Wilkinson, S. (1997). Feminist psychology. In D. Fox & I. Prilleltensky (eds.), *Critical psychology: An introduction*. London: Sage.

Wilkinson, S., & Kitzinger, C. (eds.) (1996). *Representing the other: A feminism and psychology reader*. London: Sage.

Yoder, J. D. (2003). *Women and gender: Transforming psychology*. 2nd edn. Upper Saddle River, NJ: Prentice Hall.

18

MULTICULTURAL PSYCHOLOGY

The prediction had been that by the year 2020 the size of the Hispanic population in the United States would attain parity with the African American population. The 2000 census proved this prediction wrong: there were already as many Hispanics as African Americans in the US at the dawn of the twenty-first century, each group being about thirty-six million strong (actually, Hispanics now out-number African Americans). In some regions of the country, particularly in California and Florida, the ethnic power minorities have become numerical majorities. There continue to be about one million legal immigrants to the United States annually, in addition to hundreds of thousands of illegal ones. Although high levels of immigration to North America is in keeping with past trends, a dramatic new trend is the very large numbers of immigrants from outside Western Europe. This new trend in immigration means that in terms of sheer numbers the mix of ethnicity in the US population is changing, with greater numbers of people from Asia, Latin America, and other non-European regions. The same trend is evident in other historically immigrant-receiving countries such as Australia, Canada, and New Zealand.

More muted but similar demographic changes have been taking place in Western Europe, accelerated since the 1970s by the low birth rate of indigenous Western European populations. In order for a country to maintain the same population level, an annual birth rate of at least 2.1 percent is needed. In most parts of Western Europe the birth rate has been below 2.1 percent in recent decades. Even in Italy, a Catholic country where birth control was previously illegal, the birth rate dipped below 1.5 percent during the 1990s. A consequence of this has been a need to import labor; a formidable challenge for Western European countries, many of which do not have a strong tradition of immigration. A variety of programs to bring in "temporary" or "guest" workers has been tried out in countries as large as Germany and as small as Switzerland, and very recently Western Europeans have started to look to North America for models of how "permanent" immigration might work for them (interestingly, in 2004 President Bush proposed a European-style "guest worker" program for the United States). It is clear that the tens of millions of non-Westerners in Western Europe – including millions of Turks in Germany, North Africans in France, and South Asians in the United Kingdom – are there to stay. Rather than being temporary, ethnic minorities in Western Europe are an integral part of their adopted land. The ethnic mix of Western Europe has been permanently transformed.

The changed demographics of Western societies have coincided with improved international communications and transportation, resulting in increased contact between peoples of the world. Whether such contact is direct, as when people travel and come face to face with out-group members, or indirect, as through electronic communications (email, fax, the web, telephone, and so on), there is a real sense in which the "global village" is being realized. The recognition has grown, underlined by the tragedy of 9/11, that our culturally diverse world has become much smaller, and what happens in other cultures does impact on us. This sense of a diverse but interconnected global family is intensified by the practical challenges of formulating effective policies both abroad and at home.

Multicultural psychology evolved in response to the urgent need to manage more effectively cultural diversity, in social relations generally, and educational, health, city-planning, and work arenas more specifically. At the heart of multicultural psychology are a number of propositions about identity. These propositions arise out of, on the one hand, research on inter-group relations and, on the other hand, collective (including ethnic, feminist, and gay) movements that have gained strength particularly since the 1960s. Thus, multicultural psychology is research driven but is also closely tied to some influential recent political movements arising out of the changing demographics of North America and to a lesser extent Western Europe.

But it is important to keep in mind that cultural and linguistic diversity is also a characteristic of lower-income societies, and that people in many such societies, including the population giants China and India, also face the challenge of developing adequate policies. For example, controversy and conflict over affirmative action programs, designed to improve the status of power minorities, are becoming as important in China and India as they are in North America. India has the most complex and extensive affirmative action program in the world, almost half of the places in some public universities being taken up by quotas. In some ways, the backlash against "special treatment" (such as quotas for university places) for untouchables, or *Dalits*, members of the lowest-caste in India, is similar to the backlash against special treatment for ethnic minorities in the United States, particularly in areas such as education and jobs.

In many different societies, supporters of affirmative action argue that minority status affords lower degrees of freedom and a lower range of options in education, employment, and other important sectors. Critics, however, contend that affirmative action programs are anti-democratic. Backlash has forced the dismantling of affirmative action programs in Malaysia, where quotas have favored native Malays over other ethnic groups. Affirmative action programs have only recently been introduced in parts of Brazil, to help Black and mixed-race students gain more places in universities, but already hundreds of lawsuits have been filed against the programs. Thomas Sowell conducted a systematic study of how affirmative action has worked in Malaysia, Sri Lanka, Nigeria, India, and the United States, and concluded that affirmative action has had some serious negative consequences in each society. According to Sowell, consistent across societies is that the elite in each preferred group reap by far the greatest benefits from affirmative action programs. For example, in the United States it is relatively affluent African Americans who have reaped most benefits from affirmative action. Thus, the controversy about affirmative action specifically, and the challenge of developing effective policies for managing cultural diversity more generally, is truly global.

MULTICULTURAL PSYCHOLOGY AND IDENTITY

The central focus of multicultural psychology is identity, both personal and group. Major questions concern the fate of identity when individuals belonging to different cultural groups interact. Is it inevitable that over time cultural and linguistic differences between different groups will eventually wash away and a common identity will evolve? Or, is it more likely that group differences will be maintained and perhaps even strengthened and distinct and separate identities will be upheld? These descriptive questions concern the expected trends, but multicultural psychology is also prescriptive and puts forward proposals for paths that should be taken and the policies that *should be* adopted. Multicultural psychology addresses questions about the effectiveness of different policies (such as programs to eliminate cultural differences through common educational experiences and language training) for managing cultural diversity, and the relationship between such policies and identity.

The major reason why such policies are deemed important is because of serious problems typically associated with culturally diverse societies: *prejudice*, an attitude toward others solely on the basis of group membership; *discrimination*, actual behavior directed at others on the basis of category membership; and *inter-group aggression*, behavior intended to harm another person solely because of their group membership. These problems can severely diminish quality of life and hamper relationships in social and work contexts. The policies for managing cultural diversity fall into two broad categories – assimilation and multiculturalism – and each has important implications for identity. For the most part these policies have been developed by working out and pushing back theoretical boundaries without much concern for empirical evidence, although in recent years there has been greater effort to also work in and locate a firmer empirical basis for ideas.

CRITICAL THINKING QUESTIONS

1 In what ways does international trade lead to both assimilation and multiculturalism?

2 Why are both personal and collective identity central to discussions about assimilation and multiculturalism?

ASSIMILATION AND IDENTITY

Historically the ideal form of inter-group relations popularized in the United States is assimilation, whereby groups abandon their differences and merge into the American mainstream. This strategy is seen to have a number of implications, directly or indirectly related to identity. First, it is assumed that when individuals start to see themselves as belonging to one national group, "Americans," there will be greater in-group cohesion and fewer opportunities for internal conflict. The feeling that "we are one" will overpower any former ties and allegiances to non-American groups. Greek, Vietnamese, Irish, Mexican, Nigerian, Chinese, German, and other immigrants to the United States will cut ties to their ancestral lands and languages and become loyal to their adopted land and people. Simply put, there will be no out-groups within the United States, and thus no basis for inter-group conflict.

Second, assimilation will more likely lead to a perception that "we are all alike," and thus there will be a greater likelihood for positive relations with others within the United States. This idea of similarity having positive social benefits is in line with probably the most robust relationship in social psychology, similarity-attraction. Under many different circumstances, people have been shown to be more positively attracted toward other individuals and groups that they perceive to be more similar to themselves.

On the other side of the coin, from Freud to modern researchers, the idea is endorsed that prejudice and aggression will more likely be shown against those perceived to be more dissimilar to ourselves. Most recently, evolutionary psychologists have contributed to the debate by arguing that genetic similarity is at the root of similarity-attraction. They propose that we are positively disposed toward others who are genetically similar to us and negatively disposed toward genetically dissimilar others. Thus, there exist a variety of theoretical arguments in favor of similarity-attraction, from psychodynamic to evolutionary, and also empirical evidence in support of the similarity-attraction hypothesis at both the individual and group levels.

The third reason for the historic endorsement of assimilation in the United States is the belief that it is more compatible with meritocracy. In order for every person to enjoy equality of opportunity, so the argument goes, there must be a "level playing field." This means everyone must have the same basic cultural and linguistic resources; a person who lacks such resources would not be able to take advantage of the available opportunities. For example, a person who is not in tune with the American mainstream and is not fluent in English would find it very difficult to compete successfully for higher-status jobs in the major professions in the United States. This may come about in cases where a child is born in an *ethnic economic enclave* (sections of an economy that are controlled by a cultural or linguistic group, such as exist in parts of Miami or Los Angeles, for instance), and the child can survive within the ethnic neighborhood speaking just the heritage language and competing just for job opportunities within the ethnic economic enclave.

It is also interesting to consider the relationship between the idea that assimilation will strengthen meritocracy and the ongoing criticisms of the standardized tests, such as the SAT (which used to be known as the Scholastic Aptitude Test, see chapter 7), as culturally biased. If the SAT and other such tests do discriminate against ethnic minorities, as critics contend, then a solution would be to put into place an assimilation policy so that everyone would grow up in the same cultural and linguistic context and benefit from the same opportunities. In this way, no individuals would find themselves disadvantaged because of their having grown up in marginal cultures and because of a marginal language being their first language. Thus, instead of trying to achieve culture-free tests, an impossible goal to achieve according to some critics, we should ensure that everyone benefits from the same culture and has the same advantages with respect to tests such as the SAT.

In practice, there are varieties of assimilation and the implication of assimilation for identity will depend on the particular form of assimilation that is followed. Historically, the main type of assimilation that has been popularized is what I term "minority assimilation," whereby minorities abandon their ancestral culture and language and take on the way of life of the majority. The assumption in this case is that members of the majority group change little or not at all, but minority group members become transformed by copying the majority group members. In the context of the United States, for example, minority groups would transform themselves to melt into the dominant culture of the White Anglo-Saxon Protestant (WASP) English-speaking mainstream, but the WASP culture would not change.

Minority assimilation seems to be taking place among languages on the world stage, with minority languages being abandoned and majority languages (such as Chinese, English, and Spanish) being taken up by more people. There are about 5,000–7,000 languages in the world at present, but it is estimated that by the end of the twenty-first century about fifty percent of currently existing languages will have become extinct (Crystal, 2000). Languages die largely when older speakers die and their offspring become assimilated into other (typically majority) language groups.

A second form of assimilation I have termed "melting-pot assimilation." In this case both minorities and the majority group contribute to the formation of a new and common culture, and by so doing all groups become transformed. Melting-pot assimilation is in many respects inspiring, because it implies that all cultures will have opportunities, based on their respective sizes, to contribute to the newly emerging "American" culture, and that what emerges from the melting-pot is something completely new, without ties to the prejudices and injustices of the Old World. This vision has long inspired the idea of an ideal "New Land," and has a long history. For example, when writing his famous *Letters from an American Farmer*, de Crèvecoeur (1735–1813), a Frenchman who lived for long periods in America, assumed that melting-pot assimilation would lead to a new people, the Americans. But in earlier eras the assumption was that non-Western-European people would *not* be contributors to the new American culture.

In summary, minority assimilation involves the minority group members trying to take on a mainstream identity, by copying the majority group; but in melting-pot assimilation the members of all groups develop new identities based on the cultural contributions of all the different groups.

Re-assessing assimilation

Assimilation seems intuitively appealing, because it is in many ways an attractive idea that we should all become members of one big group, a kind of universal family of humankind. Assimilation emphasizes the unity of humankind that could arise if differences were washed away. It is assumed that this would result in a situation where, to paraphrase John Donne (1571?–1631), no person is an island, complete by him- or herself; every individual is part of the whole. But critics argue that, on the basis of psychological research, one can identify fundamental flaws in assimilation policy.

One possible shortcoming is the assumption that assimilation will lead to a washing away of inter-group differences and that this will be a lower likelihood of conflict. An important question is raised: do the inter-group differences that act as the basis for conflict actually have to have an objective basis and be important according to objective criteria? One might assume that because inter-group conflict often has very serious detrimental consequences, such conflict would only result from major issues and objective causes. Nothing could be further from the truth. An impressive body of field and experimental laboratory research shows that even criteria that would objectively be viewed as trivial can form the basis of inter-group bias and violent conflict. The actual situation is rather like that depicted by Jonathan Swift in his satirical work *Gulliver's Travels*: wars can take place on the basis of one group of people breaking their eggs at the big end, and another group having a rebellion (and the audacity!) to break their eggs at the little end. For example, a major differentiation between the Tutsi and the Hutu, two groups in Rwanda who slaughtered one another in the 1990s and still are not living in peace, is on the basis of height, one group being slightly taller than the other. This slight difference is supposed to indicate group superiority and inferiority.

Experimental laboratory research using the so-called "minimal group paradigm" provides evidence to suggest that even trivial differences between groups can lead to inter-group bias. These studies, as their title suggests, are designed to minimize the significance of groups. In part one of the minimal group paradigm, individuals carry out a trivial task, such as estimating the number of dots flashed onto a screen, and are assigned to a group, X or Y, on the basis of their performance on this task, such as how many dots they reported seeing. In part two, participants are asked to allocate points to anonymous members of group X and Y. No rationale is provided for how points should be allocated, and it is explained that none of the points a participant allocates returns to himself or herself. Thus, objectively, there is no important criterion for categorization and no serious reason to show bias in favor of one group or the other in allocating points. However, findings from hundreds of studies reveal a strong trend of bias in favor of the in-group (Taylor & Moghaddam, 1994).

When we combine the findings of experimental research with practical and research experience in the field, we come to the inescapable conclusion that inter-group differences can be manufactured and given significance, even if initially they seem to be non-existent or unimportant. The socially constructed world is highly malleable; in many cases the basis for inter-group bias and conflict does not have much merit when considered objectively. For example, why has there historically been so much emphasis in Western societies on skin color? Why not ear length, or head size? The focus on skin color does not have an objective basis but is an example of socially constructed meaning: in Western societies skin color has been ascribed certain significant meanings that are associated with assumed inter-group differences and superiority/inferiority.

288   GREAT IDEAS IN PSYCHOLOGY

An implication is that assimilation will not lead to an end to inter-group differences, because no matter how far assimilation takes place and people become more and more similar, new differences can always be manufactured. The invention of inter-group differences has no boundaries, and so new bases for bias and conflict can always be found. But why should they be found? How do we explain the human tendency toward inter-group differentiation, bias, and conflict? One influential explanation, put forward as part of social identity theory, is that humans are motivated to achieve a social identity that is both positive and distinct (Tajfel & Turner, 1986). This implies, for example, that individuals will create ways to position their in-groups not only as positive but also as "different" and "special," as a way of enhancing their own identity.

A yet more pessimistic interpretation of the human tendency to show inter-group bias arises from Freud's theory. According to this viewpoint, all human relationships involve both positive and negative emotional feelings. A group consists of individuals who are emotionally tied with one another through identification with a leader. The leader helps group members to cope with negative emotional feelings by displacing such feelings onto targets outside the group. The more dissimilar an out-group, the more likely it will become the target of aggression. Freud's approach can be summed up by saying that it will be possible to bind people together in love as long as there are some other people left over to hate. This is in line with the idea that no matter how far assimilation policy is put into practice, there will always be an excuse or a basis according to which some groups will be excluded and made the target of prejudice and discrimination.

Yet another possible shortcoming of minority assimilation policy is what I have termed the "good copy problem." Minority group members are encouraged and rewarded even to strive to join the majority group, but in many important ways they can only become "good copies" of the majority group. A good copy can never be as good as the real thing, and it can certainly never be better than the real thing. Consequently, minority assimilation often leads to minority group members feeling frustrated and inferior.

Thus, although assimilation policy has supporters and seems to have some benefits, it also has potential flaws. Let us now turn to the major alternative, multiculturalism policy.

CRITICAL THINKING QUESTIONS

1 Among the arguments in favor of melting-pot assimilation, which one is the most persuasive?

2 In what ways do the results of the minimal group studies suggest weaknesses in minority assimilation policy?

MULTICULTURALISM AND IDENTITY

Multiculturalism has rapidly gained favor since the 1960s as a policy for managing cultural diversity. In 1972 Canada became the first major nation officially to adopt a policy of multiculturalism, which has meant that the federal government of Canada provides support for cultural and linguistic minorities to retain their ancestral cultures and languages (for example, through support for minority language schools and minority cultural festivals). Since then, Australia and New Zealand have adapted the Canadian model to their own conditions, and it could be argued that multicultural policy has been adopted, albeit unofficially, in a number of other Western and non-Western societies. For example, in at least some regions of India and China, governments are supporting the retention of cultural differences.

A first assumption underlying multicultural policy is that minorities are positively motivated toward retaining their ancestral culture and language. At first sight this seems a non-problematic assumption. However, there are important reasons why some minorities, or at least some individual members of particular minorities, may be ambivalent toward, or even want to abandon, their ancestral culture and language. First, in some cases the ancestral culture may have characteristics, such as sexist values, that are not favorable for at least some members. For example, some immigrant women from fundamentalist Islamic countries are often very motivated to abandon the sexist aspects of their ancestral culture, such as the enforced veiling of women and their exclusion from certain important domains, ranging from professions and politics to sports and recreation. To be more specific, Title IX (part of the 1972 US Education Act stipulating that no person will because of their sex be denied the benefits of an educational program that receives direct federal financial support) and the equal treatment of women in sports contradict fundamentalist interpretations of Islam and gender roles. Second, some immigrants may face discrimination in the adopted land, because of prejudices against their race, religion, or other group characteristics. In such cases, they may be motivated to become less rather than more visible, and in order to become less visible they may well want to abandon their ancestral culture and try to melt into the mainstream.

A second assumption underlying multiculturalism concerns the so-called "multiculturalism hypothesis," which proposes that when group members feel pride and confidence in their own group heritage, they will be more open and accepting toward out-groups. Thus, by providing support for minority groups and helping them to develop in-group pride and confidence, it is assumed, the government is creating conditions for more harmonious inter-group relations. The jury is still out on the validity of this hypothesis, in part because the few empirical studies on this topic have had mixed results. For example, a study involving Hispanic, African American and White participants showed that stronger identification with the ethnic in-group was associated with lower tolerance for out-group members among Hispanics and Whites but not African Americans (Negy, Shreve, Jensen & Uddin, 2003). The authors interpreted this to mean that the multiculturalism hypothesis was not supported for White and Hispanic participants; but other studies have found wider support for the multiculturalism hypothesis (e.g. Verkuyten, 2005).

A first shortcoming with the multiculturalism hypothesis is that it seems to have targeted the wrong groups. Typically, the most influential source of inter-group discrimination and bias in culturally diverse societies are members of the more powerful majority group, rather than minority group members. Minority group members can also show inter-group bias, but their lack of power means that more typically they are the victims rather than the perpetrators. Thus, helping minority group members to feel more pride and confidence in their heritage does not tackle the most important source of inter-group discrimination. Indeed, helping minorities to show more pride in their heritage cultures may make them a more visible target for discrimination.

Second, the multiculturalism hypothesis assumes that prejudice and discrimination can be decreased by increasing pride and confidence in the in-group. The direct implication is that prejudice and discrimination arise because individuals feel a lack of pride and confidence in the in-group. Both practical cases and psychological research lead us to question this assumption. In terms of practical cases, one could argue that, to take an extreme case, the Nazis did have pride and confidence in themselves, but they were anything but open and accepting toward out-groups. Similarly, the members of various terrorist and extremist groups, such as the Ku Klux Klan (KKK), seem to have pride and confidence in their in-group but again are not known for their warm and accepting behavior toward out-group members. A response to this argument could be that deep down, perhaps unconsciously, the members of such groups actually lack confidence and pride, and that is why they attack minorities. From this perspective, a person such as Adolf Hitler is actually insecure and lacking in confidence, and this leads to hostility toward out-groups.

A major weakness of inter-group research is that psychologists have treated self esteem as a stable trait that indicates levels of confidence and pride. Accordingly, researchers have looked at the association between measures of self esteem and inter-group bias, with mixed results (Brown, 2002). An alternative is to view self esteem as context dependent and as arising out of social relationships. Indeed, the policy of multiculturalism assumes that confidence and pride are context dependent; how otherwise could the policy propose that the confidence and pride of minorities could be bolstered through government programs?

Still another alternative is to see the problem of prejudice and inter-group hostility as arising out of something other than low self esteem. One interesting argument, first articulated by Roy Baumeister, is that a combination of inflated and unstable self esteem can be a source of intolerance toward out-groups. For example, if I imagine that I am a great soccer player and my team is the best, this is definitely an inflated view of myself and my team. It is also unstable, because the moment my team faces a serious challenge, it becomes obvious that there is no solid basis for my high opinion of myself and my team. My sandcastle collapses. One possible reaction is to express intense hostility, and sometimes extreme violence, against out-groups, particularly those I see to be vulnerable.

Multiculturalism also faces criticism because it seems to be necessarily associated with cultural relativism, the view that everything has to be judged only in the context of the culture in which it exists. Multiculturalism requires that support be provided for diverse cultures without making judgments about the quality of each culture. From this perspective, there are no valid universal criteria according to which we can make judgments about different cultural practices: we can only make judgments from within cultures, using local criteria. For example, from this perspective the behavior of a man toward a woman can only be judged from the perspective of local values, so that in traditional sexist societies a man who punishes his wife for not behaving "correctly" is acting within his rights. Or, to use a Western example, from a cultural relativist perspective the language of hip-hop, rap, and other minority music cultures can only be judged from within each minority culture. Outsiders have no right to criticize hip-hop and other minority music as "sexist" or "racist," or to claim that it incites violence.

Cultural relativism is unacceptable because it requires that we abandon the principle that all humans, including women and all other power minorities, have certain fundamental rights and duties, and that behavior in all cultures must be judged according to a set of basic universal laws. Cultural relativism put into practice would mean we would have to put aside completely the *Universal Declaration of Human Rights* and other such efforts to achieve universal standards of justice. This route would prove disastrous for those with less power, because they would not have even the possibility of getting protection from international law and institutions supporting universal standards of justice. For example, at present persecuted minorities at least have the possibility of being helped via the intervention of external forces, as happened in Bosnia, and leaders who are responsible for war crimes and genocide face the possibility of facing charges at international courts. If even this, albeit remote, possibility is taken away (using the argument that those outside a culture have no right to judge the behavior of those who share a distinct culture), then the less powerful members of cultural groups will become even more vulnerable.

But there are areas, such as those of social relations, politeness, and the arts, in which cultural relativism has more merit. For example, in Persian culture it is considered correct behavior for guests to refuse food offered to them at least two or three times before accepting, and it is polite behavior for hosts repeatedly to offer food to guests even after they have repeatedly refused the food. Such behavior would be considered impolite and even rude in some Western contexts. But in this type of case, it seems that relativism is valid and it makes little sense to argue that the politeness rules of one culture are superior to those of another. Or, consider the realm of art and aesthetics: traditional Japanese theater differs a great deal from traditional Western theater, just as decorative Islamic art is in major ways different from decorative Western art, but it does not make sense to make judgments across cultures in these areas.

In practice the varieties of multiculturalism can be conceived as lying on a continuum, with "laissez-faire" (where there is little or no government intervention) at one extreme and "active" (where there is direct government intervention) at the other extreme. Laissez-faire multiculturalism comes about when majority groups neither support nor suppress cultural differences. Consequently, cultural diversity persists and may even thrive, but not as a result of direct government intervention. On the other hand, this laissez-faire approach may lead to a weak sense of ethnic heritage identity among minorities. In active multiculturalism, majority groups actively support the ancestral cultures and languages of minorities. The same society can adopt a range of styles with respect to different aspects of culture, such as an active style with respect to language but a laissez-faire style with respect to clothing.

CRITICAL THINKING QUESTIONS

1   Is laissez-faire multiculturalism in practice the same as minority assimilation?

2   Describe a study to test the multiculturalism hypothesis

CONCLUDING COMMENT

The internationalization of trade, improved transportation and communications systems, and the large-scale movement of populations across national borders is leading to greater contact between different cultural, linguistic, religious, and ethnic groups. Associated with these changes are ever-increasing threats of inter-group conflict, and new forms of extremist reactions, such as terrorism (Moghaddam, 2005). The challenge of developing policies for managing diversity is now global, and not just a challenge that confronts historically immigrant-receiving countries such as the United States. There is need for far greater discussion about this challenge at the international level so that we can share experiences and work more effectively toward a common vision of a world at peace.

CRITICAL THINKING QUESTIONS

1   Is cultural relativism inevitably part of multiculturalism?

2   "Multiculturalism is an effective policy in business, but not in the arts or in education". Do you agree?

FURTHER READING

Baumeister, R. F., & Heatherton, T. F. (1996). Self-regulation failure: An overview. *Psychological Inquiry, 7*, 1–15.

Brown, R. (2002). *Group processes*, 2nd edn. Oxford: Blackwell.

Buenker, J. D., & Ratner, L. A. (eds.) (1992). *Multiculturalism in the United States: A comparative guide to acculturation and ethnicity*. New York: Greenwood Press.

Crystal, D. (2000). *Language death*. Cambridge: Cambridge University Press.

Dathorne, O. R. (1994). *In Europe's image: The need for American multiculturalism*. Wesport, CT: Bergin & Garvey.

Gaede, S. D. (1993). *When tolerance is no virtue: Political correctness, multiculturalism, and the future of truth*. Downers Grove, IL: InterVarsity Press.

Grimes, B. F. (2000). *Ethnologue*, 14th edn. Dallas, Texas: SIL International.

Hirschman, C., Kasinitz, P., & De Wind, J. (eds.) (1999). *The handbook of international immigration: The American experience*. New York: Russell Sage.

Hogg, M. A., & Tindale, S. (eds.) (2003). *Group processes*. Oxford: Blackwell.

Mahajan, G. (2002). *The multicultural path: Issues of diversity and discrimination in democracy*. Thousand Oaks, CA: Sage.

McMurtrie, B. (2004). The quota quandry: The United States is not the only country struggling with affirmative action in university admissions. *Chronicle of Higher Education*, 14 February, A38–A43.

Moghaddam, F. M. (2005). The staircase to terrorism. *American Psychologist, 60*, 161–169.

Negy, C., Shreve, T. L., Jensen, B. J., & Uddin, N. (2003). Ethnic identity, self-esteem, and ethnocentrism: A study of social identity versus multicultural theory and development. *Cultural Diversity and Ethnic minority Psychology, 9*, 333–344.

Nettle, D., & Romaine, S. (2000). *Vanishing voices: The extinction of the world's languages*. Oxford: Oxford University Press.

Sowell, T. (2004). *Affirmative action around the world: An empirical study*. New Haven: Yale University Press.

Tajfel, H., & Turner, J. C. (1986). The social identity theory of intergroup behavior. In S. Worchel & G. Austin (eds.) *Psychology of Intergroup relations* (pp. 7–24). Chicago: Nelson-Hall.

Taylor, C. (1992). *Multiculturalism and "the politics of recognition."* Princeton: Princeton University Press.

Taylor, D. M. (2002). *The quest for identity*. Westport, CT: Praeger.

Taylor, D. M., & Moghaddam, F. M. (1994). *Theories of intergroup relations: International social psychological perspectives*, 2nd edn. Westport, CT: Praeger.

Verkuyten, M. (2005). Ethnic identification and group evaluation among minority and majority groups: Testing the multiculturalism hypothesis. *Journal of Personality and Social Psychology, 88*, 121–138

Walzer, M. (1997). *On toleration*. New Haven: Yale University Press.

19

EVOLUTIONARY PSYCHOLOGY

The new millennium was initiated with the United States leading a coalition of forces to war in Afghanistan and Iraq, at the same time that dozens of other major violent conflicts raged in different parts of the world. A look back at human history shows that the present era is not much different from past eras: humans have continued to wage war against one another, improvements in technology simply increasing the number of people killed in wars. The twentieth century saw spectacular progress in science and technology, and in the application of this technology to killing larger numbers of fellow humans. The use of the atom bomb, twice dropped on Japanese cities at the end of the Second World War, ushered in a new era, signaling unparalleled capabilities for humans to annihilate humans. The "Star Wars" weapons being developed for use in the next few decades will no doubt improve on our present atomic capabilities to kill one another.

At the same time that war continues to devastate and impoverish some human societies, there are unmistakable signs that humans also devote a great deal of effort to helping others. This is reflected in the work of countless individuals and groups, from local, national, and international charities to organizations such as *Amnesty International* (an international group dedicated to justice, and particularly supportive of political prisoners). For now, the point I want to highlight is that although *aggression*, behavior intended to harm others, is a marked characteristic of humans, so too is helping, compassion, empathy, and various other forms of constructive, pro-social behavior.

A review of evidence about human aggression and human helping behavior raises questions such as: How did humans become so aggressive? Why are we aggressive? On the other hand, we also help one another. Why? How did we come to be helpful to others? Such questions about how and why human mind and behavior evolved in particular ways are the subject of *evolutionary psychology*, an influential new school of psychology.

There are two main reasons why I am assessing evolutionary psychology as a great idea, even though I have not done the same for the other major schools of psychology, such as the psychoanalytic, behaviorist, and cognitive schools. First, the other major schools are well represented through the individual ideas discussed in this book, such as "learning" (behaviorism), "the unconscious" (psychoanalysis), and "artificial intelligence" (cognitive psychology). Second, unlike the cases of these other schools, the individual ideas of evolutionary psychology have not yet developed fully enough to be considered independently. Evolutionary psychology is the most recent major school of psychology, having come into its own only since the 1990s. This new school has built on the foundations laid by *ethology*, the study of animals in their natural environments, *sociobiology*, the study of the evolution of behavior, and *cognitive science*, the study of brain and mental processes. Evolutionary psychology is in some ways more expansive than these three approaches, being concerned with the evolution of both mind and overt behavior.

The launching pad for evolutionary psychology is the theory of evolution as set forth in Charles Darwin's (1809–82) landmark work *On the Origin of Species by Means of Natural Selection* (1859). The basic tenets of the theory were independently put forward by Darwin and another Englishman, Alfred Wallace (1823–1913), a year earlier, but the credit has been given to Darwin because he had amassed the evidence to make a convincing case in support of the theory. I begin by considering Darwinian theory and the cultural context in which it arose. Darwin both worked out and worked in (as discussed in chapter 1). Next, I identify a number of important implications of this theory for psychology. Modern evolutionary psychology has attempted to fuse together evolutionary theory and genetics and to bring the resultant knowledge to bear on human mind and behavior. A fundamental issue is the extent to which evolutionary psychology is justified in claiming a genetic basis for behavior and mental life, and this question we also consider. In the terminology introduced in chapter 1, to what extent do genetic factors restrict degrees of freedom in different realms of human behavior, such as intelligence, personality, and so on?

Although evolutionary psychology has attracted a great deal of attention, both in academic discussion and in the mass media, the major ideas in evolutionary psychology do not lend themselves to empirical investigation. One of the shortcomings of evolutionary psychology is that its interpretations tend to be after the fact, looking back at what has happened and re-telling the story of events through the particular conceptual lens of evolutionary psychology. In response to critics who contend that evolutionary psychology does not give enough importance to cultural factors, evolutionary psychologists put forward the counter-claim that culture itself is a result of evolution. Although the interpretations of evolutionary psychology tend to be intriguing and even fascinating, evolutionary psychologists seldom engage in scientific hypothesis testing. In defense of the field, it could be claimed that evolutionary psychology is still very young and it will gain empirical repute over time.

THE HISTORICAL CONTEXT OF DARWIN'S EVOLUTIONARY THEORY

The theory of evolution is a product of nineteenth-century Western culture. We saw that the theory was put forward simultaneously by Wallace and Darwin, but even before this a number of Western thinkers, including Charles Darwin's grandfather Erasmus Darwin, had proposed that all living organisms have a common ancestry and that organisms change over time to adapt to their environments. What Erasmus Darwin and other proponents of evolution lacked was an explanation of how evolution comes about, together with hard evidence in support of their explanation. Both gaps were eventually filled by Charles Darwin after he returned from his famous five-year (1831–36) voyage around the world.

Perhaps the first important outcome of Darwin's voyage was that it raised the key questions in his mind that, if addressed, would lead to a theory of evolution. Darwin's voyage took him to a number of geographically isolated places, including the Galapagos Islands, a group of volcanic islands situated off the coast of Equador. His voyage also took him to Australia. Darwin noticed that in each land mass he visited, from the small ones in the Galapagos to the continent of Australia, lived animals that were unique in some special way. Why had animals evolved to be different in so many ways? Why were there animals in Australia, such as the duck-billed platypus (an egg-laying mammal), that could not be found anywhere else? What was to be made of the fossil evidence showing that many animals that had roamed the earth were now extinct? In his letters to family and friends back home, Darwin makes many excited references to his fossil finds, reporting, "I have been very lucky with fossil bones" (24 November 1831) and "I have just got scent of some fossil bones of a Mammoth!, what they may be, I do not know, but if gold or galloping will get them, they shall be mine" (24 July to 7 November 1834). The enormous diversity of samples he gathered raises many questions about how and why life forms took the shapes they did. The answers that Darwin gave were in fundamental ways shaped by the cultural climate of his era.

Britain was undergoing enormous transformation in economic, political, and social spheres. Starting in the second half of the eighteenth century, the modernization of farming forced hundreds of thousands of people to migrate from the countryside to seek employment in new industrial urban centers, where work and living conditions were for the most part terrible. Children as young as six years of age worked long hours in harsh environmental conditions in coal mines, textile factories, and the like. Life expectancy for most people was less than half of what it is in the twenty-first century. Despite harsh living conditions, the first three decades of the nineteenth century saw a doubling of the British population. Dramatic increases in the numbers of poor people led to fierce debates about government welfare policies. One group, which included the highly popular writer Harriet Martineau, argued that charity and government support for the poor could backfire because it would only encourage the poor to have more children, who would become an additional burden on tax payers. As it happens, Darwin's sisters gave him some of Martineau's writings to read during his long voyage.

Martineau and others of her political persuasion had found scientific support for their views in the writings of Thomas Malthus (1766–1834), an economist and a priest. Malthus presented evidence in support of the argument that whereas food production increases arithmetically (e.g. 2, 3, 4, 5...), population increases geometrically (e.g., 2, 4, 8, 16...). The result, according to Malthus, is a cycle of population increase and famine, followed by population decline and relative prosperity. After each famine, the population increases would level off for a period of time, with the result that food production would catch up. However, as food prices fell in relation to wages, the rate of population increase would pick up until, once again, there were far too many mouths to feed and famine would spread across the land. This "Malthusian cycle" was in line with the writings of major economists of the time.

Even the economist Adam Smith (1723–90), the author of *The Wealth of Nations*, was apprehensive about the plight of the masses in the new industrial society. Smith is generally considered an economic optimist because of his view that divisions of labor and free market competition would create greater wealth, but he believed that in free market conditions the wages of workers would stay at a minimal level. This is partly because population increases meant that there was always an abundant supply of workers relative to the demand, and also because workers had little power compared with the factory owners.

The Malthusian cycle directly implied that in human societies there was a fierce competition for survival. In this competitive environment some individuals succeed and rise to the top, while many others sink to the bottom or even perish. Individual variations make a difference between survival and extinction. Darwin incorporated this idea into his theory of evolution, which can be boiled down to six basic tenets. The launching pad for the theory is the observation that the members of any species reproduce new organisms in excess of the actual numbers that can survive given limited resources. A consequence of this overproduction is that a fierce competition for survival ensues. Within any species there are differences between individuals on a variety of characteristics. Some such characteristics are neutral, meaning that they do not influence survival outcomes, but others have either a negative or positive influence, meaning they either lessen or improve survival chances. Individuals that have more adaptive characteristics are more likely to reproduce and so to pass on their characteristics to future generations. Thus, there will be a change in the characteristics of species in the direction of the most advantageous variants. Darwin's theory, then, depicts a situation in which the winners in evolution are those organisms which survive to reproduce a greater number of offspring, so that their characteristics spread and eventually alter the characteristics of the entire population.

Darwin's theory and psychology

Darwin's theory has a number of important implications for psychology, but cultural conditions have meant that some such implications have become far more fully realized than others. In general, those implications have been more fully realized that fit in with the traditional causal and reductionist model of psychology. In particular, enormous focus has been placed on the possible inheritance of biological characteristics that are assumed to determine psychological functioning. Thus, intra-individual biological characteristics (e.g. genetic inheritance) are assumed causally to determine behavior (e.g. performance in tests of intelligence). This assumption among psychologists has had consequences both for psychological research and for public policy influenced by psychological research.

In the domain of psychological research, far more emphasis has been placed on identifying and highlighting the influence of inherited factors on behavior than the influence of environmental factors. An important example of this is in the domain of intelligence. One interpretation of Darwinian theory that had early and continued support from traditional psychology is that psychological characteristics such as intelligence are largely inherited. Most psychologists believe that both heredity and environment play a role in intelligence, but there is debate about the relative importance of each. Francis Galton (1822–1911) pioneered research trying to prove the hereditary basis of intelligence, and this program remains strong today (see chapter 7). Research in this tradition has had profound and pervasive impact on public policy.

In some areas this impact has been explicit and, because of its transparent and typically simplistic nature, it has been easier to combat. For example, after the First World War data from mass testing of US military personnel were used to justify an immigration policy that discriminated against certain ethnic groups, on the claim that such groups are born with lower intelligence and their entry into the United States would lower the intelligence level of the general population. The pillars holding up this argument did not prove to be robust; for example, the generally accepted position, reflected by the Flynn effect (see chapter 7) is that, as individuals become acclimatized to modern Western culture, their scores on standard intelligence tests improve – showing that environmental factors are key to performance on IQ tests. In the case of immigrants there is an even more mundane explanation: their scores improve when they become proficient in English and can better understand the test questions.

Another policy impact that has been easier to combat because it has been explicit and simplistic, but dangerous, is associated with the eugenics movement, concerned with the improvement of the human stock through selective breeding. For thousands of years humans have used selective breeding to develop horses that run faster, cows that give more milk, and thousands of other specialized animal characteristics. Now, proponents argued, we should apply the same technique to humans themselves. The wider implications of this kind of thinking can be devastating, as evidenced by Nazi racial policies.

Some other causal and reductionist ideas about what Darwinian theory implies for psychology have been more difficult to counter. For example, evolutionary theory depicts animals and humans on a continuum, and one interpretation is that we can learn about human behavior by studying animal behavior. This simplifies the task of research psychologists because, first, research on animals has to meet far less strict ethical standards than research on humans and, second, research on rats, pigeons, and other animals typically used in psychology requires less space and other material resources than research on humans. Since the overt behavior of both humans and animals is objectively measurable, and adaptive behavior survives but non-adaptive behavior becomes extinct, psychologists should focus on behavior. Using this line of reasoning, behaviorists dominated academic psychology for almost fifty years in the earlier twentieth century, searching for stimulus–response (cause–effect) relations that would explain individual behavior (see chapter 6).

But other implications of Darwin's theory have remained underdeveloped. For example, from the Darwinian idea that organisms adapt in relation to their environmental conditions arises the implication, not yet fully realized in psychology, that intelligence and abilities in general have to be understood in relation to context. The Yanomamo and other tribes living in the Amazon jungle region have adapted to their particular living conditions, just as humans working on Wall Street have adapted to the conditions of their particular jungle. The kind of intelligence shown by individuals in each group, such as the ability to recognize a wide variety of local plants and wildlife in the Amazon region or the ability to identify timely opportunities to buy and sell stocks and shares on Wall Street, is to a large extent context specific. But this lesson from Darwinian theory remains neglected.

CRITICAL THINKING QUESTIONS

1 What is it about the theory of Malthus that led both Darwin and Wallace to the theory of evolution?

2 Why do you think the idea of inherited psychological characteristics has received so much attention?

GENETICS AND EVOLUTIONARY PSYCHOLOGY

The most fundamental difference between a psychology based on classic Darwinian theory and modern evolutionary psychology is the attempt by evolutionary psychologists to incorporate the science of genetics and to identify genes as the causes of behavior. Darwin and his contemporaries did not know about the genetic mechanisms involved in evolution; this knowledge came after the research of Gregor Mendel (1822–84) became widely known, which happened decades after Mendel's death. Mendel's revolutionary discovery was that inheritance does not occur through a blending of different characteristics of the parents in the offspring, as was traditionally assumed. Rather, heredity works through the transmittance of genes, discrete units of heredity composed of deoxyribonucleic acid (DNA).

A gene is part of a chromosome. Each cell in a human body contains twenty-three pairs of chromosomes, with the exception of egg or sperm cells, which have unpaired chromosomes that become paired at fertilization. The pairwise combination of genes (one from the father, one from the mother) in chromosomes determines inherited characteristics. If a pair of genes is *homozygous*, meaning they are the same, then the characteristic they carry (e.g. eye color) will be passed on. If a pair of genes is *heterozygous*, meaning they are different, then the dominant gene will exert influence and the recessive gene will not. But a person who is heterozygous for a given gene will still carry the recessive gene and may pass on that gene to an offspring.

Genetics and modern neuroscience (see chapter 4) seem to promise a solid scientific basis for psychology. This promise has meant that many general psychology texts, and of course all evolutionary psychology texts, include a fairly detailed discussion of genetic principles in their early chapters. The implication, sometimes made explicit, is that psychological science should be based on the foundations of genetics.

The idea of evolutionary psychology is founded on the premise that genes causally determine behavior. This revolutionary idea involves a shift from the level of the group and the individual to that of the gene. It is proposed that evolutionary processes do not benefit human groups or individuals; they benefit particular genes. Humans are considered as convenient vehicles for carrying genes: the struggle is not about the survival of us as individuals or the survival of our different groups, but about the survival of the genes we carry. Likewise, competition is not between different individuals and groups of people, but between

different gene pools. But our role as individuals and groups of people is important, because the survival and success of the genes we carry depend on how successful we are at reproduction. If we are successful at having children and caring for our children until they reach reproduc-
~~tive ages then our genes will upread for them propagation~~

In some cases the genes we carry may not be directly helpful to us as individuals, but may prove useful for the next generation and in this way help our genes to spread. In this regard the example that has been discussed most extensively is *altruism*, behavior intended to help others without expectation of benefits in return. Imagine that Steve, his wife June, and their daughters Truce and Angela are passengers on a ship that has been severely damaged by storm and is fast sinking. When they reach the last lifeboat, they find that there are only two places left and the lifeboat is about to be launched from the ship. They have no time to lose and must immediately make a decision as to who will get into the lifeboat and be saved. Steve and June immediately put their daughters on the boat and sacrifice themselves.

It may appear that Steve and June are acting against evolutionary principles, because they are not engaging in the struggle to survive; instead, they seem to be letting weaker others (their young daughters) get ahead of them in the race to survive. However, according to evolutionary psychology the behavior of Steve and June makes perfect sense because ultimately they are programed to be concerned for the survival of not themselves but their genes. Because their genes are carried by their children, it makes sense that they should maximize the possibility of their children surviving and thus further spreading their genes.

From one perspective, then, evolutionary psychology does not allow for altruism as traditionally defined. This is because the persons helping others are assumed to act in ways that maximize the chances of their own genes surviving and spreading. In essence, there is an expectation of getting something in return for helping others. Altruism as traditionally defined is not supposed to involve such expectations. However, evolutionary psychologists assume that this expectation is not something we are aware of when we make our choices to take one course of action rather than another.

From an alternative perspective, evolutionary psychology does allow for altruism. This is because evolutionary psychology assumes that choices in helping behavior are guided by a whispering within, the silent but powerful genes, without one being consciously aware of why one is making particular choices. When Roger helps Karl (to whom he is related by blood) to start a new business, he is not consciously expecting anything in return. Because Roger is unaware of the silent forces that (according to evolutionary psychology) influence his choices to maximize the possibility of his genes being passed on, one might conclude that he actually is acting altruistically.

Genes, biparental investment, and gender differences

Just as evolutionary psychologists have argued that altruism is guided by genetic similarity, on the assumption that we are altruistic toward others who are genetically similar to us, they have argued that aggression follows the same pattern, so that we show aggression toward genetically dissimilar others. But the "we" in this case is males in particular. At both the collective and individual levels, physical aggression by males is much greater than by females. Major wars involving nation states are fought between armies that are either wholly or mainly made up of males. Violent crime, such as murder, armed robbery, rape, and the like, is also mainly committed by males rather than females. Other forms of aggression sanctioned by some states, such as torture, are also almost exclusively carried out by males. Typically, aggression is shown by males against other males; for example, armies of men fight other armies of men. A major exception to this trend is rape, where the victim is almost always female.

The evolutionary function of male aggression, so the argument goes, is to beat out competitor males for access to females. An extreme form of this is what took place in "ethnic-cleansing" wars in Bosnia in the 1990s: males killed other males belonging to ethnic out-groups, and systematically raped the women they captured. This same pattern of males killing rival males and raping females has been reported among traditional peoples living in more natural conditions, such as the Yanomamo of the Amazon jungle. But we should be careful to highlight similarities as well as differences between males and females.

In order to explain such trends, evolutionary psychology takes as its point of departure differences in the best possible strategies available to males and females for passing on their genes. First, consider some differences. Females have a limited number of child-bearing years, roughly a twenty-five-year period from about the teens to around the age of forty, although individual differences and modern technology mean that it could be longer in particular cases. However, because of the nine-month pregnancy period, the number of children females can have in this roughly twenty-five year period is severely limited. In contrast, males can have an almost infinite number of children, the actual number being limited mainly by the number of female partners available to them and capable of bearing children.

This gender difference in the number of children that men and women can have, it is claimed, implies differences in the behaviors adopted by males and females for passing on genes. Most visible is the difference on aggression, discussed above, but also relevant is cross-cultural research showing that females give more importance than do men to the financial prospects of potential mates. In contrast, men place more emphasis in the physical attractiveness of potential mates. Given that resources tend to be accumulated as men grow older, and physical attractiveness is associated with youth, it follows that women should choose to marry older men (who have had more time to accumulate resources) and men should prefer younger women (who are at the height of physical health and reproductive fitness). This trend is reflected in the age gap between husbands and wives, with men being older, in scores of Western and non-Western societies on all continents.

Another biological difference that, according to evolutionary psychologists, influences gender differences in behavior is the level of certainty that males and females have about being the parents of "their" children (at least, before the era of DNA testing). A female can be one hundred percent certain that she is the mother of her children, but a man cannot be so certain: there is always a possibility that he is not the father of children born to his partner. This difference has behavioral implications, according to evolutionary psychologists. Males will be more concerned about the sexual fidelity of their partners; they will show higher levels of jealousy and be more upset if they see signs of sexual infidelity in their partner. From this perspective, it makes sense that female virginity should be highly valued by males.

Whereas traditional accounts of evolutionary psychology have emphasized supposed gender differences, evolutionary psychology has also given attention to gender similarities. A mother and a father are similar in that they are both invested in the survival of their children. In practice, we find that males and females maximize the possibility of passing on their genes through *biparental investment*, a man and a woman cooperating and both significantly investing in their offspring. Men do not generally abandon their children, because they are aware that the children will do a lot better with both parents investing resources in them and sharing the burdens of child rearing. This is clear in the economic, emotional, and other advantages of two-parent families over single-parent families. In essence, both parents achieve better reproductive fitness by staying together to rear offspring.

Similarly, both parents shop around for "good genes" (to use the language of evolutionary psychology), and it is an over-simplification to say that females shop for a resourceful, reliable partner and men shop for a young, physically attractive partner. In the context of North America and Western Europe, at least, the experience of women in their twenties is very different from women in their forties and older. Young women are performing about as well as young men in the education system and in the employment sector. These younger women are about as equally successful as younger men in gathering resources to contribute to the dual-career family.

CRITICAL THINKING QUESTIONS

1 What is a major difference between Darwinian evolution and evolutionary psychology?

2 How would evolutionary psychology look on the double standard traditionally applied to men and women in the area of sexual conduct, so that a man who has affairs is lauded as a "playboy" but a woman who does the same is decried as a "slut"?

GENES AS CAUSES OF BEHAVIOR

Evolutionary psychology rests on the assumption that there is a causal link between genes and behavior. This claim has found strong support with respect to characteristics such as eye color or the ability to curl one's tongue, but much weaker support (or no serious support, critics contend) with respect to styles of thought and action. Maureen's brown eyes can be linked through genetics to her parents and grand-parents, but her love of mountain climbing and fast sports cars is not explained in the same way. Evolutionary psychologists claim that the genetic basis of behavior does exist and will be discovered, but this discovery is challenging because the causal link is indirect: genes causally determine behavior through different paths, such as genetic mutation as well as the impact of genes on proteins.

Another characteristic of research and writing in the realm of genes and behavior is that we are cautioned against the idea that any behavior is *caused* by one specific gene. Rather, we are warned, the situation is much more complex than that. At the same time, however, announcements ull are constantly being made about discoveries of links between specific genes and particular behaviors, such as a possible "IQ gene" that apparently enhances memory (Tang et al., 1999).

On the other hand, critics argue that any claim that behavior is directly caused by genes is too simplistic. The influence of genes on behavior is likely to be indirect. This influence is highly complex and realized through the interaction of genes with each other and with the environment, and the turning on and shutting down of genes at different times during the life cycle. This complexity and the important role of the environment, and particularly the cumulated role of human cultures, are underlined by the fact that humans have very few unique genes.

The Stanford University biologist Paul Ehrlich (2000) has claimed that humans have only about 100,000 genes, and that is not nearly enough to control the approximately 100–1,000 trillion connections (synapses) between the nerve cells in the human brain, even if this is all that genes did in the human body (which it is not). Ehrlich makes a pertinent and important point, but even his estimates are too lenient on those who claim a gene–behavior causal link. The results of the Human Genome Project (2001) confirmed that there are actually only about twenty to twenty-five thousand protein-coding genes in the human genome, about a third of Ehrlich's estimate. We humans have only a few hundred more genes than the mice we study in our laboratories. With so few unique genes, human uniqueness must arise out of a very complex set of interactions among genes and between genes and the environment.

It is too simplistic to assume that the explanation for human behaviors, such as in the realm of aggression, is to be discovered in genes. This becomes even more apparent when we consider actual cases of large-scale aggression, such as the two world wars during the twentieth century. Evolutionary psychologists contend that people are aggressive against genetically dissimilar others (because they want to prevent genetically dissimilar others from passing on their genes), and it is instructive to review this contention in the light of alliances during the most destructive wars. The British and the Germans were adversaries in both world wars, yet these two groups would be expected to be allies if any kind of physical characteristics were the criterion. Fighting alongside the British were such groups as the Indians and Gurkhas, while the allies of the Germans included the Japanese and Italians. Surely such alliances are explained more by ideological rather than biological patterns (for example, the Indian and Gurkha troops fought alongside the British because of historic ties to the British Empire; Germany, Japan and Italy were allies because they were dictatorships). A still larger problem is the assumption that people can actually discern genotypic characteristics of a person from their outward appearance.

Genes as causal factors: a re-assessment

Clearly, there are major limitations to the view that there is a direct causal relationship between genes and human thinking and action. The difference between humans and mice is several hundred genes, but in terms of cultural characteristics we are incomparable with mice. There is no doubt that genes can influence human thought and action, but such influence is indirect and manifested through complex inter-actions both among the genes themselves, and between genes and the environment. The environment has a fundamentally important role in the timing and manner of the expression of genes, and thus any discussion of genetic influence must incorporate the environment. The credibility of genes as direct causal agents is also called into question by patterns of collective aggression: major wars around the world follow patterns of ideological rather than genetic similarity. However, defenders of the position that genes causally determine behavior often argue that there has not yet been enough time to discover the direct causal role of genes in domains such as intelligence. This argument puts us back in a "wait and see" situation: we are asked to have faith in the possibility that future research will reveal how genes determine human behavior.

But in some areas of inter-personal relations, the evolutionary psychology viewpoint does seem to provide an interesting alternative. For example, parents show higher altruism and lower aggression toward their biological children than toward their adopted children. In many parts of the world it is taken for granted that people will show positive bias in favor of blood relatives, particularly in terms of allocating resources. The inheritance of wealth by blood relatives is one important example: it is viewed as unnatural for a person not to leave their wealth, or at least the bulk of it, to their own biological children. No doubt both custom and genetics play a role.

Similarly, certain gender differences in sexual behavior to some ⹑⹑⹑, in ways that seem compatible with evolutionary psychology explanations. For example, a double standard still seems to apply to sexual infidelity: men still seem to be judged less harshly than women if they have sexual affairs outside marriage. Similarly, the emotional reactions of men and women to infidelity still seem to differ, men showing stronger reactions against sexual infidelity and women showing stronger reactions against emotional ties between their partner and another female. These trends are in line with evolutionary psychology arguments to the effect that biological differences between men and women have direct psychological consequences, shaping gender differences in thought and action.

However, some differences that existed just a few decades ago seem to have been swept aside by changed gender roles in Western societies, bringing into question the rigidity of "biologically based" differences generally. For example, when asked the question: "If a man (woman) had all the other qualities you desired, would you marry this person if you were not in love with him (her)?" men used to be far more inclined than women to answer "no." In the United States the vast majority of both young men and women now say "no." Women used to be more inclined to answer "yes," in line with an evolutionary psychology explanation that women give more priority to selecting a male partner who is dependable and resourceful, rather than romantically attractive. In recent years women, like men, have more strongly expressed attitudes endorsing romantic love as a basis for selecting a partner. The disappearances of such gender differences is indicative of broader changes in gender roles, associated with the availability of contraceptives, the parity of women in higher education (at least fifty percent of students attending most major universities, in Western societies and some non-Western ones, are female), and far greater equality of job opportunity in the United States and some other countries. These changes suggest that some other gender differences, such as performance on spacial, mathematical, and verbal tasks, may also be influenced by cultural change, rather than being strictly determined by biological factors.

CRITICAL THINKING QUESTIONS

1 The Human Genome Project has shown the number of human genes to be far fewer than generally expected. What does this imply about the role of genes and environmental factors in human thought and action?

2 Gender differences have narrowed in a number of behavioral domains over the last century. Imagine you were a researcher studying gender differences in 1900. What kinds of assumptions might you make about female–male psychological differences? How would your assumptions about gender differences differ if you were researching the topic in 2000? If the same trends continue, what kinds of gender differences do you believe will exist in the year 2100?

CONCLUDING COMMENT

Evolutionary psychology is an exciting new movement that has gained influence since the 1990s, building on classical Darwinism, sociobiology, ethology, and related traditions. This new school of psychology depicts genes as causally determining behavior and argues that gender differences in thought and action arise out of differences in the best strategies for men and women to pass on their genes. Some aspects of inter-personal relations, such as the sacrifices people make for blood relatives, fit with evolutionary psychology expectations in intriguing ways. However, evolutionary psychology tends to provide explanations after the fact and does not lend itself well to empiricism. In short, fundamental questions remain about the viability of this new science. The number of protein-coding genes in the human genome is far less than had been expected, and the number of genes unique to humans is minuscule. An implication is that genes exert their influence indirectly through highly complex interactions, and the environment plays a fundamentally important role in the timing and nature of gene expression. Rather than direct causal connections between genes and behavior, future research will probably reveal indirect, diffuse, and multidirectional influences.

CRITICAL THINKING QUESTIONS

1 "Evolutionary psychology is better at explaining altruism and aggression at the inter-personal level (for example, within and between family members) than at the large-scale level (for example, between nation states)." Explain your agreement or disagreement with this statement.

2 Why do evolutionary psychologists expect to find behavioral differences across gender groups?

FURTHER READING

Barkow, J., Cosmides, L., & Tooby, J. (eds.) (1992). *The adapted mind: Evolutionary psychology and the generation of culture.* New York: Oxford University Press.

Burkhardt, F. (ed.) (1996). *Charles Darwin's letters: A selection.* Cambridge, England: Cambridge University Press.

Buss, D. M. (1989). Sex differences in human mate selection: Evolutionary hypotheses tested in 37 cultures. *Behavioral and Brain Sciences, 12*, 1–49.

Buss, D. M. (1994). *The evolution of desire.* New York: Basic Books.

Chagnon, N. (1992). *Yanomamo,* 4th edn. New York: Harcourt Brace Jovanovich.

Crawford, C., & Krebs, D. L. (eds.) (1998). *Handbook of evolutionary psychology: Ideas, issues, and applications.* Mahwah, NJ: Lawrence Erlbaum.

Darwin, C. (1859/1993). *The origin of species by natural selection or the preservation of favored races in the struggle for life.* New York: Modern Library.

Desmond, A., & Moore, J. (1991). *Darwin: The life of a tormented evolutionist.* New York: Warner Books.

Ehrlich, P. R. (2000). *Human natures: Genes, cultures, and the human prospect.* Washington: Shearwater.

Gaulin, S. J. C. (2001). *Psychology: An evolutionary approach.* Upper Saddle River, NJ: Prentice Hall.

International Humane Genome Sequencing Consortium (2004). Finishing the euchromatic sequence of the human genome. *Nature, 431,* 931–945.

Malthus, T. R. (1983). *Essay on the principle of population as it affects the future improvement of society.* London: J. M. Dent.

Palmer, J. A., & Palmer, L. K. (2002). *Evolutionary psychology: The ultimate origins of human behavior.* Boston: Allyn & Bacon.

Tang, Y. P., Shimizu, E., Dube, G. R., Rampon, C., Kerchner, G. A., Zhue, M., Liu, G., & Tsien, J. Z. (1999). Genetic enhancement of learning and memory in mice. *Nature, 401*, 63–69.

Trivers, R. (1971). The evolution of reciprocal altruism. *Quarterly Review of Biology, 46*, 35–56.

20
SOCIAL CONSTRUCTIONISM

For over two thousand years, from the time of Hippocrates (c. 400 BCE) to well past the Renaissance in Western Europe, the idea that a mix and balance of bodily fluids determine personality type was widely believed (see chapter 13). This idea is based on the ancient Greek conception of the four elements: earth, water, fire, and air. Combinations of basic elements, such as hot and cold, wet and dry, and so on, make up the four humors – blood, black and yellow bile, and phlegm – which shape personality. For example, too much yellow bile was thought to produce the choleric type, which is hot and dry: individuals who are quickly angered and aggressive. From the beginning of the twentieth century, as Freud's influence increased, a very different construction of personality became influential. Instead of focusing on bodily fluids, the new Freudian system envisaged three groups of forces: the *id*, instinctual forces that strive for immediate satisfaction; the *ego*, a negotiator between the demands of the id and the demands of the real world; and the *superego*, the internalized morality of society (see chapter 5). The Freudian construction of personality is now far more influential than the idea of bodily fluids.

These two contrasting constructions of personality, each widely influential in different historical eras, illustrate variations in the ways that we can make and re-make our worlds. Such constructions are used by people to categorize others, and to expect certain types of behavior from them. Moreover, such constructions are used by people to manage their own personality; to present themselves to others as particular "types". Thus, this example points to how, in generating and upholding constructions of psychological reality, individuals also regulate their own behavior.

Consider a second example, this time involving the social construction of social reality in two different societies. Our focus here is on the basis on which social status is assessed. In Shi'a Muslim society in Iran, as well as in parts of Iraq and Pakistan, a distinction is made between Sayyeds, descendants of the Prophet, and others. Mullas who are Sayyeds wear black turbans; non-Sayyeds wear white turbans. Sayyeds enjoy special prestige and privileges, such as being the recipients of certain Islamic taxes. From the perspective of this status system, the social world is divided into Sayyeds and non-Sayyeds. What would happen if a Sayyed from Shi'a Iran traveled to the Hindu regions of India? The Sayyed would find that his black turban would not lead to his being treated as one of the "special status" group, because the locals would not recognize his special status as a Sayyed. Stratification in much of India has traditionally been on the basis of a caste system, the higher castes (such as the Brahmins) having minimal contact with lower castes, particularly the untouchables. Whereas the higher castes enjoy special privileges and exclusive access to high-status jobs and other resources, the lower castes are restricted to menial jobs and denied access to power positions. What is common to both societies, Shi'a Iran and Hindu India, is stratification; what is different is the basis on which people are stratified. This example illustrates plasticity in the basis for constructions of a status hierarchy.

The implication from these and countless other available examples is that the criteria according to which our world is organized tend to be arbitrary; our world, including our conceptions of what is human, could be organized very differently. For instance, we can hold very different constructions of high status in society and the structure of personality. But countless other examples are available in our everyday lives. For example, consider the differing ways that schools are organized. In much of the United States, children in public schools are categorized into three groups, starting at age six: grades 1–5 elementary school, grades 6–8 middle school, grades 9–12 high school. But there are countless other ways of organizing schools. Why not start school at age four and end at age forty-two, or start at age ten and end at thirty? Or, instead of starting screening for college at the end of high school, children could take examinations at the end of elementary school and be streamed into two types of schools, the first providing education suitable for college-bound students and the second for students bound for jobs not requiring college education (this procedure of starting screening for college at the end of elementary school has existed for some time in the UK; see chapter 7 on the continuing eleven-plus test controversy). These kinds of variations highlight the plasticity of human life, and that very different alternative ways of organizing our lives are possible. In the terminology introduced in chapter 1, human behavior has high degrees of freedom, and change is possible within a very wide range of possibilities.

Although our world is organized in one of countless different possible ways, we come to view the particular organization of our world as the "natural" one and see it as the "normal" way that things "should be." Thus, Shi'a Muslims see it as legitimate that Sayyeds should enjoy higher social status, and Indian adherents of the caste system see it as only right that untouchables should be limited to certain undesirable jobs, just as followers of Freudian psychology believe Freud's depiction of the id, the ego, and the superego to be accurate. Similarly, children in the United States come to see it as natural that twelve years of schooling (elementary school, middle school, and high school) should precede a four-year undergraduate university program. In this way, each group comes to *objectify* their own construction, meaning that they see it as having an independent existence, of being part of a truth out there in the objective world. We can see, then, that there are as many objectifications of the world and truths as there are cultures.

But the critical stance toward objectivity also opens social constructionism to the charge that it endorses a relativistic view of the world, whereby no method of inquiry is better than any other. If the rule systems humans use are arbitrary, then on what basis can it be claimed that the social constructionist perspective deserves our attention? In a sense, relativism is the Achilles heel of social constructionism.

A related question concerns the range of topics that can effectively be examined using a social constructionist perspective. A useful way to tackle this question is to distinguish between *performance capacity*, how well individuals can carry out tasks (e.g. Can you hear that sound out there in the woods?), and *performance style*, the manner in which tasks are undertaken and the meanings ascribed to phenomena (e.g. What do you think that sound is?) (Moghaddam, 2002). For example, reaction time depends on performance capacity, but how we interpret the meaning of reaction time (for example, whether we see it as indicative of intelligence) falls in the domain of performance style. As a general rule, social constructionism is more useful in explanations of behavior that has to do with meaning systems and falls in the domain of performance style. From this perspective, the actual biological and biochemical processes traditionally studied under the topic of "physiological psychology," and more recently neuroscience, are not a suitable topic for social constructionism. However, the interpretation of such processes – what they are taken to mean – does fall under the compass of social constructionism. Even the interpretation of "findings" in hard science domains such as chemistry can be examined from this perspective (Latour & Woolgar, 1979).

THE TURN AWAY FROM POSITIVISM AND AN EXAMPLE OF RECENT RESEARCH

Social constructionism represents a turning away from *positivism*, the view that, first, there is one objective truth and, second, the truth about human behavior can be discovered inductively, accumulating data from particular cases to arrive at general theories. The positivist view of social science research is particularly rooted in the writings of David Hume (1711–76) and Auguste Comte (1798–1857), who in their different styles both emphasized the importance of using scientific methods to discover the laws of human nature. For these thinkers, scientific knowledge can only build on what is perceptible.

Positivism in this early period represents a turning away from religion and theological speculation based on beliefs about heaven, hell, angels, and other phenomena not directly perceptible. The positivist movement of the post-Renaissance era was part of a wider attempt to break free from religious orthodoxy, spearheaded by researchers intent on exploring the sensed, observable world. Along the way, researchers experienced numerous clashes with Church authorities, perhaps the most famous episodes involving Galileo Galilei (1564–1642), who was forced to recant his demonstration of Copernican theory. But critics would contend that, in their eagerness to adopt the scientific way, positivists went too far in sticking to a fixed idea of a knowable world.

A major assumption in this positivist view is that there is a single, fixed "human nature." Through empirical investigation, this "true" human nature can be discovered. An alternative view, one in which social constructionism is rooted, is represented in the writings of Giambattista Vico (1668–1744). Vico highlighted variations in human behavior across cultures and across historical eras. He also gave considerable importance to the study of language as a means of understanding human thought and values. Moreover, Vico argued that the study of human societies is fundamentally different from the study of the physical world, because humans have created human societies, and continue to recreate human societies over time. Thus, to study humans is to study a historical process with change and the construction and reconstruction of societies as a central theme.

Particularly since the 1980s, the social constructionist movement has become influential in various disciplines, including psychology. The social constructionist perspective has progressed alongside the traditional positivist perspective in psychology – like two parallel world views. It is not peculiar to psychology to have different paradigms supported by different groups in the same discipline. A famous example of this in science took place in the seventeenth century, when the heliocentric system of Copernicus (1473–1543), which proposed that the earth and the planets move round the sun, was demonstrated by Galileo. For about a century after the public condemnation of Galileo by the Inquisition, the heliocentric system and the orthodox view, that the sun and the planets move round the earth, existed side by side, until eventually all serious scientists accepted the heliocentric system.

Some critics would argue that since its pioneering days in the mid nineteenth century, modern psychology has always incorporated parallel world views and never, even in the heyday of behaviorism, accepted a single paradigm. Among the most important requirements that have to be met in order for a discipline to achieve the status of a science is agreement on, first, the subject of study, second, the methods of study, and, third, exemplars of research that represent the science. Throughout the history of modern psychology there has been serious disagreement on all three of these issues, social constructionists being the latest among those who reject the traditional psychology of the day.

Many of the research studies conducted in the social constructionist tradition have psychology as a central theme, but also cross into other disciplines, such as linguistics and micro-sociology. For example, consider Wooffitt's (1992) study of the narrative accounts people give of unidentified flying objects (UFOs), ghosts, and other extraordinary, paranormal experiences. The paranormal subjects of such accounts are approached by most of us with skepticism. Unlike when narratives are told about ordinary phenomenon, such as how the school experience is divided up ("I went to elementary school, middle school, and high school"), we are more critical and questioning of narratives concerning UFOs and the like. Also, people providing narratives of paranormal experiences are in danger of being labeled "crazy" or "wacky."

Consequently, such people have to take particular care to position themselves well in order to be persuasive.

Wooffitt discovered that most such accounts follow particular common patterns, an important component of which is the setting of the paranormal event against a background of ordinary activity and experience. Thus, narratives typically begin by saying something like "I was out taking my dog for her walk, as I usually do every evening. I stopped to chat to a neighbor in our street, then went into the park." Having set up an ordinary context and positioned the self as an "ordinary person, doing ordinary things," the narrator now typically introduces the paranormal experience. Wooffitt found that this too involves careful positioning, the paranormal phenomenon being referred to indirectly and vaguely at first, as in "I noticed something bright in the air" (rather than immediately saying, "I saw a flying saucer") or "I sensed a strange presence" (rather than "I knew it was a ghost"). This cautious, indirect strategy allows narrators to present themselves as ordinary people who have been persuaded to believe in extraordinary things by the experiences they gradually slipped into. The paranormal experiences did not arise because of them being the kind of person who is motivated to have such experiences, but because the circumstances led them to such experiences.

Note that Wooffitt's account is not causal – it is not assumed that cause–effect relations explain the thoughts and actions under investigation – and this is perhaps the most important way in which constructionism moves away from positivist psychology. The search for cause–effect relations is central to traditional psychology, whereas constructionism offers normative accounts of behavior. For example, Wooffitt explores how narratives of the paranormal are regulated by social norms and rules and follow cultural ideas and scripts about normal and abnormal phenomena. Individuals are assumed to be intentionally offering narratives of the paranormal, set against the backcloth of what is taken to be normal in everyday life.

Like much social constructionist research, Wooffitt's study leads us to re-assess our own experiences and the arbitrariness of what we are socialized to believe is the "natural order" of our ordinary world. This morning I heard a young boy say he wished the Olympic Games were held more often, but his older brother responded by saying, "Don't be silly; the Olympics have to be every four years." Social constructionism invites us to consider the view of the younger child and to recognize that there is no "natural" reason why the Olympic Games could not be held every three years or every two years (or every ten years, for that matter), or why, instead of the one-hundred-meters dash and the long jump, we could not have a twenty-meters dash and a side jump. Why is the winner of the javelin event the person who throws the javelin the farthest distance, rather than the person who is most accurate at hitting a target with a javelin? The arbitrariness of the way we organize our lives is highlighted by social constructionism, the main propositions of which are considered next.

The propositions of social constructionism

Social constructionism is based on three main propositions, presented succinctly below and explored further in the discussions that follow.

1. All phenomena that we recognize as "psychological" are properties of the flow of meaningful activities of people, typically interacting with others. Thus, thinking, remembering, deciding, and all other psychological phenomena are best understood in the context of ongoing activities of people.
2. All psychological accounts draw on normative systems (norms, rules, values, and so on). The influence of normative systems extends to accounts given by practicing and researching psychologists, as well as by lay people, and also includes scientific research methods used to study psychological phenomena, and formal reports of research findings. These all follow normative rules, conventions, and so on. By implication, scientists work out more than they typically assume, because (albeit unaware) they are in major ways influenced by the theories and concepts available at their particular time and place. Moreover, even when they try to work in and stay close to data, the very idea of what constitutes "data" is culturally defined.
3. A common social reality is constructed and upheld through the participation of individuals who are appropriately skilled in using the normative system of a culture. For example, only individuals skilled in the normative system of Shi'a Islam, and thus able to recognize and use the various cultural symbols of Shi'a Islam, could uphold the status hierarchy involving Sayyeds and others.

We begin this discussion by considering the larger recent context of social constructionism and clarifying the relationship between social constructionism and traditional psychology. Next, we consider the main implications of social constructionism.

SOCIAL CONSTRUCTIONISM AND TRENDS IN MODERN PSYCHOLOGY

From its beginnings in the mid nineteenth century, modern psychology has involved a variety of different perspectives, sometimes formalized as "schools." In any historical era, there has been a tendency for a particular perspective or school to gain greater influence, so that people regard it as the mainstream. For example, structuralism (associated with Titchener; see chapter 6) was particularly influential in the last decades of the nineteenth century, behaviorism was dominant for much of the first half of the twentieth century, and cognitive psychology has been dominant since the 1960s. However, in each historical era there are also recognizable alternative schools or viewpoints in psychology. In some cases the alternatives are considered very radical when they first appear. For example, from some perspectives behaviorism was considered radical when Watson put forward the behaviorist manifesto in 1913 (see chapter 6) and cognitive psychology seemed radical in the 1950s (see chapter 8). But both behaviorism and cognitive psychology were transformed from being the radical movement of the day to being the most influential or mainstream school a few decades later.

This is not always the case, because some progressive movements or schools always remain on the sidelines and never gain enough influence to be considered mainstream. For example, Gestalt psychology was particularly influential in the 1920s and 1930s, and even today most psychology students at least learn about the Gestalt motto – "The whole is more than the sum of its parts" – yet Gestalt psychology never achieved mainstream status. Social constructionism can be considered a radical movement that is gaining influence in psychology in the early twenty-first century, but it is not clear whether this movement will continue to gain ground and become a major force in mainstream psychology, despite the progress it has gained in much of Europe.

Social constructionism has gained influence in psychology gradually since the 1960s, in part as a result of dissatisfaction with traditional psychology on account of a number of different shortcomings that critics ascribe to it. A first shortcoming is the positivist orientation whereby traditional psychology assumes it to be the task of psychologists to discover "the facts" about an assumed "human nature." Social constructionism rejects the idea that there is a fixed human nature. Rather, social constructionism argue, in agreement with biologists such as Paul Ehrlich, that there is no fixed human nature, and that different cultural and historical conditions create varieties of different human natures. Social constructionism sees human natures as produced through social interactions, and not determined by genetic programming.

Although the main contrast between constructionism and traditional psychology is on the issue of causation, dissatisfaction with traditional psychology also focused on the issue of reductionism, the tendency to try to explain phenomena by reference to the smallest unit possible. In traditional psychology, reductionism has been associated with a tendency to try to explain behavior by reference to factors that are assumed to be fixed and internal to the individual, such as assumed hard-wired cognitive processes, or inherited temperament or intelligence. Such reductionist explanations, critics argue, assume the causes of behavior to be within the individual. Consequently, reductionism leads us to answer the question "Why is Robert unemployed?" by saying something like "Because Robert inherited low IQ" or "Because Robert lacks the right kind of personality," rather than something like "Because society does not provide the needed educational and employment opportunities for Robert and others like him." With the growth of neuroscience research, there has been increasing tendency to try to further reduce explanations of behavior, to the micro level of neurons and neurotransmitters. The implication is that Robert's being unemployed will ultimately be explained by his brain chemistry.

Critics have argued that reductionism in psychology reflects at least in part the dominance of the United States and its individualistic culture. Although modern psychology is rooted in ideas from Europe, with the emergence of behaviorism as the dominant school of academic psychology early in the twentieth century, modern psychology took on distinctly US characteristics, particularly individualism, the tendency to assume behavior is caused by factors that lie within the isolated individual. For example, if George is a billionaire and Don is penniless, the causes for their situation are within themselves: George must be highly talented and hard-working, and Don must have no talent and be lazy (rather than their situation being explained by larger conditions, such as George being the son of a billionaire, and Don the son of an unskilled, unemployed single mother). Critics argue that such American individualism explains the present state of research methods in traditional psychology, whereby in the vast majority of studies individual participants are tested in isolation in order to discover what dispositional factors cause their behavior.

The United States has been described as the only "superpower" or "First World" of psychology, exporting psychological knowledge to the other industrialized societies (the "Second World" of psychology) and the lower-income societies (the "Third World" of psychology). At the start of the twenty-first century, most psychology departments in universities around the world are strongly influenced by psychological ideas produced in and exported from the United States. Thus, social constructionism is also a turn away from what is seen as the dominance of the United States in psychology, and particularly the individualism that characterizes US culture.

As part of this turn away from reductionism and individualism, social constructionism gives importance to the idea of people and behavior emerging through social interactions. This emphasis on the social is coupled with a focus on meaning making, how people collaboratively construct and uphold interpretations of things and events. Since discourse is integral to social interactions and meaning making, social constructionism is centered on the study of discourse. The various orientations that come under the umbrella of "social constructionism" all share this concern with discourse.

Social constructionism encompasses a number of different orientations that have gained strength since the 1990s. These include: *discursive psychology*, which assumes that the most important psychological phenomena are properties of discourse or communications; *narrative psychology*, which assumes that the same conventions regulate story-telling and sequences of overt behavior; *cultural psychology*, which assumes that behavior is regulated by normative systems; and *critical psychology*, which assumes that psychology is a reflection of the dominant ideology in society. Also, the social constructionist movement encompasses newly emerging indigenous psychologies that assume psychology should in important ways become local and reflect the cultural conditions of people in a given locality.

Social constructionism also encompasses a movement toward alternative research methodologies. Particularly since the 1960s, there has been continual criticism of the traditional research methods of psychology. This point is expanded below, as part of a discussion of the main implications of social constructionism.

CRITICAL THINKING QUESTIONS

1 Provide an example of the social construction of psychological reality
(use the discussion on personality as a guide).

? How convincing do you find the social constructionist alternative to
positivism?

THE MAIN IMPLICATIONS OF SOCIAL CONSTRUCTIONISM

Social constructionism has implications for both the theoretical approach
of psychology and the methods used in psychological research. More
broadly, social constructionism has implications for the relationships
between researchers and lay people. Not all social constructionists have
exactly the same views: distinctions have been made between "hard" and
"soft," or "dark" and "light," or "strong" and "weak" positions, but I am
concerned here with generally shared views rather than extreme positions
within the social constructionist movement.

The following, then, are positions that most in the social constructionist camp would endorse.

Plasticity and change

Human beings and human societies are continually constructed
through social interactions; they are not controlled by biological
programing. A central characteristic of this process of construction is
change. As the patterns of social interactions vary over time, so do the
individual and collective lives that are constructed. In this way, societies
and the individuals in the twenty-first century differ from societies and
individuals in the sixteenth century, and both of these differ from societies and individuals in the sixth century. There are enormous variations
in the ways that human lives can be organized and human behavior can
be patterned. Social constructionism highlights the plasticity of human
behavior, and the potential for reconstructing psychological and social
reality in very different ways.

Our objectification of our social world can lead us to assume that the
way things are is the way things should naturally be. Traditionally it was
assumed that the natural state of affairs is for a family to be made up of a
man, a wife, and their children. However, cross-cultural research shows
that for some societies the natural state is for a man to have multiple

wives, in other societies the natural state is for a wife to have multiple husbands, and among some groups a family can consist of a same-sex couple and their children. Thus, rather than acknowledging a single and fixed human nature, social constructionism conceives of human natures in a continuous state of change.

Collective meaning making

People actively engage in meaning making, in the sense that they ascribe meaning to and interpret things and events. This is a social process, engaged in through interactions with others. Meaning making is a collective process, so that people collaboratively construct and collaboratively uphold meanings. For example, imagine the following conversation between two students, Jill and Cynthia:

Jill: "Sorry I'm late."
Cynthia (wearing a white lab coat): "No problem, I knew someone as responsible as you wouldn't let me down."
Jill: "Yes, well that party ended really late last night. I still have a bit of a hangover."
Cynthia: "Oh so do I. I had to leave early. Did you stay till the end?"
Jill: "No, I left around midnight with Rob. He had to go to the airport this morning. He really made a fool of himself last night."
Cynthia: "You mean when he proposed to you?"
Jill: "No, he wasn't drunk then. I mean when he tried to sing a duet with Carol."
Cynthia: "No, that wasn't Carol; it was me he sang with. I thought his singing was fine, but it was that other guy, Dave, who really sang badly."
Jill: "Oh, I'd forgotten it was you who sang with him, but I couldn't forget what a terrible voice Dave has. Truly awful!"
The two girls laugh, remembering Dave's singing.
Jill: "By the way, how long do you need me for this morning?"
Cynthia: "Should be finished in twenty minutes, easily. Come in…take a seat in the laboratory."
Jill: "Thanks…so this is your lab."
Cynthia: "Actually, it's just a small office serving as our temporary lab. You'll have to excuse the mess."
Jill: "Well, what do you want me to do? I want to be helpful. Do I need to know anything in particular?"

Cynthia: "Thanks. All you need know for now is that this is an experiment about how memory works. I'm going to flash lists of what we call nonsense syllables on that wall. Later I will ask you questions about some of those nonsense syllables."

Jill: "That's simple enough. Okay, ready when you are."

In this episode, Jill and Cynthia move back and forth between two sets of positions, first as fellow students who attended the same party the night before, and second as an experimenter and a research participant in a laboratory experiment. Jill has accepted to be a participant in an experiment run by Cynthia. The experiment is being run in a small office. Jill switches smoothly to her role as research participant, supporting Cynthia in her role as researcher. Jill could have shown a very different reaction to the situation. For example, she could have told Cynthia, "This isn't a laboratory; it's a messy little office. And I saw you half drunk at the party last night; you don't look like a serious researcher to me. And as for the meaningless nonsense syllables you are flashing onto the wall, they're not meaningless. They have meaning for me." But Jill does not react in such a way; rather, she goes along with Cynthia's positioning of her as "responsible," with the implications that has for how a "responsible" person plays the part of a research participant. Notice that Jill also accepts Cynthia's version of what the study is about. The two of them have just been collaboratively reconstructing the events of the previous evening, engaging in a real-world demonstration of how memory often works in everyday life. But Cynthia ignores this demonstration of how memory works and, instead, pushes ahead with her laboratory study on memory. Thus, the two of them collaborate to achieve a seamless transition into the laboratory experiment, where "data" will be collected on "memory."

Language is not transparent

Social constructionism places considerable importance on the study of language and symbolic communications generally. This in itself is not unique, because many traditional researchers place importance on language and language development, as does Jean Piaget, for example (see chapter 9). However, social constructionism places far more emphasis on the idea that a person's language shapes their thoughts and perceptions. In other words, language is not a transparent lens that we use to see the world "as it is." Rather, language is a warped and colored lens that determines what we see and what the world looks like to us.

This does not mean that what one can think is limited by what one can say. Instead, it means that the categorizations, distinctions, differentiations, and so on that are part of the grammar of a particular language make it more likely for thinking to take one set of directions rather than others. For example, in Farsi and a number of other languages there is no equivalent word for the English word "privacy." This does not mean that native Farsi speakers are unable to think about or to understand the idea of privacy. However, their language does not make "privacy" a very readily available idea compared with other ideas for which there are precise words in Farsi. Through its particular characteristics, language influences how the young think as they become proficient in their native tongues.

Language is already present when we arrive in this world, carrying with it particular styles of thought distinct to our culture. In this way, language provides a fundamentally important means of continuity in ways of life. Of course, language does change over time and words can come to have different meanings across different generations. For example, the word "privacy" had a different meaning for the American colonists in the seventeenth century than it does for Americans in the twenty-first century. For one thing, in the twenty-first century, despite serious efforts to curtail civil liberties in the United States, there are still some legal safeguards in support of the right to privacy that were not available in the seventeenth century. Thus, although language supports some level of continuity over time, it is also associated with change.

Another theme that receives considerable attention in social constructionism is the use of language in public and private spheres. We not only use language and other symbolic systems to communicate with others in the public domain; we also communicate within ourselves privately. What is the relationship between private experiences and public expressions? How do we communicate to others experiences that only we have access to? In addressing this question, social constructionism has been influenced particularly by Ludwig Wittgenstein's (1889–1951) so-called *Private Language Argument*.

A useful way to approach the Private Language Argument is to ask, "Is a strictly private language possible?" Yes, it is possible if I could learn words by pointing to private experiences, such as "anxiety." But if the examples are private, I could not use them to teach other people the meaning of words. How could other people look inside me to understand what I mean by a word? If we depend on pointing to examples in order to clarify the meaning of words, then we could only communicate using words with public examples.

A key distinction is between language as a descriptor of private experiences and language as a means to express those experiences. Language as we know it could not exist if it depended on using examples to point to, because it would only be possible to point to public examples ("this is a bicycle") but not private ones, such as various feelings, that are only known to oneself. A child learns to use language to express private experiences first by making natural utterances of pain, joy, and so on. When an infant girl falls and hurts her knee, she screams with pain and her mother hugs her and says, 'That was painful, yes, painful. It hurt. Let mom kiss it better." So the child gradually learns the words "painful" and "hurt," and the next time she falls she tries to use them as part of the experience of falling down. Words, then, are used to express feelings and inner states. The way in which these processes take place depend in part on local culture, which I turn to next.

Normative not causal explanations

In line with the turn away from positivism, social constructionism adopts a normative rather than a causal explanation of human behavior. This is a dramatic shift away from traditional psychology, which takes it as given that a goal of science is to discover cause–effect relations, and that the goal of scientific psychology is to discover the causes of behavior. The entire research agenda of traditional psychology, involving the manipulation of independent variables (assumed causes) in order to discover their effects on the dependent variables (assumed effects) is founded on a causal model. In the debate about causal and normative explanations, there are really two main sub-themes, to do with agency and predictability. These sub-themes can be clarified through an example of a person stopping his or her car at a red light (see chapter 2 in this book).

Jill sees that the traffic light has changed to red and she brings her car to a stop. Was her behavior "caused" by the light changing to red, in the same way that gravity causes my pencil to drop to the floor when I let go of it in mid-air? According to the social constructionist position, the answer is "No," my pencil could not decide not to fall to the ground – its course is causally determined – but Jill could decide not to stop at the red light; she could do what some other motorists sometimes do and drive through the red light. That is, she could intentionally choose to take one course of action rather than another.

But most individuals intentionally choose to follow the dominant norms of their culture, to do the right thing, such as stop at a red light, according to the local normative system. In this way, considerable regularity and predictability in behavior arise among large numbers of people. That is, we can predict with a high degree of certainty that most motorists will stop at a red light, just as we can predict with a high degree of certainty that most individuals when placed in the context of a Milgram obedience experiment will follow the orders of the authority figure and (apparently) inflict harm on another person (see chapter 16). Thus, from the viewpoint of social constructionism, the predictability that arises in most laboratory studies is explained, not by citing causes determining effects, but through reference to the tendency for most people to follow appropriate rules and norms most of the time.

Process and research methods

The turn away from positivism and the causal model has been associated with exploration of alternative research methodologies. It is typically pointed out that social constructionism is associated with qualitative rather than quantitative methods, and field rather than laboratory methods. However, the qualitative vs. quantitative and field vs. laboratory distinctions are misleading. Social constructionism does not necessarily reject quantitative or laboratory methods; rather, it rejects the traditional causal interpretations particularly associated with quantitative and laboratory methods. Behavior in a laboratory experiment can be normatively interpreted as "norm and rule following," rather than as having been causally determined by the manipulation of independent variables. The normative interpretation would emphasize not the isolated individual in a laboratory, but the meaning making that takes place through a research participant entering interactions (with the experimenter and others) in a laboratory.

The emphasis placed by social constructionism on collective meaning making through social interactions implies that research should focus on processes rather than just on outcomes. This is yet another point on which social constructionism parts company with traditional psychology. The typical psychology experiment involves a research participant spending an hour or so in isolation in a laboratory, reacting to certain events, images, commands, and so on. The dependent measures in the study are the "outcomes" or the "reactions" shown by the participant.

This neglects at least two essential characteristics of human behavior, as social constructionism depicts it. First, the social nature of human behavior is neglected: in everyday life we do not live in isolation, but among others. Second, the processes of behavior are neglected: in everyday life any particular slice of behavior is part of a long process and can be best understood in the context of that process, rather than in isolation. A study of a slice of behavior out of context, focusing on an isolated individual out of context, lacks validity, so social constructionism contends.

Thus, although the theoretical orientation of social constructionism does not necessarily exclude quantitative and laboratory methods, this orientation does imply that focus should be on the process of meaning making through social interactions. The most important of social interactions involve symbolic communications, and particularly conversations using language. Consequently, the major research method employed in the social constructionist movement has been varieties of conversational or discourse analysis. This has typically involved detailed examinations of conversations with particular attention to how those involved position themselves and others, by means of utterances that have moral force. For example, when Janet says to Tim, "As an honest person, I'm sure you agree you should give the money you found to the lost property office," an implication is that if Tim does not hand in the money, he will not be an honest person.

An important theme of all the various types of conversational and discourse analytic methods is power relationships. First, language is recognized as not just descriptive, but constructive: those who control language also have power to control how social reality is constructed. Second, the power of language places special ethical burdens on researchers, who can control how research is reported, interpreted, and publicized. In social constructionism, researchers tend to think of themselves as being in partnership with research participants, in an exploration toward constructing a picture of events. This difference between social constructionism and traditional psychology is rather similar to the difference that is claimed by humanistic therapists between themselves and traditional clinicians. Humanistic therapists see themselves in partnership with a "client" embarking on an exploration of experiences, rather than being in charge of a patient and directing events to find "the truth" (it is important to keep in mind that, although the way a therapist is trained will influence the efficacy of therapy, often even more important is the skill of the individual therapist).

Power and relativism

Are some constructions of reality more valid than others? From a relativist perspective the answer to this question is "No," all constructions of reality are equally valid. Some versions of reality are more widely accepted, but this is not because they are more valid. Rather, it is because those who enjoy greater power support and propagate particular versions of reality. For example, consider the well-known saying "One person's freedom fighter is another person's terrorist." For some people, Yasser Arafat, the late Palestinian Liberation Organization (PLO) leader, is known as a Nobel Peace Prize winner and supporter of justice; for others he was a terrorist leader. The depiction of Yasser Arafat in the mass media depends on who controls the mass media. Thus, from a relativist perspective the version of reality that is generally accepted is not more valid than others; it is simply endorsed by power groups.

But the underlying assumptions of social constructionism do not necessarily lead to an endorsement of relativism. Feminist social constructionists came to this conclusion some time ago, because it is clear that the struggle against discrimination, sexism, and other kinds of injustices could not make progress on a relativist platform. If all values are relative, then how can one justify asking for change in social relationships between men and women, Blacks and Whites, Native Americans and others, and so on? Clearly, one has first to set priorities, such as "all human beings have a right to a fair trial, equality of opportunity, freedom of speech," then to become an activist for change to achieve the identified priorities.

A relativist position works in favor of those who enjoy greater power, rather than those with less power. In a situation where all values are treated as having equal merit, those who have less power do not have a moral basis on which to agitate to improve their situation. Power becomes the only means by which values and positions are justified.

Caution in assuming universals

Another important implication of adopting a social constructionist viewpoint is that greater caution is needed in assuming universals. Social constructionism places emphasis on the role of normative systems, including conventions, values, rules, norms, in the shaping of psychological accounts, by both professional and lay people. This implies that psychologists must take great care when attempting to generalize from a finding in one or some contexts to other contexts. Universality may arise more as a construction of the researcher than a psychological characteristic of humankind. For example, social constructionists argue that the Big Five factor model of personality does not have universal validity; it is simply a construction valid among some small samples of people, mostly in universities (see chapter 13).

Defenders of traditional psychology may object and claim that psychological research is objective and not influenced by normative systems. In response to such claims, social constructionists could point to the research of Bruno Latour and others, demonstrating how "fact finding" is influenced by normative systems even in *bona fide* sciences such as chemistry. Relative to chemistry and other hard sciences, psychology has a subject-matter, human beings, that is far more variable across time and context. Just because X is true for some samples of people in some parts of the world at some times, it does not follow that X is true for all people in all parts of the world at all times.

CRITICAL THINKING QUESTIONS

1 From among the listed implications of social constructionism, which do you think is the most important and which the least important?

2 "Jean brought her car to a stop at the stop sign." Explain how a normative explanation differs from a causal one in accounting for Jean stopping her car.

CONCLUDING COMMENT

Social constructionism represents a growing challenge to traditional psychology, with considerable influence outside North America, and particularly in parts of Latin America, Asia, and Western Europe. In North America, social constructionism has made more headway in communications departments and cultural studies centers than in psychology departments, but there are some indications that this movement is still gaining momentum: for example, the increased popularity of qualitative research methods and the emergence of new research journals such as *Culture & Psychology* and *Theory and Psychology*.

Social constructionism highlights the arbitrary nature of the rules and norms we use to regulate our lives, and the relative nature of values. The movement is open to attack from those who see problems with relativism, and this includes some feminists (see chapter 17). For example, if all rules are arbitrary, on what basis can we condemn sexism, against females or males? Confronted by such questions, some researchers influenced by the social constructionist movement have explicitly rejected relativism and affirmed that not all values have equal merit. Such affirmations are part of an effort to develop social constructionist perspectives that are more explicitly committed to particular ideas of a just society. At the same time, constructionist psychologists are gaining in influence, particularly among younger researchers. Despite the objections of traditionalists, constructionist psychology has emerged as an exciting, and in some forms a radical, alternative to positivist psychology.

CRITICAL THINKING QUESTIONS

1 Why is relativism not necessarily beneficial for minority movements?

2 What are the implications of social constructionism for research methods?

FURTHER READING

Readings that reflect developments leading to social constructionism

Austin, J. L. (1962). *How to do things with words.* London: Oxford University Press.

Berger, P., & Luckmann, T. (1966). *The social construction of reality.* New York: Doubleday.

Foucault, M. (1979). *Discipline and punish.* Harmondsworth, England: Penguin.

Harré, R., & Secord, P. F. (1972). *The explanation of social behavior.* Oxford: Blackwell.

Kelly, G. (1955). *The psychology of personal constructs.* New York: Norton.

Vico, G. (1725/1948). *The new science,* trans. T. G. Bergin & M. H. Fish. Ithaca, NY: Cornell University Press.

Wittgenstein, L. (1953). *Philosophical investigations,* trans. G. E. M. Anscombe & G. H. Von Wright. Oxford: Blackwell.

Readings more directly representing varieties of social constructionism

Billig, M. (1999). *Freudian repression.* Cambridge, England: Cambridge University Press.

Bruner, J. S. (1986). *Actual minds, possible worlds.* Cambridge, MA.: Harvard University Press.

Bruner, J. S. (1991). The narrative construction of reality. *Critical Inquiry,* Autumn, 1–21.

Burr, V. (2003). *Social constructionism.* London: Taylor & Francis.

Danziger, K. (1997). The varieties of social constructionism. *Theory and Psychology, 7,* 399–416.

Gergen, K. J. (1985). The social constructionist movement in modern psychology. *American Psychologist, 40,* 266–275.

Gergen, K. J. (1999). *An invitation to social construction.* London: Sage.

Harré, R., & Gillet, G. (1994). *The discursive mind.* London and Thousand Oaks, CA: Sage.

Harré, R., & Stearns, P. (eds.) (1995). *Discursive psychology in practice.* London, and Thousand Oaks, CA: Sage.

Hart, C. W. M., Pilling, A. R., & Goodale, J. C. (2001). *The Tiwi of Northern Australia,* 3rd edn. Belmont, CA.: Wadsworth.

Latour, B. (1987). *Science in action.* Milton Keynes, England: Open University Press.

Latour, B., & Woolgar, S. (1979). *Laboratory life: The social construction of scientific facts.* Beverly Hills, CA: Sage.

Moghaddam, F. M. (2002). *The individual and society: A cultural integration.* New York: Worth.

Nightingale, D. J., & Cromby, J. (eds.) (1999). *Social constructionist psychology: A critical analysis of theory and practice.* Buckingham, England: Open University Press.

Parker, I. (ed.) (1998). *Social constructionism, discourse, and realism.* London: Sage.

Potter, J. (1996). *Representing reality: Discourse, rhetoric and social construction.* London: Sage.

Sarbin, T. R. (ed.) (1986). *Narrative psychology: The storied nature of human conduct.* New York: Praeger.

Wetherell. M., Taylor, S., & Yates, S. J. (ed.) (2001). *Discourse theory and practice: A reader*. London: Sage.

Wooffitt, R. (1992). *Telling tales of the unexpected: The organization of factual discourse*. London: Harvester/Wheatsheaf.

INDEX